AUSTRALIA
a new more inclusive history

MICHAEL S. PAHOFF

Published in Australia by

Copyright © Michael S. Pahoff 2021

The moral rights of the author have been asserted.
All rights reserved. No part of this publication may be reproduced, stored in or introduced into a retrieval system or transmitted in any form or by any means (electronic, mechanical, photocopying, recording or otherwise) without the prior written permission of the copyright owner of this book.

Cover design, typesetting: WorkingType
www.workingtype.com.au
Typeset in Skolar Latin 11/18

1st edition, 2021.

ISBN: 978-0-6451629-6-7

Contents

Prologue	1
PART ONE: PRE-HISTORIC BEGINNINGS	3
Pangea to Australia	5
Origins of Australian Flora	9
Origins of Australia's unique animals	11
First People	13
The Dreaming — The Aboriginal Creation Stories	16
500 Nations	21
Aboriginal Tribal Nations	23
Aboriginal language	25
Aboriginal Arts	29
Aboriginal economics — hunter-gatherer v agriculturalist	30
Indigenous weather knowledge	32
Neolithic Indian Migrants, circa 4000 BC	34
PART TWO: EURASIAN EXPLORATION, DISCOVERY, AND COLONISATION	37
Eurasian Discoverers	39
Some notable explorers after Cook	44
Cook's expedition	45
British settlement	50
Arthur Phillip — the First Fleet — a problem with convicts	50
Indigenous leaders during early Australian settlement	54
The Second Fleet	56
Early Colonial Rebellions	57
Early female leaders in the colony	61
Mapping & colonising Australia	65
Bass and Flinders — circumnavigating Australia	67
Van Diemen's Land — the new colonies	70

Opening the Blue Mountains	
— Blaxland, Wentworth & Lawson (1813)	73
Governor Brisbane,	78
John Oxley — To the Northern Rivers (1817-18),	
Moreton Bay (1823)	79
Henry Miller — Redcliffe, Brisbane — 1824	81
Hume & Hovell — Journey to Port Phillip (1824)	82
Charles Sturt — The Murray River (1829-30)	85
James Stirling — Perth 1829	87
Thomas Mitchell — Western NSW (1831-36)	89
Pawel Strzelecki- The Snowy Mountains	
and Mount Kosciuszko (1839-40)	92
Wurundjeri, Kulin, and Birrarung — Melbourne	94
Batman, Billibellary & Melbourne (1835)	94
Adelaide and the Kaurna	99
Aboriginal resistance and massacres	113
Pemulwuy's War (1790–1802)	119
Tedbury's War (1808–1809)	121
Nepean War (1814–1816)	121
The Risdon Massacre — Van Diemen's Land (1804)	122
Musquito's War — NSW 1805-13,	
Van Diemen's Land (1814-25)	123
The Black (Tasmanian) War (1824-1832)	124
The Cape Grim Massacre (1828)	125
The Bathurst Massacre (1824)	127
Protector of Aborigines and Native Police	127
The Myall Creek Massacre (1838)	128
The Rufus Creek Massacre (1841)	129
The Evans Head Massacre (1842)	130
The Kangaroo Creek Poisoning (1847)	130
The East Ballina Massacre (1853)	130
South Ballina Poisoning (1860s)	130
The Flying Foam Massacre (1868)	131
Jandamarra — West Australia (1894-97)	131

PART THREE: THE SEARCH FOR IDENTITY — 133

- A snapshot of Australia, circa 1850 — 135
  - Industry in colonial Australia — 138
- Communities in colonial Australia — 144
  - Torres Strait Islanders — 144
  - Other communities — 146
- Religion in colonial Australia — 149
- Early sport in Australia — 154
  - Rowing — 154
  - Horse Racing — 155
  - Cricket — 155
- Early Art in Australia — 159
- Early Literature in Australia — 163
- Early music in Australia — 164
- The Gold Rushes from 1851 — 165
  - Early gold finds (1820-50) — 165
  - The NSW Gold Rush (1851-1893) — 166
  - The Victorian Gold Rush (1851-69) — 168
  - The Eureka Stockade Rebellion (1854) — 170
  - Queensland Gold Rush (1857-1904) — 176
  - South Australia (1868-93) — 177
  - Northern Territory (1871-1909) — 177
  - Western Australia (1885-1899) — 177
- Free settlement
- — the taking of Australia — 179
  - Irish immigration — the Potato Famine (1850s) — 180
  - German immigration — the "Forty-Eighters" on — 182
  - Chinese immigration during the gold rush era — 183
- Bushrangers — 185
  - John Caesar, Pemulwuy's War (1795-1802) — 185
  - 1860s — Frank Gardiner, John Peisley, John Gilbert, Ben Hall, Dan Morgan, Captain Thunderbolt — 186
  - 1870s — Captain Moonlight, the Kelly Gang — 192
  - The Kelly Gang (1878-1880) — 193
  - 1900 — Governor Brothers (Aboriginal bushrangers) — 201

Women bushrangers	202
Towards Federation	
— economy, art & sport	204
Science and industry	204
Art, Literature and Music in the late 1800s.	207
The Stage in colonial Australia	213
Dame Nellie Melba	213
Sport in the late 1800s	216
PART FOUR: THE FEDERATION OF AUSTRALIA	**227**
Contributing factors	229
Henry Parkes — the father of Australian federation	229
Edmond Barton	232
Alfred Deakin	232
The Franchise Act	
— Women's right to vote	234
Dinosaur find — 1903	235
Federation Sport	236
Empire considerations	239
The Second Boer War, South Africa, 1899-1901	239
The Boxer Rebellion, China, 1900-1901	242
Rear-Admiral Sir William Creswell	
— Father of the Australian Navy	243
A question of immigration — The White Australia Policy	244
The Stolen Generations	249
A new capital city — Canberra	252
The World's First Labour Government 1904	256
Mawson and the Antarctic	258
The First World War	261
Gallipoli (1915)	264
France (1916-18) — Monash	268
Palestine (1917-18)	272
World War One for Australia	275
Chinese Australians in World War One	276
Indigenous Australians in World War One	277

Australia after the war	279
The formation of the Returned Services League (RSL)	279
Spanish Flu	282
Immigration post war	283
New projects	286
Australian Aviation — early beginnings	293
Australian automobiles — early beginnings	296
Art and Literature — new technologies and ideas	298
Famous early international Australian actors	302
The Great Depression in Australia	305
Australian Sport before and during 'The Great Depression'.	305
Netball in Australia	314
Mary Poppins — P.L.Travers & Mary Sheppard	315
The Second World War	318
Egypt & Libya	320
The End of the Second World War	337
PART FIVE: MODERN AUSTRALIA TAKES SHAPE	**339**
A wave of immigration	341
The Chifley Government	342
Caldwell, the Assisted Migration Program 1945 — 10 Pound Poms	343
The Foundation of the Liberal Party	346
The 1950s in Australia	347
The Snowy Mountain Scheme — 1949-1972	349
The Melbourne Olympics 1956	349
The Cold War	353
Indigenous Civil Rights	355
The 1960s — Australian Reform, Civil Rights, the Vietnam War and popular music	359
The Ord River Project	361
The Decimalisation and Metrication of Australia	362
Neville Bonner	369
The Vietnam War (1962-1975)	370

The Arts in '60s Australia	372
Florence Broadhurst	374
Two Great Australian Sportswomen	377
Australia and Women's Lib — Greer, Reddy & Roxon	379
Free Trade and Anti-Censorship — 1970s	381
Trans-Tasman Agreement	
— New Zealand and Pacific Island migration	382
1975 — Constitutional Crisis	384
The HIV/AIDS Epidemic	386
New Waves of Immigration	389
Multiculturalism, the ABC Charter, and SBS	395
1983 — Australia and its droughts	402
1986 — Australia becomes	
truly independent	406
Uluru returned (1985)	407
Mabo v Queensland (1986 & 1992)	409
1990s — Was it "the Recession we had to have"?	411
Nicky Winmar — 1993	411
The Internet and Online development	412
PART SIX: THE NEW MILLENNIUM	**415**
The Y2K Bug	417
Sydney 2000 Summer Olympics	417
Further waves of immigration	420
2K Australian music rules the world	422
A great array of players	425
Stolen Generations, Deaths in custody, and Sorry	432
Palm Island Death in Custody 2004	433
Sorry — 2008	434
A Champion Indigenous Footballer	435
Australia's first female Prime Minister	437
Australia's first NBA Hall of Fame inductee	438
Same-sex Marriage	443
Euthanasia	444
Covid-19	445

PART SEVEN: FUTURE CHALLENGES — 449

    Immigration — 451
    Indigenous Rights — 452
    Pandemics — 457
    Infrastructure, Land Use, and Climate Change — 458
    Corporate Governance — 463
    Australian independence
    — constitutional monarchy v republic — 465

APPENDICES — 467

    Appendix 1
    — Australian Governor Generals and Prime Ministers — 467
    Appendix 2A
    — List of New South Wales Governors and Premiers — 469
    Appendix 2B
    — List of Tasmanian Governors and Premiers — 472
    Appendix 2C
    — List of Western Australian Governors and Premiers — 475
    Appendix 2D
    — List of South Australian Governors and Premiers — 477
    Appendix 2E
    — List of Victorian Governors and Premiers — 480
    Appendix 2F
    — List of Queensland Governors and Premiers — 483
    Appendix 3
    — Events in Australia and the rest of the world — 486

References: — 496
Acknowledgements: — 501

Prologue

I write this new more inclusive history of Australia because it fills a gap in what we have not included and still continue to omit in Australia's history.

As a child of the 1960s, I read much of my history from the wonderful collection of books published by Hamlyn. Australian history in primary and secondary school began with James Cook and the Endeavour followed shortly after by the First Fleet, the explorers, bushrangers, gold rushes then Federation. At school we were taught an Anglicised version of Australian history, and we accepted it as a continuation of a history that began with ancient Britons being conquered by ancient Romans, Anglo-Saxons, Vikings, and Normans. The Aborigine in Australia was relegated to that of the ancient Briton, conquered and assimilated to an irrelevant section of pre-history.

There were two major events that drew my attention to Aboriginal Australians. The first was the 1967 Referendum that gave indigenous Australians the vote. The second was Lionel Rose winning the world bantam weight championship in 1968. These events elevated the identity of Aboriginal Australians to something more than what I had seen on television documentaries. As I learnt more, I became aware of a whole aspect of Australian history that was not included in my early Australian story books. Aspects such as Aboriginal history, peoples, language, arts, heroes and leaders, outlaws were all missing and needed to be included.

Another aspect of my early education in Australian history was that convicts, soldiers, and early settlers came from the British Isles.

Some Chinese had arrived during the gold rush and other Europeans began arriving after the First and Second World Wars. Immediately, this created doubt in my own mind. Although, parts of the maternal side of my family arrived from England in Victoria's early history, the paternal side of my family arrived before the First World War. The history was not wrong but those who were writing it were omitting significant sections.

In adulthood, it has been my great pleasure to meet many diverse Australians and learn that their histories have been also minimised or omitted from general Australian histories and confined only to specific stories of individual communities.

In the last half century, Australia has adopted multiculturalism as a national policy, although it has enjoyed the fruits and rewards of multiculturalism long before then. Further, I have been enlightened by the great works of noted Aboriginal leaders such as Charles Perkins, Noel Pearson and many others.

During the process of researching and writing this book, I have learnt more as I have delved deeper into the stories of those often on the fringe of general Australian histories. I hope to bring these stories to you now, hoping to provide a new more inclusive history of Australia.

PART ONE

PRE-HISTORIC BEGINNINGS

Pangea to Australia

Like most of the continents on Earth, Australia hasn't always been in the same position on the globe, distant from other continents. Once, all the continents of the world were connected into one giant supercontinent, Pangea.

Scientific discovery of Earth's origins began about 200 years ago. Before then, different people had their own ideas about how the land, seas, vegetation, and animals were created. Many of these creation stories and belief systems formed the different religions we have today. Scientists estimate that the Earth began 4.6 billion years ago, or 4,600,000,000 years ago, which was around the same age as the Sun and the rest of the planets in our solar system. For its first 4 billion years, Earth existed in what was called Pre-Cambrian time, where it fluctuated between being volcanic hot and ice cold.

Around 600 million years ago, as the Earth's climate stabilised into conditions similar to now, the very first organisms began in the great oceans. This was called the Paleozoic Era and lasted for 380 million years. It was at this time that all the land on Earth was connected together and called Pangea. Around Pangea was a great ocean, and it was the beginnings of some creatures that still exist today — sponges and corals, worms, molluscs, and protozoa.

The following table describes the changes on our Earth, from Pangea to now.

Years ago	Eras	Periods	Land & Sea	Creatures
4.6 billion years ago		Pre-Cambrian	Earth begins — Mix of lava and ice	Early proteins & cells
600 million years ago	Paleozoic Era	Cambrian	Earth temperature stabilises, oceans form	Algae & plankton, sponges, corals, worms, molluscs, trilobytes & protozoa
500 million years ago		Ordovician	Spores appear	Fishoids & eurypterids
430 million years ago		Silurian	Warm dry land, vascular plants (lycopods)	Armoured fish, starfish & snails
410 million years ago		Devonian	Fern forests	Lobe-fins, crabs, bugs & insects
350 million years ago		Carboniferous	Pangea is formed. Conifers & mosses	Sharks, amphibians, ray-finned fish & scorpions. Sexual reproduction begins.
285 million years ago		Permian	Large trees	Mammal-like reptiles & 'stem' reptiles

Years ago	Eras	Periods	Land & Sea	Creatures
230 million years ago	Mesozoic Era	Triassic	Gingko trees	Tiny mammals, crocodiles
205 million years ago		Jurassic	Pangea breaks apart into Laurasia & Gondwana	Early dinosaurs
140 million years ago		Cretaceous	Laurasia & Gondwana break apart into separate continents. Flowers	Dinosaurs & flying reptiles
68 million years ago	Cenozoic Era	Tertiary	Our continents are moving into position. Grasses & cereals	Birds, hippos & rhinos, apes, cats, dogs & bears, dolphins & whales
3 million years ago		Quaternary	Continents in position, though land bridges between continents exist.	Marsupials & primates (early humans)

Break-Up of Pangaea: 200 Million Years Ago to Present

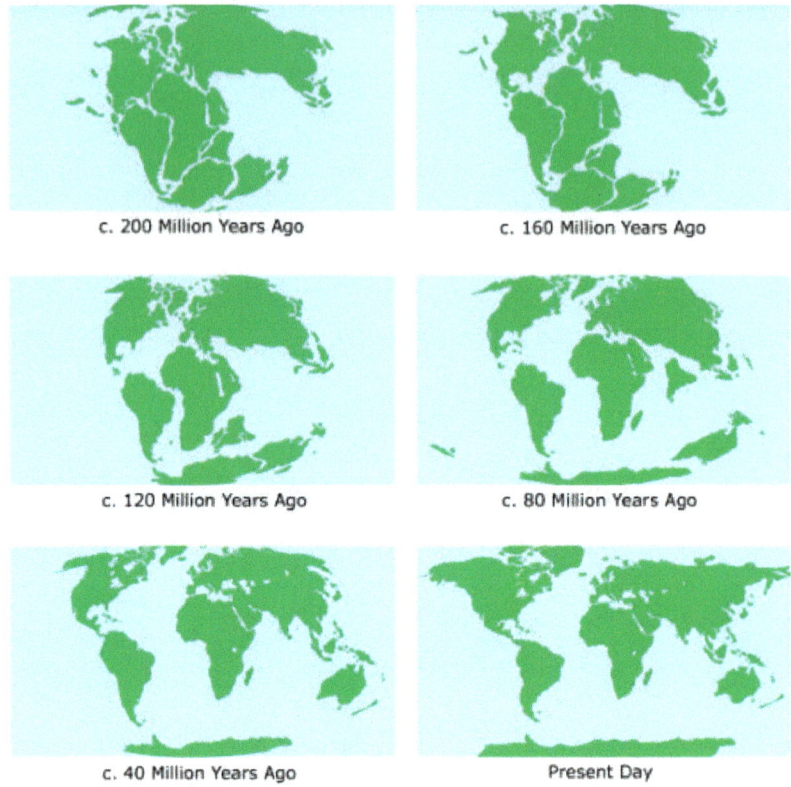

Origins of Australian Flora

Australia's flora comprises over 20,000 vascular (land) plants, 14,000 non-vascular (water) plants, 250,000 species of fungi (yeasts and moulds), and over 3,000 lichens (algae). Australia's most prominent flora are hard leaf seeded plants such as Acacia (wattle) and Eucalyptus (gum trees).

Australia's flora can be traced to the Jurassic period, over 200 million years ago (MYA), when Pangea had broken up into two separate supercontinents, Gondwana and Laurasia. At this time ferns and conifers had already become established. Current examples of this period can be found in the rainforests of Tasmania.

Gondwana broke apart during the Cretaceous period, 140 MYA, and the Australian continental plate drifted eastwards away from Antarctica. The special features of Australian flora reflect this transition, as flowering plants emerged. From 25 to 10 MYA, pollen records indicate the proliferation of Eucalypts, Casuarina, and Banksia-type flowering plants.

The tracing of the charcoal remains of vegetation across Australia from around 50,000 years ago indicates that human habitation in Australia existed at that time.

Tasmanian rainforests reflect the conifers and ferns of Gondwana, 200 MYA.	Eucalypts (gum trees) emerged over 100 MYA.	Acacia (wattle), Australia's national flower emerged over 10 MYA.

Origins of Australia's unique animals

Fauna in Australia consists of mammals, reptiles, fish and insects of which about 90% of each are both unique and native to Australia. However, flying birds, known for their intercontinental migrations, are not. Non-flying birds, such as emus and cassowaries are. The uniqueness of Australian animals indicate that they developed later than 50 MYA, when it had already split apart from Antarctica and become isolated.

Gouldian Finch

Azure Kingfisher

Superb Lyrebird

Australia was part of the supercontinent Gondwana, which included South America, Africa, India and Antarctica. The mammal type known as marsupials — warm-blooded, furry vertebrates that suckle their young — are common across these continents. Therefore, this common link indicates that marsupials originated more than 140 MYA. The platypus and echidna, known as Monotremes (one hole), lay eggs and suckle their young. They are closely related to porcupines and other anteaters, which might indicate that this species of mammal may have originated before the division of continents. Australian crocodiles, related to other crocodiles and alligators found in Asia, Africa and the Americas, originated earlier to over 250 MYA, when the original supercontinent Pangea existed.

    Platypus   Echidna   Crocodile

As a result of Australia's arid climate, marsupials could proliferate. These include kangaroos, wallabies, quokkas, possums, quolls, numbats, the Tasmanian devil, and the Tasmanian tiger (thylacine). Macropods (large legs), such as kangaroos and wallabies, can cover large distances across arid lands between billabongs (natural water ponds). The koala and wombat are very closely related. Both are herbivores, koalas living in trees, while wombats live on the ground.

Kangaroo   Possum   Koala   Wombat

Australia is also noted for having a large number of venomous animals, including many poisonous snakes, spiders, scorpions, platypus, octopus, jellyfish, and stingrays. The most-deadly animals are:

Box jellyfish   Redback spider   Taipan snake   Sydney funnel-
                                                                                    web spider

First People

Scientists believe that early humans began in the Great Rift Valley of East Africa — modern day Ethiopia, Uganda, Kenya, among other countries. The Great Rift Valley contained forests, grasses & cereals, and animals. As the climate changed, and the forests lessened, and the primates came down from the trees in search of food, such as berries & cereals from plants, and meat from animals, they became hunter gatherers. Scientists call these primates or early humans 'Australopithicus', meaning Southern ape. 'Lucy' a partial skeleton of an 'Australopithicus' was discovered in 1974 in Ethiopia. Scientists believe that 'Lucy' is a common ancestor of all humans on Earth.

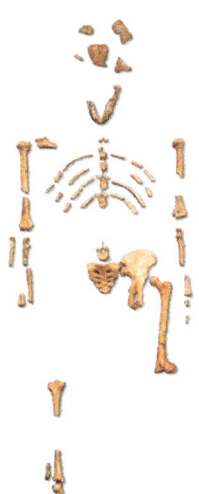

Reconstruction of the fossil skeleton of 'Lucy' Australopithicus.

Image of Australopithicus

About 500,000 years ago, as early humans developed, migrations of early humans began. Early human groups developed skills and slowly migrated into new areas in search of food. 'Homo Habilis' (Handy man) created stone tools. 'Homo Erectus' (Erect man) migrated long distances. 'Homo Sapiens' (Wise man) began about 300,000 years ago. Other sub-branches of early humans, such as 'Neanderthals', were found to have settled in Eurasia. These were followed by 'Cro-Magnon' (Cave men).

Scientists believe that as the last major Ice Age receded, early humans travelled out of Africa. One of the earliest groups, 'Upper Paleolithic' (Old Stone Age) humans, travelled out of Africa over 65,000 years ago, crossed southern Asia, and across land bridges into Australia. These humans that settled in Australia are the indigenous ancestors of Australia's Aborigines.

Humans also settled in Europe, once it became warm enough, around 45,000 years ago. They settled in eastern Asia about 25,000 years ago. Humans crossed a land bridge from eastern Asia into North America about 15,000 years ago, then into South America about 12,000 years ago. The last group of humans to settle in new territory migrated and settled into New Zealand and the Pacific Islands about 5,000 years ago.

The pre-history of Australia is considered to begin with the earliest human settlement in Australia about 60,000 years ago, through to the first European colonisation in 1788. The reason it is called pre-history is because there is no definitive documentation recording the events of the period, and our knowledge is generally composed of folklore, or stories handed down verbally from generation to generation, and through archaeological discovery.

The ancestors of Aboriginal Australians settled in Australia about 60,000 years ago. They were hunters and gatherers. They used tools made of stone, bone and wood. However, as the Ice Age receded further the oceans rose. The land bridge between Asia and the Australian continent submerged and disappeared. The Australian continent became isolated from the rest of the world. This meant that the Aborigines never got to learn about later inventions, such as working with metals like bronze and iron, until European settlement in the 1700's, less than 300 years ago.

Photograph of fossil skeleton found at Lake Mungo.

The earliest archaeological discovery of human existence in Australia was at Lake Mungo, located 760 kilometres due west of Sydney. The fossil skeleton remains of a woman were found in 1969, and later the fossil skeleton remains of a man were discovered in 1974. They have been dated to be over 40,000 years old.

Similar discoveries have been made in Western Australia, including the Juukan Gorge area and caves.

Carbon-dating indicates that the area around Sydney has been inhabited for at least 30,000 years. An archaeological dig in the modern suburb of Parramatta, in western Sydney, indicated that ancient Aboriginal people used charcoal, stone tools and campfires. In Penrith, in far-western Sydney, numerous Aboriginal stone tools were found in Cranebrook Terrace gravel sediments dating back almost 50,000 years. Archaeological evidence found on the upper banks of the Swan River in Western Australia indicates ancient Aboriginal settlement from about 30,000 years ago.

In south-eastern Australia, archaeological finds around the suburb of Keilor in Melbourne have been dated as 30,000 years old. Cloggs Cave, a limestone cave along the Snowy River, near Buchan in Eastern Victoria, is the site of ancient Aboriginal remains from 17,000 years ago. In Tasmania, which was still connected to the Australian mainland by land-bridge, there have also been significant ancient Aboriginal finds. Those found in the Cave Bay Cave on Hunter Island have been dated as 18,500 years ago. Ancient Aboriginal fossils have also been found at Fraser Cave and Beginner's Luck Cave in southern Tasmania, dating back 20,000 years.

The Dreaming — The Aboriginal Creation Stories

Early hunter gatherers considered that the physical world, its land, mountains, rivers, seas, plants and animals had a supernatural quality. There was a belief that all things possessed a spirit, in the same way that people do, so early humans created stories to explain how everything came into being and how everything is connected. This is what we now call religion, a system of belief.

The first world religion was a form of 'Shamanism', which began about 100,000 years ago. It is the system of belief that the ancestors of Australian Aborigines brought with them when they settled. Shamanism still exists today in some parts of indigenous Asia and America. The Aboriginal creation stories are called 'The Dreaming' or 'Dreamtime'.

The Dreaming tells of how the ancestral beings shaped the land and embedded their spirits in the land. It says that the land is alive, and the power of The Dreaming is eternal and ever-present, and that we can access that power. The Dreaming tells of how the rainbow serpent emerged from beneath the ground to cut out huge mountains, ridges, and gorges.

There are many Dreamtime stories, and they vary depending on the tribes and areas around Australia. Here are some examples.

A Creation Story of the Ngiyaampaa country in western New South Wales.

Long ago, in the beginning, there was nothing, and the spirit of our ancestral being 'Guthi-Guthi' lived up in the sky.

He came down to create a special land filled with people, animals and birds.

Guthi-Guthi came down and created land, he set down borders and the sacred sites. He set down the birthing places from where all the Dreamings came from.

Guthi-Guthi set a foot on each of two mountains — Gunderbooka and Grenfell — and he looked out over the land and saw that it was bare. Guthi-Guthi knew that the water-serpent 'Weowie' was trapped inside a mountain, Mount Minara. So Guthi-Guthi called out to the water-serpent, "Weowie, Weowie!" But the water-serpent was trapped inside the mountain and couldn't hear.

Guthi-Guthi went back up to the sky and again called out, "Weowie, Weowie," but again the water-serpent did not hear. So Guthi-Guthi came down from the sky like thunder and crashed on the mountain. The Mountain split apart and Weowie the water-serpent came out. Where the water-serpent went, he made river and streams, and cut gorges out of the land.

When it was done, Weowie crawled back into the mountain, and that's where he lives to this day, in Mount Minara.

However, after that, they wanted water to come down from the north, to run through all of the country. It was up to the Old Pundu, the Cod, to drag the water down from the north and create a river, the Darling River.

So Old Pundu came out with his little mate Mudlark and they set off up north and they created the big river that flowed through the country down to the sea.

So, this country was created, and the first two tribes to put down and settle here were Eaglehawk and Crow. And from these tribes came many more tribes. So, the Ngiyaampaa and the Barkandji peoples came from the Eaglehawk and Crow.

A Creation story from the Yuin-Monaro people of the far south coast of New South Wales.

A long time ago, the Great Spirit, Darama, came down to earth and made all the animals and birds, and he gave them all names. He also made a man and a woman, Toonkoo and Ngaardi. Toonkoo and Ngaardi lived on a mountain.

One day, Toonkoo told Ngaardi that he was going out hunting for kangaroos and emus. While Toonkoo went hunting, Ngaardi stayed home to make some bush tucker. She waited and waited for Toonkoo to return, but he didn't. Ngaardi started worrying then crying. As the tears fell from her face, they created the rivers and creeks that ran down the mountain. She waited all day for Toonkoo to return with food, but he never came back.

While Toonkoo was out hunting, he threw a spear and got a kangaroo. When he walked a bit further and came across the Great Spirit, Darama, up in the sky. Watching him, Toonkoo aimed his spear and threw it at Darama, but Darama caught it, then threw it back at Toonkoo. As it came down, the spear turned into a boomerang. That's how we got boomerangs.

Toonkoo continued hunting but was still angry at Darama, so Darama put him on the moon. As the moon was coming up, Ngaardi was still crying. As the moon came up over the horizon, she looked up into the face of the full moon and saw Toonkoo.

There, on the mountain, she laid down. She said to herself that if Toonkoo ever came back, he would find her heart on the mountain. Today, her heart is the red flower that we call the Waratah.

The story of how the water got to the plains, from the Butchulla people of Fraser Island

Along way back to the beginning of time, everything was new, and there was a tribe of Aboriginal people living on a mountain. It was a beautiful place, but everyone was worried because it had not rained for a long time, and they were running out of water. All the wells, except for one, were empty.

The last time it had rained, the water had just run down the side of the mountain out to the sea. Now, on the other side of the mountain, the plains were dry, and nothing grew.

Two members of the tribe, two greedy men, Weeri and Walawidbit, decided to steal the last of the water then run away with it.

In secret, they made a large water carrier, called an 'eel-a-mun'. One night, while the tribe slept, they stole the water and hurried away.

In the morning, when the other woke up, all the water was gone. There was no water for the little children and babies, the old people, and it was very hot.

The Elders called all the people together. It was then that they noticed that Weeri and Walawidbit were missing.

Looking around, they found their tracks, and the warriors quickly followed these tracks down the other side of the mountain, and they could see Weeri and Walawidbit in the distance.

As the watercarrier, 'eel-a-mun', was very heavy, Weeri and Walawidbit were walking slowly. They thought they were safe. However, when they saw the warriors chasing after them, they began to run too.

The best spearmen from the warriors ran to a cliff that jutted out over the plains and threw all their spears. One hit the eel-a-mun and it dropped off. It made a hole in the water-carrier. On and on, across the plains, Weeri and Walawidbit continued to run. They did not notice that the water was leaking out until the water-carrier was almost empty. By the time they noticed, the warriors had caught up with them.

When Weeri and Walawidbit were caught, the warriors took them back home and the Elders called a meeting. They decided that Weeri and Walawidbit had to be punished for stealing, and for thinking about themselves first and not the tribe.

A clever man, Wonmutta, made some very strong magic, and Weeri changed into the very first emu. He went running down the mountains onto the plains in shame. Walawidbit was changed into the very first blue-tongued lizard, and he crawled away to hide in the rocks.

But a wonderful thing happened. Wherever the water had leaked out of the watercarrier, eel-a-mun, there were now beautiful waterholes, called billabongs. There was grass and flowers and the plains, and lovely water lilies growing by the billabongs. And there were shrubs and trees too.

Soon the birds came, and everyone was happy because there was lots of water for everyone.

The Creation of Budj Bim by the Djardgurdwurung people of south-western Victoria

At the start of the Dreaming, four Creator Beings were sent by the Great Creator Spirit to make the different features across the land. The Creator Beings were of giant form and first arrived at a secret sacred location in the Stony Rises area just to the south of Lake Condah.

These four Creator Beings took the shape of men and became the first of a long line of law men who had special spiritual and ceremonial powers and responsibilities (shamans). The Djardgurdwurung people believe the descendants of these four men carried on these powers, responsibilities, and rituals through the generations until today.

Three of the original law men moved to other parts of the land, to the north and to the west. The fourth law man crouched down, and his giant body transformed to make the peaks of Tappoc and Budj Bim (Mt Napier and Mt Eccles respectively). When Budj Bim erupted with lava and stones some 30,000 years ago, the Djardgurdwurung people witnessed the Creator Being revealing himself to the land. This story has been passed down as folklore through the generations.

The significance of this story is that modern archaeologists have used new scientific evidence to verify the eruptions and have dated these to around 37,000 years ago. This means that the Djardgurdwurung people must have been already living in the area for that time and more, which makes this story one of the oldest oral traditions in existence, predating creation stories from other continents.

Other surviving traditions refer to geological events such as volcanic eruptions, earthquakes and meteorite impacts that have been transformed into other creation stories passed down as the Dreaming or Dreamtime stories.

500 Nations

The Aboriginal Study, a paper published in 2016, by Professor Eske Willerslev of the University of Cambridge has confirmed that modern Aboriginal Australians are directly genetically related to the first inhabitants of Australia.

In this genomic study of 83 Aboriginal Australians (speakers of the Pama-Nyangan languages) and 23 Papuans from the New Guinea Highlands, they were directly genetically connected to the original humans that migrated from Africa more than 70,000 years ago, but also genetically isolated and therefore diverged from Eurasians between 50-70,000 years ago. This may mean that when we look at Aboriginal communities prior to European colonisation, we are looking at what our other human communities around the inhabited world also looked like some 70,000 years ago.

For 60,000 years the ancestors of the Aboriginal people of Australia continued to grow. It is estimated that there were between 250 to 700 nations or clans. Estimates of the pre-European population of

Australia range from 300,000 to 1,000,000 people. Also, there are estimates that there were about 250 to 300 languages, and up to 600 dialects.

The politics of the 500 Nations

The politics of early Aboriginal society would not be recognisable by most Western observers as there appear to be no records of kings or formal governments. The unit was the family — children, parents, siblings, uncles, aunties. Related families would form the clan or tribe. The clan had a totem (tribal symbol), usually an animal. Family 'Elders' would lead the tribe, with a 'Chief', strongly influenced by 'shamans', who were religious healers.

Intra-tribal disputes were often resolved by "one-on-one" combat, while inter-tribal disputes led to limited battles, in terms of warriors, weapons, and time.

Modern map of Australia divided into its Indigenous nations, pre-European settlement, provided by the Australian Institute of Aboriginal and Torres Strait Islander Studies (AIATSIS) website.

Aboriginal Tribal Nations

As previously written, there were between 250 to 700 nations or clans. Many of these come under larger umbrellas of people, as follows:

Koori — represents the Aboriginal people living in the south-east of Australia from southern NSW to Victoria.

Noongar — represents the Aboriginal people living in south-west Australia.

Murri — the Aboriginal people of northern NSW and Queensland.

Palawa — the Aboriginal people of Tasmania

Yolngu — Aboriginal people of the Northern Territory.

Due to the disintegration of many Aboriginal communities, it is extremely difficult to list each Aboriginal tribal nation, but these are the ones centred around the current Australian cities.

The Kulin nation, centred in and around Melbourne, is Victoria's most noted Aboriginal nation. It was composed of five tribes — the Boonwurrung (Port Melbourne to Moe), Woiwurrung (northern Melbourne), Taungurong (Central Victoria), Djadjawurrung (Bendigo and Maryborough), and Wathaurong (Ballarat and Geelong).

Also, we know the Gunai or Kurnai nation was located, east of the Kulin, in Gippsland and consisted of five tribes — the Brataulung (Wilson's Promontory), the Braiakuaung (Sale), the Brabiralung (Bairnsdale), the Tatungalung (Ninety Mile Beach), and the Krauatungalung (south-eastern coast to Point Hicks).

Details of Victorian nations and languages can be found at https://vacl.org.au/home

The tribes of Aboriginal people around Sydney were the Tharawal (southwest), Dharug (west), Eora (central Sydney), Kuring-gai (north). The Yuggera people lived around Brisbane.

The Kaurna people lived around Adelaide.

The Wajuk clan of the Noongar people lived around Perth.

The Larrakia clan lived around Darwin.

While in Hobart, the Nuennone lived south and the Paredarerme lived in the north.

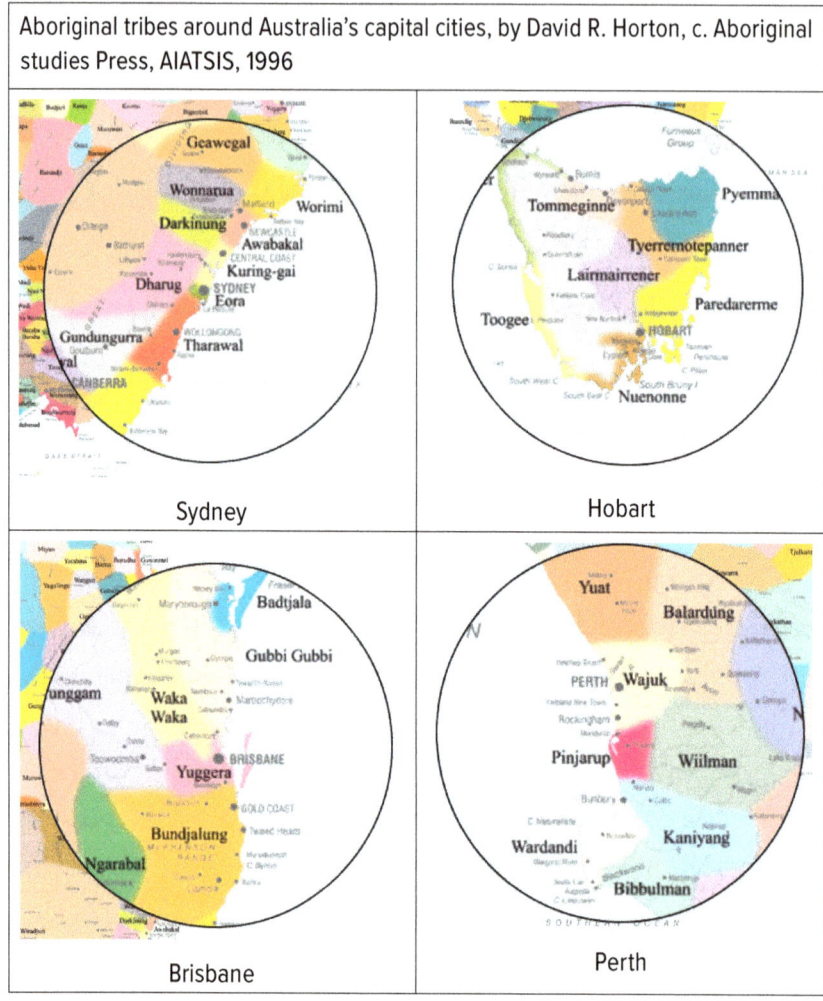

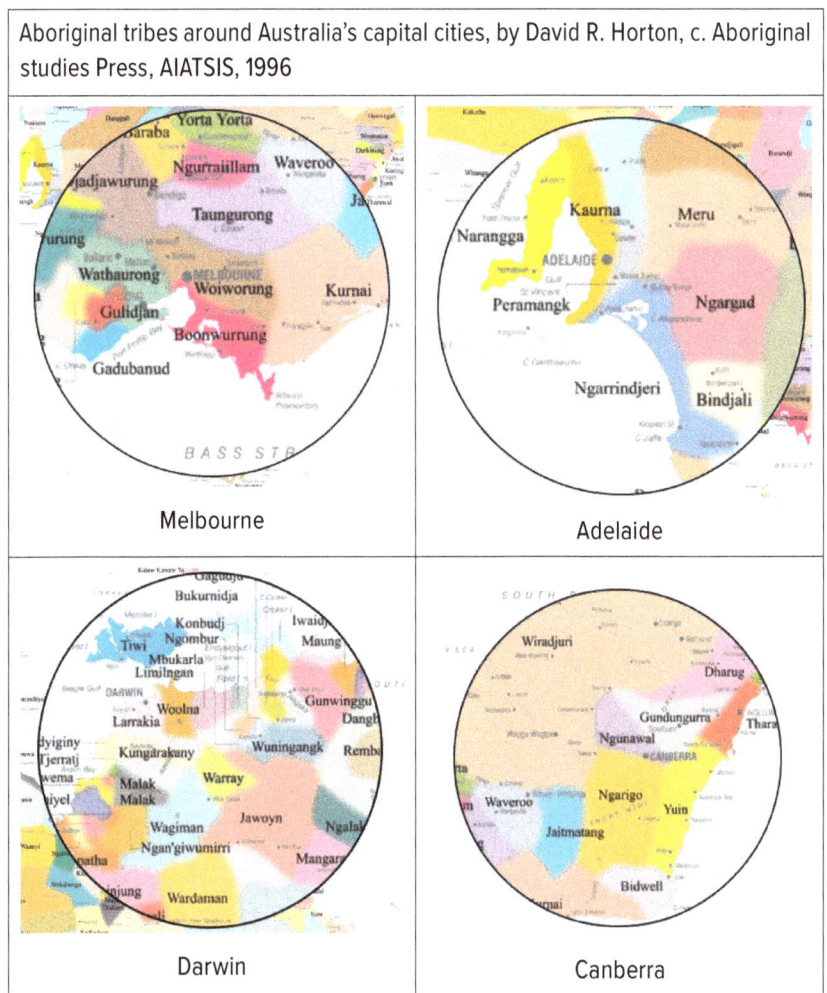

Aboriginal tribes around Australia's capital cities, by David R. Horton, c. Aboriginal studies Press, AIATSIS, 1996

Aboriginal language

The Pama-Nyangan language group is common for almost all Aboriginal Australians, except for those in the very north of Australia. Of the 250-300 languages that once existed, only about 46 of those languages today have 100 speakers or more. The Macro-Gunwinyguan language group is located in Arnhem Land in the north of the Northern Territory. This variation in languages bases between Pama-Nyangan and Macro-Gunwinyguan indicate that Aboriginal migration was not homogeneous and that there was more than one wave of migration to Australia. Recent archaeological and genetic discoveries indicate an Indian migration to northern Australia some 4000 years ago, influencing language and agricultural practices.

In New South Wales (NSW), there are 2 active Aboriginal languages — Wiradjuri (southern NSW) and Gamilaraay (central-northern NSW).

In South Australia (SA), there are 4 active languages — Pitjantjatjara (northern and south-west SA), Yankunjatjara (western desert, SA), Adnyamathanha (central SA), and Ngarrindjerri (southern SA).

In Queensland (Qld), there are also 4 active languages — Guugu Yimidhirr, Wik-Munkan, Kuku Yalanji, and Kuuk Thayore — all located in the Cape York Peninsula (northern Qld).

In Western Australia (WA), there are 17 active Aboriginal languages. Of these the most spoken languages are Ngaanjatjarra (eastern WA), Martu Wangka (central WA), Noongar (south-west WA), Yinjibarndi (northwest WA), and Bardi (Kimberleys area).

In the Northern Territory (NT), there are 19 active languages. Of these the most spoken languages are Upper Arrernte (Alice Springs), Dhuwal (northern NT), Pitjantjatjara (southern NT), Warlpiri (central NT), Murrinh Patha (northwest NT), Tiwi (Tiwi Islands, off NT north coast), and Kunwinjku (western Arnhem Land, northern NT).

In Victoria and Tasmania, there are no more active Aboriginal languages. Wurundjeri was the Aboriginal language spoken by the Kulin nation that was located in and around Melbourne, Victoria. Palawa Kani was the name given to Aboriginal Tasmania, although it is unsure as to whether this was the language.

The word 'hello' can be said in a number of different ways according to region and language, as follows:

"Ninna Marni" — Kuarna, South Australia

"Palyah" — Pitjantjatjara, Central Australia

"Parma zee" — Yolnu Matha, Arnhem Land, Northern Territory

"Mayyam" — Mirriam Mir, Torres Strait Islands

"Galang gnuruindhau" — Turrbal, Brisbane, Queensland

"Budyeri kamaru" — Gadigal (Eora), Sydney, New South Wales

"Jingiwallah" — Budjalung, Northern Rivers, New South Wales

"Wominjeka" — Wurundjeri, Melbourne, Victoria

"Yah" — Palawa Kani, Tasmania

"Wayiba" and "Wanthiwa" — Yinjibarndi, Pilbara, Western Australia

"Jooeh" — Martu Wangka, Western Desert, Western Australia

"Kaya" — Noongar, Fremantle, Western Australia

The variations in these indigenous versions of 'hello' indicate just how distinctive each language is.

Further information about Australian Aboriginal languages can be gained on the Australian Institute of Aboriginal and Torres Strait Islander Studies website.

Words of the Noongar people of southern Western Australia are found on the Noongar Culture website — https://www.noongarculture.org.au/. Some of these words are as follows:

Pronouns	People	Time/Seasons	Verbs	Adjectives	Abstract
Ngany (I/me)	Koolang (child)	Kedalup (day)	Djinang (look/see)	Boola (large)	Kaya (hello)
Noonookurt (you)	Koolangka (children)	Beerit (twilight)	Nih (listen)	Koomba (big)	Wandju (welcome)
Ngalak (we/us)	Maam (man/father)	Kedalak (night)	Wankiny (talk)	Boolariny (plenty/lots)	Balai (beware)
Ngalang (our)	Yorga (woman)	Yeye (now/today)	Walinj (cry)	Dabakarn (slow)	Bardan (spirit)
Bari (he/she)	Ngarngk (mother)	Benang (tomorrow)	Yakiny (stand)	Djerung (fat)	Nidja (here)
Balup (them)	Deman (grandmother)	Boorda (later)	Koorliny (come)	Karlawooliny (hot)	Winja (where)
Balang (those)	Dembart (grandfather)	Boordawon (soon)	Dalyaniny (go/gone)	Boodja-Dooga (dusty)	Yira (up)
	Djook/Djookian (sister/s)	Koora (long ago)	Boolyaka (leave)	Kwobardak (pretty/beautiful)	Bo (long way)
	Ngoon/Ngoonee (brother/s)	Birak (summer)	Bardanginy (run)	Moorditj (hard)	Kaartdijin (knowledge)
	Konk (uncle)	Bunara (autumn)	Baranginy (catch)	Noorti (smelly)	Kenyak (that's enough)
	Koorta (husband/wife)	Makuru (early winter)	Barkininy (bite)		Nortj (dead)
	Moort (family)	Djilba (late winter)	Barminy (hit)		Uart (nothing)
	Noongar (person/people)	Kambarang (spring)	Boorniny (cut)		
			Djooboori (swim)		
			Dookerniny (cook)		
			Ke-ning (dance)		
			Waabiny (play)		

Body parts	Items	Nature	Animals	Prepositions	Feelings
Djoorla (bones)	Booka (coats)	Keip (water)	Djert (birds)	Kardup (beneath/under)	Djiripin (happy)
Kart (head)	Boorn (wood/stick)	Kinjarling (rain)	Mopoke (owl)		Moolyip (upset)
Moolymaree (face)	Boya (rock/stones)	Bilya (river)	Yerdarap (duck)		Kwaba (good)
Meeyal (eyes)	Choota (bag)	Binjar (swamp/lake)	Warlitj (eagle)		Warlung (healthy)
Dwank (ears)	Darp (knife)	Wardan (sea/ocean)	Weitj (emu)		Minditj (sick)
Mooly (nose)	Gidjie (spear)	Boodja (country)	Gooljak (swan)		Karnya (shame)
Ngorlak (teeth)	Kali, Kylie (boomerang)	Boodjara (country of origin)	Djildjit (fish)		Kart-warra (silly/stupid)
Darliny (tongue)	Koitj (axe)	Karl (fire)	Kwilana (dolphin)		Koboolweert (hungry)
Yet (chin)		Djarima (forest)	Djilgi (prawn)		Koboolkorl (full/satisfied)
Wort (throat)		Djinda (star)	Kooyar (frog)		
Nanuk (neck)		Goorda (island)	Yakkan (turtle)		
Narnak (beard)		Kata (hill)	Yonga (kangaroo)		
Ngoornt (chest)		Ngarngk (sun)	Dwert/Dwerda (dog/dingo)		
Koboorl (stomach)		Meeuk (moon)	Karda (goanna)		
Djoop (kidney)		Mulgar (thunder)	Koomoori (possum)		
Koort (heart)		Walken (rainbow)	Kwenda (bandicoot)		
Kwelak (hip)			Nyingarn (echidna)		
Kwan (backside)			Djilyaro (bees)		
Maart (leg)			Kara (spider)		
Yartj (thigh)					
Boonitj (knee)					
Djen/Djena (foot/feet)					
Kwoliny (wrist)					
Maar (hand)					
Marak (finger)					

Aboriginal Arts

Australia has always had a strong artistic and theatrical tradition. Modern Australian Aboriginal art is currently growing in popularity and authentic pieces can command large prices at sale or auction. The 'corroboree' or 'caribberie' (Eora) is an Australian Aboriginal ceremonial meeting. It is an Australian Aboriginal dance ceremony which takes the form of sacred 'Dreamtime' ritual or informal gathering. It includes music, dance, make up and costume.

Archaeological discoveries of Aboriginal art indicate that it has existed as long as the Aboriginal population in Australia. The 'Gwion Gwion' rock paintings were discovered by pastoralist Joseph Bradshaw in the Kimberley region of Western Australia in 1891. These rock paintings have been dated to around 25,000 years ago. Although, there are unrelated rock paintings that date even earlier. Of over 8,000 examples of 'Gwion Gwion'-like rock paintings, most have been damaged or ruined as a result of Western Australian government land management actions and that of mining companies. Modern Aboriginal art varies from traditional styles by Clifford Possum Tjapaltjarri, Gloria Petyarre, Christine Napanangka Michaels, Marcia Purdie, Rover Thomas, Tommy Mitchell, Bill Whiskey and John Mawurndjal to more international styles by Albert Namatjira, Kudditji Kngwarreye and Lin Onus.

A South Australian Corroboree (1864), painting by WR Thomas, Art Gallery of South Australia

Rock pictures from 'Gwion Gwion' paintings, circa 25,000 years ago.

The Spirits Jimpi and Manginta, by Paddy Jaminji and Rover Thomas, https://janetthomas.wordpress.com/

Aboriginal economics — hunter-gatherer v agriculturalist

There has been much recent conjecture regarding the historical Anglo-European view of Aboriginal Australia as being one of "hunter-gatherers". This notion portrays the traditional inhabitants of this country as seemingly unchanged from the time that Aboriginal migration is estimated to have occurred over 50,000 years ago. But can a whole continent of people remain static over so many millenia? This view may have arisen as part of the British policy of "terra nullius" over Australia, that the land was unoccupied by a 'civilised' society, denigrating its traditional inhabitants to savages.

Through language groups, we know that there was a first wave of Pama-Nyangan-speaking people who are estimated to have arrived more than 50,000 years ago, which would have pre-dated the advent of agriculture. However, the later migration of Macro-Gunwinyguan-speaking people may have seen the introduction of some form of agriculture to traditional Australian society.

Bruce Pascoe, in his books Dark Emu: Black Seeds: Agriculture or Accident? (2014) and Young Dark Emu: A Truer History (2019) indicate a very-different pre-European economy in Australia, one that included farming and agriculture, and trade. Pascoe's accounts are based on carefully recounting records of the early Australian colonial explorers, especially those of Thomas Mitchell, who witnessed women in the traditional communities harvesting onions and yams and cultivating the land.

Furthermore, we are aware of the traditional Aboriginal practice of "burning off" the land with controlled bushfires in an effort to maintain and secure sedentary communities from the ravages of uncontrolled bushfires. Certainly, the balance of agricultural activity with that of hunting and gathering would depend on how arable the various regions of the continent settled were — tropical, temperate, and semi-desert regions.

Also, just as Australia has many unique species of fauna — kangaroo, koala, platypus — so is its flora, grains and vegetables that were not recognisable to traditional Anglo-European knowledge and custom.

And one could go further to speculate that Aboriginal agricultural practices may have developed in their own unique manner.

Finally, we know that the traditional society in Australia did trade with external communities ranging from the Torres Strait to the Makassar (southern Indonesia) to even as far as explorers and traders from China, where relics have been identified in northern Australia, well-before European settlement. With trade, comes communication and the passing of knowledge, including agricultural methods.

It is hard to accurately describe the full detail of Aboriginal economies prior to European settlement, however we can recognise that it has not been static since the initial immigration of over 50,000 years ago and that it has been influenced by its post-agricultural-advent neighbours, as observed by the very early European explorers and current archaeologists.

Indigenous Weather Knowledge

The Australian Bureau of Meteorology (BOM) website provides an excellent explanation of how indigenous weather knowledge was far more complex than the European seasons. Whereas the European seasons are four equally divided times of the year, in terms of months — Summer (December to February), Autumn (March to May), Winter (June to August) and Spring (September to November), the indigenous seasons were not uniform over the continent and more accurately reflected the climate patterns of local regions.

The map of Australia, below, shows the diverse nature of climate across the continent and how these cannot be uniformly classified into four equal seasons.

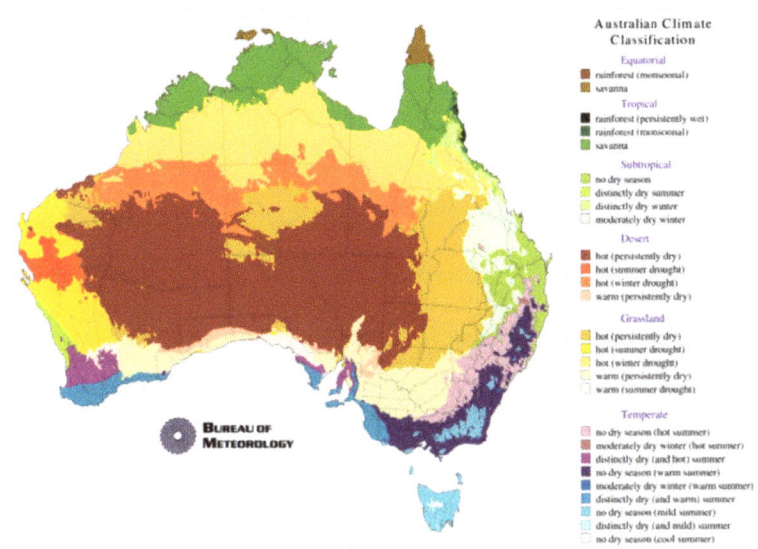

Tiwi seasons (far north)

In the Tiwi Islands, north of Darwin, in the Northern Territory, there are only three Tiwi seasons — Jamutakari, the wet season (December to February); Kumunupunari, the dry season (March to August); and, Tiyari, hot and wet season (September to November).

Nyoongar seasons (south west)

In the Nyoongar region of south-western Australia, there are six seasons — Birak, first summer (December to January, burning time); Bunuru, second and hottest summer (February to March); Djeran, cooler season (April to May); Makuru, cold and wet season (June to July); Djilba, first spring (August to September); and, Kambarang, second and drier spring (October to November).

Kaurna seasons (around Adelaide)

The Kaurna people have four seasons, but the timing is different to the European seasons — Warltati, hot season (January to March); Parnati, windy season (April to June); Kudlila, wet season (July to September); and, Wirltuti, mild and warm season (October to December).

Walabunnba seasons (Alice Springs, Central Australia)
The Walabunnba people of Central Australia have two seasons only — Watangka, hot season (October to March); and Yurluurrp, dry but cooler season (April to September).

Gariwerd seasons (Grampians, Victoria)
The Gariwerd calendar of the central highlands of Victoria has six seasons — Kooyang (Eel season), hot and dry (January to March), Gwangal Moronn (Honeybee season), warm season (March to May); Chunnup (Cockatoo season), freezing cold (May to July); Larneuk (Nesting bird season), wet and changing weather (July to August); Petyan (Wildflower season), warmer spring days (September to November); and, Ballambar (Butterfly season), hot and dry (November to January).

The various indigenous seasons reflect local climate and indicate the changes in fauna and flora, and when appropriate burning off times should occur.

Neolithic Indian Migrants, circa 4000 BC
As written earlier, there are recent archaeological and genetic studies that support the notion that there was an Indian migration to northern Australia some 4,000 years ago. In 2012, a genetic study by Irina Pugash of the Max Planck Institute for Evolutionary Anthropology suggested Indian explorers had settled and assimilated with the indigenous population. The timing of the migration coincided with a genetic change in the indigenous population of the northern Australia. It also coincided with a change in the types of tools and food processing discovered by archaeological digs in the same region. It may also

account for the difference of the Macro-Gunwinyguan language group in the Arnhem Land region of Australia. There are two theories on how the genetic transfer took place: 1) That it occurred directly from India to Australia; and 2) that it was an indirect transfer through Indonesia. It may account for the introduction of agricultural procedures that flowed through Australia that were noted later by the British explorer, Major Mitchell, in the early 1800s. The main concern regarding this theory is one of timing. The Neolithic Era, usually associated with these 'New Stone Age" technology is around 10,000 BC, 12,000 years ago, not 4,000 years ago. Also, if the migration was 4,000 years ago, there appears to be a unreconcilable absence of early metals technology that usually appears in archaeological finds of this time period. One might speculate that the Neolithic Era came to Australia later than it did in other parts of the world, which might be explained using Blainey's 'tyranny of distance'.

'Tyranny of distance' refers to the influence of distance in slowing the development of remote communities, such as the indigenous communities of Australia and New Zealand. Three key factors identified in influencing the speed at which a civilisation develops are: 1) competition, 2) communication, and 3) resources. Remote communities are removed from competition and the related external threats of neighbouring advantages in technology. Also, distance slows or halts the communication of new technologies or systems. The positive aspect is that distance assists in protecting and preserving established communities, from disease as well as wars.

PART TWO

EURASIAN EXPLORATION, DISCOVERY, AND COLONISATION

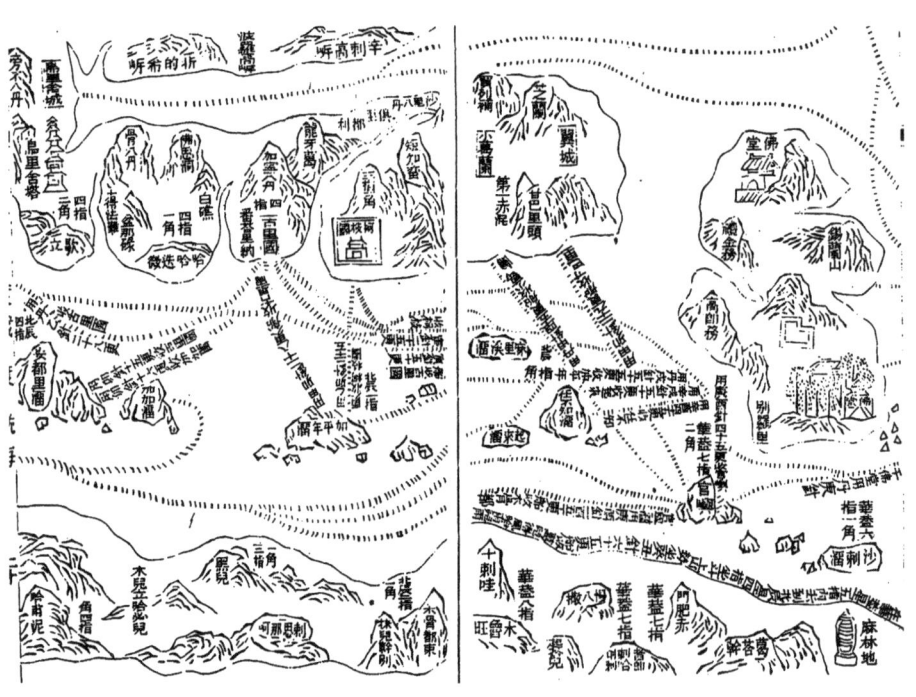

Zheng He's sailing charts, the Mao Kun map, were published in a book entitled the Wubei Zhi. A section of the Wubei Zhi oriented east: India in the upper left, Sri Lanka upper right, and Africa along the bottom.

Eurasian Discoverers

Much is made of Captain Cook in Australian history books but there were quite a few Eurasian discoverers to Australia before him. The first noted explorer was a Chinese admiral with over 300 ships.

European exploration for Australia begins with the European colonisation of south-eastern Asia. Portuguese and Dutch explorers claimed the areas of and around modern Indonesia. Through their discoveries, these explorers came across records and maps of a great southern land. The Dutch set up a corporation to transact business with these colonies, the Dutch East India Company. Later, as Britain, expanded its colonial empire, it established the British East India Company to transact colonial business.

Zheng He (1371-1433) was a Chinese explorer, diplomat, and admiral during the Ming dynasty, at the time of the Chinese Emperor Yongle. Zheng set out on seven voyages between 1405 and 1433. His early voyages were focused on Java, Indonesia, and it is on one of them that he may have visited Australia. His maps indicate the existence of a great southern land, south-east of Java. Zheng sailed in a large fleet.

Cristovao de Mendonca (1475-1532) was a Portuguese nobleman and explorer. Mendonca, with three caravels, sailed in search of Marco Polo's fabled islands of gold between 1521 and 1524 and charted the east coast of Australia. One of Mendonca's caravels was wrecked near the coast of Warrnambool and is said by some to be the 'mahogany ship' of Australian folklore. The Dieppe maps, a group of 16th century French maps charting the eastern coast of Australia, are considered to be evidence of Mendonca's travels and the inspiration for James Cook's voyage of discovery.

Willem Janszoon (a.k.a Jansz), (1570-1630) was a Dutch navigator and colonial governor. Janszoon is recognised as the first European to have sailed to Australia. Sailing on the ship named the Duyfken (meaning Little Dove), Janszoon landed at the Pennefather River on the west coast of Cape York, near Weipa, Queensland, in 1606, a week before Torres arrived.

Luis Vaz de Torres (1565-1608?) was a Spanish explorer. In 1605, Torres originally set out with a Portugese navigator named De Queiros but they were separated. It was De Queiros who may have originally come up with the name Australia. In 1606, Torres sailed south of New Guinea into the strait that now bears his name and would have seen Cape York. There is no record of him landing. We do not know when Torres died, but he disappears from history in 1608.

Eurasian Discoverers

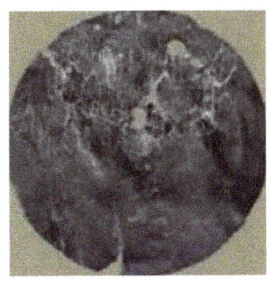

Dirk Hartog (1580-1621) was a Dutch explorer. He was employed by the Dutch East India Company between 1616 and 1618. Hartog's group was the second European expedition to land in Australia. In 1616, as part of a greater expedition, Hartog's ship, the Eendracht, became separated from the rest and was making its way towards Batavia (now Jakarta, Indonesia), when it landed on an island in Sharks Bay, Western Australia. He left an inscribed plate (left) to mark his landing on Dirk Hartog Island. After scouting the area for a few days, Hartog left and later reported that the area was not worth further exploration.

Frederick de Houtman (1571-1627) was also a Dutch explorer, who sailed along the western coast of Australia on his way to Batavia. He was also an astronomer and charted 12 different constellations in the southern hemisphere sky during his voyages. Also working for the Dutch East India Company, in 1619, De Houtman on the ship Dordrecht sailed past Perth and landed again at Sharks Bay. According to maps of his time, De Houtman identified that the coastline at Sharks Bay matched the land of Boeach or Locach as previously described in 'The Travels of Marco Polo'.

Abel Tasman (1603-1659) was also a Dutch sailor and merchant, and also worked for the Dutch East India Company between 1642 and 1644. Inspired by 'The Travels of Marco Polo', Governor-General of the Dutch East Indies, Anthony Van Diemen, in Batavia, ordered Tasman to explore the area described in the book as Boeach (also Beach). In 1642, Tasman, on the ship Zeehaen, sailed south of Australia to discover Tasmania (which Tasman named Van Diemen's Land, but was later changed), then onto New Zealand. In 1644, Tasman sailed and chartered the Australian northern coast from near Exmouth all the way to the top of Cape York.

Willem de Vlamingh (1640-1698?) was another Dutch sea captain to work for the Dutch East India Company. In 1696, De Vlamingh was sent to New Holland with three ships — Geelvink, Nijptang and Veseltje — to search for any survivors of the missing capital ship Ridderschap van Holland that disappeared on its way to Batavia with over 300 passengers and crew in 1694. Although failing to find any survivors, De Vlamingh landed at Rottnest Island, sailed up the Swan River, then onto Dirk Hartog Island, where he swapped Hartog's original plate for a newer pewter one. The original plate is on display in the Rijksmuseum in Amsterdam, Holland.

William Dampier (1651-1715) was an English privateer (pirate), explorer, naturalist (fauna and flora) and navigator, and was the first Englishman to explore Australia. He was the first person to circum-navigate the world three times. On his first trip, on the Cygnet in 1688, Dampier stopped at Kings Sound, at the mouth of the Fitzroy River in Western Australia. On his second trip, captaining the HMS Roebuck in 1699, he sailed along the Western Australia coast from Sharks Bay to Roebuck Bay, then onto other islands around New Guinea, such as New Hanover, New Ireland and New Britain. After his trip, Dampier was court-martialled for cruelty and dismissed from the English navy. Dampier also wrote a book, 'A New Voyage Round the World' in 1697.

Makassan Trepangers, Indonesian fishermen from Sulawesi, are known to have come to Australia on fishing trips from about 1720 along the northern coast of Australia, although some reports put the date from 1640. Trepang is an Indonesian word for 'sea-cucumber' which is an invertebrate worm-like creature that lives on the sea floor. In 1803, Matthew Flinders on his trip around Australia encountered Pobasso, the chief of a group of Makassan Trepangers near Nhulunbuy on the Arnhem Land coast.

Eurasian Discoverers

Louis Antoine, Comte de Bougainville (1729-1811) was a French admiral and explorer. Early in his career, Bougainville was aide-de-camp to the Marquis de Montcalm in Canada during the Seven Years War (1756-63). In 1766, he was given two ships — Boudeuse and Etoile — by Louis XV and ordered to circum-navigate the world. In 1767, Bougainville sailed close to the Great Barrier Reef before turning towards the Solomon Islands. Bougainville Island in the Pacific is named after him.

James Cook (1728-1779) was a British sea captain, explorer, navigator and cartographer. Cook was also in Canada during the Seven Years War, mapping the St Lawrence River. On his first voyage (1768-71), Cook was engaged by the British Admiralty to travel to Tahiti, to view the transit of Venus across the path of the Sun, then onto New Zealand and Australia, where he travelled and chartered the east coast from Point Hicks, through the Great Barrier Reef, then across the Torres Strait, back to Britain. He stopped near Cooktown to repair his ship, the Endeavour. Cook captained two other great ocean voyages. He died in the Sandwich Islands (Hawaii) during his third voyage.

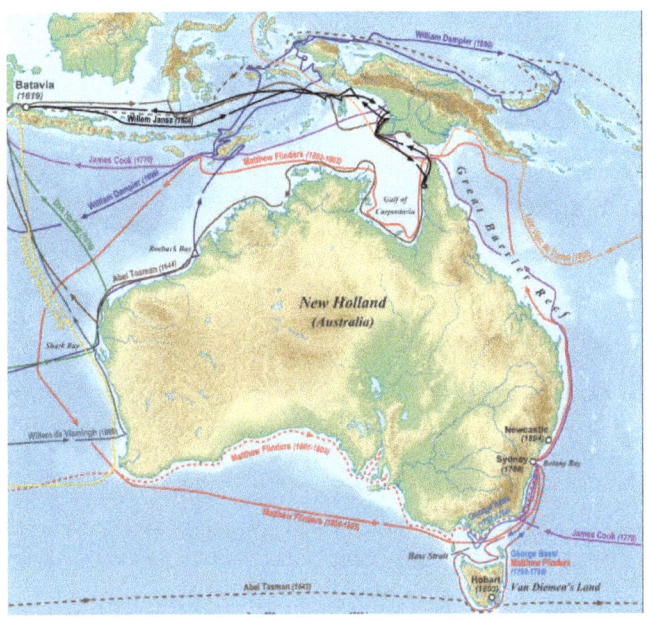

Some notable explorers after Cook

Marc-Joseph Marion Du Fresne (1724-1772) was a French explorer who made important discoveries in the southern Indian Ocean, Tasmania and New Zealand. In 1771, he was given two ships — Mascarin and Marquis de Castries — hoping to find Terra Australis. Sailing the same route as Abel Tasman, he sighted the western coast of Van Diemen's Land in March 1772. The ships anchored at Frederick Henry Bay or at Blackman's Bay, which precisely is uncertain. He was killed by Maoris shortly after landing in New Zealand. Marion Bay is named after him.

Tobias Furneaux (1735-1781) was a British navigator and Royal Navy officer. He was also the first man to circumnavigate the world in both directions. Furneaux accompanied Cook on his second voyage (1772-1775) and commanded the second ship, Adventure.

During the voyage, Furneaux became separated from Cook, and separately charted the south and east coasts of Van Diemen's Land. The Furneaux group of islands, including Flinders Island, were named after him.

Antione Bruni d'Entrecasteaux (1735-1793) was a French naval officer, explorer and colonial governor. In 1791, he was sent in command of the French ship Recherche to search for the missing La Perouse expedition. In April 1792, he anchored in Recherche Bay on the southern coast of van Diemen's Land. The expedition spent almost two months gaining supplies and collecting documents and specimens of fauna and flora, including the Blue Gum, Tasmania's floral emblem.

Sir John Hayes (1768-1831) was an officer in the British East India Company. In 1793, on his way from Calcutta to New Guinea to collect tradeable spices, he struck adverse winds and detoured down the western and southern coasts of Australia. He landed at Adventure Bay and explored the surrounding areas. Hayes was unaware of d'Entrecasteaux's expedition and renamed many of the geographical features, including the Derwent River.

Nicholas Baudin (1754-1803) was a French explorer, cartographer, and naturalist. In 1800, Napoleon selected Baudin to lead an expedition of two ships — Geographe and Naturaliste — captained by Admiral Hamelin, with nine botanists to explore New Holland. He reached the south-west coast of Australia in May 1801 and collected over 2,500 specimens. In April 1802, he met Matthew Flinders at Encounter Bay. Baudin died in Mauritius in 1803 during his return to France. Baudin Beach, Baudin Rocks and Nicholas Baudin Island bear his name.

Cook's expedition

Cook's expedition has been recognised officially as the one that discovered and claimed the Australian continent for Great Britain; therefore, it is this one that we will expand on.

It begins not with James Cook, but with Andrew Dalrymple (1737-1808) a Scottish geographer and hydrographer (mapper of oceans, creator of charts) for the British Admiralty. Dalrymple was employed in 1752 as a clerk for the British East India Company. In 1762, he was translating some documents that had been captured in the Philippines. The documents contained a testimony by De Torres of a great continent south of New Guinea. On his return to London in 1765, Dalrymple was elected a Fellow of the Royal Society and petitioned to lead an expedition to discover this great continent. As Dalrymple was not in the British Navy, the British Admiralty appointed James Cook, a renowned cartographer in the British Navy to lead the expedition. Dalrymple gave all his documents to Joseph Banks to use on the journey.

The HMB (bark) Endeavour, Cook's ship for the expedition, was a collier, a bulk cargo ship used for the transport of coal. One can speculate that it was chosen for its carrying capacity on such a long voyage, although this isn't verified. Other members of the expedition were:

Joseph Banks (1743-1820) — botanist — already a Fellow of the Royal

Society. Banks had experience in studying the natural history (fauna and flora) of Newfoundland and Labrador, Canada, in 1768. His duty was to document the natural history of the 'unknown' continent. He was later awarded a baronet in 1781, and elected President of the society in 1784 for his accomplishments.

Lieutenant Zachary Hickes (1739-1771) was second-in-command to Cook. He died on the voyage and was buried at sea. Strangely, although both Point Hicks (Australia) and Hicks Bay (New Zealand) were named after him, the 'e' in Hickes was omitted.

Charles Green (1734-1771) was a British astronomer. Green died on the voyage too.

Daniel Solander (1733-1782) was a Swedish naturalist, and held a doctorate from Uppsala University, Sweden.

Herman Sporing (1733-1771) was a Finnish explorer, draughtsman, botanist and naturalist. He also died on the voyage.

Other notables on the voyage were: William Monkhouse, surgeon; John Thomson, cook (as in galley chef); Alexander Buchan and Sydney Parkinson, both artists; Mr Reading, bosun's mate; James Magra, midshipman; Mr Orton, clerk; Mr Weir, quartermaster and about 80 others.

Cook's voyage had two parts. The first part was open, to view and document the transit of Venus between the Earth and the Sun from Tahiti in June 1769. The second part, whose envelope was not to be opened until the transit was complete (to hide it from espionage) was to locate and document the 'unknown' continent (Latin: Terra Incognita).

Cook's voyage was also part of an overall project by the British Admiralty in tackling the prevention and risk of scurvy, a fatal disease that had killed most of the crews on long voyages. The Admiralty were experimenting with supplements to crews' diets whilst on voyage. In Cook's case, the crew of the Endeavour were supplied with 40 bushels of malt (2,690 kgs), 1000 pounds (450 kgs) of portable soup, vinegar, mustard, wheat, sauerkraut (German pickled cabbage). Cook also paid strict attention to airing and drying the lower decks and keeping his men warm and well slept.

The voyage began on August 26, 1768, it sailed across the Atlantic Ocean, along the east coast of South America, rounded Cape Horn and sailed across the southern Pacific to make it to Tahiti in time to view the transit of Venus on June 3, 1769. While in Tahiti, Cook met and conversed with a Tahitian prince, named Omai, and another, named Tupaia. In their meetings, the Tahitians described and positioned the major islands of the Pacific for Cook to chart. In September 1769, the Endeavour arrived at New Zealand. Cook was the first European explorer to do so since Abel Tasman 127 years earlier. The Endeavour and its crew spent the next six months circum-navigating and Cook charting the islands of New Zealand.

According to Cook's log, at 6am on April 20, 1770, the Australian coast was sighted at Point Hicks, making landfall. The Endeavour then proceeded and landed a week later in Botany Bay, located in southern Sydney. It was there on April 29, as Cook landed, around 2pm, a younger man and an elder man of the Gweagal tribe walked up to meet them. The crew offered gifts, but these were not accepted. The two men walked away but were fired upon by the crew. They ran back to their huts, gathered more warriors, spears were thrown, more shots were fired, but records indicate that little harm was done. It was here that Banks, Solander and Sporing made some study of the local fauna and flora. Later, Banks was to recommend Botany bay as the suitable location for a settlement.

The Gweagal Shield, an exhibit encased in glass at the British Museum is a relic of first contact between the British and the indigenous people of Australia. Note the bullet hole in the shield which occurred when Cook's men opened fire.

The Endeavour sailed further north into Sydney Harbour, which Cook named Port Jackson. Upon landing, an older and younger Aboriginal person walked up to the landing party. A shot was fired, which wounded the older Aboriginal man. They ran off but returned with others. Spears were thrown, muskets fired, and again the Aborigines ran off. Later, Cook's party followed them to a village where they found Aboriginal children playing. Cook and his landing party left gifts then returned to ship.

The Endeavour continued northwards and landed at Bustard Bay on May 23. Cook noted in his journal that in the distance there were quite a number of campfires exuding smoke, further evidence of Aboriginal occupation. On June 11, while sailing through the Great Barrier Reef, the ship ran aground on a reef and was damaged, and the voyage was delayed for seven weeks as the ship was repaired, near today's Cooktown. During this time, Banks, Solander and Sporing made extensive studies of the fauna and flora. It was here that the word 'kangaroo' entered the English language, taken from name given by the local Guugu Yimidhirr people (gangurru).

Once repairs were complete, the Endeavour sailed further north along the coast to the top of the Cape York Peninsula, stopping at Possession Island, called Bedanug by the local Kaurareg people. From there, Cook set course for Batavia (Jakarta, Indonesia). It was noted by Cook in his journal on October 15 that although there had been two occurrences of scurvy — Charles Green and the Tahitian Tupaia — there had been no lives lost. It was when they reached Batavia, unfortunately during a malaria outbreak that Sporing, Green and Tupaia contracted further illness and died. After departing Batavia, the Endeavour made its way home to England. After rounding the Cape of Good Hope, while in the south Atlantic, Lt. Hicks contracted fever and died. He was buried at sea by the island of St. Helena. On July 10, seaman Nicholas Young sighted the English coast. The Endeavour continued up the English Channel and anchored at the Downs on July 12. The Endeavour had been at sea for almost three years. Cook went ashore in Deal, Kent. His return was unexpected because the English press had been publishing stories for quite some time that the Endeavour had been lost at sea.

When Cook claimed the Australian continent, the King of Great Britain was 'Mad' King George III (b.1738, K.1760-1820) and the Prime Minister of Great Britain was Lord North (b.1732, PM.1770-1782, d.1792).

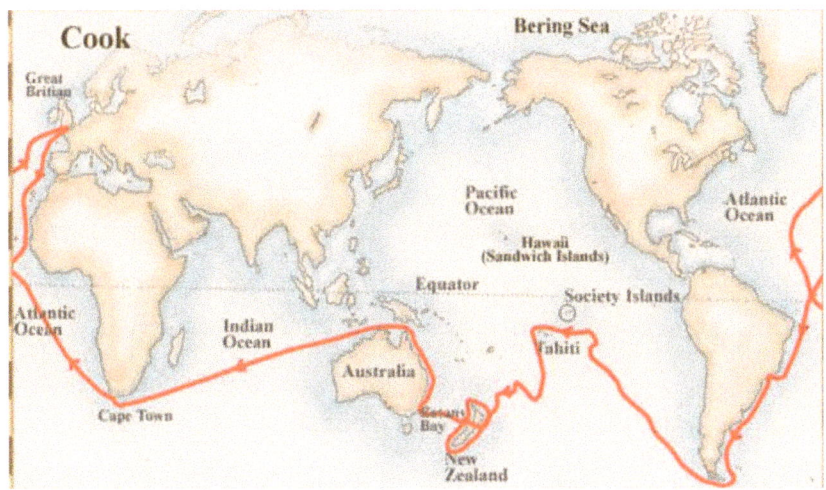

Cook's first voyage

British settlement

The European settlement of Australia needs to be viewed in context by understanding Britain's political position after the American War of Independence.

In 1782, a preliminary treaty was agreed to in Paris that ended the American War of Independence. With the Treaty of Paris, ratified by the United States of America in 1783, Great Britain found itself without a destination to send its convicts. Since Cook's expedition, Sir Joseph Banks, now President of the Royal Society (of scientists and philosophers) had been advocating for a British settlement in New South Wales. In December 1785, the Westminster Parliament gave orders for a penal colony to be established in New South Wales on land claimed by James Cook.

Arthur Phillip — the First Fleet — a problem with convicts

The First Fleet was commanded by Commodore Arthur Phillip. He was given authority to establish the colony, set down regulations for the colony, and to make land grants. Under his command were two British naval escorts, HMS Supply and HMS Sirius; two convict transports or barks, Alexander, Charlotte, Friendship, Lady Penrhyn, Prince of Wales and Scarborough; and three store ships, Golden Grove, Fishburn and Borrowdale. The fleet set out on May 13, 1787. Along with Arthur Phillip, his officers and crews, were about 800 convicts — 600 male and 200 female convicts (24 female convicts were off-loaded at the Cape of Good Hope. This made a total of 1,420 officers, passengers, crew, marines, marines' families, convicts — men, women and children.

Apart from the discovery of a planned mutiny on the Scarborough, the voyage was a well-behaved one. After departing Portsmouth, the fleet stopped at Teneriffe on June 3, where it paused for a week. It then departed for Rio De Janeiro, which it arrived at on August 5th, and stayed for a month. Conditions were very hot, and prolonged stays were needed to ensure the health and safety of all. The fleet reached the Cape of Good Hope in South Africa on October 13. This was the last before heading on to Australia, so large numbers of animals and supplies were taken on board all of the ships. The 24 female convicts of the Friendship were left at the Cape of Good Hope to make enough room to store all the supplies. The fleet set sail from the cape, using the 'Roaring Forties', winds of high speed to propel the sailing ships. The Friendship was recorded as sailing 133 miles (215 kms) in one day. Van Diemen's Land was sighted by the Friendship on January 4, 1788. The HMS Supply was intended to arrive earlier that the rest of the fleet for the purpose of finding a suitable location to site the colony; however, the other ships arrived unexpectedly soon after, without the necessary reconnaissance being achieved.

The HMS Supply was the first ship of the First Fleet to arrive at Botany Bay. It arrived on January 18, 1788, after 250 days of sailing. The whole fleet had arrived by January 20. Of the 1,420 who had left, some had died; however, the 1,336 that arrived included 20 babies born on the trip. The voyage had travelled over 15,000 miles, 24,000 kilometres, and not one ship had been lost.

It was soon discovered that Botany Bay was not a suitable place to begin a settlement. The bay was unprotected and too shallow to anchor the ships near the shore. There was insufficient fresh water to supply over 1,000 people for any length of time, and the soil was poor. It was here that first contact was made with the Aboriginal (Koori) people of the Eora tribe. On January 21st, Phillip set off on three small boats to explore the bays further to the north. Phillip decided that the suitable site for the new colony was to be 12 kilometres north, at Port Jackson. Phillip and his party returned to Botany Bay on January 23. On January 24, two ships of the French La Perouse expedition were sighted off Botany Bay. The French ships stayed until March 10 undergoing repairs. After departing for their return to France, both French ships were shipwrecked on the Solomon Islands.

On January 26, the First Fleet weighed anchor from Botany Bay and arrived at Port Jackson later that day. At Port Jackson, Arthur Phillip with the crew of HMS Supply raised the British flag and named the settlement Sydney Cove, after the then British Home Secretary, Lord Sydney. Crew, passengers and convicts of the other ships looked on from above and below the decks of their ships. On that day, the new arrivals made contact with the Cadigal people, specifically the Bidjigal clan, who already lived around the Port Jackson area. January 26 is the date that marks Australia Day.

When Arthur Phillip founded the settlement of Sydney Cove at Port Jackson, the King of Great Britain was still 'Mad' King George III, and the Prime Minister of Great Britain was now the renowned William Pitt, the Younger, (b.1759, PM.1783-1801, 1804-1806, d.1806).

Commodore Arthur Phillip

Raising of the 'Union Jack' at Port Jackson in 1788.

There was no treaty signed between Arthur Phillip and the indigenous people at Port Jackson. Although Philip intended to treat the Aboriginal people well, conflict did break out. On February 15, 1788, a small party set sail on the HMS Supply to set up a small settlement at Norfolk Island. Between 1790 and 1810, Pemulwuy of the Bidjigal clan led a series of attacks on the new settlement. This was the beginning of conflict between European settlers and the Aboriginal people that lasted over a century, and still exists politically today. When European settlement began in 1788, there is estimated to have been between 250 to 700 Aboriginal nations or clans, and between 300,000 to 1,000,000 Aboriginal people. Through what has come to be known as the Australian Holocaust, by the year 1900, the Aboriginal population of Australia had declined to less than 120,000.

A mix of nationalities

An assumption that the First Fleet was composed of British convicts, is almost entirely true. However, the First Fleet contained some small diversity of nationalities and ethnic groups. According to various records, there were:

- 12 Blacks of African, American or West Indian origin
- 2 Channel Islanders
- 141 with Irish surnames or of Irish origin
- 9 Jews of British nationality
- 14 North Americans
- 33 of Scottish origin
- 9 of Welsh origin, and
- Others with origins from Madagascar, Norway, Italy, Germany, France, Sweden, Portugal and Holland.

Indigenous leaders during early Australian settlement

Bennelong

Woollarawarre Bennelong (c.1764-1813) was a senior Koori of the Wangal clan of the Eora people, who lived in the area south of the Parramatta River. They had close ties to the Wallumedegal clan, living on the west side of the river.

Bennelong was captured in November 1789 under the orders of Arthur Phillip for the purpose of making him an intermediary between the Koori people and the new settlers. Bennelong would have been aged around 25. Phillip had attempted this a few months earlier with another Koori, Arabanoo, but the latter had died quickly of smallpox. Bennelong was married to Barangaroo, who died in 1791. They lived in a hut built on a site now known as Bennelong Point, the location of the Sydney Opera House.

Bennelong learnt English and taught Phillip about Koori culture and language. In 1792, Bennelong and another Koori, Yemmerrawanne sailed with Phillip to England, where they were presented to Lord Sydney. Bennelong and Yemmerrawanne fell ill in England, and the latter died there. Bennelong returned to Australia in 1795 on the HMS Reliance. On board the Reliance was surgeon and later explorer George Bass on his first trip to the colony. Bennelong taught Bass some of his language during the voyage. On his return, Bennelong resumed his position as the intermediary for Phillip's replacement, Governor Hunter, and advised and educated him on Koori culture. In the early 1800s, Bennelong lived with about 100 of the Wangal clan on Wallumedegal land, north of the Parramatta River at Kissing Point. It was there that he died in 1813 at near 50 years. Bennelong Point, where his hut stood, is named after him.

Bennelong Point, circa 1800

Bennelong Point now

Pemulwuy

Pemulwuy (c.1750-1802) was a Koori man who is noted to be the first leader of Koori resistance against European settlement. He was of the Bidjigal clan of the Eora people. In 1790, he began a rebellion that developed into a 12-year guerrilla war against the British colony until his death in 1802. In 1790, during an encounter with a group from the Bidjigal clan, a Captain McIntyre was speared. It was thought by many, including Bennelong, that McIntyre had previously killed Bidjigal people. In retaliation, Governor Phillip ordered Captain Tench to massacre and behead a dozen Bidjigal people and send the severed heads back to the village.

Pemulwuy persuaded the Eora, Dharug and Thrawal tribes to unite in rebellion. In 1792, raids were made on settlers at Parramatta, Georges River, Prospect, Toongabbie, Brickfield and the Hawkesbury River. In 1795, Pemulwuy was wounded and captured in a raid at Botany Bay, but later escaped. The rebellion continued until 1801, when Governor King ordered that Pemulwuy should be taken 'dead or alive'. Pemulwuy was killed in 1802. Governor King ordered that Pemulwuy be decapitated and his head was preserved in spirits and sent to Sir Joseph Banks in London. After Pemulwuy's death, Governor King invited the Aboriginal people back into the settled areas. However, Pemulwuy's son, Tedbury continued the struggle until being killed in 1810. Pemulwuy's skull has been requested for repatriation by the Sydney Aboriginal people, but it is yet to be located.

Bennelong   Arabanoo   Pemulwuy

The Second Fleet

The Second Fleet serves as an interesting comparison with the First fleet. Whereas the First Fleet was planned and managed by the Royal Navy, the Second Fleet was a privatised venture, contracted out to the firm Camden, Calvert and King, who had gained a reputation previously for their operations in the slave trade. Whereas the aim of the First Fleet was to deliver the convicts safely, the aim of the Second Fleet was to deliver the convicts as quickly and cheaply as possible. It consisted of one escort ship — HMS Guardian (converted to carry convicts); four convict ships — Lady Juliana, Surprize, Neptune and Scarborough; and one supply ship — Justinian. Only the Scarborough had sailed with the First Fleet. There appears to be no overall commander of the Second Fleet, but a collection of ship captains.

The store ship, Justinian, departed on June 28, 1789, sailed separately, taking about 290 days and arrived at Sydney Cove on April 15, 1790. Lady Juliana departed a month later, on July 29, taking almost 310 days and arrived at Sydney Cove on June 3, 1790. Guardian departed on September 12, 1789 but was disabled and never made it to Sydney Cove. Its convicts were transferred to the Neptune. The other three ships — Surprize, Neptune and Scarborough — departed together January 19, 1790, and arrived respectively on June 26, 27 and 28; taking 158, 159 and 160 days. Of just over 1,000 convicts that departed, just over 250 died on the trip, almost 500 arrived sick, mostly from scurvy, and only about 250 arrived well. Of the 500 sick convicts that arrived, over 100 were to die at Sydney Cove shortly after. It was documented by Captain Hill in his noted criticism of the fleet, one of only three Royal Navy officers accompanying the voyage, that on Neptune, the convicts were kept chained, starved and not allowed on deck.

For all the criticism of the Second fleet, it is noted for transporting a volunteer regiment that was to become known as the New South Wales (NSW) Corps. It also carried two men who were to have a significant effect on the new colony's future. The first was D'Arcy Wentworth, father of William Charles Wentworth, and John Macarthur, then a young lieutenant in the NSW Corps.

Early Colonial Rebellions

Although the convict colony at Sydney Cove was under strict military control, this did not mean that the colony was free from disturbance. In the first few years, life for both settlers, and more so for the convicts, was difficult. Similar to the earlier British settlement of North America, stockades, buildings, farmland, wells, and other facilities needed to be constructed. The convicts were used as the labour force for building the settlement. Amongst the officers and settlers that had arrived with the fleets, there was a competition to possess more and more of the 'newly-found' land. Captains Arthur Phillip, John Hunter, Philip King and William Bligh were each Royal Navy officers, and each was successively charged with allotting property, keeping order, and promoting goodwill. Unfortunately, as a result of competing interests, there were rebellions within the colony.

The Castle Hill Rebellion (1804)

The Castle Hill Rebellion, also known as the Battle of Vinegar Hill, occurred in 1804. Many of the convicts arriving in the new colony had been involved in the Irish Rebellion of 1798, and their punishment was transportation from Great Britain to the convict colony of New South Wales. Phillip Cunningham and William Johnston had both been captains in the United Irishmen's Forces. In 1804, as convicts, the two men led about 300 convicts, mostly Irish, in a rebellion against the colonial government. In March 1804, the rebels seized the government farm at Castle Hill, overpowered the guards, and gained much-needed arms. The rebels chose the slogan 'Death or Liberty', which had previously been used in the 1798 Irish Rebellion. The rebellion lasted another two days. Unwisely for the rebels, they had stumbled onto a supply of liquor at the farm and became hopelessly drunk.

Major George Johnston of the New South Wales Corps parleyed with Cunningham to have a conference and come to a resolution. Immediately, Major Johnston took Cunningham prisoner, and the rest of the New South Wales Corps stormed the rebel encampment. Over twenty convicts were killed, the others were captured and arrested. The day after, Governor King ordered martial law. Cunningham and seven other ringleaders were hanged without trial. The other members of the rebellion were flogged and sent to a new convict settlement on the Coal River, later named Newcastle.

The Mutiny on the Bounty (1787)

Although quite separate to the convict colony at Sydney Cove, the outcome of the Mutiny on the Bounty, and its captain, William Bligh, later Governor of New South Wales, would be linked.

In 1787, Captain William Bligh had been sent on a mission, commanding the HMS Bounty to collect 'breadfruit' in Tahiti to be transported to the Caribbean for cultivation. While in Tahiti, his crew became accustomed to the tropical lifestyle and had also formed relationships with the Tahitians. When the HMS Bounty left Tahiti, the crew, led by First Mate Fletcher Christian, mutinied. Bligh with members of the loyal crew were put aside on a lifeboat, while the mutineers returned to Tahiti to collect provisions and their Tahitian wives. After leaving Tahiti, the mutineers sighted an uncharted island. Christian realised that Pitcairn Island had been located on the maps in the wrong place. This was the perfect place for the mutineers to settle without fear of discovery. Miraculously, Captain Bligh and his loyal crew on the lifeboat sailed over 1,000 miles to Batavia, where they caught a ship to England. The Royal Navy sent the HMS Pandora to seek out the mutineers; however, they were never discovered.

Captain Bligh must have thought to himself that he would never want to be involved in another mutiny again.

The Rum Rebellion (1808)

On January 26, 1808, on exactly the 20th anniversary of the new colony, Major George Johnston, head of the New South Wales Corps, led 400 soldiers from their barracks and arrested Governor Bligh. This was the same Governor Bligh that had endured the 'Mutiny on the Bounty'.

Bligh was the fourth and last Royal Navy officer to govern the NSW convict colony. When he arrived, it was in a poor state, damaged by floods and lacking supplies. Bligh went to work to restore the colony. He immediately set up flood-relief for the farmers and agreed that the government stores would buy all the crops that the farmers harvested. He even set up a 'model' farm by the Hawkesbury River. However, he did make all promissory notes issued to the farmers payable in currency only, not goods. Further, Bligh tightened control over visiting ships and their cargoes, this included quantities of rum that had been illicitly used for trading in grain, food and other goods. Bligh's reforms drew the ire of the New South Wales Corps.

John Macarthur (1767-1834) was the leader of the opposition to Bligh's reforms. Macarthur had come to the new colony in the Second Fleet as an officer in the New South Wales Corps. Afterwards, he had left the regiment and had become a farmer and owned estates in Parramatta and Camden. Macarthur is noted as the first Australian pastoralist to bring 'merinos' (Spanish sheep) to Australia because merinos could cope better with the arid Australian heat than the British types of sheep. Macarthur is known as the 'father of the Australian wool industry'.

Bligh did have supporters from the British settlers in the Hawkesbury River region, who he had aided during the floods. When word of the rebellion came to the notice of the British Government, it was quickly put down. Major Johnston was court-martialled. The New South Wales Corps was withdrawn from the colony, and Macarthur was exiled from the colony for eight years. Bligh was relieved from duty as governor of New South Wales and was promoted to Admiral until his retirement. During his time in exile, Macarthur organised the transportation of merinos from Spain to his estate in Camden.

Major General Lachlan Macquarie was appointed in Bligh's place as Governor of New South Wales. Rather than being a Royal Navy officer, Macquarie was a British Army officer who had previous success as an administrator in Scotland. He had also fought in both the American Revolutionary War and the Napoleonic Wars. Macquarie was the NSW Governor from 1810 to 1821, and had an important role in the social, economic and architectural development of the colony.

Early female leaders in the colony

Elizabeth Macarthur (nee Veale, 1766-1850)

During Macarthur's exile, it was his wife, Elizabeth, who managed the family estates at Parramatta and Camden during Macarthur's exile. In 1788, Elizabeth Veale, daughter of a Devon farming family, married a handsome but penniless army officer. In 1790, she sailed with him to the newly founded colony at Sydney Cove. She never returned to England but, with her husband, carved out a vast agricultural empire. Although her husband, John Macarthur, is credited with pioneering Australia's wool industry, it was Elizabeth who managed the estate for over a dozen years of her husband's absence. In all, she gave birth to eight children, of which seven survived. It was Elizabeth who salvaged her disgraced husband's reputation after his court-martial. It was Elizabeth who entertained a young Charles Darwin visiting Sydney. It was Elizabeth who befriended explorer Matthew Flinders. It was Elizabeth who wined and dined a succession of New South Wales Governors and their wives, from Arthur Phillip in 1790 to Sir Charles Fitzroy in 1840. It was Elizabeth who managed the introduction of merinos onto the Macarthur estates.

For her achievements, the Elizabeth Macarthur Agricultural Institute is named in her honour. It is the largest agricultural centre of excellence operated by the New South Wales Department of Primary Industries, employing 200 scientists, and is located at Camden Park, the Macarthur Camden estate.

Esther Abrahams (1767-1846)

Esther Abrahams was the 'de facto' wife of Major George Johnston of the NSW Corps, and with her daughter is identified as one of nine Jewish persons aboard the First Fleet. Esther was a Londoner, who at 20 years of age had been tried while pregnant at the 'Old Bailey' and transported on the First Fleet. On the voyage, she met George Johnston and he offered both her and her daughter protection. In all, Esther bore seven children. Because of George's position, he and Esther were granted large tracts of land around the Annandale region of Sydney. In 1809, in George's absence on court-martial in England, Esther was granted 570 acres in her own right, and 2,000 acres that she was awarded conditionally with George located on the Nepean River, Cabramatta and Bankstown. It was Esther, like Elizabeth Macarthur, who managed the estates in her husband's absence. On his return to New South Wales in 1813, George married Esther. In 2002, the pavilion at Bicentennial Park in Johnston Street, Annandale, was dedicated to her. Esther Abraham's portrait is displayed in Sydney's Jewish Museum.

Caroline Chisholm (1808-1877)

Born in England, Caroline Chisholm was a progressive humanitarian known mostly for her care of female immigrants. Reared with a strong ethic of obligation towards others, Caroline Chisholm followed her husband Archibald Chisholm, a British soldier, to India in 1832. It was there that she initially became involved with the welfare of many of the young girls, daughters of British soldiers and settlers in India, by setting up practical education for them in literacy, religion, morals, housekeeping and nursing.

In 1838, Caroline followed her husband on furlough to Sydney, New South Wales. Again, she set up support systems for immigrants, especially young girls who were arriving in Sydney penniless, without friends or family. In 1840, her husband returned to his regiment in India but with his encouragement, Caroline stayed in Sydney and set up a home for young women. In her seven years in New South Wales,

Caroline Chisholm is noted to have placed over 10,000 immigrants in homes and jobs. She delivered formal reports on the living standards of immigrants to the Legislative Council in Sydney and, on her return to England, to the House of Lords in London. Her reports were used by a rising journalist Charles Dickens.

In 1849, with the help of Lord Shaftesbury and Sir Sydney Herbert, Caroline Chisholm founded the Family Colonisation Loan Society to loan half the fare of those families wishing to emigrate to Australia. In 1854, the Chisholm family returned to Australia, where they settled in Kyneton, just outside of Melbourne until 1865, when they finally returned to London. It has been said that she inspired the character of Mrs Jellyby in Charles Dicken's novel 'Bleak House'. Caroline Chisholm is remembered by a suburb in Canberra, her face on the Australian $5 note, and the federal electorate in Victoria.

Governors of New South Wales appointed by King George III (1760-1820)	
Captain Arthur Phillip, RN	February 7, 1778 — December 10, 1792
Captain John Hunter, RN	September 11, 1795 — September 27, 1800
Captain Philip Gidley King, RN	September 28, 1800 — August 12, 1806
Captain William Bligh, RN	August 13, 1806 — January 26, 1808
Major General Lachlan Macquarie, CB	January 1, 1810 — December 1, 1821

William Bligh   Lachlan Macquarie   John Macarthur

Caroline Chisholm   Elizabeth Macarthur   Esther Abrahams

Mapping & colonising Australia

After the new colony at Sydney Cove began in 1788, Arthur Phillip's next aim was to explore the areas around the settlement. Phillip entrusted much of this early exploration to two marine officers, Watkin Tench and William Dawes.

Watkin Tench

Watkin Tench (1758-1833) was not only a British Marine officer but was a keen explorer and author. Tench wrote two accounts of his experiences in New South Wales, 'Narrative of the Expedition to Botany Bay' and 'Complete account of the settlement of Port Jackson'. Like many of his comrades, Tench served in the American Revolutionary War before sailing in the First Fleet aboard the Charlotte. Tench was the first European to discover the Nepean River. In his account of life in Port Jackson, he documented the brutal treatment of the Aboriginal women. He wrote about the Cadigal and Cammeraygal people, and befriended Bennelong and Barangaroo. At the end of his four-year contract, Tench returned to Britain, fought in the Napoleonic Wars, wrote further journals, and retired a Lieutenant-General.

William Dawes

William Dawes (1762-1836) was also British Marine officer, as well as an astronomer, engineer, botanist, surveyor, explorer, abolitionist, and colonial administrator. Dawes sailed with the First fleet aboard the Sirius He worked as an engineer and surveyor in the new colony and built his observatory at what is now Dawes Point, under the southern entrance of the Sydney Harbour bridge. Dawes laid out the batteries along the entrance to Sydney Cove and laid out the first streets and allotments in Sydney. He explored west of Sydney along the Nepean River and made the first but unsuccessful attempt to cross the Blue Mountains. He studied the Eora people and learnt their language when he took an Eora girl, Patyegarang (Grey Kangaroo) into his home. When Dawes refused to take part in the punitive action to hunt down Pemulwuy, knowing that the dead MacIntyre had been hunting Aborigines, he came into conflict with Governor Phillip and was sent back to England. Dawes later worked against slavery in Britain. Dawes died destitute.

Patyegarang

Patyegarang (Grey Kangaroo), a young Aboriginal woman, was thought to be the first to teach her language to the new European settlers. She might be considered the Australian counterpart to the American story of Pocahontas. Patyegarang was of the Cammeraygal clan of the Eora people and spoke Cadigal as her language and was 15 when she met and became language-tutor to Lt. William Dawes. Patyegarang introduced Dawes to the language of the Dharug and Eora people. Dawes compiled the language into several notebooks. He taught her English.

When Dawes returned to England, the story of Patyegarang was lost until Phyllis Mander Jones, an Australian librarian, working at the University of London's School of Oriental and African Studies around 1970, came across three of Dawes's notebooks which revealed the lost language and his story with Patyegarang. In 2008, Kate Grenville wrote the novel 'The Lieutenant', based on the story of Patyegarang and Dawes.

A portrait of an unknown Cammeraygal woman, circa 1800-1804, possibly Patygarang. (Parramatta Heritage Trust.)

Bass and Flinders — circumnavigating Australia

George Bass and Matthew Flinders were great maritime explorers who circumnavigated and chartered the Australian coastline.

George Bass (1771-1803) was a British surgeon and Australian explorer. Bass trained in medicine and joined the Royal Navy as a surgeon in 1794. In 1795, he arrived at Sydney Cove as ship's surgeon aboard the HMS Reliance. On the voyage were Matthew Flinders, John Hunter (sailing as Arthur Phillip's successor, the next NSW Governor), Bennelong (returning from his trip to London), and his surgical assistant William Martin. On the Reliance, Bass had brought with him a small boat, 2.4 metres (8 foot) long, 1.5 metres (5 foot) wide, which he called the Tom Thumb. It was Bass's aim to do some exploring around the new colony.

Matthew Flinders (1774-1814) was a British navigator, cartographer, and a captain in the Royal Navy. Flinders made three trips to Australia. As a boy, Flinders had been inspired by Daniel Defoe's Robinson Crusoe and wanted to sail the sea. At 15 years, he joined the Royal Navy. He sailed on many voyages, including William Bligh's second voyage to transport breadfruit from Tahiti to the Caribbean. Bligh's first voyage had been the infamous 'mutiny on the Bounty'. In 1795, Flinders arrived at Sydney Cove as midshipman aboard the HMS Reliance.

In October 1795, Bass and Flinders, with William Martin, set sail on the Tom Thumb out of Port Jackson to Botany Bay then went onto sail further up the Georges River into areas that had not been explored. On their return, reporting to the new governor, John Hunter, it was decided to create a new colony there at what was to become known as Bank's Town (after Joseph Banks). In 1796, in another small boat that they also called the Tom Thumb, they sailed as far as Lake Illawarra, which they called Tom Thumb Lagoon.

In 1797, without Flinders, Bass sailed further along the south-eastern coast and along the Gippsland coast, past Cape Howe and Wilson's Promontory, to Westernport Bay. On the trip, he also noted the Kiama Blowhole. Bass reported that he believed Van Diemen's Land was separate from the Australian mainland but hadn't proved it.

In 1798, Flinders and Bass sailed on the sloop Norfolk and circumnavigated Van Diemen's Land. They sailed along the estuary of the Derwent River that had previously been charted by Captain John Hayes of the British East India Company in 1793. Based on Flinders' report, the decision was made to create a new settlement on the estuary of the Derwent River, now Hobart, and to name the waters between the mainland and Van Diemen's Land as Bass Strait. The largest island in Bass Strait was named Flinders Island.

In 1799, Flinders sailed north this time and landed at Moreton Bay, near Clontarf and Redcliffe, which he named after its red cliffs.

In 1801, Flinders returned to London where his report was given much attention, especially by Sir Joseph Banks, President of the Royal Society. Later that year, Flinders was given command the HMS Investigator and the task of charting the entire coastline of the Australian mainland. For the journey, Flinders took a young William Westall, who would draught most of the charts and pictures along the way. It would be 10 years before he returned to England.

Flinders' journey around the Australian coastline took two years. Initially sighting land at Cape Leeuwin, he charted the entire southern coast through Bass Strait then onto Port Jackson. In April 1802, he met with the French explorer Nicholas Baudin at Encounter Bay, near Kangaroo Island. Later, he sailed north, charting the east coast including the Great Barrier Reef, continuing through the Torres Strait to Timor. He sailed down the western coast of Australia and returned to Port Jackson. While returning to England in 1803, he was captured by the French at Mauritius, a French colony, and not freed until 1810. He arrived in England ill and died before the publication of his writings 'A Voyage to Terra Australis'. It was on Flinders' recommendation that the British Admiralty decided to refer to the new continent as Australia.

Flinders was buried at the old London General Cemetery, under today's Euston Station. At the time of writing, 2019, archaeologists had just located his remains before a rebuild of the station was to commence.

In 1803, on contract with Governor King to supply provisions to the Sydney colony, George Bass and his crew, while on voyage, were never seen or heard of again. There are stories of them being captured by the Spanish off the coast of Chile. Although his ship was recovered from the Spanish two years later, these stories are not proven.

King Bungaree

Bungaree (1775-1830), born in the Broken Bay area of north Sydney, of the Kuringgai people, is recorded as one of Australia's earliest explorers. He is rarely noted in colonial histories of Australia, however he was the first recorded Aboriginal person to circumnavigate the continent of Australia and the first recorded person listed as Australian.

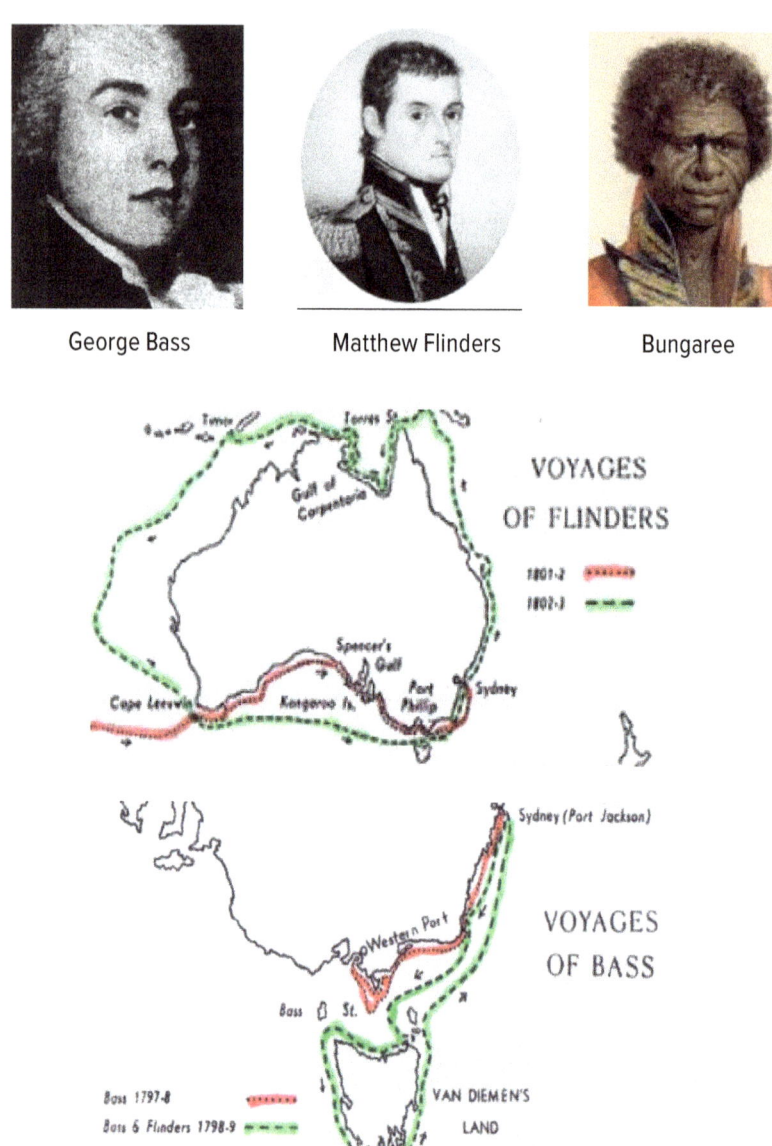

George Bass · Matthew Flinders · Bungaree

Matthew Flinders noted that Bungaree was an important member of his expeditions and helped him communicate with many of the different indigenous peoples during his expeditions.

Bungaree arrived in Sydney with the remains of his tribe after their camp had been destroyed by settlers. He joined the crew of the HMS Reliance, on a trip to Norfolk Island in 1798, where he met and gained the confidence of Matthew Flinders. Bungaree sailed with Flinders on a survey of Hervey Bay and Bribie Island (Queensland). From 1801 to 1803, Bungaree accompanied Flinders on his circumnavigation of Australia as the only indigenous member of the crew. Flinders credited Bungaree on a number of occasions of saving the crew and the expedition from disaster (see map on facing page).

In 1815, Governor Macquarie awarded Bungaree with 6 hectares (15 acres) of land at Georges Head, north of Sydney, and referred to him as "Chief of the Broken Bay tribe."

Van Diemen's Land — the new colonies

The British government felt that the French had shown interest in Van Diemen's Land for some time. Due to the political pressures of the Napoleonic Wars, it was decided to settle it as a priority.

In 1803, Lt. John Bowen (1780-1827) established a colony at Risdon Vale in 1803 on the Derwent River. The following year, Lt. Col. David Collins (1756-1810) moved the settlement from Risdon Vale to Sullivan's Cove. Collins named the new settlement Hobart Town, after Lord Robert Hobart, then British Secretary of State for War and the Colonies.

On May 3, 1804, approximately 300 Aboriginal people were moving through Risdon hunting kangaroo. On seeing such large numbers, the British soldiers fired on them. Early reports estimated about 50 natives killed but later reports estimated the number as hundreds. It was a massacre.

Also, in 1804, Lt. Col. William Paterson (1756-1810) established a settlement at Port Dalrymple at the heads of the Tamar River. Initially the settlement was on the eastern side of the Tamar (George Town). Again, on the following day, November 12, 1804, an Aboriginal group approached Paterson's camp in a friendly manner. They were fired on by the soldiers, with fatalities. Later, after further exploration of the

North Esk and South Esk Rivers, he moved the settlement to the excellent pastures at the gorge of the South Esk River, which was named York Town, later Launceston.

John Bowen   *David Collins*   *William Paterson*

The Solomon Brothers

About 70,000 convicts were transported to the penal colony of Van Diemen's Land from 1804 to 1850. One of these convicts was to inspire one of Charles Dickens' most well-known characters, the infamous Jew, Fagin, of Oliver Twist. Isaac 'Ikey' Solomon was a known 'fence', a receiver and seller of stolen goods. In 1819, Ikey Solomon and his brother, Judah, were found guilty and transported to Van Diemen's Land. After his sentence, 'Ikey' settled with his family in New Norfolk. However, he died poor and estranged from his family.

Ikey's brother Judah was a clever businessman. He took the opportunity of a small new colony that required the regular supply of essential and luxury items. Judah became a shopkeeper. Although still a convict, he was listed as a founding investor in the Bank of Van Diemen's Land and later was a founder of the first synagogue in Argyle Street, Hobart. He died a wealthy man and is listed as a valuable member of the Hobart community.

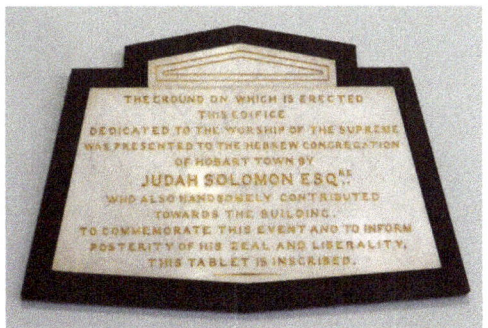

Sketch of Isaac 'Ikey' Solomon

Plaque commemorating Judah Solomon's foundation of the Argyle Street Synagogue.

Excerpt of photo of Argyle Street Synagogue, now demolished (Hobart Synagogue).

Opening the Blue Mountains — Blaxland, Wentworth & Lawson (1813)

From Sydney's founding as a British settlement in 1788, it existed with a western barrier, the Blue Mountains, a rugged region west of Sydney containing steep cliffs, eucalyptus forests and breathtaking waterfalls. It forms part of the Great Dividing Range, a mountain range that runs from the state of Victoria in the south, through NSW, into Queensland in the north. It separates the narrow east coast from the rest of Australia. Archaeologists believe that the Blue Mountains were formed about one million years ago as part of the Kosciusko Uplift during the Pliocene Epoch of the Quaternary Period. The pressure of the uplift raised the area in a monoclinal (step-like) fold, reaching a height of 3,000 feet. In 1788, Captain Phillip had named them the "Carmarthan Hills' after the area in southern Wales, UK; however, the name changed due to the blue haze that the mountains emitted. Prior to European settlement, the area had been settled by the Dharug tribe of the Aboriginal people. Previous explorers had determined that there was a large continent over the Blue Mountains but finding a path through them was the challenge.

Gregory Blaxland   *William Wentworth*   *William Lawson*

Three Sisters, Blue Mountains   *Jamison Valley, Blue Mountains*

Wentworth Falls

In 1813, the fast-growing colony was struggling due to droughts over the previous two years. The newly established settlers saw an opportunity to gain more fertile farmland over the mountains. With permission from Governor Macquarie, on 11 May 1813, three explorers, four servants, four pack horses and five dogs set off from Emu Plains in search of a path through the Blue Mountains. The explorers were Gregory Blaxland (1778-1853), a pioneer farmer from England; William Charles Wentworth (1770-1872), an explorer, politician, author and journalist, born on Norfolk Island (off the Australian east coast); and William Lawson (1774-1850), explorer, grazier and politician, also from England.

During the 27-day expedition, the group crossed the Nepean River and methodically made their way up the ridges rather than the valleys. They crossed Mount York and onto Mount Blaxland, near the town of Lithgow, on the western side of the mountains. There, the explorers found vast forests and grasslands that could support the growing colony for the next thirty years.

The following year, in 1814, William Cox (1764-1837), a British soldier, engineer and explorer, with the help of two Aboriginal men, Colebee and Joe, eight guards, and a team of thirty convicts, built a road 160 kms (100 miles) across the Blue Mountains in less than a year. The Aboriginal men were from the Dharug tribe, Colebee from the Boorooberongal clan and Joe from the Mulgoa clan.

Later, in 1815, George Evans discovered the Lachlan and Macquarie rivers, flowing inland from the mountains.

William Cox

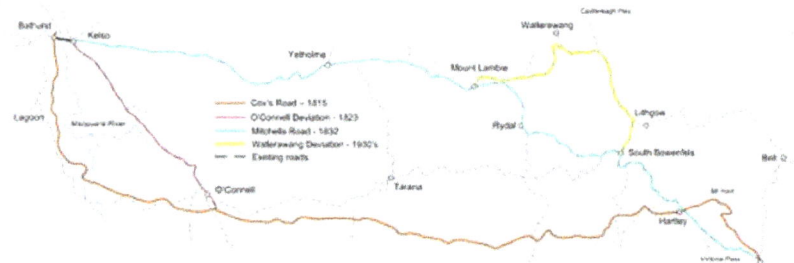

Cox's road across the Blue Mountains (in brown).

Wentworth's link to Homebush

Homebush was the site of the 2000 Sydney Olympic Games. In Australian history, Homebush was home of the Wangal people of the Dharug tribe. It also has strong colonial links to early British settlement. D'Arcy Wentworth (1762-1827), father of Willian Charles Wentworth, arrived in Australia arrived aboard the Second Fleet as Assistant Surgeon to the colony of New South Wales. Like other settlers, Wentworth used 'Terra nullius' (nobody's land) to advantage and obtained land through the New South Wales colonial government, ousted the resident Dharug tribe, and founded the Wentworth Estate at Homebush around 1800. Upon his passing, the Estate was inherited by Willian Charles Wentworth, who purchased additional land in Sydney's eastern suburbs and built Vaucluse House. In 1841, the Homebush Racecourse was built on the Wentworth Estate and operated until 1880. Homebush was the site chosen to locate the 2000 Sydney Olympics.

Mak Sai Ying — the first Chinese in Australia

There have been reports of Chinese fishermen coming to Australia as early as the 15th Century, searching the northern coastline for sandalwood, and trepang (sea-cucumber). Chinese maps since that time have recorded an outline of the Australian coast. Matthew Flinders, on his expedition around Australia, on the HMS Investigator in 1802-1803), noted that the local Aboriginal people of the Gulf of Carpentaria were familiar with some of the firearms and iron tools his crew were carrying. He also recorded his finding of pieces of earthenware and other pottery of Chinese origin.

Mak Sai Ying (1796-1880), also known as John Pong Shying, was born in Guangzhou, Canton. He is credited as the first Chinese person to settle in Australia and arrived as a free settler in 1818. Ying was a carpenter and lived with John Blaxland at his Newington Estate. Three years later, 1821, Ying worked for Elizabeth Macarthur at Elizabeth Farm. Later, he is known to have purchased land in Parramatta. In 1829, John Shying, as he became known, was granted a licence to open a public bar, The Lion, in Parramatta. He also owned the Peacock Inn in Parramatta. In 1832, he briefly returned to China, but was back in

Sydney five years later. Shying's descendant, Barry Shying, and his grandson Nick live in Melbourne.

With the ending of the convict system in the 1840s, there was a growing labour shortage and more Chinese 'Coolies' were encouraged to come to New South Wales. In 1848, a large group arrived on the ship Nimrod at Miller's Point in Sydney. They had come from Xiamen, a port city south of Guangzhou. By 1852, more than 1,500 Chinese people lived in Sydney.

Governor Brisbane,

By the early 1820s, the colony at Sydney had grown to over 10,000 soldiers, convicts and settlers. The city became conflicted as to whether it was to remain a convict colony or whether it was to become a free city. The British government has appointed John Bigge (1780-1843), an English judge and royal commissioner, to lead an inquiry into the effectiveness of Sydney as a convict colony. During the early 1820s, Commissioner Bigge submitted three reports criticising the Macquarie governorship and recommending additional convict settlements at Port Curtis (Rockhampton), Port Bowen and Moreton Bay.

In 1821, Governor Brisbane took over from Macquarie. Sir Thomas Brisbane (1773-1860), born in Scotland, was a British Army officer, astronomer, and administrator. He studied astronomy at the University of Edinburgh and was elected as a fellow to the Royal Society of London in 1810. Early in his military career, Brisbane had served as a brigade commander, with Arthur Wellesley, the Duke of Wellington, in the Peninsular War. He commanded a brigade in America during the War of 1812, then returned to Europe to command an army division in France after Napoleon's defeat at Waterloo. In 1820, Brisbane successfully applied for the position of Governor of the Colony of New South Wales.

When Brisbane arrived in Sydney to take over governorship, he came across a confused administrative mess. Far more land had been granted to settlers than was available and much of the land was being occupied without title by squatters. Brisbane needed more land to immediately pacify discord amongst the growing number of new arrivals that had received title in London to lands that had already been occupied by squatters. In 1822, Brisbane began issuing 'tickets-of occupation' that allowed squatters to permanently occupy untitled lands prior to survey. In 1823, he ordered Oxley to explore and survey new territories in northern New South Wales. In 1824, he ordered Hume and Hovell to explore and survey new territories in southern New South Wales. More Aboriginal people were being killed and dispersed, as their land was taken by the new colony.

John Oxley — To the Northern Rivers (1817-18), Moreton Bay (1823)

John Oxley (1784-1828), born in England, was a Royal Navy officer, and an explorer and surveyor of Australia. He served as Surveyor-General of New South Wales. He is best known for his expeditions of the Northern Rivers of New South Wales, and the area around Moreton Bay and the Brisbane river.

In 1799, at 15 years, he entered the Royal Navy as a midshipman and travelled to Australia in 1802. Aboard the HMS Buffalo, he participated in surveying the area around Westernport Bay. In 1806, at 22 years, Oxley commanded the Estramina on a trip to Van Diemen's Land. After returning to England, in 1807, he was made first lieutenant of the HMS Porpoise, carrying home the deposed Governor Bligh. In 1812, Oxley took up the position of Surveyor General of New South Wales and was granted 1,000 acres (400 ha) near Camden.

In 1817, after successive crossings of the Blue Mountains, Governor Macquarie ordered Oxley to explore the Lachlan and Macquarie rivers, as these rivers flowed westwards and inland rather than towards the coast. In each of his expeditions of the Lachlan (1817) and of the Macquarie (1818) rivers, Oxley was impeded and halted by flooding marshes and concluded that both rivers ended in an inland sea. In his 1817 expedition, Oxley just fell short of coming across the Murrumbidgee river and its rich farming lands. However, on his 1818 expedition, after being impeded by flooded marshes once again, Oxley turned eastwards and discovered the rich farming land of the Peel river, near Tamworth, and the magnificent waterfalls that are now known as Aspley Falls.

John Oxley

In 1823, Governor Brisbane ordered Oxley to locate an appropriate site for a new convict colony, north of Sydney. On this expedition, Oxley travelled and explored along the Tweed river. There he came across two escaped convicts living in the local Aboriginal community, probably of the Bundjalung people. Here, he was shown and named the Brisbane river and recommended this area as the preferred site for the new convict colony, which was initially called Moreton Bay, then Brisbane. A monument at North Quay commemorates his landing place in Brisbane. Oxley suffered continually from illness after his expeditions and died five years later.

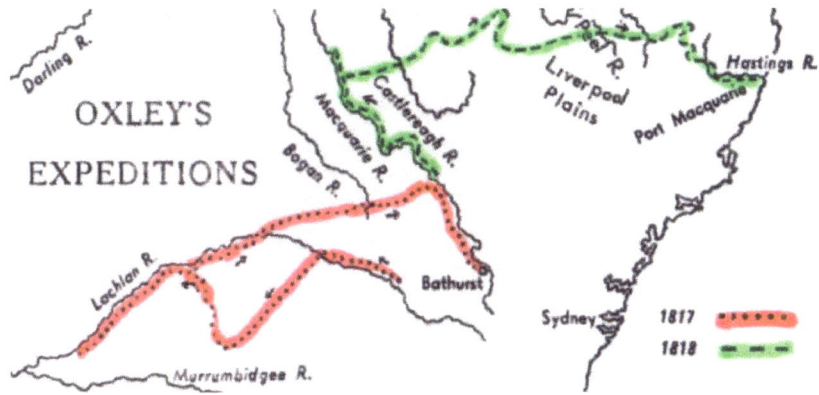

Map of Oxley's 1817 Lachlan river and 1818 Macquarie river expeditions.

Henry Miller — Redcliffe, Brisbane — 1824

In September 1824, under orders from Governor Brisbane, a new convict settlement was established in Redcliffe. However, it was moved to a new location along the river that led into Moreton Bay. Both the river and the new convict settlement at Moreton Bay were eventually named after Governor Brisbane.

The settlement at Moreton Bay was established by Captain Henry Miller. Miller (1785-1866) was born in Ireland and was an officer in the British 40th Regiment, prior to his assignment to the Colony of New South Wales. Like Governor Brisbane, Miller had served in the Peninsular War, was part of Pakenham's unsuccessful attack at the Battle of New Orleans (1814) and had returned to Europe in time to be at the Battle of Waterloo (1815). Miller held charge of the Moreton Bay settlement for 18 months, before handing it onto Captain Peter Bishop. When his regiment returned to England, Miller elected to remain in Australia and was then transferred to Hobart where he stayed for the remainder of his life.

Captain Henry Miller

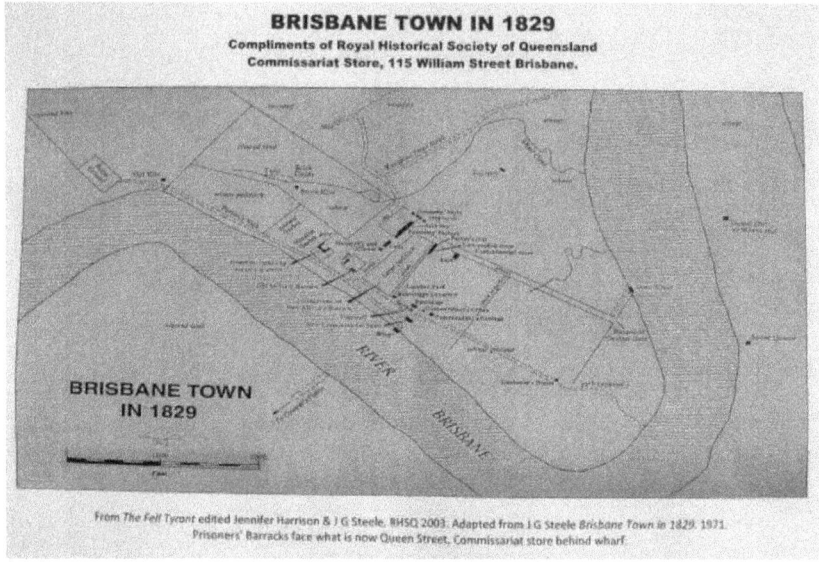

Hume & Hovell — Journey to Port Phillip (1824)

In 1824, Governor Brisbane commissioned Hamilton Hume and Willian Hovell to explore the sources of the Lachlan and Macquarie rivers, previously explored by John Oxley, in southern New South Wales. Oxley had asserted that this land was uninhabitable. Brisbane disagreed and was prepared to offer land grants to those who would establish a settlement at Wilson's Promontory and to those who would travel overland. Hume and Hovell took up the offer to travel southwards from Sydney.

Hamilton Hume (1797-1873) was born in Parramatta, then west of Sydney, now a Sydney suburb. In his early teenage years, Hume began exploring around Bathurst. In 1818, he went with Oxley to Jervis Bay. In 1822, he accompanied Alexander Berry who was establishing an estate on the southern coast of New South Wales, near Nowra.

William Hovell (1786-1875) was born in England. Hovell moved to Australia in 1813. He acquired captaincy of a ship to trade along the east coast of Australia. In 1816, Hovell was shipwrecked in Bass Strait. In 1819, he acquired land in Sydney and began exploring south of there.

Hamilton Hume *William Hovell*

Hume and Hovell, with six others, departed on 17 October 1824 from Hume's homestead on Lake George. The next day they arrived in Cooma, and the following day by the Yass Plains. Over the next couple of days, they travelled further than Oxley had and, with difficulty, crossed the flooded Murrumbidgee river. On 24th, reaching a mountain barrier, the expedition split in two, but Hovell later re-joined with Hume once he discovered no further access. By the end of October, they were gazing at the Australian Alps, never previously seen by European explorers. By mid-November, they had reached the Hume River, later called the Murray river, and the rich tablelands around Albury. On the 17th, the expedition crossed the Hume river and continued onwards past Mt Buffalo, through the Ovens valley, and crossed the Ovens and Goulburn rivers. Both Hume and Hovel journalised the beauty of the area and its value for farming.

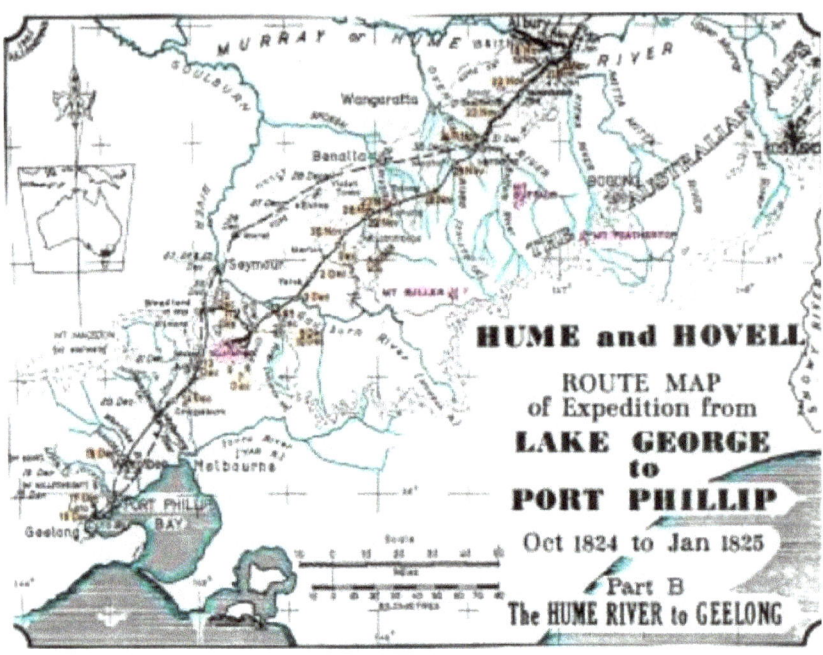

Onward, the party trekked on an Aboriginal pathway that roughly ran through today's Yea and Flowerdale onto Mt Piper, near Broadford. They continued southwards to the junction where the Maribyrnong river meets Jackson's Creek, eventually arriving at Corio Bay, which the local Aboriginal people of the Wathaurong and Gulidjan tribes called 'Iramoo'. Due to damaged instruments, Hume and Hovell thought they had arrived at Westernport Bay, but it was in fact Port Phillip Bay. There, they spent a few days recuperating before returning to Sydney by 18 January 1825. The route that the Hume and Hovell expedition travelled along has now become the Hume highway.

Charles Sturt – The Murray River (1829-30)

Charles Napier Sturt (1795-1860) born in Bengal, India, was a British Army officer and Australian explorer. Sturt led two expeditions that explored the western flowing rivers between Sydney and Adelaide.

Charles Sturt

While serving in the British army after the Napoleonic Wars, Sturt sailed to Australia in 1827 as part of an escort for convicts. Once in Sydney, it did not take Sturt long to win the confidence of Governor Darling. Darling appointed Sturt a major of brigade and military secretary. Also befriending Oxley and Hume, Sturt sought permission from Darling to further explore the west-flowing rivers of New South Wales, which he gained.

In November 1828, Sturt's expedition, including Hume as an assistant, trekked its way up the Macquarie, Bogan and Castlereagh Rivers to discover the Darling River. Although Sturt did not travel down the Darling, it confirmed that there was no inland sea in the north-west of New South Wales as had been previously asserted by Oxley.

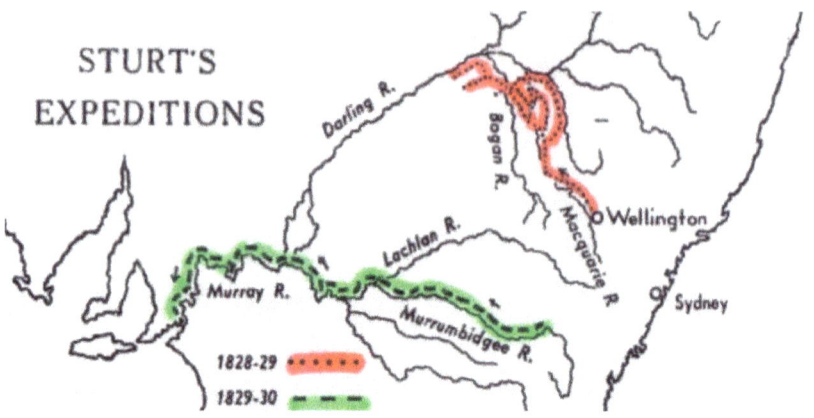

In 1829, Darling approved Sturt's proposal to explore the Murrumbidgee River discovered by Hume and Hovell. In January 1830, the new expedition made its way along the Murrumbidgee and found that it ran into a much larger river which Sturt named the Murray River. In fact, this was the same river that Hume and Hovell had previous forded upstream and named the Hume River. The party continued along the Murray until they discovered that it joined the Darling river. Sturt asserted that the west-flowing rivers eventually ran into the Murray River. In February 1830, the group came upon a large lake that Sturt named Lake Alexandrina. A few days later, they arrived at the mouth of the Murray by the sea. Sturt was disappointed to find a that the mouth was a series of shallow marshes, lagoons and sandbars that were unsuitable for shipping. This time, Sturt and his party had to row upstream against the current. Nearly running out of supplies, the expedition eventually returned to Sydney after travelling by small boat some 3,000 kilometres. Sturt lost his eyesight for some months, as a result of the arduous return journey.

After his expeditions, Sturt served briefly as commander on Norfolk Island before returning on sick leave to Britain. Later, he returned to New South Wales and was granted 5,000 acres on the Ginninderra

Creek, which he named Belconnen. In 1838, Sturt led another expedition down the Murray and surveyed Adelaide as the appropriate location to site the capital of the new colony of South Australia.

James Stirling — Perth 1829

James Stirling (1791-1865), born in Scotland, was a British naval officer and colonial administrator. Stirling persuaded the British government to establish a new colony on the mouth of the Swan River. Along with Thomas Peel, a cousin of British Prime Minister Sir Robert Peel, a consortium was created and granted 1,000,000 acres of land along the Swan River that belonged to the Whadjuk tribe of the Noongar people. The consortium was privately funded by an ex-convict, merchant and financier, and Sydney Jew by the name of Solomon Levey. The Swan River Colony was established in 1829 with Stirling as its first Governor and military commander. He founded the city of Perth and a port at Fremantle and explored the area of the Swan river in a merciless and bloody fashion.

Cayute — Battle of Pinjarra, Perth (1834)

Due to the founding of the new settlement of Perth, the resident Whadjuk tribe had become displaced and sought refuge on the land of the Pindjarup tribe. This caused conflict. As more Whadjuk people, followed closely by European settlers, came onto Pindjarup land. Thomas Peel arrived with 300 settlers and servants to set up an estate on Pindjarup land along the Murray River, south of Perth. The new settlers began displacing the Pindjarup from their land and they began to starve.

The leader of Pindjarup people was Cayute, also known as Galyute or Wongir. He led a raid at Shenton's Mill, in South Perth, in search of supplies. Following the raid, at Peel's insistence, Captain Ellis led a party that captured Cayute and two others, Yedong and Monang. They were taken back to Fremantle Prison, publicly flogged, then released. Soon after, Cayute led a raid on Peel's property at Mandurah, killing a servant and injuring two British soldiers. The editor of the Perth Gazette, Charles McFaull, called for severe action.

On 28 October 1834, a troop of 25 soldiers led by Stirling and Peel arrived at the Pindjarup camp and massacred the inhabitants. This is known as the Battle of Pinjarra or the Pinjarra Massacre. The Pinjarup did fight back. Captain Ellis was mortally wounded. Cayute escaped and avoided capture. There was a report of him in a raid in 1840, but there are no records of Cayute after that time.

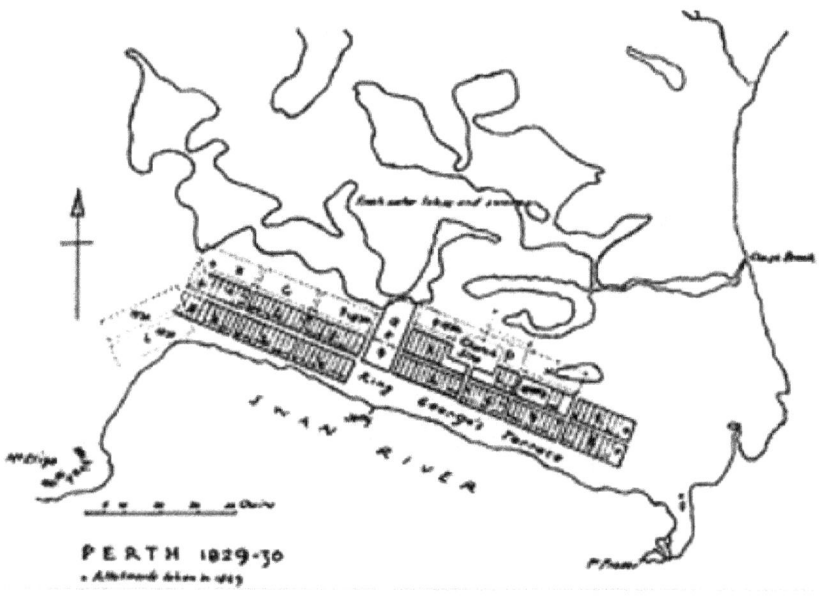

Perth 1829-1830

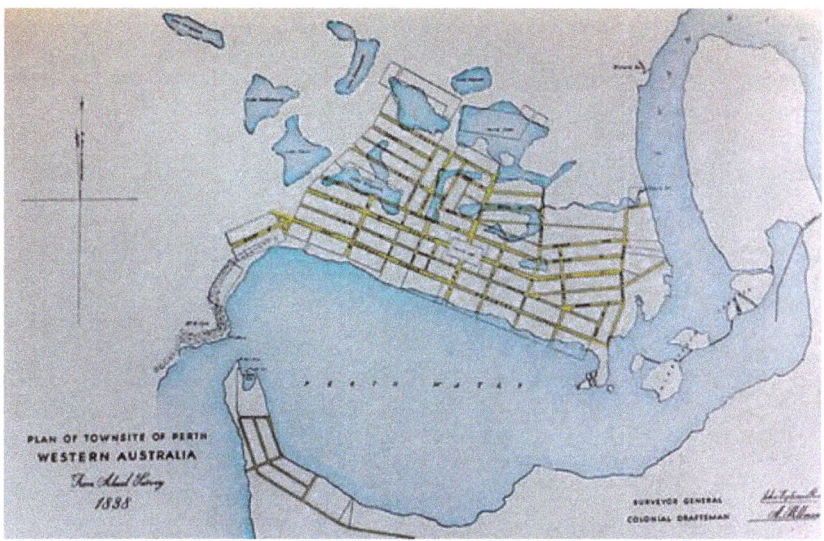
Perth 1838

Thomas Mitchell — Western NSW (1831-36)

Thomas Mitchell (1792-1855), born in Scotland, was a surveyor and explorer of eastern Australia. Initially a British Army officer, Mitchell came to the colony of New South Wales to take up the role of assistant to John Oxley, then succeeded him as Surveyor General when Oxley died. His first job was to update all the maps of Sydney, including the central city, Point Piper, Darling Point, and Port Jackson. Then, he set about re-mapping the entire Colony of New South Wales, which grown by then to 19 counties.

During his tenure as Surveyor General, Mitchell embarked on four major expeditions to map eastern Australia. The first expedition (1831-1832) explored up to the Gwydir River, inland of the Northern Rivers, up to what is now the Queensland border. He took with him the local Kamilaroi people to assist in finding water and keeping peace along the way.

Mitchell's second expedition (1835) aimed to explore the Darling River up to where it connects with the Murray River; however, growing hostility with Aboriginal tribes into whose land he was intruding, caused him to abandon it. On one occasion, his expedition is recorded to have killed 4 Aboriginal people, including a woman with a baby on her back, then killed an unknown number fleeing across the Darling River.

Major Sir Thomas Mitchell

His third expedition (1836) travelled westwards along the Lachlan River to Swan Hill, which he named. Along the way, he took Turandurey a woman of the Muthi Muthi tribe of the Riverina area as a guide. Again, encountering hostile resistance, this time from the Barkindji tribe, his expedition group with rifle fire forced 150 people into the Murray River. His 16 men fired 80 rounds at the fleeing group. After the massacre, Mitchell turned southwards and travelled down to the southern coast at Portland, where he found a farm that had been recently established by the Henty brothers, Edward and Frank. After reprovisioning, Mitchell went in a north-easterly direction back through Mount Macedon, which he named, then onto Yass, then Sydney.

On his fourth expedition (1845-1846), Mitchell travelled into the central Queensland area looking for a river that ran all the way to the Gulf of Carpentaria. Although he discovered the Warrago, Nogoa, Belyando, Victoria and Barcoo rivers. He also crossed the Burdekin River discovered by Ludwig Leichhardt a year earlier. He did not find a river that ran into the Gulf.

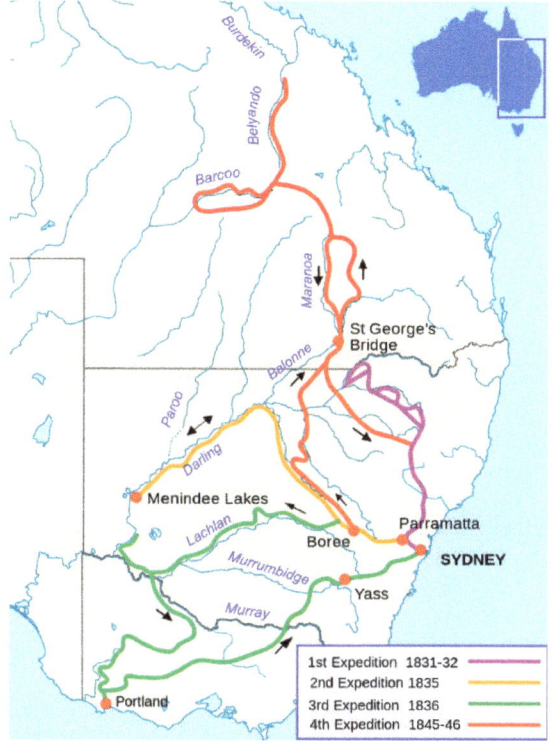

Mitchell's four expeditions.

It is primarily from Mitchell's records of his expeditions that provide evidence of traditional agricultural among the Aboriginal communities he had observed. The recordings of these observation form the basis of evidence for Bruce Pascoe, in his books Dark Emu: Black Seeds: Agriculture or Accident? (2014) and Young Dark Emu: A Truer History (2019).

Pawel Strzelecki- The Snowy Mountains and Mount Kosciuszko (1839-40)

Pawel Strzelecki (1797-1873) was a Polish explorer and geologist. Born to dispossessed Polish nobility, Strzelecki served for a short time in the Prussian cavalry, as a tutor, then as manager of the estate of a Lithuanian noble family. When the old prince died, Strzelecki was in dispute with the new prince over entitlements. The matter was settled, and Strzelecki took off in 1835 on travels through Europe to Britain, Africa, the Americas, New Zealand. He arrived in Australia in 1839 and immediately visited his old friend James Macarthur at Camden. Upon hearing of Strzelecki's credentials, Governor Gipps requested him to survey the region of eastern Gippsland.

In 1839, Strzelecki discovered gold but was persuaded by Gipps to keep it quiet. Later in 1839, Strzelecki set out into the Australian Alps to explore the Snowy Mountains with James Macarthur, James Riley and two Aboriginal trackers — Charlie Tarra and Jackey. In 1840, they climbed to the peak of Mount Kosciuszko, which Strzelecki named after the Polish hero Tadeusz Kosciuszko, who had fought in the American Revolutionary War (1775-1783) and resisted in the Third Polish Partition (1794-1795). Strzelecki's expedition descended the La Trobe River into Gippsland towards Westernport. They were saved from starvation by their Aboriginal guide Jackey and arrived in Melbourne 1840.

From 1840-1842, Strzelecki explored and mapped all of Van Diemen's Land. After, he returned to Britain, via China. In 1845, Strzelecki became a British citizen. In Ireland in 1846, he was appointed chief agent of the British Relief Association charged with the distribution of supplies during the Irish Famine. In 1849, Strzelecki was awarded a gold medal from the Royal Geographic Society and made a fellow of the Royal Society. With Florence Nightingale, he assisted in the recovery of British soldiers during the Crimean War (1853-1856) and was knighted in 1869. Strzelecki was buried in Kensal Green Cemetery, London, but was later reburied in Posnan, Poland, in 1997.

Pawel Strzelecki

Statue of Strzelecki at Jindabyne

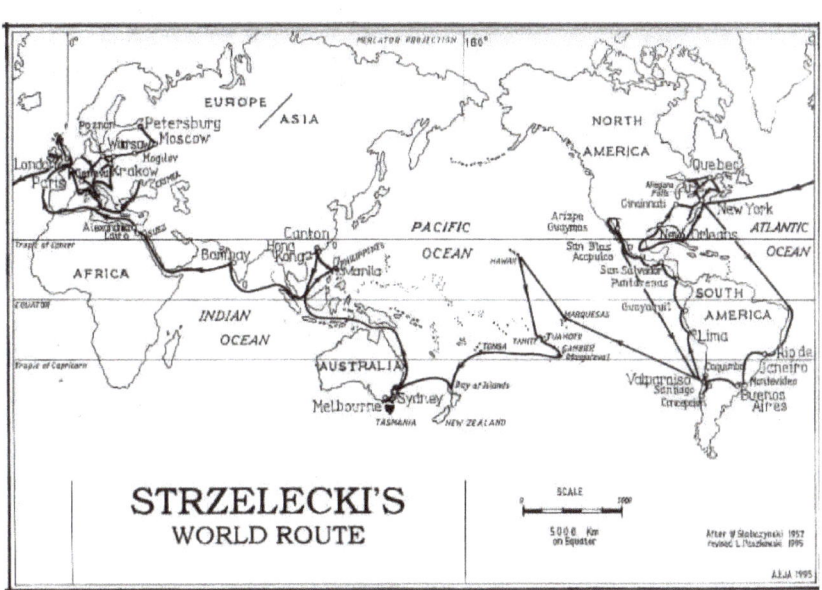
Strzelecki's world travels (1835-1849)

Wurundjeri, Kulin, and Birrarung — Melbourne

The Kulin Alliance is a confederation of five tribes that occupied the areas around the current city of Melbourne. The tribes included the Boonwurrung, south of the Yarra; the Woiworong, north of the Yarra; the Taungurong, north-east of Melbourne; the Djadjawurung, north-west of Melbourne, including Bendigo; and the Wathaurong, west of Melbourne, including Geelong. This may be considered a similar alliance to the Iroquois confederacy of five tribes — the Mohawk, Oneida, Onondaga, Cayuga and Seneca — of American history. Wurundjeri are the indigenous people and the language of the Kulin Alliance. Birrarung is the indigenous name for the Yarra River in Wurundjeri language.

John Batman — Melbourne (1835).

John Batman (1801-1839) was born in Parramatta, and was a grazier, explorer and entrepreneur. In 1821, at age 20, Batman, with his brother Henry, acquired a large property in the north-east of Van Diemen's Land. During his time there, Batman captured two bushrangers, Thomas Jeffries and Matthew Brady, and was actively involved in the rounding up and slaughtering of Tasmanian Aborigines, from 1829 to 1830, to expand his properties to 7,000 acres. In one instance, in a report by Tasmanian Colonial Governor, George Arthur, Batman captured then 'cold-bloodedly' shot them.

To expand his properties further, Batman sought land grants in the Westernport area. In 1835, to stake his claim, he sailed into Port Phillip Bay then into the Yarra River. There he stated, "This will be the place for a village." He named it Batmania, but it was later renamed after the then British Prime Minister, Lord Melbourne. It is documented that Batman negotiated a treaty with the Kulin peoples, also known as the Dutigalla Treaty. In exchange for all the land between Melbourne and Geelong, Batman provided tools, blankets and food. Although an unfair treaty, it is the only instance in Australian colonial history of a European treaty with the Aboriginal people. As it was, Governor Bourke deemed the treaty invalid, did not recognise it, and merely claimed the land again as 'Terra nullius'.

Batman set up a property on Batman's Hill, located at the western end of Collins Street. His health declined quickly, and he died three years later. He was buried in the Old Melbourne Cemetery, now site of the Queen Victoria Market, but was later exhumed and reburied in the Fawkner Cemetery.

John Pascoe Fawkner

John Pascoe Fawkner (1792-1869), born in London, was an early pioneer, businessman and politician in Melbourne. Fawkner financed a party of free settlers from Van Diemen's Land to Batmania (Melbourne) in 1835. After Victoria became an independent colony in 1851, Fawkner sat on its Legislative Council, and founded two of Melbourne's early newspapers. The Melbourne suburb of Fawkner is named after him, as well as Fawkner Cemetery, and Fawkner Park.

Robert Hoddle

Robert Hoddle (1794-1881), born in London, was a surveyor and artist. He was Surveyor General for the Port Phillip District from 1837 to 1853. Hoddle designed the Hoddle Grid of streets that make up the CBD of Melbourne.

Billibellary

Billibellary (1799-1846) was a leader of the Woiworong tribe, located north of the Yarra River, at the time of the European settlement of Melbourne. He was also a noted songwriter. Billibellary's influence has been noted to extend well beyond the tribal lands of the Woiworong. His family lived near today's Yarra Bend on the Merri Creek. He was one of eight 'ngurungaeta' (tribal leaders) to sign a treaty with John Batman. Billibellary's achievement, in friendship with colonial administrator William Thomas, was to feed and protect his people, and keep peace with the new European settlers who were taking tribal lands during his lifetime. In this capacity, he served in the Native Police Corps to protect his people, but later resigned when it was found to have captured and killed Aboriginal people. He died of a respiratory illness and was buried near Dight Falls, near where the Merri Creek runs off the Yarra River.

John Batman

John Pascoe Fawkner

Robert Hoddle

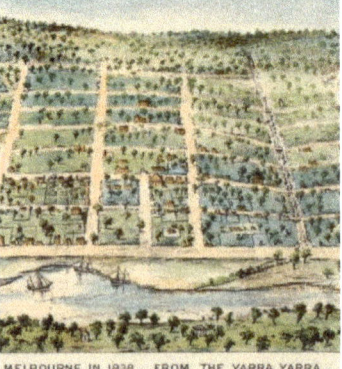
Part of the Hoddle Grid of Melbourne.

Derrimut

Derrimut (1810-1864) was a leader of the Boonwurrung tribe, located south of the Yarra River, at the time of the European settlement of Melbourne. Derrimut, like Billibellary, attempted to protect his people from incoming European settlers. After losing the land immediately south of the Yarra River, Derrimut fought in the late 1850s and early 1860s to protect the Boonwurrung homelands around the current day Melbourne suburb of Mordialloc. When the lands around Mordialloc were taken by settlers in the 1860s, Derrimut, with remnants of the Boonwurrung and Woiworong tribes were relocated to Coranderrk Mission Station, an Aboriginal reservation near Healesville. Derrimut died at 54 years, most probably of depression at the Melbourne Benevolent Asylum in 1864. He is buried in the Melbourne General Cemetery in North Carlton. The Melbourne suburb of Derrimut is named after him, although it is located on Wathaurong tribal land, not Boonwurrung land.

Billibellary   *Derrimut*

Simon Wonga

Simon Wonga (1824-1874) was the son of Billibellary. At 11 years, he went with his father to make a treaty with John Batman. In 1840, he was injured and cared for by Susannah, the wife of his father's friend and colonial administrator William Thomas. In 1851, he became Ngurungaeta of the Wurundjeri people. In 1859, he unsuccessfully attempted to negotiate a new homeland for the Taungurong tribe along the Goulburn River, but did succeed in securing tenancy of land, but not freehold, at Coranderrk Mission Station, near Healesville. The Melbourne suburb of Wonga Park is named after him.

Simon Wonga   *William Barak*

William Barak

William Barak (1824-1903) was the last Ngurungaeta of the Wurundjeri people. His father, Bebejern, was also leader of the Wurundjeri people. Barak attended the Yarra Mission School from 1837 to 1839. He joined the Native Mounted Police in 1844. In 1863, Barak moved to the Coranderrk Mission Station. Upon the death of Simon Wonga, Barak became the last Ngurungaeta of the Wurundjeri people. He was also noted for his artworks. He died at almost 80 years and is buried at Coranderrk Cemetery.

The Butcher of Gippsland

The Gippsland area is situated along the east coast of Victoria and the south-eastern coast of Australia. Between 1840 and 1850, a series of repeated massacres occurred against the Gunai Kurnai people. The significant perpetrator of these massacres was Angus McMillan, "Butcher of Gippsland". McMillan was born in Skye, Scotland, in hardship and deprivation and migrated to Australia in 1838. In 1840, seeing the opportunity of claiming the vast Gippsland area for himself, McMillan set about massacring and dispersing its occupants — the Gunai Kurnai people. These massacres were kept secret so that the perpetrators, McMillan's "highland brigade", would not be prosecuted.

McMillan is alleged to have kept hessian bags full of the skulls of murdered people. An 1845 census listed McMillan's holdings in Gippsland as six acres. By 1856, his holdings had increased to 150,000 acres, with one of the state's largest holdings of sheep and cattle. However, bushfires and mismanagement meant that McMillan was in debt and had to sell his estate and he died, leaving his wife and children destitute. In 1948, the federal electorate of McMillan was named after him but was subsequently changed in 2018 to that of Monash, due to recognition of the Gippsland massacres. The Gippsland massacres are portrayed in Andrea James' play, 'The Black Woman of Gippsland'. There are currently hundreds of submissions to remove all monuments to "the butcher of Gippsland".

Adelaide and the Kaurna

Prior to European settlement, the area along the eastern coast of St Vincent's Gulf was occupied by the Kaurna tribe. The tribal lands extended from modern-day Port Pirrie in the north, through Adelaide, to Victor Harbour in the south, but does not include the Yorke Peninsula. The Kaurna are sometimes referred to as the Garner tribe. Kaurna also refers to their dialect spoken, belonging to the Thura-Yura language spoken by the Aboriginal peoples around the greater St Vincent and Spencer Gulf region.

The Kaurna were not a large tribe and were surrounded by other tribes such as the Narangga, who lived on the Yorke Peninsula; the Ngadjuri, who lived east of the Karna; the Ngarrindjeri, who lived further south along the 'Coorong'; The Meru, living further east; and the Ngargad and Bindjali tribes in the south east of South Australia.

Unlike the rest of Australia, South Australia, by way of the South Australia Act 1834, was not considered to be 'Terra nullius'. Although the Act recognised the permanent ownership of the region by the Aboriginal people, it was ignored by the early European authorities, settlers and squatters. In 2000, the Kaurna Yerta Corporation lodged a native title claim with the South Australian government. In 2018, it was determined that they were given title to the area from Myponga (near Victor Harbour) to Lower Light (near Gawler), which included Adelaide. However, an earlier 2009 claim for $50 million in rent owed was rejected.

William Light — Adelaide (1836)

William Light (1786-1839), born in Kuala Kedah, Malaysia, was British Army and Naval officer, an artist, and the first Surveyor-General of the Colony of South Australia. In 1836, William Light charted the Port Adelaide River, selected the location of Adelaide as the colony's capital, and designed the layout of the streets and parks in the Adelaide city centre. He chose the location of Adelaide as the colony's capital because it was sited next to the Torrens River and because it received consistent rainfall due to the Adelaide Hills. Light died in Adelaide in 1839 and is buried at West Terrace Cemetery.

Edward John Eyre — The Great Australian Bight (1841)

Edward John Eyre (1815-1901), born in England, was an explorer and colonial administrator. Before he was 18 years, Eyre had emigrated to Sydney. Not long after, he bought a giant flock of 1,000 sheep and 600 cattle, transported them to Adelaide and sold them in the new colony for a large profit.

William Light

Edward John Eyre

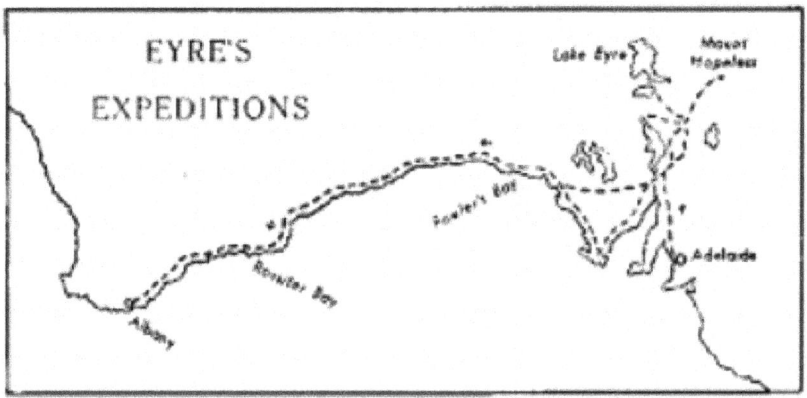

In 1839, with the money gained from his sale, Eyre, now 23 years, set out to explore South Australia in two expeditions. The first was north of Adelaide into the Flinders Ranges around the area of Wilpena Pound. The second expedition was from Port Lincoln to the Gawler Ranges, the latter of which he named after South Australia's then governor, then across the Nullarbor Plain, along the Great Australian Bite to Ceduna. He intended to travel further west but ran short of water.

In 1841, Eyre travelled west across the entire Nullarbor Plain, along the Great Australian Bite beyond Ceduna to Albany. His companion,

John Baxter, was killed on the expedition. Eyre and his other companion Wylie, probably from the Minarig tribe around modern-day Albany, survived the journey. Wylie chose to remain with his tribe.

Eyre later served as a colonial governor in New Zealand and in Jamaica. It was in Jamaica that he ruthlessly put down a rebellion killing over 500 people and burning down 1,000 houses. He used this brutal influence to reform the local government and made it a crown colony. Lake Eyre and the Eyre Peninsula in South Australia, and the Eyre Highway, the main highway from South Australia to Western Australia, are named after him. A statue of him can be found in Victoria Terrace in Adelaide.

Charles Sturt revisited — Central Australia (1845)

Earlier, we covered Charles Sturt's two earlier expeditions of 1828-29 along the Macquarie River to the Darling River, and 1829-30 along the Murrumbidgee and Murray rivers.

In 1844, Darling attempted the most perilous of his expeditions into Central Australia in search of a rumoured great inland sea. The great inland sea may have been Lake Eyre that disappears during prolonged droughts. With 15 men, including John McDouall Stuart, and 200 sheep, Sturt's group travelled along the Darling and Murray rivers to Broken Hill, then onto the Simpson Desert. It was there that the expedition broke down, Sturt contracted scurvy, and the group returned to Sydney. In 1849, Sturt was appointed Colonial Secretary but resigned in 1851 due to declining health.

Charles Sturt University in New South Wales, the suburb of Sturt in Adelaide, the Sturt Highway from Wagga Wagga to Adelaide, among other acknowledgements, are named after him.

Ludwig Leichhardt — Northern Australia (1844-48)

Ludwig Leichhardt (1813-1848), born in Germany, was an explorer and naturalist. In 1842, Leichhardt arrived in Sydney to study the geography and wildlife of the area, with a view to exploring inland Australia.

In 1844, Leichhardt led an expedition 4,800 kilometres (3,000 miles) from Moreton Bay (Brisbane) along the Queensland and Northern Territory coast to Port Esslington, near Darwin. He was awarded a medal from the Paris Geographical Society for his expedition, although he did not get to receive it.

In 1847, Leichhardt attempted an expedition from the Darling Downs, in south-eastern Queensland, across Australia to Perth. However, the expedition was halted after 800 kilometres due to heavy rain and malarial fever. Instead, a few weeks later, the group explored the area inland along the Condamine River.

In 1848, Leichhardt attempted his Darling Downs to Perth crossing again and disappeared, never to be heard from again. In 1900 a small brass plate with the inscription Ludwig Leichhardt 1848 was discovered near the Great Sandy Desert, near the Pilbara Region and Kimberley Ranges of north-western Western Australia. The brass plate was authenticated in 2006. There is also a story from the Wallumbilla tribe of the Maranoa region of Queensland about a white man leading a large group of mules and bullocks along the river. The Aboriginals surrounded the group and massacred everyone in it. Yet this does not explain how relics from the expedition came to be found in Western Australia.

Leichhardt is acknowledged by a suburb in each of Sydney and Brisbane, and the Leichhardt Highway and Leichhardt River in Queensland.

Ludwig Leichhardt

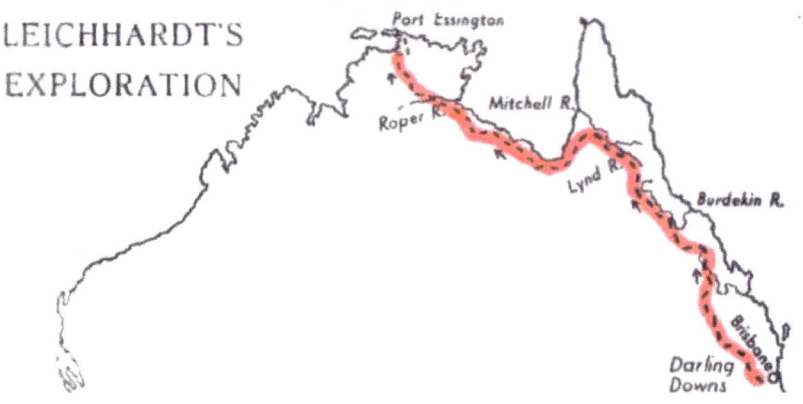

Augustus Gregory — Western Australia (1846-48)

Augustus Charles Gregory (1819-1905), born in England, was a surveyor and politician. With his younger brothers, Frank (1821-1888) and Henry (1823-?), he explored across Australia.

Initially, his family emigrated to Western Australia and gained several grants of land along the Swan River. Working with his older brother, Joshua (1815-1850), he acquired experience as a surveyor and joined the Government of Western Australia Survey Office.

In 1846, Gregory led his first expedition into the area north of Perth, covering just over 1,500 kilometres (1,000 miles) in 47 days.

Augustus Gregory

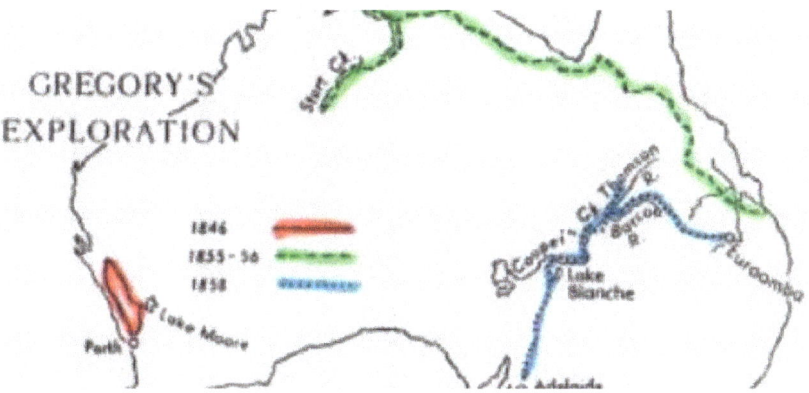

In 1848, he led another expedition along the Western Australian coast past the Murchison River in search of new pasture lands. However, after crossing the river, his group were turned back due to water supply difficulties, yet they had covered almost 2,500 kilometres (1,500 miles) in ten weeks.

In 1856, he commanded an expedition that began at Port Essington, on the north coast, near Darwin, initially traveling west to and around Lake Gregory in northern Western Australia. After, the expedition travelled eastward along northern Australia into Queensland, arriving in Brisbane some 16 months later, covering over 8,000 kilometres (5,000 miles) across rugged land.

In 1858, Gregory led his last expedition, hired by the New South Wales government to search for remains of the missing Leichhardt expedition. It began near Brisbane and lasted four months, following the Barcoo River and Cooper's Creek into South Australia to Adelaide. Along the Barcoo River, he had found a tree marked with the letter 'L'.

In 1859, Gregory was appointed the Surveyor-General for Queensland, was awarded the Founder's Gold Medal by the Royal Geographic Society, and was eventually knighted in 1903. He died in 1905. His honours include a Queensland electorate; a town, a river, and a highway in Queensland; and a town in Western Australia — all named Gregory.

John McGillivray — The Great Barrier Reef (1846-50)

John McGillivray (1821-1867), born in Scotland, was a naturalist and explorer. Between 1843 and 1850, McGillivray sailed on several voyages, mainly along the area of the Great Barrier Reef and the Torres Strait. On those trips, he collected many types of fauna and flora. Later, living in Grafton, Queensland, he extended his collection. Some of his collection can be found displayed in the British Museum in London.

Edmund Kennedy — Cape York (1847-48)

Edmund Kennedy (1818-1848), born in Guernsey, Channel Islands, was a surveyor and explorer. In 1840, he arrived in Sydney and took up the role as an assistant surveyor in New South Wales. In 1845, Kennedy received his first opportunity as an explorer, accompanying Thomas Mitchell on his fourth expedition into northern New South Wales. Mitchell was so impressed with Kennedy's leadership qualities that he took him on his 1857 expedition into central Queensland.

In 1848, in charge of his own expedition, Kennedy was ordered to explore the east coast of Cape York in the far north of Queensland, to reach its most northerly point then travel along its western coast. It was anticipated that the journey would take eighteen months. The group were dropped off in the May of 1848 by ship at Rockingham Bay, between Townsville and Cairns but were immediately beset by challenging rainforest terrain. After nine weeks, they had travelled only 60 kilometres (40 miles). Also, food and supplies had gone missing, presumed stolen. Further, they missed a rendezvous with a supply ship. By mid-November they had reached Weymouth Bay in poor condition. Kennedy with four others, including his Aboriginal guide Jackey Jackey, continued north. The rest remained at Weymouth Bay. Around December 13, Kennedy was speared during a melee with Aboriginals. Only Jackey Jackey survived ten days with no provisions and trekked the remaining 30 kilometres to reach the tip of Cape York and meet the supply ship. The ship returned to Weymouth Bay to find only two survivors of from the remaining group. Kennedy is honoured by a Queensland electorate and highway.

Edmund Kennedy

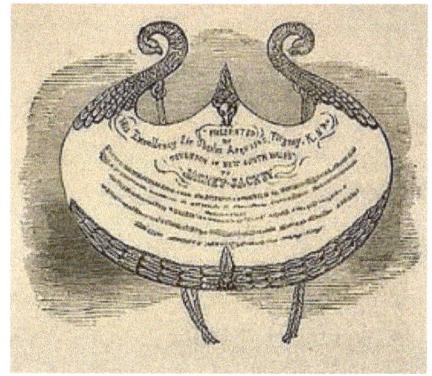

Jackey Jackey's silver breastplate

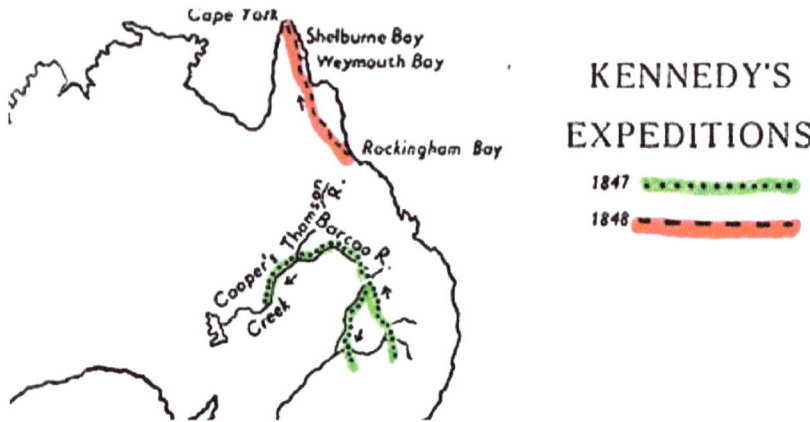

Jackey Jackey (Galmahra)

Jackey Jackey (1833-1854), born around Muswellbrook, NSW, was an Aboriginal guide. He is also known by his indigenous name, Galmahra, and was a member of the Wonnarua people. He was a guide in the Surveyor-General's Department of New South Wales. He was the sole survivor of Edmund Kennedy's 1848 Cape York expedition. For his heroic deeds, Jackey Jackey was awarded a solid silver breastplate. He is honoured with a creek and a mountain range in Cape York, Queensland.

John McDouall Stuart — Adelaide to Darwin (1859-62)

John McDouall Stuart (1815-1866), born in Scotland, was a surveyor and explorer. Stuart migrated to Adelaide in 1838. In 1844, he joined Charles Sturt's expedition into Central Australia, where he learnt the complexities of travelling in 'waterless' terrain. From 1846 to 1858, Stuart practised as a surveyor in Port Lincoln.

In 1858, Stuart commanded his first expedition, over three months, into the area around Coober Pedy belonging to the Banggarla, Kokatha and Wirangu tribes. He gave his diaries and maps of over 100,000 square kilometres to the South Australian Government, who claimed the land for themselves. Stuart was granted 2,500 square kilometres of this territory.

John McDouall Stuart

In 1860, Stuart led another expedition, 16 months long, past the MacDonnell Ranges (Tjotitja) into the centre of Australia. Here, he raised a flag as "a sign to natives that the dawn of liberty, civilisation and Christianity was about to break on them". The furthest point the group reached was Attack Creek, halfway between Alice Springs and Katherine.

In 1861, given news that a group from Melbourne, led by Burke and Wills, were attempting to travel overland to Darwin, the South Australian government financed Stuart on a new trip to beat them. This time,

Stuart reached Stuart's Plain, close to the Gulf of Carpentaria, but didn't make it all the way, before falling back to Adelaide. For his efforts, Stuart received the 1861 Gold Medal from the Royal Geographic Society.

Stuart still believed he could go all the way and in October 1861, he made another attempt. This time Stuart was well prepared and met most challenges. His group arrived at Attack Creek in March 1864, Sturt's Plain in April. However, after this, his journey began to falter, but made the Indian Ocean, near Darwin, in July. Ill with scurvy and near blind, Stuart arrived back in Adelaide in December.

The next year, he returned to visit his sister in England. There he died and was buried at Kensal Green Cemetery, London. The Stuart Highway, running from Darwin to Port Augusta, is named after him. The towns of Stuart and Stuart Plains were later changed to Alice Springs and Coober Pedy respectively.

Burke & Wills — Melbourne to Gulf of Carpentaria (1860-61)
The Burke and Wills Expedition (1860-1861), a journey from Melbourne overland to the Gulf of Carpentaria, was financed by the Royal Society of Victoria. It began with 19 men, but only one, an Irishman John King, survived.

Robert O'Hara Burke (1821-1861), born in Ireland, was a soldier, police officer and explorer. William John Wills (1834-1861), born in England, was a surveyor, surgeon and explorer.

Although well supplied, the expedition lacked anyone with any experience in trekking the Australian bushlands. The expedition started slowly but did make good time after reorganising itself at Menindee on the Darling River. It made good progress to Coopers Creek, where it set up a depot. From there, Burke and Wills, with two others, travelled alone. They reached the Flinders River, near the Gulf of Carpentaria, but swamplands kept them from reaching the coast.

The four returned to the depot at Coopers Creek exhausted to find that it had been abandoned only hours earlier. It was there that Burke and Wills died. Both were honoured by the federal electorates of Burke and Wills.

Robert O'Hara Burke   William John Wills

Painting (left) of Burke and Wills arriving at the deserted camp at Coopers Creek, by John Longstaff

Alexander Forrest — the Kimberley Region (1879)

Before European settlement, the Kimberley region had been occupied by the Gooniyandi, Walmatjarri, Jaru, Kija and Gurindji peoples for thousands of years. The first European to arrive in the Kimberley was Alexander Forrest whose family was to have a very significant impact in Western Australia.

Alexander Forrest (1849-1901) was born in Picton, inland from Bunbury in Western Australia. He was a surveyor, explorer, investor and politician. Alexander Forrest explored various areas of Western Australia, including the Kimberley region in 1879. He named the Kimberley region, the King Leopold Ranges, the Ord, Fitzroy and Margaret rivers. He claimed the area and leased out over 50 million acres to new European settlers, including the Durack Family. The Duracks set up the Lissadell, Argyle, Rosewood and Ivanhoe cattle stations. The Ivanhoe cattle station, north of Kunanurra, located on rich alluvial soils, was later to be the site for the Ord River Scheme.

His brother Sir John Forrest was the first Premier of Western Australia and was the premier that ordered the Fitzroy Crossing massacres of Aboriginal peoples during the Jandamarra rebellion (1894-1897).

Andrew Forrest (b.1961), former CEO and chairman of Fortescue Metals Group is the great-grandson of David Forrest, Alexander and John's younger brother.

Aboriginal resistance and massacres

From the time that the earliest European explorers arriving at Sydney Cove, moving out past the Blue Mountains and the settlers that came after them, the Aboriginal people were clearly the losers. The cost was initially, through 'Terra nullius', a loss of recognition and identity. This was followed by the loss of life and land, taken by disease, massacres, expulsion, and the British soldiers and new settlers.

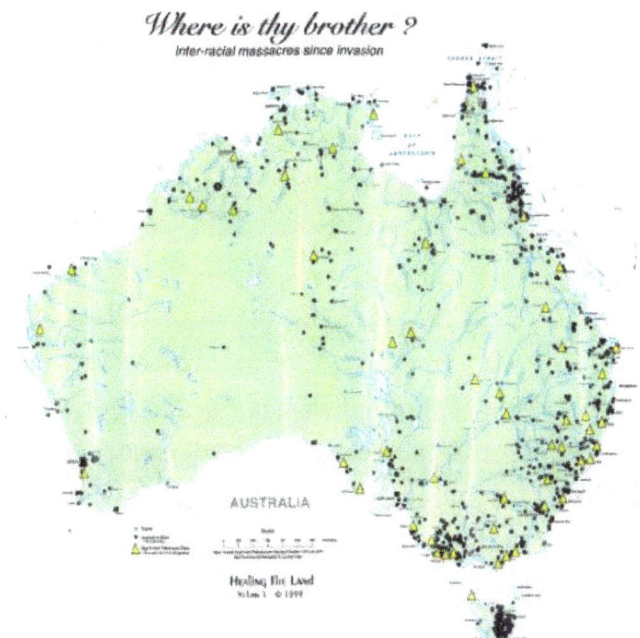

Australian massacre map, Judith Monticone, 1999

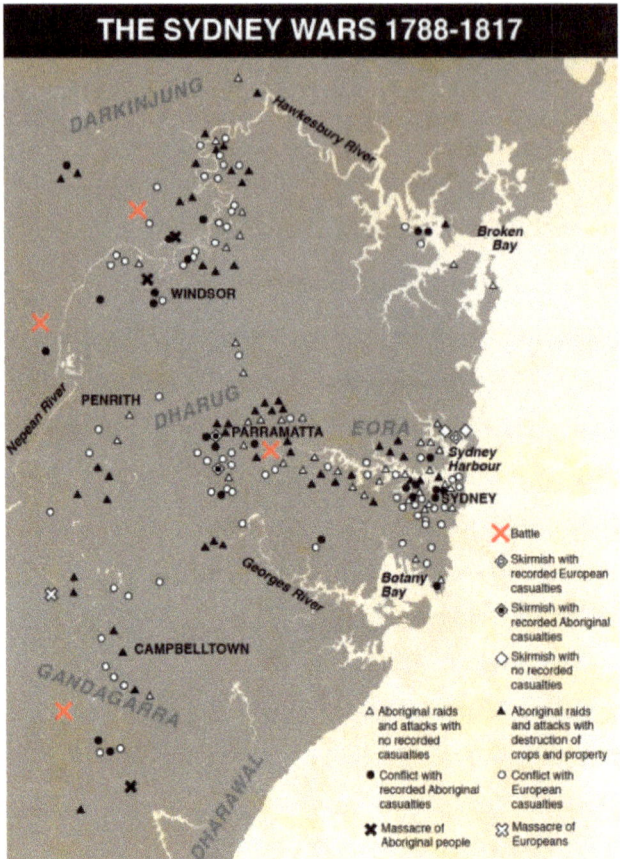

When Captain Cook landed at Botany Bay in 1770, he mistook Aboriginal indifference to him as an excuse for 'Terra nullius'. By the time Captain Phillip landed at Sydney Cove in 1788, Aboriginal indifference had changed to partial resistance. Some, like Bennelong, sought opportunity with the new occupiers. Others, such as Pemulwuy, sought resistance to occupation. The massacres of the Eora tribe began in 1788.

Later, as the colony expanded beyond the Blue Mountains, Governor Macquarie led a policy of settler occupation of Aboriginal lands and ordered expeditions to annihilate the local Aboriginal tribes of the Dharug, Gandagarra and Darkinjung, and take their land under the guise of 'Terra nullius'.

List of Aboriginal Frontier Massacres

New South Wales:

July 1791 — Prospect Hill and The Ponds, 50 Aboriginal deaths estimated, other dispersed

April 1794 — Hawkesbury River, 7 dead, one Aboriginal boy dragged through fire, thrown in river, shot dead, others dispersed

May 1795 — Hawkesbury River, 15 Bediagal killed estimated, including a child and newborn baby

September 1795 — Hawkesbury River, 5 killed, unknown number wounded

March 1797 — Battle of Parramatta, 5 killed, unknown number wounded

March 1799 — Hunter River, 4 Awabakal men killed

April 1816 — Appin Massacre, unknown number either shot or forced off cliffs to their death

1824 — Bathurst Massacre, 16 Wiradjuri killed

1827 — Hunter Valley, 12 Gringai killed

1832 — Bawley Point, 4 killed, including elderly couple and pregnant woman

1835 — Williams Valley — unknown number of Gringai forced off cliff, remainder shot dead

July 1835 — Mitchell expedition, Darling River, 5 killed including woman with baby. Others killed fleeing across river.

May 1836 — Mitchell expedition, Murray river, unknown number driven into river and killed fleeing.

January 1838 — Waterloo Creek massacre, estimated 50 killed

June 1838 — Myall creek massacre, estimated 28 killed

Mid-1838 — Gwydir River, unknown number massacred

November 1838 — Moree, 9 Gamilaraay people killed

July 1838 — Murray River, 14 people killed

1838 — 1851 — Macleay River, estimated 15 separate massacres, unknown number of Djangadi killed

June 1841 — Macleay River, 20 killed

August 1841 — Rufus River Massacre, estimated 40 killed

1842 — Evans Head Massacre, estimated 100 Bundjalung killed

November 1847 — Kangaroo Creek poisoning, 23 people died in agony

April 1849 — Darling River, 5 killed

1849 — Hospital Creek Massacre, unknown number killed

1849 — Butchers tree, unknown number killed

1854 — East Ballina Massacre, 40 killed, many more wounded

June 1895 — Fernmount poisoning, 6 died in agony

Tasmania

May 1804 — Risdon Cove Massacre, unknown number slaughtered

February 1828 — Cape Grim Massacre, over 30 Pennemukeer killed

1828 – 1832 — Black War, genocide of unknown number of estimated 20,000 people

Victoria

1833 – 1834 — Convincing Ground Massacre, estimated 200 Gunditjmara killed by whalers, only two members of Kilcarer clan survived

April 1838 — Benalla, estimated 100 Koori killed

May-June 1839 — Campaspe Plains Massacre, 6 Djadjawurung killed

June 1839 — Murdering Gully Massacre, estimated 40 killed

1840-1850 — Gippsland massacres, estimated 1,000 Kurnai killed

Massacre map, Victoria 1836–1850

Victorian massacres map, Koori Heritage Trust

February 1840 — Westernport, 9 Kurnai killed

1843 — Warrigal Creek Massacre, 100-150 Kurnai killed

1844 — Shady Creek Massacre, 70 Kurnai killed

1848 — Port Fairy, last group of Ganubanud tribe massacred

Western Australia

1830 — Fremantle, unknown number killed

1834 — Pinjarra Massacre, over 25 killed

August 1836 — York area, over 10 killed

August 1841 — Lake Minimup, over 50 killed

June 1854 — Greenough area, unknown number killed

1865 — Kimberley area, 20 killed

1867 — Battle of Minderoo, unknown number killed by mounted troops

1868 — Flying Foam Massacre, estimated 150 killed

1887 — Halls Creek, genocide of Djara, Konejandi and Walmadjari tribes

1893 — Behn River, over 50 killed

1890-1926 — Kimberley — The Killing Times, hundreds killed

1906-1907 — Canning Stock Route, unknown number of Mardu women and men raped and massacred

1915 — Mistake Creek Massacre, 7 Kija killed

1922 — Sturt Creek Massacre, over 10 killed

1924 — Bedford Downs Massacre, Gija and Worla men poisoned, died in agony

June 1926 — Forrest River Massacre, 20 killed

1960 — Great Sandy Desert, Walmajarri men, women and children systematically massacred

South Australia

1848 — Avenue Range Station Massacre, Mount Gambier, over 10 Bungandidj killed

1849 — Waterloo Bay Massacre, 10 Nauo killed

Queensland

1842 — Whiteside poisoning, Brisbane Valley, over 50 died in agony, poisoned by settlers

1842 — Kilcoy poisoning, estimated 60 died in agony

November 1848 — Canning Creek, 3 women and a child killed by 7 white men

1849 — Upper Burnett, over 100 killed

1849 — Balonne River, unknown number killed

1850 — Paddy Island, hundreds killed

January 1856 — Mount Larcombe, 250 men, women and children surrounded and slaughtered

March 1858 — Hornet Bank station, 300 Yeeman killed

1860 — North Bundaberg, 20 killed, other dispersed

March 1860 — Bendemere, 15 killed

February 1861 — Manumbar, 6-10 old men killed

October-November 1861 — Central Highlands, estimated 170 people killed

July 1865 — Rockhampton, 18 Darumbal ambushed and killed at ceremonial gathering

1867 — Goulbolba Hill Massacre, large massacre of men, women and children, unknown number killed

April 1867 — The Leap Massacre, Mackay, 200 men, women and children forced to jump off cliff

July 1867 — Rockhampton, 8 killed, including elderly and children

1872 — Skull Hole, Bladensburg, over 200 killed

1873 — Battle Camp Collision, miners kill unknown number

1874-1875 — Blackfellow's Creek, miners kill unknown number

1878 — Cook district, estimated 75 killed

1879 — Selwyn Range, estimated 300 Kalkadoon killed

1879 — Cape Bedford, 28 Guugu-Yimidhirr shot and drowned

1884 — Battle Mountain, Mount Isa, 200 Kalkadoon killed

1884-1885 — Coppermine massacres, unknown number killed

1888 — Diamantina River, 200 killed

1918 — Bentinck Island, over 100 of Kaiadilt clan raped, killed or drowned

Northern Territory

December 1827 — Raffles Bay, over 30 killed fleeing to beach, women bayoneted

1874 — Barrow Creek Massacre, Kaititja tribe wiped out

1875 — Massacre of Running Waters, settlers kill estimated 100 Arrernte

1880-90 — Arnhem Land, Yolngu men, women and children poisoned and died in agony

1928 — Coniston Massacre, estimated 17 Walpiri killed

Here is a recount of some of the noted Aboriginal wars and massacres that are so often missing from earlier 'sanitised' versions of Australian history. Also, some of the noted Aboriginal leaders who led courageous but ultimately futile resistance.

Pemulwuy's War (1790-1802)

The first noted conflict between the early British soldiers and settlers and the indigenous people of Australia was named Pemulwuy's war, after a spiritual chief of the Bidjigal clan of the Eora people. Born in 1750, Pemulwuy was about 40 years old when the war broke out. Prior to the war, Pemulwuy had organised the hunting and supply of meat to the new colony. In 1790, Pemulwuy was forced into a guerrilla war with the colonists that lasted twelve years until his assassination in 1802.

In 1790, a small shooting party, including Governor Phillip's gamekeeper, John McIntyre, left for Botany Bay. During the night, the party was met by an Aboriginal group, referred to in the report by Captain Watkin Tench as 'Indians'. Although the Aboriginal group retreated, McIntyre followed them and was subsequently speared but survived. The group was chased by the hunting party but escaped. Upon receiving the report Phillip ordered Tench to raid and massacre the Bidjigal camps. It had been suggested by Bennelong to Tench that McIntyre had previously hunted and killed Bidjigal people and that this was only an act of retaliation. Tench managed to convince Phillip that the mission should be only the capture of the guilty group and that no indiscriminate raids should occur. Tench's proposal was accepted, but in a three-day mission, he failed to capture the group. Over the next year, Pemulwuy organised the Eora, Dharug and Tharawal people into a rebellion. From 1792, Pemulwuy led raiding parties against settlers along the Parramatta and Hawkesbury rivers. In June 1795, the Battle of Richmond Hill was fought between about 70 marines of the New South Wales Corps and an equal number of Dharug warriors led by Pemulwuy. Although the colonists claimed a victory, it was not decisive. In December 1795, Pemulwuy's warriors attacked a working party at Botany Bay. He was wounded and captured but escaped later. During Pemulway's rebellion, the colonists took the opportunity to expel the local Aboriginees and take the land around Parramatta. In 1797, Pemulwuy recommenced his rebellion. In March 1797, the Battle of Parramatta saw Pemulwuy lead 100 Bidjigul warriors against a garrison at a government farm at Toongabbie. In the battle, 32 warriors and 13 soldiers were killed. Pemulwuy was wounded several times, captured but escaped again. In 1801, Governor King ordered for Pemulwuy to be brought in dead or alive. He was shot, killed and beheaded by a British sailor the following year. His head was sent by Governor King to Sir Joseph Banks in London.

Tedbury's War (1808-1809)

Upon Pemulwuy's death, the rebellion was continued by his son, Tedbury. This is where information is less reliable, although Pemulwuy is identified as a chief of the Bidjigal clan of the Eora people, his son Tedbury is recorded as a member of the Dharug. Born in 1780, Tedbury was 22 years when his father was killed. It is unclear whether Tedbury participated in Pemulwuy's rebellion. In 1805, he was captured and tried before a magistrate then released. It is also recorded that in 1808,

Tedbury was an ally of John Macarthur and was a regular visitor to Elizabeth Farm. In 1809, he was accused of the robbery of a traveller along Parramatta Road, and in September 1809 led an attack on the farm of the Bond family on the Georges River. Although recorded as the Battle of Bond's Farm, it was not an organised battle between warriors and soldiers.

In February 1810, in view of witnesses, Tedbury threw a spear at Edward Luttrell's sister. Luttrell shot Tedbury. Lutrell was charged with assault on Tedbury but acquitted. Tedbury died of his wounds shortly after. In November 1811, Robert Luttrell, Edward's brother, was clubbed to death by Tedbury's fellow Dharug warriors. This was in reprisal for the Luttrell's capture and taking of the Dharug women.

Nepean War (1814–1816)

In 1812, a drought, in and around the areas of the Hawkesbury and Nepean rivers, meant that local Aborigines and settlers were coming into conflict over food. Aboriginal people were being accused of stealing from the settlers and violence ensued. In the town of Appin, there were a number of recorded incidents, including the killing of an Aboriginal boy by soldiers at Broughton's farm; the spearing of a soldier by warriors; and the raid on a camp by settlers and the killing and dismembering of Aboriginal women and children, near John Kennedy's farm. In July 1814, two Aboriginal children were killed at Daly's Mulgoa farm, when Mrs Daly fired at them. By 1816, Governor Macquarie sent two detachments to Appin on a seek and destroy mission of all Aboriginal camps and people. Known as the Appin Massacre, the camps were destroyed, and all captured and killed Aboriginals were beheaded. In late 1816, settlers were driven from their Hunter Valley farms. Governor Macquarie indemnified any soldier in the killing of any Aboriginal people and offered rewards of land grants for this.

In reprisal, over 500 Aboriginal people were massacred. Journals by George Bowman (1824) and John Lang (1834) recorded how soldiers were indiscriminately killing Aboriginal men, women and children, and of how the rivers ran red with blood.

The Risdon Massacre — Van Diemen's Land (1804)

Tasmania was originally connected to the mainland of Australia. The first human inhabitants arrived about 40,000 years ago. Around 6,000 years ago, when global water levels rose, Tasmania was separated from the mainland, much in the same way that Ireland and Great Britain became separated from mainland Europe.

Prior to European settlement in Tasmania in 1803, there were seven distinct Aboriginal groups. In the north were the Peerapper, Tommeginne, Tyerrernotepanner and Pyemmairrener peoples. In the centre were the Lairmairrener. Along the south and east coast were the Toogee, Nuennone and Paradarerme. Although it is recorded today that Tasmanian Aboriginals spoke a language called Palawa, each of the groups had their own variation or dialect. Estimates of the number of Tasmanian Aboriginals prior to European settlement vary as low as 3,000 up to 23,000.

With the establishment of the first military outpost on Van Diemen's Land at Risdon in 1803, there had been several bloody encounters between British soldiers and Aboriginal people of the area. Although David Collins, the first lieutenant governor of the colony, had received instruction from London that any acts of violence against Aboriginal people would be punished, he did not communicate nor enforce this order. In May 1804, a detachment of soldiers fired into a group of about 100 people. Witnesses claimed that 50 men, women and children had died, with the bodies being burned afterwards. There was no action taken against the soldiers.

From 1807 to 1813, 600 colonists were transported from Norfolk Island to areas along the Derwent and Tamar rivers, occupying over 12,000 hectares with 5,000 cattle and over 30,000 sheep. The new colonists used violence to claim more land, killing Aboriginal men and women, and taking their children as servants. By 1824, there were over 12,000 colonists occupying about one third of Van Diemen's Land, 175,000 hectares. The sheep population had grown to over 200,000.

The first problem was that the increase in colonists and their animals were crowding out the Aboriginal people. The sheep were taking over the traditional kangaroo hunting grounds. The second problem was the gender imbalance amongst the colonists, with a ratio of 6 men to one woman. This led to many male colonists forcefully taking Aboriginal women into captivity. By 1824, the consequent number of violent incidents had more than doubled.

Musquito's War — NSW 1805-13, Van Diemen's Land (1814-25)

Musquito (c.1780 — 1825), born in the Port Jackson area, belonged to the Eora people. He was an indigenous resistance fighter in both New South Wales and Van Diemen's Land, and also served as a tracker for the British authorities. In 1805, after being reported as raiding settlers' properties in the Hawkesbury area, orders were issued for his arrest. Although arrested without charge, Musquito was sent to Norfolk Island for eight years.

In 1813, Musquito was sent to Van Diemen's Land. The following year, his brother, Phillip, gained Gov. Macquarie's consent for Musquito to be returned to Sydney, but he was not returned. By 1817, in Van Diemen's Land, Musquito had distinguished himself as a tracker for Lt. Gov. Sorrell, including the capture of bushranger Michael Howe. However, Sorrell had broken his promise to return Musquito to

Sydney. In turn, a marginalised Musquito left the settlements and began gathering followers in resistance. His band raided several properties along the eastern coast until he was wounded and captured by another Aboriginal tracker named Teague. In 1824, he was charged with aiding and abetting in the murder of a stockkeeper and hanged the following year, inciting further violence between the Aborigines and the settlers. Musquito was the subject of a collection of paintings by Aboriginal artist Lin Onus and displayed at the Cooee Art Gallery. Screen Australia has announced that it is funding a film by director Dylan River made of Musquito's story.

The Black (Tasmanian) War (1824-1832)

The Black War refers to a period of violent conflict between European settlers and Aboriginal people in Van Diemen's Land from the mid-1820s until 1832. In 1824, George Arthur, the newly appointed Governor of the colony, issued a proclamation for the protection of Aboriginal people and the prosecution of European settlers who wantonly massacred them. However, this did not stem the number of conflicts between the declining number Aboriginal peoples and the ever-increasing number of European settlers. The conflict was fought using guerrilla tactics by both sides. In November 1828, martial law was declared against Aboriginal people, but this did not end the conflict.

In March 1830, an Aborigines Committee appointed by Arthur determined that the only resolution to the conflict would be the complete destruction of Aboriginal communities and culture in Tasmania.

The Black Line (1830)

In October 1830, the Black Line of over 2,000 soldiers, settlers and convicts began the organised massacre, surrender and removal of all Tasmanian Aboriginal people from their remaining traditional lands.

A bounty was placed on each Aboriginal person killed. By November, it is estimated that only 200 Aboriginal people remained in Tasmania, mainly in the heavy rainforests of the west coast. By 1832, the last of these surrendered.

The Cape Grim Massacre (1828)

The Cape Grim Massacre occurred on 10 February 1828. Cape Grim is located on the extreme north-western coast of Tasmania near Hunter Island. The massacre had been preceded by the killing of Aborigines who were attempting to protect their women from being molested by shepherds belonging to the Van Diemen's Land Company. In retaliation, the Aborigines destroyed a flock of about 100 sheep belonging to the company. Against this, in early February, the company killed a dozen Aborigines but that was not enough. On February 10, a group of Aboriginal Tasmanians were collecting food along the beach. In an ambush, the Van Diemen's Land Company shepherds shot about 30 Aboriginal hunters cornered on a cliff. The shepherds threw the bodies of the dead hunters onto the beach below, then the shepherds massacred the women and children camped on the beach. When the massacre was reported to the magistrate, Edward Curr, who was also the company manager, he ordered that no investigation be made of the incident.

Mannalargenna

Mannalalargenna (1770-1835) was an Aboriginal Tasmanian. He was an elder of the Plangermaireener tribe of north-eastern Van Diemen's Land, around what is now the Piper River or Ben Lomond area. Mannalalargenna led the Aboriginal resistance against the European settlers. He was not killed during the conflict but was promised amnesty if he and his remaining warriors surrendered. Instead, immediately after surrender, Mannalalargenna was clapped in chains and transported to Flinders Island. He died on Wybalenna Island in 1835, still in captivity.

Mannalalargenna married off his sister and four daughters to seamen from the Furneaux Islands. Today, many Aboriginal Australians can trace their ancestry to these marriages. Mannalalargenna Day is celebrated in early December at Little Musselroe Bay since 2015 as a memorial to lost and remaining Aboriginal Tasmanian culture.

Truganini   *Mannalalargenna*

Truganini

Truganini (1812-1876), born on Bruny Island, is considered to be the last full-blooded Aboriginal Tasmanian. She was the daughter of Mangana, the chief of the Bruny Island people. In 1829, after the massacre of her people by soldiers and settlers, where she was also raped, Truganini was removed to the Aboriginal reservation at Flinders Island. Later, she was moved to the Colony of Port Phillip. In her last days, she begged to be buried respectfully. Despite this, within two years, her skeleton was placed on display by the Royal Society of Tasmania.

The Bathurst Massacre (1824)

The Bathurst War, also known as the Bathurst Massacres, occurred in central New South Wales in 1824. It was fought between the Wiradjuri people, led by Windradyne, and the New South Wales Corps, led by Major Morisset. The beginnings of the massacre were a repeated theme of traditional Aboriginal lands being taken by settlers. The Aboriginal people looking for food on settler property. The settlers killing them. The Aboriginal people retaliating. Followed by an organised group of soldiers, armed settlers and convicts massacring them.

In August 1824, Governor Brisbane proclaimed martial law against the Wiradjuri. On September 10, a group of about 250 soldiers and armed settlers entered an empty Wiradjuri camp. The Wiradjuri were away burying some dead. Upon the return of the people to the camp, the soldiers fired at the Wiradjuri and a massacre ensued. By December, nearly all of the Wiradjuri had surrendered, and martial law was repealed. Upon this, Windradyne, still with a price on his head, surrendered too.

Protector of Aborigines and Native Police

In the 1830s, the British government began to realise that the colonisation of the new territories had put the rights of the Aboriginal people at risk.

In January 1838, Lord Glenelg, a Scottish politician, then British Secretary of State for War and the Colonies, sent to Governor Gipps the House of Commons report: Report of the Parliamentary Select Committee on Aboriginal Tribes (British Settlements). The report recommended the establishment of the position Protector of Aborigines to protect the rights of the Aboriginal people and to protect their lands from colonial encroachment. In practice, the Protector of Aborigines was a position used to slaughter Aboriginal people, force them off their lands, subject them to cruelty and injustice, and to take Aboriginal children away from their parents. Matthew Moorhouse, the first Protector of Aborigines, led the Rufus River Massacre, which slaughtered over 30 Aboriginal people. The position of Protector of Aborigines was established in each of the colonies and continued after federation. In Queensland, the last Protector of Aborigines was Patrick Killoran, who held the position until his retirement in 1986.

To enforce their will over the Aboriginal people, the Protector of Aborigines in each colony often used Native Police. These were Australian native police units, of Aboriginal troopers, often recruited under threat and force, commanded by British or colonial officers. The colonial authorities realised that colonial troopers were limited in their tracking skills, especially in remote areas. They needed the Aboriginal troopers to be effective. In many cases the Native Police were used to hunt down and kill Aboriginal people. There were instances where Native Police troopers, such as Jandamarra, were exposed to cruelty themselves or to their kinsman and rebelled. Some became bushrangers and were hunted down by the authorities.

The Myall Creek Massacre (1838)

The aftermath of the Bathurst Massacre did not end the plight of the Aboriginal people of New South Wales. The Myall Creek Massacre occurred in northern New South Wales near the Gwydir River, near Bingara. In June 1838, a group of about 35 Aboriginal people, almost entirely old men, women and children of the Wirrayaraay tribe of the Kamilaroi people sought refuge on a cattle station. These people were well known as many of their young men worked on the surrounding cattle stations and some of the children spoke English. At that time, a group of about a dozen stockmen led by a free settler named Fleming were riding about the area killing any Aboriginal people they could find. On June 9th, they rode into the station and rounded up these old men, women and children. They tied tethered and herded them across the hill to the back of the station and slaughtered them with swords. The children were beheaded. Kilmeister, who had originally invited the Aboriginal people onto the station for refuge took part in the massacre. Eventually the incident was reported to the new governor, George Gipps. After two trials, seven of the group were found guilty and hanged. The Myall Creek Massacre has been claimed to be the only time where Europeans were executed for the massacre of Aboriginal people.

The Rufus Creek Massacre (1841)

The Rufus Creek Massacre took place along the Rufus Creek near Wentworth, New South Wales, in 1841. The local Maraura people attempted to block the overland route used by settlers and stockmen across their land. It was also said that promises of compensation by the passing stockmen were not kept. The massacre of the Aborigines was led by Moorhouse, the first Protector of Aborigines. He claimed that his attack pre-empted an anticipated attack by the Aborigines. He claimed 30 to 40 Aboriginal were killed, although later documents dispute Moorhouse's claims and that there was a much larger number killed.

The Evans Head Massacre (1842)

The Evans Head Massacre occurred near the Richmond River in north-eastern New South Wales in 1842. The spark for the massacre began at Pelican Creek where five European men were discovered dead, presumed killed by the local Aboriginal people. In retaliation, Europeans killed over 100 of the Bundjalung people.

The Kangaroo Creek Poisoning (1847)

Kangaroo Creek along the Orara River were the tribal lands of the Gumbaingirr people well before Europeans had arrived. In the 1840s, the first European settlers to claim these lands were led by Forster and Blaxland, son of the early explorer, and set up the town of Grafton. In 1847, a fellow settler, Coutts, set up a station at Kangaroo Creek. In exchange for some land, Coutts offered the local Gumbaingirr people flour laced with arsenic. Many of the people died. Coutts was arrested but never charged.

The East Ballina Massacre (1853)

In 1853, at night, a group of Native Police troopers and trackers with orders surrounded a camp of between 200 to 300 Bundjalung men, women and children who were asleep. They massacred the camp with only a few being driven towards and over the nearby cliff. Later the bodies of the massacred people were thrown over the cliff. No action was taken against the perpetrators. Today's East Ballina Golf Course is located on or very near to the site of the massacre.

South Ballina Poisoning (1860s)

In the early 1860s, there were 200 people of the Arakwal tribe of the remaining Bundjalung people. Authorities provided them with poisoned flour to make damper. Some refused to eat the damper which was not local to the area. The next morning, the survivors found that over 150 of their tribe were dead. For some years after the local Aboriginal people sought retribution but were mercilessly put down by troopers, settlers and convicts.

The Flying Foam Massacre (1868)

The last noted Aboriginal massacres and uprisings took place in the Pilbara and Kimberley regions of north-western Western Australia. The Flying Foam Massacre in 1868 was recorded to have occurred upon the death of two police officers and a local workman. Although three Jaburara men were convicted and executed the violence did not end. In retaliation as many as 150 Jaburara people including children were killed by local troopers and settlers. In 2013, the first Flying Foam Massacre Remembrance Day was commemorated at the King Bay Massacre site.

Jandamarra — West Australia (1894-97)

Jandamarra was a member of the Bunuba tribe and led a series of guerrilla actions against settlers in the Kimberley region of Western Australia. In his early years, he had served as an indentured servant or slave to white settlers but had joined the police force in early adulthood. It was as a policeman he became a skilled horseman and marksman. Upon an incident in 1894, where Bunuba tribesmen had hunted some stock belonging to settlers, Jandamarra was ordered to track down his own people. Confronted by Chief Ellamarra, Jandamarra was forced to decide his loyalties, and became an armed fugitive and led the Bunuba with Ellamarra in an armed rebellion.

The Western Australian Premier, Sir John Forrest, ordered the rebellion to be crushed. Police massacred Aboriginal camps at Fitzroy Crossing. Although Ellamarra was killed and Jandamarra wounded. Jandamarra escaped and led a three-year long guerrilla warfare against the police and European settlers. The rebellion was at a stand-off until the police recruited an Aboriginal tracker called Micki in 1897. Micki was not Bunuba. He tracked, hunted and killed Jandamarra at Tunnel Creek after taking his children hostage. The white troopers cut off Jandamarra's head, where it was eventually sent to England.

Jandamarra's family buried the remainder of his body at the Napier Range. A documentary named "Jandamarra's War" was screened in 2011.

The plight of the Aboriginal people and the stolen generations will be covered later.

Part Three

The Search For Identity

A snapshot of Australia, circa 1850

By 1850, all the major colonial settlements that were to become state capitals of Australia had already been founded. These were Sydney (1788), Hobart (1804), Brisbane (1824), Perth (1829), Melbourne (1835), and Adelaide (1836). The two colonies yet to be founded that were to become territory capitals were Darwin (1869) and Canberra (1913). As each of these colonies were founded, Aboriginal habitation in community groups within these areas had already ceased and had been pushed into more remote areas.

By 1850, there were already four colonial territories, New South Wales had been named in 1770 and settled in 1788. The Colony of Van Diemen's Land was separated from New South Wales in 1825. The Swan River Colony was proclaimed in 1829, although it was renamed the Colony of Western Australia in 1832. South Australia was proclaimed as a separate province from New South Wales in 1836.

Interestingly, New South Wales took over control of New Zealand in 1839, although it split away the following year in 1840 to become the Colony of New Zealand.

In 1844, the convict settlement at Norfolk Island was transferred to the Colony of Van Diemen's Land, even though it was over 2,000 kilometres away, and was much closer to the Colony of New Zealand.

In 1846, the northern half of New South Wales was separated from it as the Colony of North Australia in 1846. Although this was revoked a year later in 1847.

The Colony of New South Wales claimed by Great Britain in 1787.

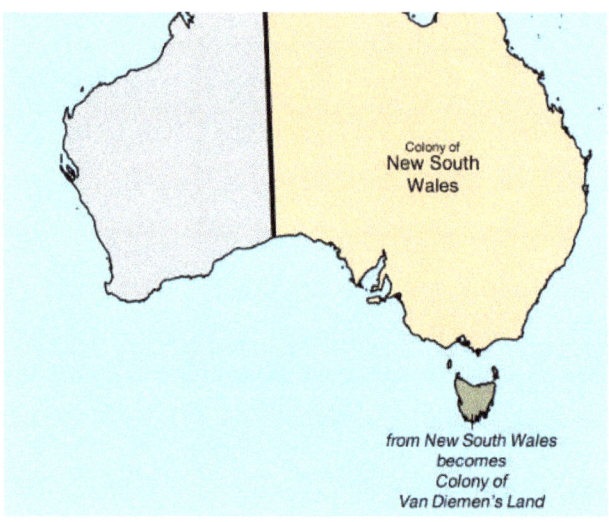

The Colony of Van Diemen's Land is separated from New South Wales in 1825.

A snapshot of Australia, circa 1850

The Swan River Colony was proclaimed in 1829 and was renamed the Colony of Western Australia in 1832.

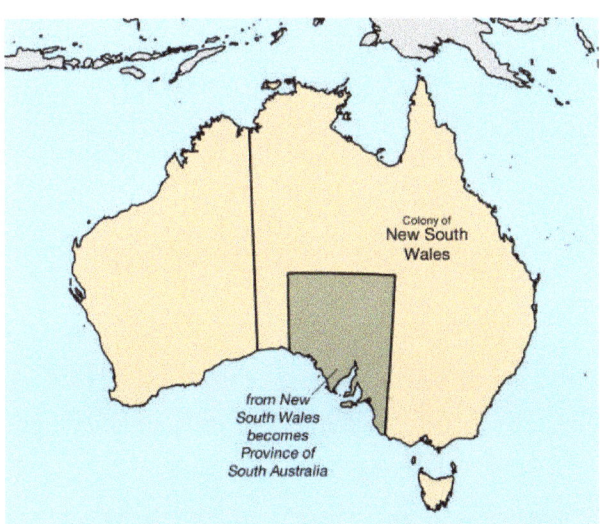

The Colony of South Australia proclaimed in 1836.

In 1850, the British Government passed the Australian Colonies Government Act, which separated the colonies and allowed each one to form their own representative government. Each was based on the New South Wales model of a two-house parliament, a legislative council and a legislative assembly. Between 1855 and 1857, constitutions for each of the colonies were proclaimed.

The Colony of Victoria, from the old Port Phillip district was proclaimed in 1851. Van Diemen's Land was renamed Tasmania in 1856. Also, Norfolk Island was split from Tasmania and became its own colony in that same year. The separate colony of Queensland, from the previous Moreton Bay settlement, was established in 1859. Also, the area that was to become the Northern Territory passed from New South Wales to Queensland (1862), then to South Australia (1863).

Industry in colonial Australia

The 1850s saw the development of interior rural areas between the colonial cities. Therefore, transport and communications were a priority. New railways, roads, paddle-steamers and telegraph links were built. In 1853, Freeman Cobb formed the stage-coach company Cobb and Co, setting up routes between Melbourne and the goldfields at Ballarat and Bendigo.

The first railway between Melbourne and Sandridge (Port Melbourne) was opened in 1854. This was followed by lines to St Kilda (1857), Geelong (1857), North Brighton (1859) and Sunbury (1859).

In 1857, Sydney opened its first railway line to Parramatta, and in 1858, Adelaide opened its first railway line to Port Adelaide.

In 1858, Melbourne, Sydney and Adelaide were linked by telegraph lines. At the same time, Hobart was linked to Launceston. In 1859, a telegraph cable was laid under the Bass Strait between Tasmania and Victoria.

The 1850s, saw the emergence on unionism in the colonies. In 1856, after the successful Eight Hour Day campaign, it was decided that a 'People's Palace should be built. In 1859, the first Trades Hall building, made from timber, was opened, sited near the current Lygon Street main entrance. In 1874, the current building was opened.

The first Trades Hall building on Lygon Street in 1859

The current Trades Hall building opened in 1874

David Jones

David Jones (1793-1873) was a Welsh-born merchant. Having worked in retail in his early life, David Jones emigrated with his family to Hobart in 1834. In 1838, he established David Jones & Co., establishing a department store in George Street, Sydney. In 1849, Jones established a new two storey shop on the corner of Barrack and George streets. This would remain the main location of David Jones until the opening of a new store in Elizabeth Street in 1928. Jones was also a founding director in 1848 of the Australian Mutual Provident Society (AMP). There are now 48 David Jones stores in Australia.

David Jones, National Portrait Gallery

Early picture of David Jones store, corner Barrack and George streets.

David Jones store, corner Barrack and George streets, circa 1900.

Grace Bros.

In 1885, brothers Albert Grace and Joseph Grace migrated from England in the 1880s. In 1885, they opened a small store in George Street, Sydney. In 1906, they opened a five-storey department store at Broadway. In 1911, they established Grace Bros Removals. In 1933, Grace Bros. opened stores in Parramatta and Bondi Junction and thereafter continued to expand into the suburbs, until taken over by Myer in 1983.

Gas in colonial Australia

The Australian Gas Light Company (AGL) was founded in Sydney in 1837 by Charles Nicholson and Ralph Mansfield. It was their aim to supply gas to light up all of Sydney's streets. However, at that time, gas was created by burning coal, not the natural gas that we have now. The first gasworks in Australia was at Miller Point at the edge of Darling Harbour, followed by smaller gasworks at Balmain and Five Dock. The Darling Harbour gasworks operated until 1922. In the 1880s, AGL built a newer and larger gasworks at Mortlake covering 32 hectares (79 acres). This gasworks operated until 1990.

Unsigned painting of the gasworks at Millers Point, circa 1873, by Samuel Elyard. State Library of NSW.

There were other competitors in the early colonial gas industry including the Parramatta Gas Company (founded 1872), the Manly Gaslight and Coke Company (1883), and the Natural Gas and Oil Company (1932), which relied on coal and had nothing to do with the use of natural gas that began in Australia in the 1960s.

Banking in colonial Australia

The current Australian Banking System relies on the Reserve Bank with the four major banks, with other bank and non-bank financial intermediaries. However, these four major banks have their roots in colonial Australia.

The first bank to be established in the colonies was the Bank of New South Wales. It was founded in Sydney in 1817, and opened further branches in Moreton Bay, Brisbane (1850), Victoria (1851), New Zealand (1861), South Australia (1877), Western Australia (1883), Tasmania (1910), and Papua (1910). In 1982 it merged with the Commercial Bank of Australia (founded 1866) to form what is now Westpac.

In competition, the Commercial Banking Company of Sydney was founded in 1834. Also, the National Bank of Australasia was formed in Melbourne in 1858. Branches were set up in each of the colonies, Tasmania (1859), London, UK (1864), Western Australia (1866), New South Wales (1885), Queensland (1920). In 1982, these two banks merged to form what is now the NAB.

The Bank of Australasia was formed in 1835, although it was a London-based bank. In 1837, the Union Bank of Australia was also established in London. It took over the struggling Launceston-based Tamar Bank and the Melbourne branch of the Derwent Bank in 1838, and opened a branch in Sydney in 1839, and in Wellington, New Zealand, in 1840. It opened other branches in Adelaide (1850), Brisbane (1858), Perth (1878). In 1892, it acquired the Bank of South Australia.

In 1951, the Union Bank of Australia and the Bank of Australasia were merged to form what is now the ANZ Bank.

In 1842, the Savings Bank of Port Phillip was established. After merging with a number of independent savings banks, it was reconstituted in 1912 as the State Savings Bank of Victoria. Following the Commonwealth Bank Act 1911, the Commonwealth Bank of Australia opened its doors in Melbourne in 1912 and was the first bank to receive a federal government guarantee. It immediately took over the State Savings Bank of Tasmania. By the following year, it had branches in all states of Australia. The Commonwealth Bank continued to expand and took on central banking powers; acquiring in 1920, the Queensland Government Savings Bank (est. 1861); in 1931, the Government Saving Bank of New South Wales (est. 1871); and the State Bank of Western Australia (est. 1863). As the bank expanded, its aims increasingly came into conflict with the Australian government, especially during the great depression of the 1930s. These conflicts resulted in a separation of duties, Reserve Bank Act 1959, and the Reserve Bank of Australia was established in 1960. In 1990, it acquired the State Savings Bank of Victoria. It continues to be known as the Commonwealth Bank of Australia or CBA.

Communities in colonial Australia

In colonial Australia, the major ancestral communities were Indigenous Aborigines, Torres Strait Islanders, British (England, Scotland and Wales), Irish, Chinese, Italians, Germans, and Greeks.

Aborigines arrived in Australia about 65,000 years ago. Although there have been relics from Asian visitors to Australia, there has been no evidence of settlements by them prior to European settlement.

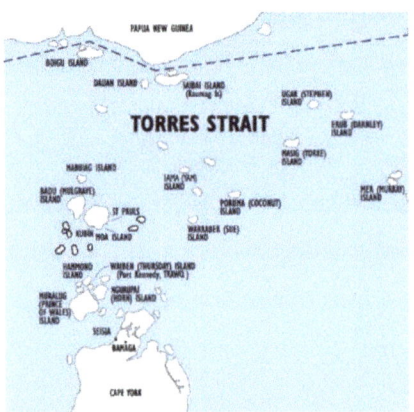

Map of Torres Strait Islands; source NATSICC

Torres Strait Islanders in traditional costume; NSW Art Gallery

Torres Strait Islanders

The Torres Strait Islanders are people that arrived much later than most of the mainland Aboriginal people and settled in the islands of the Torres Strait and northern parts of Queensland. However, it is estimated that they may have been living on the islands from between 10,000 to 2,500 years. There are about 6,000 Torres Strait Islanders living on the islands, while 42,000 live mostly in north

Queensland. Notable Torres Strait Islanders that we know today are Eddie Mabo, the land-rights campaigner; Christine Anu, the Australian pop-singer; Cynthia Lui, the first Torres Strait Islander elected to the Queensland parliament; Patty Mills the NBA basketballer; AFL players, Sam Powell-Pepper and Albert Proud; and NFL players, Sam Thaiday and Dane Gagai.

Torres Strait Islanders are quite distinct from other Aboriginal people in Australia. They have some distinct customs and language. In the western Torres Strait, islanders speak Kalaw Lagaw Ya, which is part of the Pama-Nyungan family of languages which covered most of Aboriginal Australia. However, in the eastern Torres Strait, islanders speak Meriam Mir, which is a Papuan language. Another, third language, is Torres Strait Creole, which developed from Torres Strait Pidgin English in the 1880s. Torres Strait Islanders have a lot in common with the Papuan people and are a seafaring people and trade with other islands such as Papua New Guinea. Their livelihood centres on fishing for dugong, turtles, crayfish, crabs and other shellfish. The Islanders have a long tradition of woodcarving, masks and drums, and decorating items for ceremonial use.

Prior to European settlement, Torres Strait Islanders were free to fish for themselves. However, after the European settlement of the islands and northern Queensland from 1863, European settlers took over the fishing industry and reduced the islanders to merely fishing servants, working on the European settler-owned fishing boats at subsistence level. Furthermore, Torres Strait Islander culture and beliefs were being repressed by the growing number of Christian missionaries being sent there. The Queensland government formally annexed all of the Torres Strait Islands by 1879.

Other communities

The Chinese

The first recorded Chinese migrant to Australia was Mak Sai Ying from Macau. As the Opium Wars (1839-1860) raged in China, more Chinese sought safer places in the world to live. As with the Californian goldrush of 1849, the Australian gold rush of 1851 attracted many Chinese immigrants from Macau and Canton. By 1855, there were over 10,000 Chinese migrants in colonial Australia.

In 1908, two Chinese Australians — Wally Koochew (Carlton) and George Tansing (Geelong) made their debuts in the Victorian Football League. These were followed by Ernie Foo (St Kilda, 1914) and Jack Wunhym (Footscray, 1927).

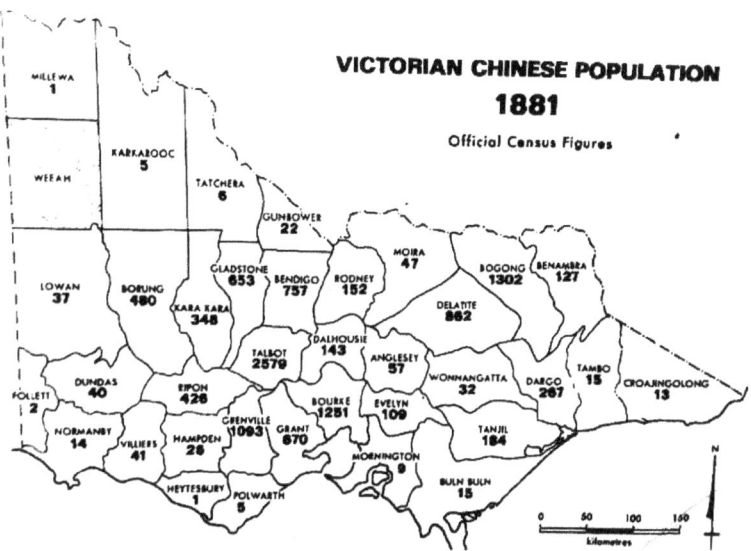

Photographs comparing distribution of Chinese population across Victorian districts, 1854 and 1881, (Golden Dragon Museum, Bendigo).

The Italians

James Mantra and Antonio Ponto sailed aboard James Cook's Endeavour voyage to Australia. Giuseppe Tuzo arrived with the first fleet and settled in Sydney. Hundreds of Italians arrived with the gold rush, including Raffaello Carboni who was present at and documented the Eureka Stockade of 1854. Italian immigration was spurred by European wars occurring in the mid-1800s, including the wars for Italian independence.

The Germans

In the 1800s, the Germans were the largest non-English speaking European community in Colonial Australia. The first known German arrived with Arthur Phillip on the First Fleet. Augustus Alt, who graduated from Marburg University in 1748, and was the first "Land

Surveyor-General" of the colony. Phillip Schaffer from Hesse arrived in 1790 and was given land for free cultivation.

In 1838, the families of six German vinedressers — Johann Justus, Friedrich Seckold, Johann Stein, Caspar Flick, Georg Gerhard, and Johann Wenz — arrived in Sydney. They worked on the vineyards belonging to the Macarthur estate at Camden. In 1838, two groups of Lutheran German immigrants, escaping religious persecution there, settled around the Adelaide hills and helped build the Barossa winemaking region. The great link between the German community and Australian winemaking had begun.

The Greeks

The first known Greeks to arrive were seven Greek sailors in 1829, convicted of piracy by a British naval court and sentenced to transportation as convicts to New South Wales. Though eventually pardoned, two of the seven remained to settle in the colony. Their names were Ghikas Bulgaris and Andonis Manolis. The first known free Greek migrant was Katerina Georgia Plessos (1809-1907). She arrived in Sydney with her husband Major James Crummer of the British Army in 1835.

In 1894, Charlie Pannam (nee Pannamopoulos) played his first game for the Collingwood Football Club, later transferring to Richmond in 1907. His sons were Albert and Charlie junior, and grandsons were Lou and Ron Richards of Collingwood Football Club notoriety.

The city of Melbourne is claimed to be the second largest Greek community in the world, next to Athens.

Religion in colonial Australia

Indigenous Australian Religion pre-1788

Prior to British settlement, Aboriginal Australians practised a form of 'Animism' which is called the 'Dreaming' or 'Dreamtime'. In the Dreaming, their ancestral beings were based on Australian native animals. These animals shaped the land and embedded their spiritual power within it for eternity. The land is alive with their power, and the power of the Dreaming is eternal and ever-present. Aboriginal Australians believed that they could access that power and enter the eternal. There are many links that can be made between the Dreaming and similar religions of that time, such as 'Shamanism' in Lapland, northern Asia and the pre-Columbian Americas.

Christianity

Christianity came to Australia with the First Fleet in 1788. Most of the Christian convicts on the First Fleet were either Catholics or Protestants. Protestants included some Methodists, while some of the Scottish soldiers and settlers were Presbyterians.

The Protestants

Richard Johnson was the first Church of England chaplain and was ordered by Arthur Phillip to improve the public morality of the colony. The first Sunday mass was held under a tree. The following week, it was held in an officer's tent. Johnson built the first church in Sydney in 1793 on the corner of Hunter and Castlereagh streets. Johnson and his wife taught between 150 to 200 children at the church during the week.

However, he did not receive reimbursement until 1797. The church was burnt down by convicts in 1798. Governor Hunter laid the foundation stone of the original St Phillip's Church on Church Hill, Lang Park in 1800 but it was not completed until 1809. This church served until 1857, when it was replaced by the current Gothic-styled church. The foundation stone for St James' Church, Hyde Park, was laid in 1819. By 1823, there were churches in Sydney, Newcastle (1818), Liverpool (1819), Windsor (1820) and Campbelltown (1823).

The Catholics

The first Catholic priests arrived in Sydney in 1800 as convicts, sentenced to transportation for participating in the 1798 rebellion in Ireland against British rule. The priests were James Dixon, James Harold and Peter O'Neill. In 1803, Dixon was freed conditionally to hold Catholic mass. However, after the Irish-led Castle Hill rebellion in 1804, permission for Dixon to hold mass was revoked. In 1820, two Catholic priests from London, John Joseph Therry and Connolly, arrived in the colony and in 1821 the foundation stone for St May's Cathedral was set by Lachlan Macquarie. John Bede Polding (1794-1877) was Sydney's first bishop from 1835 to 1877. He requested a group of nuns to be sent to the colony to provide pastoral care in women's prisons, hospitals and schools, Five Irish Sisters of Charity arrived in 1838. In 1843, upon Polding's request, the Christian Brothers arrived in Sydney to set up schools. In 1857, St Vincent's Hospital in Sydney was established as a free hospital to tend the poor. Similar hospitals were set up in each of the other colonies. During Polding's tenure, St Patrick's Cathedral on Eastern Hill in Melbourne was built in 1848 with Augustinian friar James Goold as its first bishop.

The Church Act (1836)

The Church Act of 1836 was passed during Governor Bourke's tenure. It was strongly opposed by the Protestants. Although this was intended to encourage the building of churches through the colonies, its major effect was to allow the expansion of church rights to the Catholic, Presbyterian, Wesleyan, Baptist and Jewish communities. The first purpose-built synagogue was built in an Egyptian style by James Hume in York Street in 1844.

The Jews

The first move to establish a formal Jewish identity in colonial Australia came with the forming of the 'Chevra Kadisha', a Jewish burial service, in Sydney in 1817. The first recorded Jewish religious service was held by emancipist Joseph Marcus in a private home in 1820. In 1832, the Sydney Jewish congregation was formed, with Joseph Montefiore as its first president. Organised Jewish communities were opened in Sydney (1831) and in Melbourne (1841). In 1844, the first synagogue opened in York Street, Sydney, followed by Hobart (1845), Launceston (1846), Melbourne (1847), Adelaide (1850), Brisbane (1865), and Perth (1892).

The Muslims

A trading relationship between Indonesian Muslim trepangers and indigenous Australians was well-established by the 1700s, prior to Captain Cook's visit. Further, there were 'Mohammedans' listed in colonial censuses from 1802. The first mosque was built in Australia at Marree, South Australia, in 1861. Between 1860 and 1890, a large number of Afghan camel drivers migrated and settled in Australia. Eight of these participated in the Burke and Wills expedition of 1860-61. In the 1870s, a large number of Malay pearl divers were recruited to work in Western Australia and the Northern Territory. The Great Mosque in Adelaide was built in 1888.

Photo of Australian Afghan cameleers, circa 1895, State Library of South Australia

Remains of Mosque at Maree, South Australia, originally built in 1861

The Buddhists

In 1856, a Buddhist temple was established in South Melbourne by the Sze Yap group, Chinese immigrants from Canton. This temple was also used for ceremonies from Taoism and Confucianism too. In 1870, the first Sinhalese Buddhists from Sri Lanka arrived in Queensland to work in the sugarcane plantations.

See Yup Temple, Raglan Street, South Melbourne. This temple was constructed in 1866 and the building still exists today. It replaced the original temple built in 1856.

The Hindus

Like the Muslims, a trading relationship between Indonesian Hindus and indigenous Australians was well-established by the time James Cook visited Australia. From 1788, Indian crews from the Bay of Bengal were on trading ships to the new colony. From 1816, Indian domestic servants were being brought to Australia. In the 1850s, a Hindu Sindhi merchant, Shri Pammull, built a family opal trade in Melbourne. However, it took until 1977 before the first Hindu temple was built in Australia in Auburn, Sydney.

Early sport in Australia

Prior to European colonisation, Aboriginal sport consisted of games around hunting, tracking, wrestling, spear-throwing, swimming, fishing, canoeing, and a curiously unique game played with possum-skins sewn into a ball. "Marngrook", from the Woiwurung language, is a collective term meaning 'ball game'. Marngrook with its free-flowing game, with kicking in the air and high-marking, where players on a team set up on both sides of the ball, unlike nearly all European sports, was to form one of the bases of today's "Aussie-rules" football.

With the arrival of the First Fleet, many of the popular British sports of era came into play, such as rowing, hunting, horseracing, cricket, boxing, competitive walking and cock fighting.

Rowing

In early 1788, a rowing race between the crews of each of the ships of the First Fleet marks the first official sporting event in Australia. By the early 1800s, crews from the various merchant and naval vessels would compete in row boats. In 1840, the first regatta was held on the Parramatta River. The popularity of competitive rowing continued to grow. In 1863, fours from Sydney and Melbourne completed for the first time, with Sydney winning.

In 1876, the Victorian Rowing Association was formed, the first organised body for rowing in the world. This was followed in 1870, when the Sydney Rowing Club began. In the last three decades of the 19th Century, Australia dominated world rowing championships.

Horse Racing

Lt. George Johnston, of First Fleet fame, became a prominent breeder of racehorses. Early horse racing had followed at Parramatta and in the Hawkesbury River settlement between 1807 to 1809. However, the first official horse race in Australia took place at Hyde Park in 1810 under the patronage of Governor Macquarie and organised by the officers of the 73rd Regiment. The first racecourse at Randwick opened in 1833. Homebush Racecourse on the Wentworth Estate operated from 1841 to 1880. In October 1842, the Australian Jockey Club (AJC) met to formulate the rules of racing in Australia.

Melbourne's first race meeting was held in 1838 near present-day's Southern Cross Station. The beginnings of Flemington racecourse held its first race meetings in 1840.

Cricket

From the Sydney Gazette, we learn that the first recorded cricket match in Australia took place in Sydney in December 1803. By 1826, cricket clubs in Sydney included the Currency Cricket Club (C.C.), the Military C.C. and the Australian C.C. The earliest matches were recorded to have been played at Hyde Park.

In Tasmania, the oldest club was the Derwent City CC (1835), followed by the Launceston CC (1841).

In Victoria, the oldest cricket clubs are the Melbourne CC (1838), Brighton CC (1842), Williamstown CC (1852) and Richmond CC (1854).

In Western Australia, the Perth Cricket Club was founded in 1862, and in South Australia, the Norwood and Kensington CCs were founded in 1871.

The most notable cricketer of the time, Tom Wills (1835-1880) was captain of the Richmond Cricket Club (1858-60, 1862-65), also captain of the Melbourne, captain of the Victorian Cricket Team, a founder of

Australian Rules Football, and founding Richmond Cricketers Football Club secretary and captain (1860), a predecessor to the current AFL Richmond Tigers Football Club, founded later in 1885.

Tom Wills, painted by William Handcock in 1870

Australian Rules

Tom Wills is credited with forming Australian Rules football, as well as being an avid cricketer. The game is said to have been established in Melbourne as a way to keep the cricketers occupied and fit during the winter. Although unverified, Wills may have learnt to play 'Aussie Rules' during his teenage years in the 1840s from his Aboriginal friends playing 'Marngrook' around his father's property on the Molonglo Plains of New South Wales.

There is a conflicting argument that Australian Rules Football may have been established in South Australia, where an informal game of

'Caid' was recorded to have been played by the local Irish community as early as 1843 in celebration of St Patrick's Day.

Australian Rules contains elements of Gaelic football, especially the field positions; however, Gaelic football is played on a rectangular pitch, whereas 'Aussie Rules' is played on an oval. This was probably because already existing cricket ovals were used to play football matches. The first official game was played on 7th August 1858 between Scotch College and Melbourne Grammar on Richmond paddock, next to the Melbourne Cricket Ground, on what is today known as the Punt Road Oval. The oldest surviving set of rules were drawn up in 1859, three days after the formation of the Melbourne Football Club. These were revised in 1860 and included rules for kicking, marking and bouncing the ball.

There were about 20 Aussie Rules football clubs in Victoria by the mid-1860s, including: Albert Park, Ballarat, Brunswick, Carlton, Castlemaine, Collingwood Cricketers, Geelong, Melbourne, Melbourne Grammar, Northcote, Richmond Cricketers (captained by Wills), Royal Park, Scotch College, University, Warehousemen and Williamstown. The Collingwood and Richmond teams pre-dated the current AFL clubs that were established in 1892 and 1885 respectively.

Full drawing of 'Aboriginal domestic scene' by William Blandowski, 1857.

Insert of background of sketch clearly showing youths playing 'Marngrook' the indigenous inspiration for 'Aussie Rules footy'.

Rugby Union

Although there were unofficial games before, Rugby Union did not officially begin in Australia until 1864 with the creation of the Sydney University club. In 1869, Newington College played Sydney University in the first official school match.

Tennis

Around 1860, after the advent of the lawnmower, Harry Gem and Augurio Perera conceived the idea of combining Basque Pelota (a form of outdoor squash) with the 16th Century English game of "Royal Tennis". It was originally played on a croquet lawn with a net and racquets. Tennis arrived in Australia in the mid-1870s. The first recorded tournament in Australia was played at the Melbourne Cricket Ground in January 1880 and named "The Championship of the Colony of Victoria".

Early Art in Australia

Evidence of Aboriginal rock art dates back some 30,000 years. The Gwion Gwion paintings, also known as the Bradshaw rock art, located in the Kimberley region, are considered Australia's earliest works of art. William Barak (1824-1903), one of the last traditionally educated Wurundjeri leaders, was also a noted artist.

The Gwion Gwion paintings

Corroboree, William Barak, 1895

Early colonial art, heavily influenced by British painters of the Romantic movement such as J.M.W. Turner and John Constable, was usually in the form of landscapes where variable lighting enhanced the natural forms. Early colonial painters in the colony included John Lewin (1770-1819), John Glover (1767-1849), Thomas Watling (1762-1814), William Westall (1781-1850), Augustus Earle (1793-1838), and Conrad Martens (1801-1878). They captured images of the Australian colonial landscape and its fauna and flora in that style.

George Stubbs, The Kongouro from New Holland, 1772

Thomas Watling, A Direct North General View of Sydney Cove, 1794

Conrad Martens, Campbell's Wharf, c.1857

Early Literature in Australia

Prior to European colonisation, there is no evidence of Aboriginal writing. David Unaipon (born David Ngunaitponi) (1872-1967) a preacher, inventor and author of the Ngarrindjeri people, located along the Coorong, is considered to be the first Aboriginal author. His 'Legendary Tales of the Aborigines' provided the first accounts of Aboriginal mythology.

The early colonial writings were mostly reports and descriptions of events that had taken place. An example of this was Watkin Tench, who described in two books — Narrative of the Expedition to Botany Bay and Complete Account of the Settlement at Port Jackson — his experiences as part of the First Fleet and the settling of Sydney in 1788.

William Wentworth published the first book written by an Australian, which had the extraordinarily long title of 'A Statistical, Historical, and Political Description of the Colony of New South Wales and Its Dependent Settlements in Van Diemen's Land, With a Particular Enumeration of the Advantages Which These Colonies Offer for Emigration and Their Superiority in Many Respects Over Those Possessed by the United States of America'.

The first novel written by an Australian was a crime novel by Henry Savery titled Quintus Servinton: A Tale founded upon Incidents of Real Occurrence, published in Hobart in 1830. The first Australian novel to be published and printed in mainland Australia and the first Australian novel written by a woman was a Gothic romance titled 'The Guardian: a Tale' by Anna Maria Bunn in 1838.

Early music in Australia

Indigenous Australian music is symbolised by the iconic instrument, the didgeridoo, and the community dance ceremony, the corroboree, dating back over 40,000 years. That musical expression is now seen in the contemporary music of bands like Yothu Yindi.

Post 1788, western-styled music came from the British and Irish convicts and settlers that arrived. An example of this was the Irish song, 'The Wild Colonial Boy'. It is a song about an actual Irish rebel, who is transported as a convict, becomes a bushranger, and is eventually shot dead by police. Originally, the song was about Jack Duggan and the Castlemaine was that in County Kerry, Ireland. The first Australian version was actually about Jack Donohue, an actual bushranger between 1825-30. However, later his name was changed to Jack Doolan. This music style eventually adapted into the Australian folk music and bush ballads of second half of the 19th Century and after.

The Gold Rushes from 1851

The Australian Gold Rush era is seen by many as the catalyst for an independent Australia. The gold rushes provided colonial Australia with vast wealth to build an infrastructure and attracted large immigration that provided it with a sustainable modern population. Following from the European revolutions of 1848, the gold rushes filled the new immigrants and settlers with ideas of liberty, justice, equality and independence. The gold rushes were to provide each of the colonies with the impetus and means to achieve these aims.

Early gold finds (1820-50)

Gold was first discovered in Australia in 1823 by the assistant surveyor James McBrien at Fish River, near Bathurst. Further, in 1839, Pawel Strzelecki discovered deposits of gold in his journeys beyond the Blue Mountains. However, these reports were kept quiet by order of the then Governor Gipps to keep order among the soldiers, settlers and convicts in the colony.

In 1841, the Reverend William Clarke found gold in the Cox River, near Bathurst. He also found gold in the Wollondilly River the following year. Although reports inferred an abundance of gold, Governor Gipps still preferred to stifle news of them.

In 1848, the California Gold Rush led to many people leaving Australia for California. Consequently, the New South Wales government rethought its position and sought approval from the Colonial Office in London to allow the open mining and sale of gold. The hope was to attract people back to the colony.

The NSW Gold Rush (1851-1893)

The first gold rush in Australia was begun by Edward Hargraves in May 1851 when he claimed to have discovered gold near Orange. Hargraves had experienced the California goldfields and brought new knowledge of gold prospecting techniques, such as panning and cradling to New South Wales. Hargraves was offered rewards by the colonial governments of New South Wales and Victoria to promote gold prospecting to their regions.

Edward Hargraves, painted by T.T. Balcombe

In May 1851, gold was also found at Ophir, near Orange. The number of diggers jumped from 100 in May to over 2,000 by June, and the roads to Bathurst became choked with prospectors.

Due to the large receipts of gold, the British government in 1854 established the Sydney Mint. This was the first Royal Mint established outside of Britain. In 1872, 'Holtermann's Nugget' was found by Bernard Holtermann. It was a mixture of slate and gold weighing 235 kilograms.

Bernard Holtermann and his nugget from Hill End, NSW.

By 1860, the population of NSW had risen from 20,000 to over 350,000 people. Tension rose due to a rise in the monthly mining fee to 30 shillings but was lowered when Governor Fitzroy reduced the fee by two-thirds. At Lambing Flat, now Young, the population grew to 20,000. Racial tensions grew as 2,000 of these were Chinese migrants, which led to a riot in 1861.

The Lambing Flat Riots

The Lambing Flat riots were a series of violent attacks upon the Chinese miners and their community that occurred in the Burrangong region of New South Wales, now the town of Young. The European miners were envious of the success of the Chinese miners. The Chinese miners were better organised, working together in large groups, covering much larger areas, and working harder, therefore gaining a greater return of gold for their efforts. Further, a bill intended to oust Chinese miners from the goldfields failed to be passed by the New South Wales Legislative Council. Rumours were spread by the European miners and in June 1861, some 2,000 to 3,000 European, American and Australian miners descended on about 2,000 Chinese miners. Fortunately, the Chinese miners escaped to a nearby homestead. The police arrived to repel the rioting mob. The mob's leaders were killed. Later, soldiers and sailors arrived to restore the Chinese miners' rights to their claims and were given compensation.

The Victorian Gold Rush (1851-69)

As in the case of New South Wales, there were also early discoveries of gold in Victoria at Clunes in 1841, Bundalong on the Ovens River in 1844, the Pyrenees Ranges in 1848, and the Woady Yaloak River in 1849. Like New South Wales, the Victorian government chose to stifle and discredit these early reports.

Victoria's first gold rush began in July 1851 with further discoveries at Clunes. This was followed by discoveries at Beechworth, Castlemaine, Daylesford, Ballarat and Bendigo. The Victorian Gold rush had turned a dependent colony into a world-wide attraction. Victoria's gold rush exceeded all others except for the gold rush in California.

The Victorian gold rush continually grew from 1851 and peaked in the year 1856 with an output of over 90,000 kilograms of gold, in that year alone. The total output of gold from 1851 to 1856 as reported by Victorian Mines Department was almost 1,900,000 kilograms of gold. The largest nugget found in the Victorian gold rush was the 'Welcome

Stranger' found by John Deason and Richard Oates at Moliagul, near Bendigo, in 1869. It had a gross weight 78 kilograms (2,520 troy ounces) and netted 71kilograms (2,284 troy ounces). It was eventually melted down in London in 1859. Other large nuggets were found around the Bakery Hill and Canadian Gully areas of Ballarat, including the 'Welcome Nugget' (69 kilograms) found in 1858, and the 'Lady Hotham', after the Governor's wife, (45 kilograms) in 1854.

Image of the 'Welcome Stranger' nugget replica, Museums Victoria

At the beginning of 1851, the population of Victoria was 29,000. By the end of 1851, it was 75,000 people, and by 1860, it had grown to 500,000 people, larger than NSW. Also, Melbourne with 140,000 people in 1851 became larger than Sydney, until shortly after federation in 1901. The gold rush attracted prospectors, called 'diggers', from around the world. Around Victoria were large tent camps, where people lived in slums. Great wealth was being made but many immigrants were angry that they were being charged licencing fees for mining rights yet seeing little in return. This gave rise to the Eureka Stockade, to many the first step in Australia's road to independence.

The Eureka Stockade Rebellion (1854)

The Eureka Stockade rebellion occurred on the Ballarat goldfields in Victoria. It was a rebellion by the goldminers against the colonial government of Victoria, based in Melbourne. The rebellion was caused by the Victorian colonial government imposing unpopular taxes upon the miners without giving the miners a chance to be heard — taxation without representation.

The rebellion had its roots in 1851, with the first Victorian gold find. Upon hearing of Hiscock's gold rush near Buninyong, the Governor Latrobe imposed the requirement of a miner's licence upon miners. The licence had a fee of 30 shillings per month. Within a few months, the licence fee rose to one pound per month, with the intention of raising it to three pounds per month, which led to public dissent and protest. Although the colonial government repealed its plans, the diggers, as the miners were called, began to gather arms.

Changes in the Goldfields Act of 1853 meant that diggers would have to produce their licence for inspection at any time. In Bendigo, in 1853, the Anti-Gold Licence Association was formed, leading to more protests. In 1854, the police began making twice weekly inspections of licences.

In October 1854, a Scottish miner James Scobie was murdered at Bentley's Eureka Hotel. Ten days later, when Bentley, the prime suspect and accused, was acquitted, thousands of miners gathered in protest. The hotel was burned to the ground and the Bentleys just managed to escape with their lives. The authorities began looking for the culprits of the hotel-burning and more riots ensued.

Later in October, the Diggers Rights Society was formed by the Ballarat Catholics. Soon after, Father Smyth was arrested. It was followed in November by the forming of the Ballarat Reform League by John Humffray, based on the British Chartists movement of 1838. Over 10,000 miners had gathered at Bakery Hill in Ballarat. The Ballarat

Reform League unsuccessfully attempted to resolve the crisis with Governor Hotham, so the miners decided on open resistance. This vote for open resistance is reported to have been the first 'secret ballot' cast in world history. Peter Lalor was elected the military leader of the rebels. Henry Ross designed the Southern Cross Eureka flag, which was sewn by Anastasia Hayes. The rebels formed a military stockade on Bakery Hill. Unfortunately, Lalor chose the password 'Vinegar Hill', referring to the Irish rebellion of 1798, and nearly all of the miners chose to melt away. In complete surprise, at 3 am on December 3rd, 1854, about 275 British soldiers and police, led by General Thomas, attacked and captured the stockade manned by only 190 rebel miners. About 50 miners were killed, 20 wounded, and 120 captured. Six British soldiers were killed. Henry Ross was wounded and taken prisoner. Peter Lalor was wounded but escaped.

Peter Lalor

Swearing Allegiance to the Southern Cross, Charles Doudiet

The Battle for the Eureka Stockade, J.B. Henderson

Of the 120 rebels captured, thirteen were put on trial for treason. They included one born in Australia, seven from Ireland — Timothy Hayes, John Manning, John Phelan, James Beattie, William Molloy, Michael Tuohy, and Henry Reid; an American — John Joseph; a

Jamaican — James Campbell; one Jew from Scotland — Jacob Sorenson; an Italian — Raffaello Carboni; and a Netherlander — Jan Vennick. They were brought before Chief Justice William a Beckett under the auspices of Victorian Chief Justice Redmond Barry (see Ned Kelly trial). All thirteen were acquitted.

At a separate trial, Henry Seekamp, editor of the Ballarat Times was jailed for six months. In that time, his wife, Clara Seekamp took over the newspaper and became Australia's first female newspaper editor.

A Royal Commission into the rebellion led to the replacement of the gold licences with an annual 'miner's right' and a tax on exported gold. The report also gave recommendations regarding the restriction of Chinese immigration. The Electoral Act 1856 mandated the vote for male colonists and the election of them into the Victorian Parliament's lower house, the Legislative Assembly. Both Peter Lalor and John Humffray were elected. Both served long political careers, with Lalor later becoming the Speaker of the Legislative Assembly.

After the Victorian gold rush, there were gold rushes in the other colonies. After 1860, the Victorian population began to fall as miners looked elsewhere for gold.

 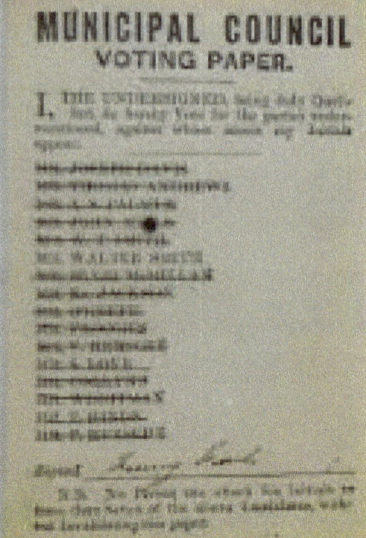

Fanny Finch

Frances Combe (1815-1863), was a Black English immigrant to Australia, who became a successful businesswoman in Castlemaine during the Victorian Goldrush. She arrived in South Australia in 1837, where she married Joseph Finch in 1838. Life for them was hard. Joseph found himself in prison, but Fanny worked to survive the hardship. They moved to Forest Creek, near Castlemaine during the gold rush in the early 1850s. There, Fanny opened a restaurant and a boarding house and became a successful businesswoman.

In 1855, there was a court case against her for selling sly grog by two policemen claiming to have been drinking in uniform at her establishment, and she was fined 50 pounds. Speculation may be that the two policemen were offended that Fanny actually asked them to pay for their grog. We know that the police force at that time was corrupt and subject to later investigation and reform.

An anonymous writer in the Mount Alexander Mail, Friday 7 Dec 1855, claims to have known Mrs Finch since her Adelaide days as "… she bore and supported the character of an industrious and praiseworthy person. Mrs Finch has also acquired great credit for the manner in which she conducted her restaurant at Forest Creek, and her refreshment at the time was the only one in which any person could get respectable accommodation".

Fanny Finch gained her greatest fame during the 1856 Castlemaine municipal elections. A law passed in 1854, gave the right of vote to any "rate paying persons". The law did not place any exclusions on female suffrage. Fanny and another female friend, who remained nameless, as rate payers, completed and signed voting cards in the city hall. The city officials chose to disallow their votes, as it was intended, though not expressed, that women should not have the right to vote. A report of the incident was made in the Melbourne Argus, describing Fanny as "the famous Mrs Finch". In 1865, the legislation was amended from "rate paying persons" to "rate paying men". Her voting card from the 1856 election is on display at the Castlemaine Art Museum.

Queensland Gold Rush (1857-1904)

In 1851, gold was also found in Queensland, near Warwick. However, the Queensland gold rush did not begin in earnest until 1858 when gold was discovered in the Fitzroy River by Maurice O'Connell, grandson of William Bligh the former governor of New South Wales. The sparsely population of Queensland swelled to about 15,000 people. The Queensland gold rush was very important, as the colony was on the point of bankruptcy.

In 1858, gold was found at Canoona near Rockhampton and in 1861, gold was discovered in central Queensland near Peak Downs, about 250 kilometres south-east of Mackay. This was followed by further discoveries near Gladstone (1862), Canal Creek (Leyburn, 1863), Charters Towers (1865), and Crocodile Creek, near Rockhampton (1865).

Richard Daintree (1832-1878), born in England, was a geologist and photographer. Daintree was the first government geologist for north Queensland and discovered many gold and coal deposits. The town of Daintree, the Daintree National Park, the Daintree River, the Daintree Rainforest and the Daintree Reef have all been named after him.

James Nash discovered gold at Gympie in 1867. The Gympie goldfield was established in 1868 and within a few months the number of diggers had swelled to 25,000. Further gold discoveries were made at Charters Towers (1871) and the Palmer River, near Cooktown (1872). At Charters Towers, a 12-year-old Aboriginal stockman, Jupiter Mosman had made the discovery. The Queensland gold rush lasted until 1904 and assured Queensland's future.

South Australia (1868-93)

In 1852, on the back of the success of the Victorian gold rush, the South Australian government offered a 1,000-pound reward for the first person to discover gold there. William Chapman had recently returned from the Victorian goldfields and with his mates, Thomas Hardiman and Henry Hampton. He found gold deposits at Echunga in the Adelaide Hills. Within a few weeks, there were 600 people camped at "Chapman's Gully". Further discoveries were made at Echunga from 1853 to 1858, with 1,200 people living there in 1868. The goldfields at Echunga continued until 1893 and had produced over 5,000 kilograms. Further gold discoveries were made near Gawler (1868), Ulooloo (1870), Waukaringa (1873), Teetulpa (1876), Wadnaminga (1888) and Tarcoola (1893), however the South Australian gold rush was not as large as that of Victoria.

Northern Territory (1871-1909)

Gold was discovered at Darwin in 1871 as workers for the Australian Overland Telegraph line were digging holes for telegraph poles. The Northern Territory gold rush lasted from 1871 to 1909 and extracted about 250 kilograms of gold.

Western Australia (1885-1899)

In 1885, Charles Hall and Jack Slattery found gold in the Kimberley region, in what was to be called Halls Gap. The gold nugget found by Hall was 870 grams (28 troy ounces). Within a short time 15,000 new prospectors had arrived. The gold rush in Western Australia had begun. The discovery at Halls Gap was followed by further discoveries near Yilgarn (1887), at Cue (1891) on the Murchison; Coolgardie (1892), and Kalgoorlie (1893). The word Yilgarn is taken from the local Aboriginal word for white quartz, where gold is often found.

The Western Australian gold rush had a huge impact on Western Australia and the other colonies. When gold was found at Halls Gap, the population of Western Australia numbered 21,000. By the end of the gold rush in 1901, the Western Australian population had grown to over 180,000 people. The gold rush had attracted people from Africa, America, Great Britain, Europe, China, India, the Pacific Islands and New Zealand. The gold rush created enough wealth in Western Australia to build railways, roads, and other infrastructure.

The gold rush had attracted many people from overseas, but it had also attracted many people from the other colonies. In the 1890s, both Melbourne and Sydney were feeling the effects of a global economic downturn and this was worsened by losing significant numbers of people moving to Western Australia.

Free settlement
— the taking of Australia

The free settlement of Australia can be looked at in two ways: 1. The migration of free settlers to Australia; and, 2. The freedom to take the land. The early Australian colonies — New South Wales, Van Diemen's Land, Western Australia — had originally been established as convict settlements. As time passed, the British soldiers and their convicts had evolved into or been replaced by settlers, from overseas or born in Australia, looking to create new lives and opportunity.

The evolution of convicts into settlers, after serving their sentences, had a significant influence on the social justice system in Australia. Many of the convicts who had arrived in the early 1800s had escaped poverty and oppression. A significant number, such as those who were transported following the Peterloo Massacre and early Chartist movements in England, had been transported for minor crimes arising from hardship and consequent social alienation. Once they had become free settlers and found prosperity in the colonies, they wanted Australia shaped from a different mould. Their model for a better home was one with more social justice and reform. As the colonies grew in prosperity and reputation, more settlers were attracted. However, the new settlements, towns and stations were not free, they came at a cost, and that cost was born by the Aboriginal people. It was their land before it was overrun by settlers.

When European settlement began in 1788, the estimate of Aboriginal population of Australia was as high as 700,000 people. By 1900, that population had fallen to about 115,000 people. The population loss of Aboriginal people over that near 110-year period was about 84%. It ranks with and possibly greater than the genocides of indigenous peoples in many places around the world and is comparable to the plight of the Native American peoples.

Those who are the descendants of overseas migrants and those who are migrants to Australia today enjoy a relatively high standard of living when compared to many other places in the world. However, many of the Aboriginal people in Australia today do not enjoy the same standard of living. Today's migrants and descendants of migrants need to realise that they have that relatively high standard of living because the land in which we now exist was taken from the Aboriginal people. We owe them for the standard of living we have that was taken from them. This is just one single issue that confronts Australia today as it comes to terms with Aboriginal reconciliation.

From a non-Aboriginal perspective, free settlement allowed European and other settlers to claim, occupy and build new settlements, cattle stations and towns. It allowed many migrants from Europe and Asia who had never owned property to do so in Australia. The gold rushes had created the wealth to build the cities, railways and roads, industry and infrastructure. In most of Australia's capital and rural cities, many of the parliament buildings, treasury buildings, town halls, court houses, universities, and other public buildings were originally established and built in the second half of the nineteenth century from the wealth of the gold rushes.

Irish immigration — the Potato Famine (1850s)

Prior to the gold rush, the British — from England and Scotland — had dominated the colonies. However, through the large-scale immigration that occurred as a result of the gold rushes, many new communities emerged, escaping the miserable plight of their previous existences. One such community were from Ireland, the Irish.

It is estimated that about 30% of the current Australian population have some Irish ancestry. Although there were over 100 convicts that arrived on the First Fleet with an Irish surname, the first significant group of Irish people to arrive in Australia were convicts transported during the Irish rebellion of 1798, a decade later. Most of these were classed as criminals although they were prisoners of war.

The 1798 Irish rebellion was sparked by the Society of United Irishmen, founded in 1791, who were Catholics, Protestants and other dissenters with an aim to remove English influence from Irish affairs. Suppression of the society in 1794 led to it meeting in secret then breaking into full rebellion in May 1798. After some early gains, the rebellion was mercilessly crushed at Vinegar Hill. The rebel leaders were summarily executed, and Britain enforced greater control over Ireland with the 1801 Act of Union which brought Ireland directly under British control. Great Britain changed its name to the United Kingdom, incorporating Ireland into union with England, Wales and Scotland.

More Irish people came as a result of further rebellions — the Rebellion of 1803 and the Young Irelander Rebellion of 1848, influenced by mass uprisings and rebellions across the major cities in Europe. Around 40,000 Irish convicts were transported to Australia between 1798 and 1850. The early Irish in Australia did not come to the colonies with the same rights and respect as afforded to other European settlers. As a result, the Irish communities found themselves apart and on the periphery of colonial society. One such Irish family were the Kelly family of Avenel, near Seymour, 115 kilometres north of Melbourne. The Kelly family was to have a significant impact on Australian history and folklore.

In the 1840s, the Irish Potato Famine brought many more Irish migrants to the colonies as free settlers. The Great Famine of Ireland ran from 1845 to 1849, with the worst year being 1847. While Ireland grew many types of crops, most were exported through private enterprise. Only potatoes were retained as the primary nourishment of the population. When the potato blight, an organic disease which affected most of northern Europe, ruined the potato crop, the Irish government, dominated by the British continued to export the other crops and let the Irish people starve. Over one million Irish people died during the Great Famine and a million more emigrated to Canada, the United States of America, Australia and other countries. During the Great Famine, Ireland's population fell by 25%. Between the Great Famine and the end of the gold rush era, the census of the Australian colonies accounted for about 250,000 people who were Irish born, over a quarter of immigrants from the United Kingdom.

German immigration — the "Forty-Eighters" on

Just as the revolutions of 1848 had impacted the Irish, they had also impacted the German peoples too. The Germans were the fourth largest group of non-English-speaking immigrants to Australia, after the English, Scots and Irish up to the year 1900.

After the 18th Century Enlightenment and successful revolutions in America and France, the middle and working classes of people across Europe sought to do away with the oppressive policies of the old divine-right monarchies and aristocracies. Revolts occurred across Europe in France, the Italian states, the German states, the Austrian Empire, Denmark, Sweden, Switzerland, Belgium, Ireland and Spain, and South America in Columbia and Chile.

In 1848, the first non-British ship carrying immigrants to Victoria was the 'Goddefroy' from Germany, and they settled in a village on the Bellarine Peninsula that they called Germantown, later Grovedale. In 1849, the 'Beulah' brought the families of German vinedressers to Sydney and the 'Parland' brought more too. Also, in 1849, the 'Princess Louise' sailed from Hamburg to Port Adelaide and brought around 160 emigres, including revolutionaries Johann Mosel, and brothers Richard and Otto Schomburgk. The emigres formed the South Australian Colonisation Society. These families settled and formed the South Australian wine industry.

Notable "Forty-Eighters" in Australia were Carl Linger, who wrote the music to The Song of Australia; Dr Moritz Schomburgk, director of the Adelaide Botanical Gardens; Hermann Buring, winemaker; and, Friedrich Krichauff, Chairman of the Agricultural Bureau.

Just before the Victorian gold rush, Louis Monasch arrived in Melbourne from Posen in Poland, held by Prussia. They spoke German. In 1865, his wife Bertha, gave birth to a boy John Monash, later to become General Sir John Monash of the Australia Corps during the First World War. In 1879, when still a boy on school holidays, the young John went to stay with his father at their shop in Jerilderie. It was just when the bushranger the Kelly gang rode in to gain supplies from his father's store. John Monash later claimed to have spent some time conversing with Ned Kelly.

Chinese immigration during the gold rush era

Most of the Chinese who came during the gold rush era came from the Canton province and the area surrounding the Pearl River delta. Life in China had been shattered by the introduction of opium into China by the British East India Company who were attempting to gain political and economic control over the country. When the British began the First Opium War (1839-1842), China was estimated to have had the largest economy in the world. When the British ended the Second

Opium War (1856-1860), the Chinese economy had been reduced by half. There were also vicious land feuds between the Imperial forces and the rebellious Taiping and Red Turban secret societies, resulting in hundreds of people being killed each month.

An indentured carpenter in Melbourne, Louis Ah Mouy or Louey Amoy, sent a letter about the Bendigo goldfields to his family in the Toi Shan district of Canton, which was called "Dai Gum San", the Big Gold mountain. Many young Chinese came to the goldfields to seek their fortune. The Chinese elders did not want whole families to be lost to China, so only the young men were allowed to go, with their wives and families staying behind. Although free settlers, many of those who came to Victoria were often bound by contract to Chinese businessmen who had provided the passage money, so some of the gold went back to the Chinese creditors. After the sum was repaid, the Chinese diggers could send their moneys to their families or find fortunes for themselves. If they defaulted, their families in China would be held responsible. Many were successful and returned home to China. Others remained in Victoria and sent their earnings back to their families in China. In 1857, over 200,000 ounces of gold was shipped back to Canton.

The Europeans in the colonies generated much antipathy towards the Chinese immigrants that in June 1855 the Victorian government levied a 10-pound head tax for each Chinese person arriving at the Victorian docks. As a result, between 1855 and 1857, ships carrying Chinese immigrants would off-load their human cargo in Port Adelaide or Robe in South Australia. These Chinese men would then walk overland some 500 kilometres to reach the Bendigo goldfields.

Chinese immigration from 1850-1900 was restricted by taxes and regulations. The 1901 Immigration Restriction Act, otherwise known as the White Australia Policy, ended Chinese immigration until after the end of the Second World War.

Bushrangers

The promise of the new colonies and the gold rushes brought many settlers. Some prospered, while some others, alienated from opportunity, were pushed to the periphery and had to survive by means outside of the law. The influence of the bushrangers to Australian history, like those of the convicts before them, was to push for social justice and to reform corrupt authorities when corruption was evident.

One of the largest bushranger gangs, the Gardiner-Hall gang, over its time had 23 members, of which 8 were either hanged or killed by policemen, with the others receiving gaol sentences. The Felons Apprehension Act 1865 allowed any bushranger specifically named under the Act to be shot and killed by any person at any time without warning.

There are many listed bushrangers, over 50 on some lists, that roamed the east coast of Australia. Most were from New South Wales, but Victoria boasted the Kelly Gang, Queensland had the Kenniff Brothers, and Tasmania had the 'Gentleman Bushranger', among others. Here are a few of the more notable bushrangers.

John Caesar, Pemulwuy's War (1795-1802)

John Caesar (1764-1796) was Australia's first bushranger. Caesar was born in either Africa or the West Indies, he was taken as an indentured servant to England in 1786. In that same year, he was tried for stealing 240 shillings and sentenced to transportation aboard the convict ship Alexander as part of the First Fleet. Working as a convict in the new colony, he gained popularity for his massive strength, hard work and insatiable appetite and was nicknamed "Black Caesar".

In 1789, he was caught stealing again, probably due to lack of supplies, and was sentenced to 'life' in the colony. He took flight from the convict colony a fortnight later but was caught. Governor Phillip saw Caesar's potential and sent him to work as a labourer on Garden Island, initially in chains and later without. Caesar escaped but was caught and sent to Norfolk Island in 1790. It was there he fathered a daughter Mary in 1792 with fellow convict Anne Power but returned to Port Jackson in 1793.

Caesar escaped and was recaptured another two times in 1794 and 1795, living on the run by stealing from both the colony and the local Eora community. In 1795, in a working party at Botany Bay, the group was attacked by the Eora leader Pemulwuy and his warriors. Caesar gained notoriety by wounding Pemulwuy. In 1795, Caesar escaped again. Governor Hunter offered a reward for his capture. In 1796, he was wounded in flight and died a few days later. He was survived by his daughter Mary Ann Fisher Power, who settled in Van Diemen's Land in 1813.

1860s — Frank Gardiner, John Peisley, John Gilbert, Ben Hall, Dan Morgan, Captain Thunderbolt

The gold rushes brought many people seeking fortune to Australia, however not all succeeded. There were those who were alienated and sought survival outside of the law. Some were a threat to established local authorities yet were popular within their own communities. Others were seen by some and themselves to be rebels rather than outlaws.

Frank Gardiner   John Gilbert   Ben Hall

Daniel Morgan   Captain Thunderbolt   Captain Moonlite

Frank Gardiner

Frank Gardiner (1830-1882), born Francis Christie in Scotland, was an Australian bushranger. With his parents, Charles and Jane Christie, he migrated to the Colony of New South Wales in 1834. His mother fell under the attention of a wealthy Scottish businessman Henry Monro, who was also migrating aboard the same ship. In 1835, Monro purchased properties south of Goulburn then northwest of Melbourne and employed Charles Christie as his overseer.

In 1850, Frank Gardiner, working as a stockman around Bendigo. With two accomplices, he stole a herd of horses from a neighbouring station. Caught, he was sentenced in 1851 to five years hard-labour at the newly completed Pentridge Prison. Shortly, he escaped, made his way from Victoria to New South Wales, where he resumed stealing horses. In 1854, he was caught and sent to Cockatoo Island where he met fellow bushranger John Peisley.

In 1860, he was granted a ticket of leave, joined up with Peisley and Ben Hall, and formed what became known as the Gardiner-Hall Gang. From 1862 to 1865, the gang is alleged to have committed over 100 robberies. In 1862, the gang bailed up the Lachlan Gold Escort and escaped with 2,700 ounces of gold (76 kilograms) and bank notes. Although some of the gold was later recovered by authorities, much of it is rumoured to be still hidden, buried near the Wheogo Station, near Eugowra, owned by family members of the gang. Gardiner escaped to Queensland, living under the assumed name Clark with Ben Hall's sister-in-law Kitty Brown, where they set up a general store in Rockhampton. However, in 1864, Gardiner was recognised, arrested, taken back to Sydney, and imprisoned for 32 years. After 10 years he was released on condition he left Australia. Gardiner travelled via Hong Kong to San Francisco, where he is rumoured to have married a rich widow, set up a saloon, and was later killed over money matters in 1882. All records of Gardiner in San Francisco were deemed to have been destroyed in the San Francisco earthquake of 1906.

Although Gardiner lived outside of the law, he is recorded as being a friendly person who was well-liked by many, including those who gave him refuge on the run and attained his early release.

John Peisley

John (Jack) Peisley (1835-1862) was the first Australian-born bushranger. Born in Bathurst to family with a dubious reputation, Peisley found himself in prison by the age of fifteen for horse stealing and cattle rustling. In 1860, after ten years in prison, he was released and immediately robbed a travelling bank officer of 500 pounds in notes. He took off into the Abercrombie Ranges, which he knew well, to become a full-time bushranger. During the next two years, Peisley lived on the run, consorting with other known outlaws. He settled old scores from his youth by wounding one man and killing another. In 1862, Peisley was eventually caught, tried and was sentenced to hanging at the gallows at Bathurst Gaol.

John Gilbert

John Gilbert (1842-1865) was born in Canada and came to Australia with his family in the hope of striking it lucky at the Victorian goldfields. The family arrived at Port Phillip in 1852. A couple of years later, at 12 years, John was working as a stable hand at his brother-in-law's property at Kilmore, Victoria, but shortly after moved to New South Wales. It was there that he came under the influence of Frank Gardiner and joined the gang, which included Ben Hall.

In late 1864, after a few robberies, the gang robbed the Gundagai Mail and shot dead a trooper. In May 1865, the Binalong police received a tip-off that two bushrangers were hiding out there. The police surrounded the woolshed at Murrumburah and Gilbert was shot dead.

Ben Hall

Ben Hall (1837-1865), like Peisley, was an Australian-born bushranger. Born in Maitland, New South Wales of parents transported for minor theft, Hall's early life appeared promising, working with his family as a stockman with horses and cattle near Murrurundi. At 19, he married Bridget (Biddy) Walsh at Bathurst and had a son Henry. Bridget was Kitty Brown's sister (see Frank Gardiner). The new family took a lease out on a property at Forbes, but in 1861-1862, drought broke out and they lost their property. The marriage broke up. Biddy and their son took off with another stockman.

Ben stayed at Murrundi and, like John Gilbert, fell under the influence of Frank Gardiner. With others, they formed the Gardiner-Hall Gang. Hall also participated in bailing up the Lachlan Gold Escort and escaped with gold and bank notes. They roamed about New South Wales committing robberies, including the Gundagai Mail murder with John Gilbert. In May 1865, the week before John Gilbert's death, travelling alone, Hall was ambushed by eight well-armed police and shot 30 times. He was buried at Forbes Cemetery a couple of days later.

Daniel Morgan

Daniel Morgan (1830-1865) was actually born John Fuller in Appin, New South Wales, to George Fuller, a seller of fruit and vegetables, and Mary Owen, and was adopted out. Through his life, he carried the names John Fuller, John Smith, Down-the-river Jack, Billie the Native, Daniel (Dan) Morgan and Mad Dog Morgan. He was well known for his erratic mood swings and violent temper. In his late teens, he was working as a stockrider around the Murrumbidgee River area.

In 1854, Morgan was sentenced to 12 years hard labour for highway robbery, served six years, was given a ticket of leave for good behaviour in 1860 but disappeared. Later that year, Morgan stole a prize horse owned by the Evans family but was tracked down by Evan Evans. In an ambush, Morgan was wounded but escaped to the Riverina area.

From 1863, Morgan became identified in several major armed robberies, including that of a police magistrate. In 1864, in a raid on the Round Hill station, he killed the overseer. A few days later, he killed a police sergeant near Tumbarumba. Later that year, while being tracked by police, he lay an ambush and killed another police sergeant.

From that time on, Morgan became known for raiding squatter properties and forcing the owners to pay their employees the loot. In 1865, after the passing of the Felons Apprehension Act, Morgan went back to settle a score with Evan Evans. In April 1865, he raided the Macpherson homestead at Peechelba, north of Wangaratta. That night, a posse of police and armed vigilantes tracked him to the homestead stockyards. In the morning, while mounting his horse to take flight, Morgan was shot in the back and killed. He was buried at Wangaratta Cemetery.

Captain Thunderbolt

Frederick Wordsworth Ward (1835-1870) was born the youngest of ten children to ex-convict Michael Ward and his wife Sophia, while the family was moving from Wilberforce to Windsor in New South Wales. Ward began working at stock stations from an early age and gained a good reputation as a strong horse handler. However, his cousin, John Garbutt, a known horse-thief, enticed him into joining his gang.

In 1856, they were soon captured and sentenced to Cockatoo Island. Released after four years, Ward and Garbutt settled in Mudgee. Garbutt married the wealthy widow of the Cooyal inn and station. Ward became friendly with Mary Ann Bugg and she fell pregnant to him. Taking her to her father's farm, Ward broke his parole and was sent back to Cockatoo Island. Mary Ann gave birth to a daughter.

In 1863, Ward escaped from Cockatoo Island and took up bushranging in the New England area of New South Wales, near Uralla. Ward was wounded behind his left knee, when attempting to ambush a group of troopers. Over the next six years, Ward roamed with his gang across northern New South Wales robbing travellers, mailmen, inns, stores and stations. In 1867, his relationship with Mary Ann Bugg ended and he was not to know that she had a son.

In May 1870, when attempting a robbery at Big Rock, near Uralla, Ward was shot and killed by Constable Walker. Although there was a dispute as to whether the man shot was Fred Ward, identification of his height, hair and eye colour, and the scar behind the left knee, supported that the body was him. Big Rock, beside the New England Highway in Uralla is now called Captain Thunderbolt's Rock. There is a permanent exhibition of Captain Thunderbolt at McCrossin's Mill Museum in Uralla.

1870s — Captain Moonlight, the Kelly Gang

Captain Moonlight

Andrew Scott (1842-1880) was born in Ireland to an Anglican priest and his wife. His father wanted young Andrew to join the priesthood, but he chose studying engineering in London instead. Legend has it that he served with Garibaldi in Italy in 1860 but this is unlikely. In November 1861, Scott and his family arrived in New Zealand. His father and brother, both ordained priests, took up positions in Christchurch. Scott initially began as a schoolteacher but enrolled in the local militia during the Maori Wars (1845-1872). He was wounded at Orakau (1864) and was charged with malingering. In his defence, he expressed his rage at the slaughter of Maori women and children by the militia, which in hindsight was probably true. He did not return to service and left for Sydney.

In 1868, Scott moved to Victoria, working as a teacher, surveyor and engineer in Bacchus Marsh and Ballarat. He befriended the local community but one night followed a friend, L.J. Bruun, local agent for the London Chartered Bank back to the Egerton branch. Wearing a mask, he forced Bruun to open the safe, took the contents, then signed a letter as Captain Moonlite absolving Bruun of guilt. He escaped to Sydney and lived off the contents until he was arrested for fraudulently passing cheques. Scott was sent to Maitland Gaol for 12 months, including time at the Parramatta Lunatic Asylum. Released in 1872, he was rearrested for the Egerton Robbery and stood before Judge Redmond

Barry, the same judge who tried Ned Kelly. Scott was given ten years hard labour at Pentridge Prison.

In 1879, Scott was released but, soon after, held up the Wantabadgery sheep station near Wagga Wagga, New South Wales, with a gang, using children as hostages. Two of his gang and one police trooper were killed. Scott was arrested, found guilty of murder, and was hanged at Darlinghurst Gaol in January 1880.

The Kelly Gang (1878-1880)

The Kelly Gang are Australia's best-known bushranger gang. The members of the Kelly Gang were Edward (Ned) Kelly, his brother Dan Kelly, Joe Byrne and Steve Hart. For two years, the Kelly Gang rode around southern New South Wales and northern Victoria, raiding towns, skirmishing and killing police, until Ned, the lone survivor, was captured during the siege at Glenrowan. However, the Kelly Gang was only a small part of the 11-years of Ned Kelly's life as an outlaw.

No other character, outside of Don Bradman, Australia's most famous sportsman, is as famous in Australian history as Ned Kelly and the Kelly Gang. There have been four films about Ned Kelly, starring Frank Mills (1906), Mick Jagger (1970), Heath Ledger (2003), and George Mackay (2019) as Ned. Some see him as a hero, others as a villain. Ned Kelly was an Australian bushranger, famous for his suit of bullet-proof armour.

Edward (Ned) Kelly

Edward (Ned) Kelly (1855-1880) born at Beveridge, Victoria, the third of eight children to John (Red) Kelly, a transported Irish convict, and Ellen Kelly, nee Quinn. He went to school at Avenel, distinguished himself at 11 when saving a drowning boy in a river and was awarded a green and gold sash by the boy's father. The next year, 1867, Ned's father died in prison leaving Ned at twelve as the eldest male. Almost immediately, the police began to turn their attention towards Ned. This was commonplace in the area as Irish squatters were constantly being victimised by more politically powerful British landowners and politicians. James Quinn, Ned's maternal grandfather, held 25,000 acres of poor country at Eleven Mile Creek, between Greta and Glenrowan. The land was coveted by many richer landowners based in Melbourne and around the local area.

In 1869, at 14, Ned was arrested for allegedly assaulting a Chinese man and held in remand for 10 days, but the charge was dismissed. The following year, Ned was arrested for being in the company of local ex-convict Harry Powers. He was charged three times with horse-stealing but each of the charges were dismissed through lack of evidence, although Kelly had been held in custody for more than a month. Some historians see this as police harassment from an early age, others that the local population sided with or were intimidated by the Kellys.

In 1870, Kelly was arrested for his part in a quarrel between a hawker, Jeremiah McCormack, and a friend, Ben Gould, and sentenced to three months hard labour. Upon release in 1871, Kelly took a horse belonging to a family visitor, Isaiah Wright, a well-known boxer, and was arrested. He did not know that the horse had been previously stolen from another. Although it was found that Kelly had been in gaol at the time of the original horse-stealing, he was still sentenced to 18 months on a down-graded charge. In 1874, he fought and beat Wright in a 'bare-knuckled' boxing match at the Imperial Hotel, Beechworth, that lasted 20 rounds.

Dan Kelly

Dan Kelly (1861-1880) was Ned's brother. He appears to have been out of trouble until he was accused by local police of stealing a saddle. The charges were dropped through lack of evidence. He was sent to prison for a month for the damage caused when arriving after a shop had closed.

The Fitzpatrick Incident

In 1878, Constable Fitzpatrick was ordered to the Kelly home to arrest Dan Kelly, Ned's brother, on suspicion of horse-stealing. The Kelly family persuaded Fitzpatrick to have dinner before returning to the police station. The group, including Bricky Williamson and brother-in-law Bill Skillion, overpowered Fitzpatrick, who was wounded in what became known as the Fitzpatrick Incident. Williamson, Skillion and Ellen Kelly, Ned and Dan's mother were arrested. They were taken before Judge Redmond Barry, who was to preside in the final trial of Ned Kelly. Although there was evidence that Fitzpatrick arrived at the Kelly's drunk and made an inappropriate pass at young Kate Kelly, Williamson and Skillion were sentenced to six years hard labour, and Ellen Kelly to three years hard labour. Fitzpatrick was later dismissed from the police force for drunkenness and perjury. After the sentences were handed down, Ned and Dan Kelly, knowing that the authorities were out to get them, took off to become bushrangers. They were joined by Steve Hart and Joe Byrne, and the Kelly Gang begun.

Steve Hart

Stephen Hart (1859-1880) was the second son of Irish immigrants. He was well-known as a jockey and won the Benalla Handicap. In 1878, Hart was convicted of horse-stealing and sentenced to 12 months at Beechworth prison. It was there that he met and befriended Dan Kelly. It is Steve Hart who is attributed with saying, "Here's to a short life and a merry one!"

Ned Kelly *Dan Kelly*

Steve Hart *Joe Byrne*

Joe Byrne

Joseph Byrne (1856-1880) was also born to Irish immigrants. His mother, Margaret, was one of the "Irish Famine Girls", given free passage to Australia as a result of the Great Irish Famine. Joe Byrne appears to have done well at school until his father's death, when Joe was in 5th grade, and was known as a "flash" writer. He also learnt Cantonese from the local Chinese gold miners. He left school in 1869 at 13 years of age. In 1871, Byrne and a friend Aaron Sherritt were arrested for horse-stealing and sentenced to six months at Beechworth prison. There, he met Jim Kelly, Ned and Dan's brother. Byrne befriended Ned Kelly in 1876.

Stringybark Creek Ambush

In October 1878, upon receiving a report that Ned and Dan Kelly were hiding in the Wombat Ranges, near Euroa, the police sent two parties out in a pincer movement to apprehend them. The second party in civilian dress was headed by Sergeant Kennedy, with Constables McIntyre, Lonigan and Scanlon in support. The police group camped overnight in some old miners' diggings by Stringybark Creek. In the morning, they went hunting kangaroos for breakfast. A gunshot alerted the Kelly Gang that they had company. The police were bailed up by the gang. Lonigan went for his revolver and was killed instantly. Kennedy and Scanlan were shot shortly after. McIntyre escaped to report the killing of the troopers. Public outrage at the police killings saw the Felon's Apprehension Act pass through the Victorian Parliament, which made it possible to apprehend the gang, dead or alive.

In December 1878, the Kelly Gang raided and robbed the bank in Euroa. They are reported to have otherwise behaved well, respecting the women, and having a whisky with the bank manager. In response, Police Captain Standish arrested 23 Kelly friends and sympathisers and held them for a month without charge in Beechworth Prison. Public opinion was now turning against the police.

In early 1879, while chasing police informant Sullivan, the gang rode into Jerilderie. The shopkeeper of the store was Louis Monash, and his young son John, later to be General Sir John Monash, was up from Melbourne on school holidays. According to Roland Perry, "An awestruck John Monash had the courage to approach Ned. According to Monash they chatted for a while. Kelly gave him a shilling to mind his horse." They locked the local police up, robbed the bank, but did no one any harm. Ned even forced Joe Byrne to return a stolen watch. In Jerilderie, Ned Kelly presented a letter he had composed listing all the injustices that had been done to him by the police. The Jerilderie Letter is held at the State Library of Victoria.

From March 1879 to mid-June 1880, nothing was heard from the Kelly Gang. Both the Felon's Apprehension Act and the Victorian government reward had been withdrawn. Many believed they had fled overseas. However, police lured the Kelly Gang out of hiding by spreading word that Kelly friend, Aaron Sherritt had turned police informant. The gang found Sherritt at his home. Byrne shot him dead.

The Siege at Glenrowan

After Sherritt's killing, news came that trains full of police were heading up from Melbourne, collecting reinforcements at Benalla then heading to Glenrowan. The Kelly Gang planned to ambush the police reinforcements. Their plan was to de-rail the train and shoot any survivors. They forced line-repairers camped nearby to remove the rails from a bend by a ravine. In Glenrowan, they held 62 hostages in the hotel to keep their plan secret. Thomas Curnow, a local schoolteacher, gained the confidence of the gang and was allowed to return home. Soon after, Curnow stopped the train with a light held to a red scarf. The rails were replaced, and the trains continued to Glenrowan. Alerted to the trains' arrival, Ned Kelly let the women and children hostages go free before the action ensued. The police surrounded the hotel.

At daybreak, Ned dressed in full armour led the attack to the police with revolvers in hand. The police shot at his unprotected legs and brought him down. Dan Kelly and Steve Hart let the men hostages go free. The police then set fire to the hotel. The charred bodies of Dan

Kelly and Steve Hart were discovered among the burnt-out ruins of the hotel. Joe Byrne's bullet-ridden body was found later.

Ned Kelly in armour

Ned Kelly at trial

The Trial and Execution of Ned Kelly

Although nearly dead from excessive bleeding, Ned Kelly survived the siege and when recovered was put on trial in Melbourne before Judge Redmond Barry, the same judge who had previously sentenced Ned's mother Ellen to three years hard labour. He was found guilty of murder and sentenced to death by hanging. Judge Barry concluded the sentence with, "May God have mercy upon your soul," to which Kelly retorted, "I will go a little further than that, and I say that I will see you there (in hell) where I go. In November 1880, Ned Kelly was hanged in Melbourne's Gaol. His mother Ellen was placed in a room beside the gallows to hear her son's last words. Her last words to him were, "Mind you die like a Kelly." His last words were, "Ah, well, I suppose it has come to this. Such is life."

The hanging of Ned Kelly

In 1881, a Royal commission into the conduct of Victoria Police was held and found widespread corruption. Many senior officers were dismissed, including Captain Standish, while other police were reprimanded. In all, 36 recommendations were delivered for police reform. Eight thousand pounds of reward money was paid out, including 50 pounds to each of the seven Aboriginal trackers. However, the respective trackers were not given their money by the government as it was deemed inappropriate to give such sums of money to those unable to use it by law.

Kelly's death resulted in police reform, land law reform in rural

Victoria, while his Jerilderie Letter is seen by some as a manifesto. Whether Ned Kelly is deemed a criminal or a political revolutionary, Ned Kelly's cultural impact on Victoria is quite visible. There are four films of Ned Kelly and innumerable stories. North-eastern Victoria is known as Kelly Country. In the 1940s, artist Sidney Nolan painted a collection based on Ned Kelly that reside at the National Gallery of Australia in Canberra. In 2001, Peter Carey won his second Booker Prize for his novel, 'The True History of the Kelly Gang.'

1900 — Governor Brothers (Aboriginal bushrangers)

The Governor Brothers were not born to a life of crime but were forced into it by the social or interracial taboos of a 'white' Australian society. Jimmy Governor (1875-1901) was born of Aboriginal parents near Denison in New South Wales. His family had a good reputation for being ward-working people within a white community. In his teens, the family moved to an Aboriginal camp near Singleton. In 1896, Jimmy, now 21 years, served as a police tracker around the Gulgong-Wollar area. However, in 1898, his life was disrupted and destroyed by prejudice.

In 1898, Jimmy Governor married a 16-year-old Ethel Page. She was 5 months' pregnant to Jimmy at the time of their wedding. Both Jimmy and Ethel were working on the Mawbrey family farm at Breelong. Upon confronting Mrs Mawbrey one evening for her racial taunts upon his wife, Jimmy is recorded to have asked Mrs Mawbrey, "Did you tell my missus that any white woman who married a blackfellow should be shot?" To which Miss Kerz, the local schoolteacher accompanying Mrs Mawbrey, replied, "Pooh, you black rubbish, you want shooting for marrying a white woman." In a fit of rage, Jimmy killed Miss Kerz, Mrs Mawbrey and three of her children. Jimmy, with his brother Joe, and friend Jack Underwood ran off into hiding.

Over the next two months, the Governor brothers began a spree of violence over an area of 3,000 kilometres of northern New South Wales, where they were reported to have committed over 80 robberies and other crimes. However, the net was closing in and Jimmy was wounded, shot in the mouth, while crossing the Forbes River. Eventually, he was captured, faced trial, and sentenced to death by hanging, which occurred after the celebrations for Federation had been completed in Darlinghurst Gaol in January 1901. Jimmy's life was commemorated in Thomas Keneally's 1972 novel, The Chant of Jimmy Blacksmith, which was later filmed by Fred Schepisi in 1978.

Women bushrangers

Mary Cockerill

Mary Cockerill (?-1819), also known as Black Mary, was Australia's first-known female bushranger and was of Aboriginal descent. Not much is recorded of Mary, except that she was kidnapped by the infamous Michael Howe and the Whitehead Gang in Tasmania in the 1810s. In 1815, when Howe and Cockerill were being chased by mounted troopers, Howe suddenly turned and shot her, thinking she was slowing him down. Mary survived but as revenge led the troopers to Howe and his gang. Howe was lured to his death in 1818. Mary died in 1819.

Mary Ann Bugg

Mary Ann Bugg (1834-1905) is Australia's most known female bushranger. Born near Gloucester, New South Wales, to James Bugg, a convict transported from England in 1825, and Charlotte of Aboriginal descent, from either the Worimi or Biripi people. Mary Ann came to know Fred Ward in Mudgee in 1860 and rode with him as part of his gang until she left him in 1867.

Jessie Hickman

Elizabeth Jessie Hunt (1890-1936) was born in Burraga, New South Wales and grew up learning bushcraft, horse riding and survival skills. By the age of fifteen, she was a successful roughrider and entertainer. However, she was jailed for stealing in 1913. She was married to Benjamin Hickman in 1920. They had a daughter but gave it up for adoption. They separated and Jessie left for the Blue Mountains. Here, in a cave in the Nullo Mountains, Jessie set up headquarters for her own gang of men, known as the "Young Bucks". They stole cattle from the local farmers and sell them at the markets at Singleton and Muswellbrook. In 1928, she was arrested at a property she had purchased at Emu Plains but was acquitted through lack of evidence. After, she settled on her Emu Plains property until she fell ill with head pains. She died of a brain tumour in 1936 in Newcastle Mental Hospital. She was buried at Sandgate Cemetery.

Mary Ann Bugg

Jessie Hickman

Towards Federation — economy, art & sport

As the 1800s drew to a close, Australia was looking less like a collection of colonies, and more like a group of sprawling cities with suburbs. In the 1880s, as more immigrants came to the key cities, especially Melbourne and Sydney, with the expectation of buying homes and farms, land prices boomed. This led to an economic boom, with more workers and investors placing their money in 'high-return' building societies and investment companies.

However, for indigenous Australians, the close of the 1800s saw them pushed out of the urban regions into the periphery of rural areas, the bush. They became an indentured servant class. The indigenous men worked as stock-hands on large rural estates, only receiving food and board for their work. The indigenous women worked as domestic servants, again receiving food and board. The owners of these rural estates felt, much like the rest of the 'white'-dominated society, that Aboriginal men and women could not be trusted and so it was accepted that paying them a wage was a 'waste of time and money'. In 1886, the Board for the Protection of Aborigines was given powers to take away indigenous children from their parents. At 13 years, they were placed in missions and trained to become indentured servants. Most of these children never saw their families again.

Science and industry

By the close of the 1800s, the colonies were largely self-sufficient, growing all its own food, but still importing many manufactured items.

This created opportunity to manufacture more items within the colonies, and export surpluses in grain, livestock and mining., exports accounted for about 20% (a fifth) of total Australian product, while imports accounted for about another 20%.

Early colonial Australian industry was largely powered by coal, However, by the 1860s-on, a growing source for power came from oil shale, an organic-rich sedimentary rock that contains petroleum. Oil shale was first reported in the Wolgan Valley of New South Wales by a French naturalist and explorer, Francois Peron, in his 'Voyage de Decouverte aux Terres Australes' (Discovery Voyage of the Southern Land), published in Paris in 1807. However, the extraction and processing of oil shale did not begin commercially until the mid-1860s and was processed for oil and gas production and other products such as paraffin and kerosene and exported to the United Kingdom, Europe and the United States of America. As the exploitation and import of crude and refined oil increased, the processing of oil shale declined.

In 1882, with the import of electrical generators, the Sydney General Post Office (GPO) and Circular Quay were illuminated with Edison incandescent light bulbs. Also, in 1882, a telephone exchange was opened at the Sydney GPO, and by 1883, all the capital cities except for Perth ran telephone exchanges. In 1887, with the introduction of refrigeration on ships, Australian produce could be shipped overseas.

New manufacturing industries blossomed with the increasing population, and the latter provided a growing labour market to service these industries. Exploitation of the growing labour force influenced workers to protect their rights and they created and joined trade unions. In 1882, the Amalgamated Miners Union was formed. In 1886, the Shearers' Union was formed and boasted 9,000 members in its first year. In response to the Shearers' Union, the Sheep Farmers' Association was formed to resist increasing wage demands.

Also, women began entering the workforce. Young women entered factories as tailoresses and seamstresses. In 1882, led by Helen Robertson, more than half the 4,000 Melbourne tailoresses went on strike against the threat of employers cutting their pay.

Helen Robertson

Helen Lothan Robertson (1848-1937), born in Glasgow, Scotland, was a tailoress and trade union official. The family migrated to Melbourne in 1853, when Helen was 5 years. At 14 years, Helen entered the workforce as a clothing machinist earning between 10 and 12 shillings per week, half the rate of male labourers. At 22, she married in Fitzroy, had six children over the next eleven years, and worked in the garment industry from home, combining it with home duties.

By 1874, Helen was already involved in union activities, and by 1880 was leading Melbourne tailoresses against oppressive work practices, called 'sweating'. In that year, Helen formed the Tailoresses' Association with help from workmates. They encountered resistance from employers, tailoresses scared of being 'blacklisted', and found little support from the Trades Hall Council. In 1882, after a Royal Commission into 'sweating' her association found greater support. In the late 1880s, the Trade Hall Council formed a Female Operatives' Hall, with Helen Robertson as a founding committee member. In 1906, the male and female tailoring unions merged, and in 1907 the Federated Clothing Trades Union was formed, with Robertson as a member of the Victorian branch executive until 1925, also serving as vice president. She died in 1937 and is buried in the Melbourne General Cemetery, in Carlton. Helen Robertson is revered as pioneer of female trade unionism.

The crisis of the 1890s

In the 1890s, more foreign funds had become available in Australia and the economic boom had become a bubble. This had resulted in a speculative land boom, with property prices rising to even higher levels. The Barings Crisis of 1890, a panic that led to world recession was primarily due to exposed funds in Argentina; however, it led to British investors withholding further funds from the Australian market. The bubble had burst, and the consequence was a recession in the Australian economy. In 1891, in Melbourne, then the largest city, 16 small banks closed, and by 1892, over 100 limited companies went into liquidation. By 1893, there was a major Australian banking crisis, with 11 commercial banks closed to prevent a run, including the National Bank of Australia and the Commercial Bank. Australia had now slipped into a major world economic depression. The Australian colonial governments had realised that they needed a united Australian government to take control of and regulate Australia's affairs. Australia was heading quickly towards federation.

Art, Literature and Music in the late 1800s.
Fine Art in Australia had a golden era in the late 1880s with the Australian impressionists. This was a distinctly Australian movement of painting and is associated with the Heidelberg School, based in an artists' camp in the Melbourne suburb. Its artists included Arthur Streeton, Walter Withers, Tom Roberts, Frederick McCubbin and Charles Conder. Streeton had been strongly influenced by the French impressionists and by the English Romantic painter J.M.W. Turner.

The wave created by the Heidelberg School was followed by the opening of Grosvenor Chambers in Collins Street, Melbourne, in 1888, built "expressly for the occupation of artists". Tom Roberts, Jane Sutherland and Clara Southern were its first occupants, followed by

Streeton, by Roberts, 1891

Golden Summer, by Streeton, 1889

Tom Roberts, 1895

Towards Federation — economy, art & sport

Shearing the Rams, Roberts, 1890

Fred McCubbin, self-portrait, 1886

The Pioneer triptych, McCubbin, 1904

Clara Southern   *The Road to Warrandyte, Southern, 1905*

Louis Abrahams and Charles Conder. Melbourne's economic downturn hit hard, and Roberts and Streeton moved to Sydney and established the Curlew Camp on the eastern shore of Little Sirius Cove in Sydney's Mosman. The Heidelberg tradition influenced Australian painting well into the 20th Century.

The late 1800s saw Australian literature dominated by Henry Lawson and A.B. (Banjo) Paterson. They were 'bush poets" writing about Australian folklore and rural life, and published in the Australian Bulletin magazine, founded in Sydney in 1880. Also, in 1874, Marcus Clark wrote the Australian classic, 'For the Term of His Natural Life'.

The literature of the late 1800s also gave rise to Australian folk music and bush ballads. Australia's unofficial national anthem, 'Waltzing Matilda', was a bush ballad written by Banjo Paterson in 1895, published as sheet music in 1903, and first recorded by John Collinson and Russell Callow in 1926.

Henry Lawson, circa 1902 *Marcus Clarke, circa 1866* *Marcus Clarke, circa 1866*

When Henry was a woman!

Ethel Florence Richardson (1870 – 1946) was a noted Australian author, who wrote under the pen-name Henry Handel Richardson. Ethel Richardson was born in East Melbourne, Victoria, and was schooled and boarded at Presbyterian Ladies College.

Her experiences there influenced her novel 'The Getting of Wisdom'. After finishing school, Richardson travelled to Leipzig, Germany, to continue her literature studies. She wrote her first novel 'Maurice Guest'. Later, Richardson wrote the three-part novel 'The Fortunes of Richard Mahony', maybe influenced by Goethe's 'The Sorrows of Young Werther'. She continued to live in Hastings, Sussex, UK, until she died.

The Canberra suburb of Richardson is named after her, as well as one of the residential halls at Monash University in Clayton, Victoria.

Isaac Nathan — the father of Australian classical music

Isaac Nathan, circa 1820

The father of Australian classical music was Isaac Nathan (1791-1864). Born in Canterbury, England, to Jewish parents, Nathan was an English composer and musicologist. In his early years, Nathan studied to be a Jewish cantor; however, in 1813, Nathan and his traditional Jewish music combined with the famous English poet, Lord Byron and his lyrics to create the noted 'Hebrew Melodies', popular for the remainder of the 19th Century. Nathan emigrated to Australia in 1841 and continued to compose and perform until his death in 1864. In 1847, Nathan's 'Don John of Austria' was the first opera composed in Australia. Nathan's music has been claimed to have influenced later composers such as Mendelssohn, Schumann, Mussorgsky and others. Contemporary Australian composer, Peter Sculthorpe, wrote an orchestral piece in 1988 dedicated to him. A portrait of Isaac Nathan can be found in the National Library of Australia.

Another early Australian composer was George Tolhurst, an English composer who resided in Australia between 1852 to 1866. Tolhurst's oratorio 'Ruth' was written in the colony of Victoria in 1864.

Other noted Australian classical composers in the late 1800s came from a wide range of European backgrounds. Most noted were Hugo Alpen, Hooper Brewster-Jones, Thomas Bulch, Alice Charbonnet-Kellermann, George Clutsman, Herbert De Pinna, John Albert Delaney, Guglielmo Enrico Lardelli, Louis Lavater, George Marshall-Hall, Stephen Moreno, George William Torrence, Cesare Cutolo, Christoan Helleman and Augustus Juncker.

The Stage in colonial Australia

The first staged theatre production in colonial Australia belongs to the First Fleet. The first production was by the convicts in 1789, The Recruiting Officer, which was written by George Farquhar in 1706.

The Theatre Royal in Sydney, built in 1827, is Australia's oldest theatre. However, it burned to the ground in 1840. In 1837, the Theatre Royal was opened in Hobart. It is still Australia's oldest still-operating theatre. The Melbourne Athenaeum opened in 1839 and the Queen's Theatre in Adelaide opened in 1841. The original building that was to become Melbourne's Princess Theatre was built during the gold rush in 1854. Many theatres were opened during the gold rush to entertain miners and mining communities. Perth's His Majesty's theatre was built in 1904. Undoubtedly, Australia's most famous theatre star of the late 1800s was Dame Nellie Melba.

Dame Nellie Melba

Dame Nellie Melba (1861-1931) was born Helen Porter Mitchell in Richmond, Victoria. Her father was David Mitchell, a successful Scottish-born builder, who built Scot's Church in Melbourne. She was taught to play the piano early in life and sung in public from the age of 6. Nellie had been her nickname. She attended Presbyterian Ladies College and received private tuition in singing and continued performing in amateur concerts. After the death of her mother in 1881, Helen Porter moved with her family to Mackay in Queensland. There she was married, had a child, separated from her husband after a year, then moved back to Melbourne to begin her singing career. In 1884, she was singing in concerts around Melbourne and, in 1886, moved to England and made her debut at Princes' Hall, London. It was about this time she adopted the name Nellie Melba. However, she didn't find success until moving to Paris then Brussels, singing at the Theatre de la Monnaie. There she sang the role of Gilda in Verdi's Rigoletto for 3,000 francs per month.

Dame Nellie Melba

In 1888, Melba returned to London to make her Covent Garden debut, but soon after returned to Paris. It was in Paris that she embarked on an affair with Prince Philippe, the Duke of Orleans. In 1893, she sang at the Metropolitan Opera in New York City for the first time. Through the 1890s, Melba starred in London, Paris and New York, singing some 25 different roles. Between 1898 and 1926, she performed 26 times at the Royal Albert Hall in London.

In 1902-03, Melba made the first of her four return tours of Australia and New Zealand. In 1909, visiting Melbourne, she purchased a property near Coldstream and built Coombe Cottage, which still stands near the corner of the Maroondah and Melba Highways, and also opened a music school, the Melbourne Conservatorium, in Richmond.

During the First World War, Melba threw her efforts into charity work and, in March 1918, was awarded Dame Commander of the Order of the British Empire (DBE). After the war, through the 1920s, Melba continued touring between continents. In 1927, her title was elevated to Dame Grand Cross of the Order of the British Empire (GBE) and she was also the first Australian to appear on the cover of Time Magazine. However, in 1929, while on a European tour that included Egypt, she contracted fever and never fully recovered. In 1931, Melba died in St Vincent's Hospital in Sydney and her funeral was held at Scot's Church, which her father had built.

Melba received many accolades for her career, including four food dishes, a suburb in Canberra, a highway in Victoria, an avenue in San Francisco, statues, music halls, her face on Australia's $100 note, and a character appearance in the television series Downton Abbey. Dame Nellie Melba was truly a great international Australian.

Sport in the late 1800s

Cricket

By the late 1800s, many of the state and premier teams and associations had already been founded. The first inter-colonial match had already been played by a visiting Victorian team to Tasmania in 1851. The match was played in Launceston, with the Tasmanian team winning by 3 wickets.

The first tour of an English team to Australia was in 1861-1862, followed by a further English tour in 1863-1864. The first tour of an Australian team to England was the famed Aboriginal tour in 1868. A tour by an English team in 1873-1874, brought the noted English cricketer W.G. Grace to Australia. The 1876-1877 tour saw the first official test played between England and Australia. In 1882, a defeat of the English team in England by Australia created 'The Ashes', which is the trophy these teams play for to this day.

Fabric print of Australia's first international cricket match played at the Melbourne Cricket Ground (MCG) in 1862, between H.H. Stephenson's English XI v Victorian XVIII. Fabric print, by Henry Burn on display at MCG.

Inset of American flag on display during match.   *Inset of spectators who paid a penny to be 'laddered' up into trees to watch game and paid two pennies to be 'laddered' down afterwards.*

The Aboriginal Cricket Tour to England 1868

In 1868, an Aboriginal cricket team, managed by Tom Wills, toured England over a six-month period. It played in 47 matches; winning 14, losing 14, and drawing 19, which was a good result. The Australian Aboriginal XI was: Johnny Mullagh (captain), Bullocky (wicketkeeper), Sundown, Dick-a-Dick, Johnny Cuzens, King Cole, Red Cap, Twopenny, Charley Dumas, Jimmy Mosquito, Tiger, Peter, and Jim Crow.

Johnny Mullagh — the first internationally recognised Aboriginal sportsperson

Johnny Mullagh (1843-1891), born in Victoria, was the leading Aboriginal cricketer of his time and led the 1868 Aboriginal cricket tour to England. Mullagh was born Unaarrimin of the Jardwadjali people on Mullagh Station in western Victoria. Mullagh played in all 47 matches, scored 1,685 runs, took 241 wickets, and substituted as a wicketkeeper. He scored 75 v M.C.C. at Lords. He was employed by the Melbourne Cricket Club as a professional cricketer in 1869/70, but his contract

First Aboriginal Australian cricket touring team in 1868 with its manager and coach, Tom Wills.

Johnny Mullagh, captain, 1868 Aboriginal cricket tour.

Charles Bannerman, Australia's first Test century maker on debut, and Dave Gregory, Australia's first Test captain in 1877.

Poster located in Toorak Rd., South Yarra (2021).

was terminated early. He suffered discrimination during his cricket career. At one game in Apsley, Victoria, he chose not to have lunch at all, rather than eating it in the kitchen away from the other players. Later, aged 38, he top-scored a defiant 36 in a second innings Victoria v Lord Harris's touring English team in 1879. The local sports ground in Harrow, Victoria, is named the Johnny Mullagh Oval and there is a memorial to him. From 2020, the best player of the Boxing Day Test is awarded the Mullagh medal. In 2021, Melbourne Cricket Club inducted Johnny Mullagh into its Australian Cricket Hall of Fame.

The First Cricket Test 1877

The first Cricket Test match was played at the Melbourne Cricket Ground between Australia and England in 1877. Australia won by 45 runs. The Australian XI was: D.W. Gregory (captain), J.M. Blackham (wicketkeeper), C. Bannerman, N. Thompson, T.P. Horan, B.B. Cooper, W.E. Midwinter, E.J. Gregory, T.W. Garrett, T. Kendall, and J.H. Hodges. Highlights for Australia in the first test were Bannerman's 165 runs, opening the batting in the first innings; Midwinter's 5/78, bowling in the first innings; followed by Kendall's 7/55 in the second innings.

The trophy for Test matches between Australia and England is called 'The Ashes', which had its origins in 1882. Australia beat England by seven runs in an England-home Test at 'the Oval', London, largely due to the efforts of Australian bowler Fred Spofforth, 7/46 and 7/44. A mock obituary was written of English cricket by Reginald S. Brooks of The Sporting Times, which read:

> *In Affectionate Remembrance of English Cricket which died at the Oval on 29 August 1882. Deeply lamented by a large circle of sorrowing friends and acquaintances. R.I.P. N.B. — The body will be cremated and the ashes taken to Australia.*

During the following 1882-83 English cricket tour of Australia, the English captain, Ivo Bligh, pledged to return with "The Ashes of English cricket." During a friendly match hosted at Rupertswood Mansion in Sunbury, Victoria, he was presented with a small terracotta urn containing the ashes of a burnt cricket bail. After Bligh's death, the urn was presented to the Marylebone Cricket Club and is on permanent display at the Lords Cricket Ground in London.

During the remainder of the 19th Century, Australia only played Test Cricket with England. South Africa played England too, but Australia didn't play South Africa. Australia and England played 56 Tests, with Australia winning 20, England winning 26, and 10 drawn. For Australia, during this time, its best batsmen were Sid Gregory (4 centuries), Percy McDonnell (3), Clem Hill (2), Frank Iredale (2), and Bill Murdoch (2). Australia's best bowlers were undoubtedly Fred Spofforth (4 times 10 wickets in a match), followed by Charlie Turner (2), and Joey Palmer (2). George Giffen was Australia's best all-rounder, and Jack Blackham, it's most notable wicketkeeper.

Horse Racing — The Melbourne Cup and Queen's Plate

The AJC founded the AJC Queen's Plate, in honour of Queen Victoria, later known as the Queen Elizabeth Stakes, which was Australia's first 'big' horserace in 1851, run over 4,800 metres or about 3 miles. The horse 'Cossack' won the first two Queen's Plates in 1851 and 1852.

The AJC moved to Randwick in 1860. New racecourses opened up in Canterbury Park in 1871, Rosehill Gardens in 1885, Warwick Farm in 1889.

The Melbourne Cup, Australia's premier horse race, was run for first time in 1861 at Flemington Racecourse. The idea for the race is accredited to Frederick Standish, who was a member of the Victorian Turf Club and was steward on the day. The horse Archer (16.3 hands) won the first Cup in 3 minutes and 52 seconds. It was ridden by John Cutts, trained and leased by Etienne De Mestre. The stake was 710 gold sovereigns and a gold watch, and 4,000 people watched the race. The following year, Archer won the second Melbourne Cup. Attendance grew at horseracing events too. By the 1877 Melbourne Cup, 75,000 people attended the race, and over 100,000 by the 1880s.

Randwick Racecourse circa 1870

Melbourne Cricket Ground circa 1854

Engraving of the finishing line of the Melbourne Cup, published in the Illustrated Australian News 1881.

Aussie Rules

Australian Rules football formalised its competition in 1877, when the South Australian Football Association then the Victorian Football Association (VFA) were founded.

The original South Australian Football Association teams were Adelaide, Bankers, Kensington, Port Adelaide, South Adelaide, South Park, Victorian and Woodville. Victorian was later renamed North Adelaide, possibly due to local animosity towards its neighbouring state.

The original VFA clubs were Albert Park, Carlton, East Melbourne, Essendon, Geelong, Hotham, Melbourne, St Kilda, South Melbourne and West Melbourne. Hotham would eventually become North Melbourne. The VFA also had a second division of Ballarat, Hawthorn, Northcote, Standard, Victoria United, Victorian Railways and Williamstown.

The first Tasmanian league was founded in 1879 around Hobart, followed by the Northern Tasmanian Football Association in 1886. Tasmanian football, like its politics, was always divided between the north, Launceston, and the south, Hobart.

The Western Australian Football Association was founded in 1885 with original teams Fremantle, Rovers, Victorians and The High School. Victorians was later renamed West Perth, and The High School became Hale School in Wembley Downs.

The 1880s saw Australian Rules football become the dominant winter sport in Australia. However, in Victoria, due to inequalities in the competition that needed reforming, the top five clubs broke away from the VFA to create their own competition in 1896. The original eight Victorian Football League (VFL) teams were Carlton, Collingwood, Essendon, Fitzroy, Geelong, Melbourne, St Kilda and South Melbourne. The VFA were left with five clubs, Footscray, North Melbourne, Port Melbourne, Richmond and Williamstown, with Brunswick quickly added after to ensure the competition could continue.

Rugby

Although unofficial games of rugby had been played earlier, the Southern Rugby Union was established in 1874. It was the original administrative body for rugby in Australia. The first intercolonial rugby match was played in 1882 between New South Wales and Queensland. The following year, the Northern Rugby Union was founded in Brisbane. Matches between New South Wales and Queensland became an annual event,

The Australian Team, 1899

Australia's first touring team, 1908-9

Dally Messenger, 1908

and New Zealand was also invited to play too. In 1892, the Southern Rugby Union changed its name to the New South Wales Rugby Football Union. The following year, The Northern Rugby Union changed its name to the Queensland Rugby Football Union.

In 1888, an unofficial and private British rugby team toured Australia and New Zealand. However, the first official international rugby match was played in 1899 between Australia and Britain at the Sydney Cricket Ground. Australia won the game 13-3, but the British team won the remaining three tests. Australia played New Zealand in an official test match for the first time in 1903 at the Sydney Cricket Ground, with New Zealand winning 22-3.

In 1907, the NSW Rugby League was formed, with Dally Messenger, 'The Master', dubbed its first champion. In 1908, Australia's first rugby team toured Britain. It was the first Australian rugby team to be nicknamed the 'Wallabies'.

The New South Wales Rugby football Union was responsible for managing all international tours until the late 1940s. In 1949, The Australian Rugby union, representing all six states of Australia was formed. The ACT Rugby Union joined in 1972, followed by the Northern Territory Rugby Union in 1978.

Soccer

Soccer was introduced to Australia by British settlers in the late 19th Century. The earliest known game of soccer was played in 1875 at the Woogaroo Lunatic Asylum, Wacol, Queensland, between the inmates and asylum workers against a visiting team from a Brisbane 'Aussie Rules' football club. There is also an unofficial game in 1879, played in Hobart by the cricket club.

The first soccer club in Australia was the Wanderers club, formed in Parramatta in 1880, and the first recorded game was between the

Wanderers and a team from the Kings School rugby team on Parramatta Common in August 1880. The wanderers club was formed by an English immigrant, John Walter Fletcher, a teacher and magistrate. In 1882, Fletcher formed the New South Wales English Football Association. The earliest Australian soccer club that still exists is the Balgownie Rangers, established in 1883, based in Wollongong. In 1883, the first inter-colonial soccer game was played between teams from New South Wales and Victoria on the East Melbourne Cricket Ground.

Soccer continued to grow in popularity as each colony formed its own competition, Victoria (1884), Queensland (1884), Western Australia (1896), Tasmania (1900) and South Australia (1902). However, it wasn't until 1911 that a national governing body was formed, called the Commonwealth Football Association.

Balgownie Rangers Football Club, Premiers 1895 & 1896
Top Row: Tom Cook (hon. pres.), Charlie York, Charlie Campbell, Jim Campbell, Harry Murdoch (pres.)
Middle Row: Bill Logan, Peter Hunter, Tom Thompson (capt.), Jimmy Syms, Bill Shaw
Front Row: Bob Vardy, Mick Fitzgibbons, Bob Campbell.

Balgownie Rangers Football Club,
from http://www.balgownierangers.com.au

Annette Kellermann (1887-1975) was an Australian swimmer, actress, and writer, and is also accredited with being the 'daughter of synchronised swimming'.

In her youth, Kellerman wore leg-braces to overcome her leg weaknesses. She began swimming to strengthen her legs and, by age 15, held the 100 yard and mile records. She was also an exhibition diver.

Annette Kellerman, Library of Congress

In 1911, aged 24, Kellerman starred in 'The Mermaid', a silent film where she wore a swimmable mermaid's outfit. Her other films included, 'A Daughter of the Gods' (1916), 'Queen of the Sea' (1918), and 'Venus of the South Seas' (1924), among many others. Her name appears on a star in the Hollywood Walk of Fame.

PART FOUR

THE FEDERATION OF AUSTRALIA

Contributing factors

The idea for the federation of Australia came from the influence of other such federations as the United States and Canada and of the British Government seeking to implement a unified military decision-making process in the Oceanic region. In the 1853, New Caledonia had become a French colony. This was followed by their interest in the New Hebrides and other Pacific islands. In the 1880s, the Germans had occupied and claimed German New Guinea. Further, there was a general paranoia that Russian Imperial ambitions might threaten Australia.

During that time, contemplation was given to unifying Australia, New Zealand, and Fiji; however, the latter two decided upon seeking their own independence.

Henry Parkes — the father of Australian federation

Sir Henry Parkes (1815-1896), born in Warwickshire, England, was an Australian politician, and served as Premier of the Colony of New South Wales, before federation. Parkes is referred to as the 'Father of Federation' and is considered the earliest leading advocate of an independent Australia. Parkes died in 1896, five years before federation was announced.

As early as 1867, Parkes, as Colonial Secretary of New South Wales, first proposed the creation of a Federal Council but was rejected. Parkes proposed it again, as New South Wales Premier in 1880. This time, he found favour.

The Intercolonial Convention of 1883 drafted a bill to be presented to the British Parliament, which passed the Federal Council of Australasia Act 1885. However, New Zealand and Britain's South Pacific islands lost interest in unifying with Australia.

The key areas of focus for the Federal Council were the application of the judicial process, trade laws and tariffs, and the management of natural resources, e.g., fisheries. The Federal Council also received opposition from Queensland in relation to regulating the importing of Pacific islanders. Queensland relied heavily on cheap labour for its sugar cane industry in much the same way the southern United States relied on slaves for its cotton industry. The growing trade union movement was also concerned about how labour and wages would be determined in a federated Australia.

In October 1889, Parkes made his famous Tenterfield Oration. *"The great question ... is ... whether the time has not now arisen for the creation on this Australian continent of an Australian Government ... Australia has now a population of three and a half millions, and the American people numbered only between three and four millions when they formed the great commonwealth of the United States. The numbers are about the same, and surely what the Americans have done by war, the Australians can bring about in peace."*

The 1891 Constitutional Convention, held in Sydney, saw 46 delegates appointed by the seven colonial parliaments approve a draft constitution largely written by Samuel Griffith and Andrew Clark, however it was not ratified by the colonial parliaments. The Griffith-Clark draft enshrined four key items, being: 1. The name, Commonwealth of Australia; 2. The separation of powers between the legislative, the executive and the judiciary; 3. The division of powers between the Federal and State governments, and; 4. The establishment of a two-house parliament of a Senate and House of Representatives.

Andrew Clark also co-founded the Hare-Clark voting system of distributing preferences that we use today in the Australian Senate. It is the method by which once a candidate has met the quota of required votes, surplus votes are distributed to the next preference using a mathematic formula.

The 1898-99 Constitutional Convention, held at various stages in Adelaide, Sydney, and Melbourne, saw popularly elected delegates approve the draft constitution. The 1898 Referendum was held, and a majority was gained in each state; however, in New South Wales the majority was not large enough for the referendum to succeed. The outstanding issue was negotiated that a new Australian capital could be located in New South Wales but had to be at least 100 miles from Sydney. In 1899, a second referendum was held and succeeded. In 1900, a third referendum was held and succeeded in Western Australia, as it had not participated in either of the previous two.

The Commonwealth of Australia Constitution Act (UK) was passed by the British Parliament and given Royal Assent by Queen Victoria in July 1900, and proclaimed in Centennial Park, Sydney on January 1st, 1901. Sir Edmund Barton was sworn in as Australia's first Prime Minister. Samuel Griffith was the first Chief Justice of Australia.

After a competition was held by the Melbourne Herald in 1900, five unrelated winners with near identical designs shared equally the 200-pound prize. The new Australian flag was adopted in September 1901; however, this version had a six-pointed Commonwealth star. An amended version with a seven-pointed Commonwealth star was adopted two years later.

The new constitution deemed that Aboriginal people were not to be counted in the national census and were therefore denied the right to vote.

Although Australia had become a federation, with the states joining together under one government, the British government could still intervene and legislate with effect in Australia or its judicial courts. This was the case until the passing of the Australia Act 1986, when the Australian parliament and courts became fully independent of the British system.

Sir Henry Parkes   Sir Samuel Griffith   Andrew Clark

Sir Edmund Barton   Alfred Deakin

Edmond Barton

Sir Edmond Barton (1849-1920), born in Glebe, New South Wales, was a politician and judge, and served as Australia's first Prime Minister, serving one term from 1901-1903. In 1903, Barton resigned to become a founding member of the High Court of Australia, where he served until his death.

Alfred Deakin

Alfred Deakin (1856-1919), born in Fitzroy, Victoria, was a barrister and politician, and served as Australia's second Prime Minister, serving three separate terms. Deakin was Victoria's leading advocate for Australian federation.

The opening of the first Parliament of Australia occurred in Melbourne at the Melbourne Exhibition Building on May 9, 1901. After the opening, parliament sat at Victorian Parliament House in Spring Street for the next 26 years until the opening of the first Parliament House in Canberra in 1927.

Photograph, Opening of the first Parliament of Australia, Museums Victoria Collection.

Inset of The Big Picture, opening of the first Parliament of Australia, 1901, by Tom Roberts. (The Duke of Cornwall and York, later King George V, addresses the audience.)

The Franchise Act — Women's right to vote

The Commonwealth Franchise Act 1902 gave women the right to vote and stand in federal elections, except those who were "aboriginal natives" of Australia, Africa, Asia and the Pacific islands. By 1911, all the states had adopted the legislation. However, it did take almost two decades for the first woman to be elected to a parliament. In 1921, Edith Cowan (1861-1932) was elected to the Western Australian Legislative Assembly.

Enid Lyons

Dorothy Tangney

Carmen Lawrence

Joan Kirner

Julia Gillard

In 1943, Enid Lyons (HR) and Dorothy Tangney (Senate), were the first women to be elected to the Australian Parliament. In 1949, Lyons was the first woman to hold a cabinet seat.

In 1990, Carmen Lawrence was elected Premier of Queensland, the first female Premier to hold office and, shortly after, Joan Kirner became Premier of Victoria.

In 2010, Julia Gillard became the first female Prime Minister of Australia.

Dinosaur find — 1903

While the new nation's attentions were focused on how the federation was developing, in 1903, a geologist by the name of William Hamilton Ferguson (1861-1957) was mapping the coastal area around Inverloch in Victoria. It was a few kilometres west at Eagle's Nest that he uncovered the first dinosaur fossil discovered in Australia, a carnivorous raptor. However, it was not until some 75 years later that the site was explored further, and more dinosaur discoveries were made.

Federation Sport

The late 19th Century had seen a surge in the creation of formal sporting organisations — clubs, associations and competitions, including a revival of the Ancient Greek Olympic Games. In 1896, in Athens, Greece, the first of the modern summer Olympic Games was held. There was no better way for Australians to display their new national identity than through representation in international sport.

The Modern Olympics

In 1894, Frenchman Pierre de Coubertin presented his vision of a modern Olympics Games, based on those of Ancient Greece. However, Coubertin's vision did not include women competing. Another Frenchman Michel Breal put forward his idea of a long race to commemorate the run of the ancient Greek Pheidippides from the ancient battlefield at Marathon to the Pnyx (a meeting place on a hill in Athens) to announce the Greek victory over the invading Persians in 490 BC. This idea became the modern marathon a race of 40 kilometres, 25 miles. History tells us that Spyridon Louis of Greece won the first marathon in 2 hours 58 minutes and 50 seconds. However, very few know that a Greek woman, Stamata Revithi was prevented by Olympic officials from entering the event. Revithi may have also been known by journalists under the name Melpomene. She was poor and thought competing in the race might bring her opportunity. She ran by herself the next day, witnessed by three local officials, completed the run in 5½ hours but was prevented by local policemen from entering the stadium in Athens. Journalists reported on Revithi before the race but after, she was lost to history.

Edwin Flack

Edwin Flack (1873-1935) migrated from London to Melbourne in 1878 and is considered Australia's first Olympian. He was a middle-distance runner and tennis player. Flack won gold in in the 1896 Athens Summer Olympic Games in the 800 metre and the 1,500 metre sprints. He competed in the marathon and was leading until he dropped out of the race with three kilometres to run. Flack also won a bronze medal for doubles tennis.

Edwin Flack, Athletics Australia

Fanny Durack, National Library of Australia

Fanny Durack

Sarah Frances "Fanny" Durack (1889-1956), born in Sydney, was arguably Australia's greatest freestyle swimmer. She was the world's best female swimmer of her time of freestyle over all distances, including the mile marathon. From 1912 to 1920, Durack held the world record for 100 metres freestyle, and held the world record for 200 metres from 1915 to 1921.

In the 1912 Stockholm Summer Olympics, the first to have women's swimming, Durack set a new world record for 100-metre freestyle and was the first Australian woman to win a gold medal in swimming. The only other Australian woman to win a gold medal in swimming prior to the 1956 Melbourne Olympics was Clare Dennis for the 200-metre breaststroke in the 1932 Los Angeles Olympics.

Just prior to the 1920 Antwerp Olympics, Durack suffered appendicitis, was operated on, then contracted typhoid fever and pneumonia. Although she recovered, she never swam in an Olympics again. Durack died in 1956 and is buried at Waverley Cemetery. The Fanny Durack Aquatic Centre in Petersham is named in her honour as is Fanny Durack Avenue at Sydney's Olympic Park.

Empire considerations

One of the key factors in the federation of Australia was the recognition by the British government that there needed to be a unifying independent command in the Pacific region. One of the ways that Australia could show its independence and self-reliance was to recruit, train and deploy its own military forces.

Previously, individual states had offered troops or ships for military service, or individual Australians were recruited into foreign armies. In 1861, during the Taranaki Wars in New Zealand, the Victorian government offered the HMCSS Victoria for patrol duties and logistical support. For the invasion of Waikato in late 1863, the New Zealand government recruited about 2,500 Australians with the promise of farmland from the confiscated regions. A New South Wales contingent of about 750 infantry and artillery soldiers and officers served in the Sudan War of 1885.

The Second Boer War, South Africa, 1899-1901

The Second Boer War in South Africa followed the earlier but shorter First Boer War (1880-81). The Boers were descendants of the original German Dutch-speaking (Afrikaans) farmers who had settled with the Dutch East India Company on the Cape of Good Hope in South Africa. During the Napoleonic Wars, the British claimed the Cape for themselves. About 15,000 Boers elected to embark on the 'Great Trek' from Cape Colony and resettled in the Transvaal and Orange Free States. The discovery of gold, diamonds and other minerals by Cecil Rhodes and others led to the British attempting to annex further Boer land, which led to the Boer Wars. Note, before Boer settlement, South Africa was ruled by the indigenous Zulu people. Both Boer and British colonisation reduced the Zulu people to slaves and indentured servants. Furthermore, it was during the Boer Wars that the British created the internment system of detention or concentration camps that was used widespreadly during World War Two.

During the Second Boer war, NSW Lancers, who had been training in England, were the first to see action at Belmont in November 1899. The following month, contingents of infantry from Victoria, South Australia, Western Australia and Tasmania arrived in Cape Town and were united into an Australian Regiment under the command of Col. John Charles Hoad. For increased mobility, the regiment was converted into mounted infantry. Five hundred Queensland and New South Wales Lancers were deployed during the Siege of Kimberley in February 1900. The Australian Regiment, as part of the British column under Lord Methuen, was effectively deployed during the battles of Modder River and Paardeberg. With continued success, the regiment formed part of the force that entered Bloemfontein (March), Mafeking (May), and Pretoria (June), then fought a battle at Diamond Hill. Five hundred Australians were under siege at Elands River (August 1900), where they held on until being relieved. By mid-1901, the Boers were in full retreat and various Australian units saw action in the north-west of South Africa. Not all encounters were successful. Heavy casualties were suffered during the ambush near Middleburg (June 1901), Gun Hill (October) and Onverwacht (1902).

Upon Federation in 1901, eight new Commonwealth horse battalions were sent to South Africa, but the war had ended before they were deployed. Some Australians joined irregular South African units and were therefore subject to British justice. Such was the case of Lts. Harry "The Breaker" Morant and Peter Handcock who were court-martialled and executed for war crimes against South African civilians. Controversy followed the execution of Morant and Handcock as to whether, as alleged, they had been scapegoated by British military authorities looking to avoid responsibility for civilian killings. Subsequent investigations indicate that responsibility should have been brought upon Captain Alfred Taylor, a regular British officer, ruthless mass murderer, cattle rustler, and profiteer. The court-martial was portrayed in the Bruce Beresford film, Breaker Morant (1980), starring Edward Woodward, Jack Thompson and noted others.

Lt. Harry "The Breaker" Morant (Australian War Memorial)

Poster from the film, Breaker Morant (1980).

Overall, 16,000 Australians served in Australian units in South Africa, with another 10,000 recruited into other Imperial units. Of these, about 500 were killed, 700 wounded, and six received the Victoria Cross, the highest and most prestigious award in the British military system.

Officer, NSW Infantry, 1885

Colonel, NSW Artillery, 1886

Officer, Adelaide Lancers, 1900

Officer, First Australian Horse, Boer War, 1900

Australian Nursing Service, Boer War, 1900

The Boxer Rebellion, China, 1900-1901

Britain also requested help from the Australian colonies during the Boxer Rebellion; however, most of its army units were already deployed in South Africa. A naval force of about 500 Victorians and New South Welshmen were sent in the South Australian ship HMCS Protector, under Capt. William Creswell. Arriving in Tientsin, the group was used for surveying and logistical duties, returning to Australia the following year.

Rear-Admiral Sir William Creswell — Father of the Australian Navy

Willian Creswell (1852-1933) born in Gibraltar, is considered to be the "father" of the Australian Royal Navy. Creswell joined the Royal Navy as a cadet at age 13, and served in the Channel Fleet, China, Malaya, India and Zanzibar. Creswell emigrated to Australia in 1878 as a pastoralist to the Northern Territory but was quickly dismayed. He found a posting aboard the South Australian naval ship HMCS Protector, which served in the Boxer Rebellion in China. From 1895, Creswell was agitating for an independent Australian naval force. After Federation, in 1904, Creswell was appointed Naval Officer Commanding the Commonwealth Naval Forces, given the responsibility of forming a unified Australian Royal Navy. In 1911, he was promoted to rear-admiral, following his service in ship construction, shore support and convoy formation. When the First World War was declared in 1914, Australia could thank Creswell for the Australian Navy being ready for service.

A question of immigration — The White Australia Policy

Prior to federation, British, European and Chinese miners had competed against each other on the goldfields, and the labour unions were opposing the migration of low-paid South Sea Islanders to work on the sugar plantations. Consequently, the colonial governments were under pressure to restrict foreign workers.

Soon after federation 1901, the Barton government enacted the Immigration Restriction Act. It had been drafted by Alfred Deakin, who was to become Australia's second prime minister. The act gave preference to British migrants over others.

> "That end, put in plain and equivocal terms ... means the prohibition of all alien coloured migration, and more, it means at the earliest time, by reasonable and just means, the deportation or reduction of the number of aliens now in our midst. The two things go hand in hand, and are the necessary complement of a single policy — the policy of securing a 'white Australia'." (Attorney General Alfred Deakin, 12 September 1901)

Further, Deakin sought to justify the policy by identifying the strengths of the Asian migrants, as follows:

> "It is not the bad qualities, but the good qualities of these alien races that make them so dangerous to us. It is their inexhaustible energy, their power of applying themselves to new tasks, their endurance and low standard of living that make them such competitors."

The British government had opposed any expression of an explicit racial policy within the legislation; and, all legislation passed by the

Australian government had to be ratified by the British government in London. To circumvent this opposition, the Australian government had removed any explicit references to race. In its place, a controlling mechanism was inserted instead, that an immigrant needed to pass a dictation test that could be given in any European language as decided at any time by any immigration officer.

"The Mongolian Octopus" cartoon, The Bulletin, 1886, National Museum of Australia

Australian pineapples being advertised for their 'white Australian' qualities, although they were most probably sewn, tended and harvested by South Pacific Islanders.

Although the British government was displeased with the legislation, it decided not to intervene. Although there were many politicians from both sides of Australian politics that supported the White-Australia Policy, there was one strong voice by Tasmanian Free-Trade Party member, Donald Cameron, who stated:

"No race on ... this earth has been treated in a more shameful manner than have the Chinese ... They were forced at the point of a bayonet to admit Englishmen ... into China. Now if we compel them to admit our people ... why in the name of justice should we refuse to admit them here?"

Following the Immigration Act 1901, the Australian parliament passed the Pacific Islanders Labourers Act 1901, the result of which led to the deportation of about 7,500 South Pacific Islanders from Queensland plantations.

Australia was not the only country to enforce a policy of 'white' domination. In 1896, South Africa passed laws where all Africans were required to wear a badge and required a special pass to travel. In 1905, the General Pass Regulations Act denied Africans the vote and limited them to fixed areas. Further, in the United States of America, in 1896, the Plessy v Ferguson Supreme Court case upheld a Louisiana law that required segregation of "persons of colour" on railroad cars. This was later applied to schools, hotels, restaurants, and other establishments until 1954, when the decision was reversed in Brown v Board of Education. None of this mitigates the shame upon Australia for letting the White Australia Policy occur.

The White Australia Policy continued for over 50 years. It began to fall apart after a surge in migration to Australia after the Second World War and was fully dismantled by the Holt government in 1966.

The dictation test, as a controlling mechanism, was not only used against non-European peoples but also to keep out European political dissidents. Such was the noted case in 1934 of Egon Erwin Kisch, a radical Czechoslovakian journalist.

Egon Erwin Kisch (1885-1948)

Kisch was born into a wealthy, German-speaking Jewish family in Prague. He took an interest in crime and studied journalism then began writing for the Prague-based newspaper, Bohemia. During the First World War, he fought in the Austro-Hungarian army but was imprisoned for his letters that exposed and criticised the way the Austrians were fighting the war. He was imprisoned and later emerged as radical in the failed Vienna revolution of 1918. He became a communist in 1919. From 1921 to 1930, Kisch worked as a journalist in Berlin, and often spoke publicly about his communist views and against fascism.

In 1933, following the burning of the Berlin parliament building, the Reichstag Fire, Kisch was arrested and sent to Spandau Prison; however, as a Czechoslovakian citizen, he was released but expelled from Germany. He sailed to Britain but was refused entry to land because of his political views. In 1934, Kisch sailed to Australia as a delegate to the All-Australian Congress Against War and Fascism. Due to the ban placed on him in Britain, Kisch was refused entry at both Fremantle and Melbourne. In desperation, Kisch threw himself off the ship in Melbourne and landed on the dock breaking his leg.

Although bundled back onto the ship, the Australian left-wing politics went into overdrive. By the time the ship arrived in Sydney, its captain was charged with illegally detaining Kisch. Justice Evatt, then a High Court Judge (1930-1940), Australian Attorney General (1941-1949) and later Leader of the Australian Labor Party (1950-1960) ordered his release. Upon his release, Kisch was re-arrested and under the Immigration Act forced to take the dictation test. Kisch, a well-educated international journalist, spoke many European languages and passed a few of the dictation tests. One can only guess that he was given multiple tests in different European languages to achieve a particular political aim by the authorities. Finally, the immigration officer, from northern Scotland, decided to run a dictation test in Scottish Gaelic, spoken by 1% of Scots. English is the major language in Scotland, as it is for all of Britain. Kisch failed the test. The case went to the High Court and the case against Kisch was thrown out. In February 1935, Kisch spoke to 18,000 people on the Sydney Domain about the dangers of Hitler's regime and of future war.

During the war, Kisch lived in Mexico then returned to Prague after the war, where he died two years later. Since the war, Kisch's work has been lauded and in 1977, Stern, a German magazine, founded the

Egon Erwin Kisch Prize in his honour. Kisch also appears as a minor character in Frank Hardy's Power Without Glory (1950).

Kisch in Melbourne in 1934. State Library, NSW.

Picture of Kisch taken at Sydney Domain, speaking to 18,000. State Library, NSW.

The Stolen Generations

Donald Cameron stated that, "No race on ... this earth has been treated in a more shameful manner than have the Chinese...", yet even he did not account for the plight of the Australian Aboriginal people. When the First Fleet arrived in Australia in 1788, the Aboriginal population was estimated to range from 300,000 to 1,000,000 people, the median point being 650,000. By federation, the number had declined to less than 100,000 and is referred to by many as the 'Australian Holocaust', the genocide of the Australian Aboriginal people.

In 1889, an early settler, Samuel McLeod wrote:

"On arriving at Roebourne (Pilbara, W.A.) we saw gangs of unfortunate Aborigines chained to wheelbarrows with bullock chains ... The effect of the chains can be imagined in a climate where the stones get so hot they cannot be handled. The sight was too painful for most of us from a free land."

However, the oppression and discrimination extended past the settlers and was entrenched within the executive and judiciary of government. In 1905, a Western Australian Royal Commission on The Condition of the Natives by Dr Walter Roth presented to both Houses of Parliament, wrote:

"Cattle killing is the chief offence for which natives are being sentenced in the northern parts of the State; indeed, the portion it bears to other crimes committed by them is about 90 per cent ... In connection with the arrest of Aborigines accused of this crime, your Commissioner has received evidence which demonstrates a most brutal and outrageous

condition of affairs... Blacks may be arrested without instructions, authority or information...

Not knowing how many blacks he is going to arrest, the police can only take chains sufficient for about 15 natives; if a large number are reported guilty, he will take chains to hold from about twenty-five to thirty. Chains ... are fixed to the neck. Children from fourteen to sixteen years are neck-chained..., chains are used for female natives not only at night, but sometimes during the day. These women are the unwilling witnesses arrested illegally for the Crown."

A neck-chained gang of Aboriginal women at Wyndham, circa 1900. The J.S. Battye Library

Chained gang, Wyndham Police Station, East Kimberley, Western Australia, 1905

As early as the 19th Century, colonial authorities were realising that the Aboriginal people were headed for extinction and that action was needed. Unfortunately, their decision was to take away Aboriginal children from their parents, placing them in church-run missions.

In 1869, the Victorian Aboriginal Protection Act included the earliest legislation allowing authorities to remove children from their parents. In 1897, the Queensland government passed the Aboriginals Protection and Restriction of the Sale of Opium Act.

In 1909, the South Australian Protector of Aborigines lobbied for the power to remove Aboriginal children without a court hearing. In 1915, the New South Wales Aborigines Protection Amending Act allowed for the removal of Aboriginal children without having to establish in court that they were neglected. These were extended under the authority of various Acts in each of the State governments after federation.

The removal of children applied to 'half-caste' or mixed-race children. It was thought by the authorities that 'mixed race' children could be trained to work and assimilate into a white society, and that 'full-blood' Aboriginal children had no way of sustaining themselves and were doomed to extinction. It was conducted between 1905 to 1967, although there is evidence of it still occurring into the 1970s. It is estimated that at least 100,000 children were removed from their parents.

Each of the states had their institutions. Some of these included the Moore River Native Settlement and Beagle Bay Mission in Western Australia, the Doomadgee Aboriginal mission in Queensland, the Ebenezer Mission in Victoria, the Wellington Valley Mission in New South Wales, and the Garden Point Mission in the Northern Territory.

Recounts and narratives of the Stolen Generations and the removal of these children from their parents can be found in the Anthony Hill novel 'The Burnt Stick' and the Phillip Noyce film 'Rabbit-Proof Fence', based on the book by Doris Pilkington Garimara, among other excellent books, plays and films.

A new capital city — Canberra

In the negotiations that preceded federation, the delegates from New South Wales were not prepared to agree unless Sydney or New South Wales was recognised in the federation. At the time, in the 1890s, Melbourne was Australia's largest city in population, having overtaken Sydney during the Gold Rush era. A compromise was made for a new capital city for Australia that, according to section 125 of the Constitution, was in New South Wales but at least 100 miles from Sydney.

As a result of survey work conducted by Charles Scrivener in 1908, Canberra was chosen as the site of Australia's new capital city, narrowly defeating the town of Dalgety, near the New South Wales / Victorian border. The process began in 1911 when the New South Wales government ceded about 2,500 square kilometres along the Molonglo River to the Australian government. The Federal Capital Territory, later Australian Capital Territory was created.

Prior to European settlement, the greater Canberra area had been home to the Ngunawal and Ngarigo peoples. It is estimated that there were at least 300 to 400 Aboriginal people living in the Canberra area prior to European settlement. Archaeological evidence indicates that the area had been inhabited for over 20,000 years. The area was first explored by Europeans — Charles Smith, Joseph Wild and James Vaughan — in 1820. European settlement of the Canberra area began in 1824, when Joshua Moore was granted a 'ticket of occupation' for 2,000 acres in the area covering today's Civic and Dickson suburbs. A building was erected on what is now the Acton Peninsula named 'Canberry Cottage'. For his efforts, he was given another 1,000 acres.

The name, Canberra, Canberry or Camberry, meaning 'meeting place' was given by its traditional owners, as were Yarrowlumla and Tageranong. In 1843, the estate was acquired by Arthur Jeffreys, who replaced the cottage with the larger Acton House, which later was demolished in 1911 for the old Canberra Hospital and later, in 2001, the National Museum of Australia.

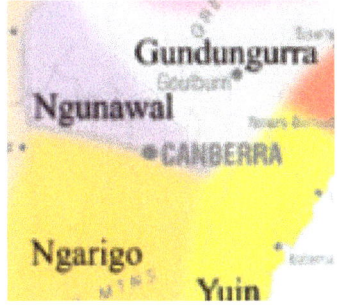

The Indigenous surrounds of the greater Canberra area according to the AIATSIS map.

Picture of the old Acton House, circa 1900. National Library of Australia.

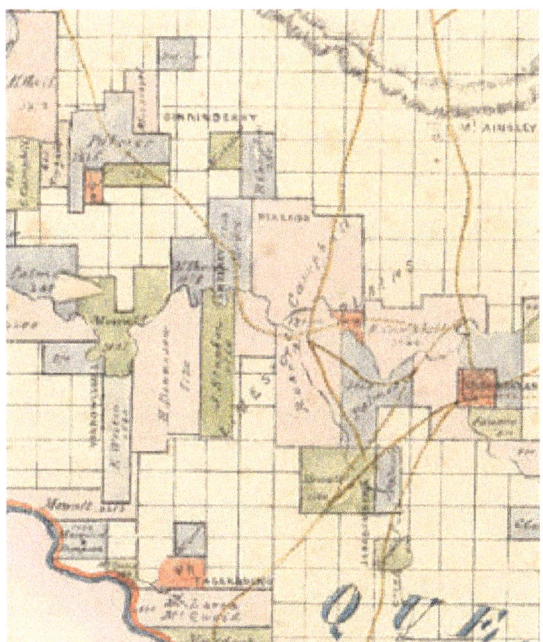

Map of Canberra area, circa 1843.

Photo of the National Museum of Australia on the site of the old Acton House.

An international competition held in 1911 was the process for designing the look of the new capital city in Canberra. The winning design was created by Chicago architects Walter Burley Griffin and Marion Mahony Griffin. Of their plan, he famously remarked:

"I have planned a city that is not like any other in the world. I have planned it not in a way that I expected any government authorities in the world would accept. I have planned an ideal city — a city that meets my ideal of the city of the future."

The design was based on a large triangle with two axes that straddled a water axis. The Parliamentary Triangle ran from the old Parliament House on Capital Hill, along Commonwealth Avenue, to the Civic Centre around City Hill, along Constitution Avenue to the Defence Precinct on Russell Hill, then along Kings Avenue back to Capital Hill. Many government buildings and offices, including National Library and High Court are located in the triangle. The design is said to have been inspired by the work of their fellow-Chicago architect, Danial Burnham, in his 1909 Plan of Chicago.

The man-made lake that Canberra is built on is called Lake Burley Griffin.

The Griffin design for the new city of Canberra, circa 1912.

Walter Burley Griffin and
Marion Mahony Griffin

In 28 years, the Griffins designed over 350 buildings. They were heavily influenced by the Prairie School, otherwise known as the Chicago group. In the 1920s, the Griffins pioneered the 'Knitlock Construction Method' in Australia, also used by Frank Lloyd Wright in the United States of America.

The World's First Labour Government 1904

John Christian Watson (1867-1941), born John Christian Tanck in Valparaiso, Chile, was an Australian politician. He served as Australia's third Prime Minister. He formed Australia's first Labour Party government as well as the world's first Labour Party government at a national level. His parents separated in 1869, and he went with his mother to New Zealand, where she was re-married to a British-born George Watson, and attended Oamaru State School in North Otago

Watson emigrated to Australia in 1886, at nineteen. He became known as Chris Watson and was active in the typographical union and a founding member of the Labour Electoral League of New South Wales. Watson was elected President of the Sydney Trades and Labour Council and President of the Labour Party Conference by age twenty-four. He assisted in pioneering the Caucus solidarity system, was one of the first Labour members of the New South Wales Parliament, was elected to the first national parliament in 1901, and appointed as Labour's leader in the House of Representatives. Upon successfully defeating Deakin's draconian Conciliation and Arbitration Bill, Deakin resigned as Prime Minister and Watson formed a minority government in 1904. Although praised by many, including Deakin, for his 'Soundness of judgement, clearness of argument and fairness to opponents', Watson's minority government lasted only four months.

Watson later resigned from parliament in 1907 and was expelled from the Australian Labor Party in 1916 for voting in favour of conscription during the First World War. (Note, Labor dropped the 'u' from its name in 1912.) Later, Watson went into business, becoming the director of several big companies, eventually being appointed as chairman to the board of oil giant Ampol.

*Chris Watson,
National Library of Australia*

Mawson and the Antarctic

Legend of the Antarctic in western history finds its origins in ancient times. Marinus of Tyre, a Hellenised Phoenician in the 2nd Century AD, is attributed with the term 'Antarctic', meaning the opposite of the Arctic, south pole to north pole. The term became intertwined with 'Terra Australis Incognita', the unknown southern land or continent.

Similar to the case of the European discovery of Australia, there is record of other Europeans arriving in Antarctica prior to James Cook passing through the Antarctic Circle in 1773 on his second great voyage. According to Dutch maritime records, Dirck Gerritsz Pomp at around 1600 was the first Dutch sailor to visit Antarctica, as well as being the first Dutchman to visit Japan and China. The Spanish sailor Gabriel de Castilla claimed to have sailed past Antartica in 1606. Other explorers to encounter the greater- Antarctic zone were Anthony de la Roche (1675), Edmond Hailey (1700), Charles Bouvet de Lozier (1739), Yves Joseph Kerguelen (1771), James Cook (1773) and William Smith (1819). However, the first confirmed sighting of Antarctica was a Russian expedition by the Imperial Navy, led by the Admirals von Bellingshausen and Mikhail Lazarev in 1820. This was followed by what is coined the 'Heroic Age of Antarctic Exploration'. In 1905, an expedition by the British William Spiers Bruce set up the first permanent base on the Antarctic continent. Notably, the first to the South Pole, saw a race between the Norwegian expedition of Roald Amundsen and that of the British Robert Falcon Scott. Amundsen won the race on December 14, 1911. Scott arrived at the South Pole a month later, but he did not survive the return journey.

Between 1911-14, the Australasian Antarctic Expedition, led by Douglas Mawson, an Australian geologist, explorer and academic, concentrated on mapping and survey work along the coastline from Cape Adare to Mt Grauss. Mawson had served in an earlier expedition by the British Ernest Shackleton (1907-09). Mawson is credited with discovering Commonwealth Bay, the Ninnis Glacier, Mertz Glacier, and Queen Mary Land. Due to poor weather conditions, Mawson's expedition could not be collected by ship, so it was forced to remain for another year, which became a great survival story in David Roberts' book, 'Alone on the Ice: The Greatest Survival Story in the History of Exploration'.

For his efforts, Mawson was knighted and received a Founder's Gold Medal by the Royal Geographical Society, and the David Livingstone Centenary Medal from the American Geographical Society. Mawson appeared on the Australian $100 note. Mawson Station in Antarctica is named after him. Mawson's artefacts from his expedition are permanently displayed in the South Australian Museum.

Mawson in 1914, State Library of South Australia

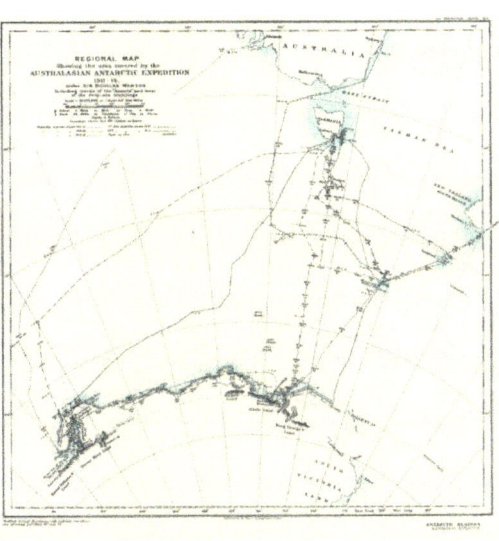

Map of Mawson expedition (1911-14), published by Royal Geographical Society

Mawson Station, Antarctica

Mawson on Australian $100 note

The First World War

For the second half of the 19th Century, Europe had been seething under growing social, economic and political pressure. This pressure had brought a number of revolutions across Europe and threatened the old dynastic empires. Consequently, the major empires formed into two competing alliances, the 'Triple Entente' of the British, French and Russian empires on one side, against the 'Triple Alliance' of the German, and Austro-Hungarian empires and Italy. Later, Italy withdrew and changed sides, and the Turkish (Ottoman) Empire replaced it. The world economic crisis of the 1890s, which had also affected Australia, put further pressure on the politics of Europe.

1914 Europe

Cartoon depicting the Triple Entente v Triple Alliance

The explosion of war broke out in August 1914, when the heir to the Austro-Hungarian Empire, Archduke Franz Ferdinand, and his wife Sofie were assassinated in the Bosnian capital of Sarajevo by a Serbian national, Gavrilo Princip. Princip and his accomplices were arrested. Austria declared war on Serbia, then the alliance system kicked in. Serbia was allied to Russia, so Russia declared war on Austria. Germany was allied to Austria, so declared war on Russia. France, allied to Russia, declared war on Germany and Austria. When German troops crossed the Belgian frontier in a 'flanking' invasion of France, Britain declared war on Germany. Turkey, allied to Germany, declared war on Russia, France and Britain. When war was declared, Australia and New Zealand, as part of the British Empire, declared war on its side. The war was to last over four years, August 1914 to November 1918. The total number of military and civilian casualties in the First World war numbered 40 million. The war also resulted in revolutions that ended the Russian (Romanov), Austrian (Hapsburg), Turkish (Ottoman), and German (Hohenzollern) empires and dynasties.

During the First World War, Australia participated on land in three major locations, Gallipoli, France and Palestine. Its first action was taking possession of German New Guinea in September 1914. However, its first notable confrontation was at sea near the Cocos (Keeling) Islands in the Indian Ocean in November 1914. The HMAS Sydney was part of an escort for the convoy of Australian troops from Albany, Western Australia, to Egypt. On the way, Captain John Glossop, commanding the Sydney, received a distress call from the transmitting station on Direction Island that the German light cruiser, SMS Emden, was attacking it. The Sydney sped away from the escort to meet the Emden. On November 9, 1914, the Sydney engaged fire with the Emden, commanded by Captain von Muller, and forced the Emden to beach itself and surrender. In the battle, 670 rounds of ammunition were fired, with 100 hits. The Sydney had been hit 16 times with three Australians killed, while the Emden was hit 84 times with 134 Germans killed.

Picture of the HMAS Sydney, circa 1914

Captain John Glossop

Captain John Glossop

John Collings Taswell Glossop (1871-1934) born in England. He served in the Royal Navy from 1884 to 1921. Initially serving in the Channel Fleet, Glossop visited Australia for the first time as a midshipman aboard the HMS Orlando. Glossop served in a handful of ships aboard the Australian Squadron before returning to England in 1900. In 1902, he was given his first command, the gunboat HMS Lizard. Glossop returned to Australia in 1908, in command of the cruiser HMS Prometheus. In 1913, Glossop was transferred upon request to the Royal Australian Navy and was given command of the new Australian Navy cruiser HMAS Sydney. In November 1914, the HMAS Sydney fought and captured the German cruiser SMS Emden. In 1915, Glossop was awarded a Companion of the Order of the Bath (CB), the Japanese Order of the Rising Sun, and the French Legion of Honour. In 1920, Glossop reverted to the Royal Navy. In 1921, he was promoted to Rear Admiral, but retired the next day. In 1926, Glossop was appointed Vice Admiral on the retired list.

Gallipoli (1915)

The First World War opened with a series of open battles as Germany invaded France through Belgium and fought a strategically defensive war against a Russian army that had superior numbers but had inferior weaponry. By the end of 1914, on the western front, the French, with British assistance, fought the Germans to a stalemate and both sides dug into defensive lines of trenches that ran from the English Channel, through Belgium and France, to the Swiss border. The same stalemate had occurred on the eastern front as the Germans, Austrians and Russians also dug into long trenches. Russia also had the problem that it lacked for modern industry and needed to be supplied with weapons from France and Britain, but the only open ports were the northern ports in the Arctic Sea, which were closed during Winter. Russia, France and Britain desperately needed access to a Russian warm-water port. Russia had its warm-water Black Sea ports, but access was blocked by the Turkish Empire that controlled the Bosphorus Strait that linked the Mediterranean Sea with the Black Sea.

The Gallipoli campaign was designed by Winston Churchill, then the British First Lord of the Admiralty. Its aim was to open the Bosphorus Strait, otherwise known as the Dardanelles, by a combined sea and land attack. The British and French navies would sail up the strait and attack its port-city of Istanbul, while British and French soldiers would attack the land peninsula that ran along the western side of the strait, the Gallipoli Peninsula. This was to be an amphibious assault, sea and land, which was extremely difficult, even if everything went right. The French and British spent over four months in Egypt training for the campaign. However, few things went right in the Gallipoli Campaign, and it was a massive defeat for the British, French, and its allies the Australians and New Zealanders.

The naval assault on the forts along the Bosphorus by the French and British navies in February 1915 did not succeed, as the Turks had already mined the waters. The navies made another attempt in March, which resulted in the French Bouvet, the HMS Irresistible and the HMS Ocean being sunk, with other battleships, the HMS Inflexible, and the French ships, Suffren and Galois, being badly damaged. The naval assault up the strait to Istanbul was called off. Now it was the turn of the amphibious assault on the Gallipoli Peninsula from the sea. However, the amphibious assault was not planned to occur until April, which gave the Turks an extra four weeks to build roads, redoubts, and trenches, and deploy soldiers and artillery, in preparation for an imminent attack. That extra four weeks would be crucial in its outcome.

The ANZACs

The first landing of troops on the Gallipoli Peninsula began on 25 April 1915. The Mediterranean Expeditionary Force (MEF) led by the British General Sir Ian Hamilton numbered 78,000 troops. It landed on five beaches along the peninsula from Cape Helles in the south, to 12 miles north-west at what became known as Anzac Cove. The MEF would be opposed by the 60,000-strong Turkish 5th Army, under the command of the German General Liman von Sanders. Hamilton planned to land two divisions of the Australian and New Zealand Army Corps (ANZACs) under General Sir William Birdwood, at night on a beach just south of ANZAC Cove that had a gentle rise up to a low ridge. Unfortunately, the sea current pushed the landing boats a mile and a half north to a narrow beach under steep cliffs. When the troops landed, there was little resistance but, in the night, the troops became confused and made little headway on the hills above the beach. The Turkish divisional commander, Colonel Mustafa Kemal Bey, later Kemal Ataturk, on his own initiative, led an immediate counterattack that swept the ANZACS back onto the ridges around the beach. Birdwood and his divisional commanders, Generals Bridges and Godley, recommended a withdrawal. Hamilton overruled them, and there the ANZACs dug trenches and caves around and into the cliffs to shelter from the Turkish fire. My maternal grandfather, Lt. Dr. Michael Southwick (Sorokiewitch), aged 21 years and only graduated as a surgeon the November before, served as one of "Kitchener's 100", as a British army surgeon on the hospital ships, then the island and Lesbos, operating on and often amputating the limbs of the wounded soldiers.

A second attempt was made in August 1915, with reinforcements, and a new amphibious assault was made further north at Suvla Bay; however, it too failed to make any ground. In December, the Allied command decided to withdraw from Gallipoli. The withdrawal was much better planned and implemented than the assault. Not one soldier was killed during the evacuation.

Map of Gallipoli location, Australian War Memorial

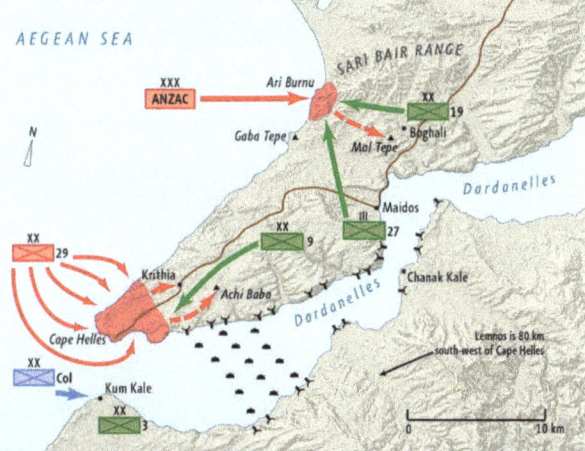

Map of Gallipoli invasion, New Zealand History

View on the trenches from the beach, Christchurch City Libraries

Overall, casualties were shared equally between the Turks and the Allies, each side lost about 50,000 killed and 100,000 wounded. Of the killed, almost 9,000 were Australians. There was much bravery by all soldiers from both sides at Gallipoli. One story is of the Australian stretcher-bearer named John Simpson Kirkpatrick and his donkey, collecting and carrying wounded soldiers from the valley to the medical station at Anzac Cove, until he too was killed in May 1915. The ANZACS were refitted and shipped to France to fight on the western front. JFC Fuller, the British officer and historian, wrote of Gallipoli:

"...there was no judgement; no clear strategic analysis of the initial problem; no proper calculation of its tactical requirements; and no true attempt to balance the means at hand with the end in view."

France (1916-18) — Monash

The Australian soldiers began arriving in France from April 1916. By June, all five divisions had been deployed south of Armentieres as part of the British 4th Army, under the command of the British General Rawlinson. They arrived just in time to participate in one of the bloodiest battles in western military history, the Battle of the Somme. The Australian 5th Division attacked the German position at Fromelles in July, suffering 5,500 casualties. The Australian 1st Division attacked Posieres two days later and suffered 5,000 casualties. It was relieved by the Australian 2nd Division, which attacked Mouquet Farm in August, suffering 6,300 casualties. The Battle of the Somme lasted until November 1916. Total casualties on both sides numbered over 1,000,000. Of those casualties, 20,000 were Australian. Through 1917, the Australians fought at Bullencourt (March), Messines (June), Ypres (September), Passchendale (October). Some had been limited successes, but they had suffered another 55,000 casualties.

John Monash

General Sir John Monash (1865-1931) born in Melbourne, was an Australian of German-Jewish descent. He was schooled at Scotch College and graduated a Master of Engineering in 1893 at Melbourne University. His father owned the Jerilderie General Store and Monash claimed that he met Ned Kelly there in 1879. Monash worked as a civil engineer and, in business, pioneered the Monier method of building roads and bridges with reinforced concrete. The military was Monash's hobby, and he served as part of the militia (army reserve) from university through to the First World War. It was on a visit to Australia that the British General Sir Ian Hamilton befriended Monash, which was to reward Monash in the future.

Upon the outbreak of war, Monash became an officer and was soon placed in command of Australia's 4th Brigade and served at Gallipoli. However, his early military years were clouded under the rumour that he was a German spy, and his performances as an officer were being continually criticised behind his back by Australian journalists Charles Bean and Keith Murdoch (father of Rupert Murdoch).

Roland Perry writes that Bean and Murdoch sent their misconceived reports to Australian Prime Minister Billy Hughes, who travelled to London to 'sack' Monash. Instead, when he arrived, Hughes received reports from the British military office that lauded Monash's planning, implementation and other military talents, hence changing Hughes' mind.

After Gallipoli, while Monash was training the Australian 3rd Division in England, Hamilton introduced him to King George V. When his division was deployed on the western front, his division's training came to the fore. With each battle — Messines, Broodseinde, Passchendaele — Monash's reputation for detailed planning and implementation was growing. 1918 was Monash's year. Another success at Villers-Bretonneux, Monash won the full confidence of the British Staff and was given authority to plan general offensives for the British Army. He was also winning over the confidence of his previous critic Charles Bean, who wrote that Monash was more effective the higher he rose, in order to use his greater capacity for planning, organisation, technology and tactics.

General Monash during WW1

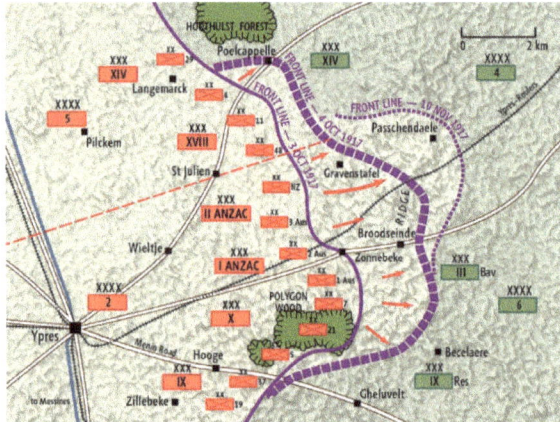

Battles of Broodseinde and Passchendale on map, New Zealand History

Statue of Sir John Monash, King's Domain, Melbourne

Monash was also given command of all the Australian divisions, which were finally put together into the one Australian Corps. It was the largest individual corps on the Western Front. Monash went to work again on tactics combining the use of logistics, infantry, artillery, airplanes, and tanks. This meant having the airplanes drop supplies of food and ammunition at forward targets, so when the infantry arrived, they could be resupplied.

In June 1918, Monash began a golden run at Hamel. In August, he won at Amiens. It was the first decisive Allied victory of the war. The German chief commander General Ludendorff described it as the day that Germany lost the war. King George V came to the battlefield and bestowed Monash as a Knight Commander of the Order of the Bath (KCB), the first time a British monarch had done so in 200 years.

At Chuignes, Mont St Quentin, Peronne and Hargicourt, Monash continued his winning run. By October, Monash was planning and implementing operations for over 200,000 men, including 50,000 new American reinforcements. In the Battle of the Hindenburg Line, the Allies smashed the Germans and broke its last line of defence. The next month, Germany surrendered.

For his efforts in the war, Monash was awarded with the Knight Grand Cross of the Order of St Michael and St George, Knight Commander of the Order of the Bath, Grand Officer of the Legion of Honour (France), the Croix de Guerre (Belgium), and the Distinguished Service Medal (USA). Although the war had ended, Monash was ordered to remain in London. Roland Perry speculated that the Hughes government feared the outcome if Monash returned and ran against the government in the oncoming election. Once he did return, Monash worked to increase the benefits to ex-servicemen and supported the influence of the Returned Service League. Later, Monash was to lead the State Electricity Commission of Victoria and was appointed Vice-Chancellor of the University of Melbourne.

Palestine (1917-18)

After Gallipoli, while the Australian infantry forces went to France, the mounted forces stayed in Egypt as part of the British forces, under General Allenby. He was set with the task of invading the Turkish Empire through Palestine. In command of the Australian Mounted Division was Harry Chauvel.

Chauvel and Beersheba

General Sir Henry (Harry) George Chauvel (1865-1945) born in Tabulam, New South Wales, was a soldier, and son of a grazier. Born of his father's 5,000-hectare property (12,000 acres), Chauvel was educated at Sydney Grammar School, then Toowoomba Grammar School, after his father sold his property due to drought and purchased a smaller property in Queensland. After touring Europe in 1889, Chauvel joined the Queensland Mounted Infantry. In 1899, he commanded a company of Queensland Mounted Infantry that relieved the Siege of Kimberley. By the end of the Boer War, Chauvel's successes had earned him a Companion of the Order of St Michael and St George (CMG). After the Boer War and federation, Chauvel became an officer in the mounted section of the newly formed Australian army. Over the next few years, he was given the responsibility for training new mounted infantry units across Australia.

Upon the outbreak of the First World War, Chauvel went to Egypt commanding the First Light Horse Brigade. In May 1915, the brigade was sent as dismounted infantry reinforcements to Gallipoli, and was placed, with the Monash's 4th Brigade, in Godley's 2nd Division. In 1915, Chauvel was twice promoted, Brigadier General in July, then Major General in November, where he was also appointed Companion of the Order of the Bath.

In March 1916, Chauvel assumed command of the Australian

Mounted Division, located on the Suez Canal defences. At the Battle of Romani, in August 1916, Chauvel and his mounted division achieved the first decisive victory against the Turks. At Magdhaba, in December 1916, it was Chauvel's plan of attack that won the battle. In January 1917, Chauvel achieved another important victory at Rafa, upon which he was awarded a Knight Commander of the Order of St Michael and St George.

In March 1917, the First Battle of Gaza, Chauvel's cavalry charge took the town, but he was ordered to withdraw due to lack of supporting troops. In April, the Second Battle of Gaza did not achieve success and the commanding officer, the Canadian General Dobell, was replaced. However, Chauvel was promoted to lieutenant general and given command of the newly formed Desert Mounted Corps, under the overall command of the British General Allenby.

Australian soldiers riding through Jerusalem 1918, prisoners in tow.

In October 1917, at the Battle of Beersheba, Chauvel and his Desert Mounted Corps played a critical role in a battle that 'went down to the wire'. The Desert Mounted Corps won the battle in what is recorded as the last of history's great and successful cavalry charges. Films that recorded this famous cavalry charge at Beersheba were 'Forty Thousand Horsemen', made by Harry's nephew Charles Chauvel in 1940, and 'The Lighthorsemen' by Simon Wincer in 1987. For his victory at Beersheba, and for the subsequent capture of Jerusalem, Chauvel was appointed a Knight Commander of the Order of the Bath, the same award given later to General Monash.

In September 1918, the Desert Mountain Corps formed part of a surprise attack at the Battle of Megiddo, destroying the Turkish army in three days, capturing the Golan Heights and Damascus by October 1st, then capturing Aleppo by October 25th. Turkey surrendered five days later.

In 1919, Chauvel was awarded a Knight Grand Cross of the Order of St Michael and St George and the French Military Cross. At his investiture in London, King George V dubbed him 'Sir Harry'.

Painting of Lt Gen. Harry Chauvel by James Peter Quinn, 1919

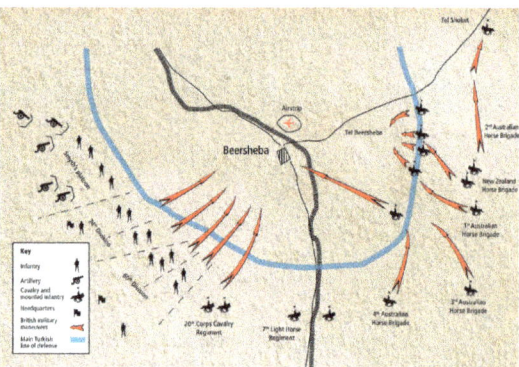

Battle of Beersheba map; World Maps; cavalry attack from the right.

The Charge of the Australian Light Horse at Beersheba, 1917; painted by George Lambert in 1920, at the Palestine Gallery in the Australian War Memorial.

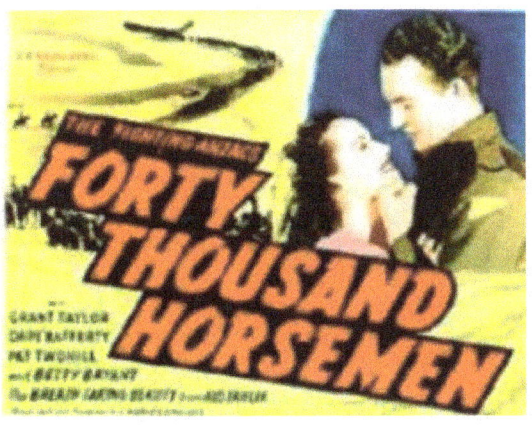

Film poster of 'Forty Thousand Horsemen' (1940), by Charles Chauvel, starring Grant Taylor and Chips Rafferty. (Australian War Memorial)

World War One for Australia

The First World War, the Great War or, more ironically, the "War to end all wars" gave Australia a sense of identity. Australia had gone to war in its own name, though not independently. During the course of the war, its armed forces had evolved into a unified force, the Australia Corps, and gained a strong reputation as courageous and innovative fighters. Australia was beginning to weave a story, a history of its own.

Between 1914 and 1919, over 400,000 Australians served in the Australian army during World War One, fighting in allegiance with Britain. Of these, over 330,000 served overseas. Countless more Australians enlisted directly into the British army. The Australian army suffered over 60,000 killed, and another 150,000 wounded. Furthermore, 130,000 horses had left Australia to serve in World War One. Due to Australia's strict equine laws, only one came home. Only Sandy, the horse of Major-General Sir William Bridges, who was killed at Gallipoli, returned to Australia. The other surviving horses were either sold at auction in Palestine or France, or put down.

Australians saw combat in many places — the capture of German New Guinea, the Mesopotamian campaign, Gallipoli, the Senussi campaign in northern Africa, Sinai and Palestine, France and Belgium,

Persia, the Caucasus campaign, the Egyptian Revolution of 1919, and in the Russian Civil War following its revolution.

During the First World War, the Australian Government under Prime Minister Billy Hughes decided to put the conscription issue to the Australian people as a referendum, first in 1916, then again in 1917. Both times the referendums were defeated.

Chinese Australians in World War One

When war was declared, the Chinese-Australian community rallied behind the flag and over two hundred of their community enlisted. About half of these came from Victoria. Of the two hundred-odd Chinese Australian solders, over forty died.

Lt. Frank Currie   *Pte. Hugh Currie*

One noted Chinese-Australian soldier, Benjamin Moy Ling, stated: "If Australia is good enough to live in, it is good enough to fight for." Benjamin Moy Ling served as a sapper in the Australian army.

William Edward "Billy" Sing was also a noted Chinese-Australian soldier, especially as a sniper in the Gallipoli Campaign. However, after the war, Billy fell on hard times and died in obscure poverty.

The Currie brothers of Bendigo in Victoria fought with distinction during the First World War. They were the grandsons of Lee Jacgung, a gold miner, originally from Guangzhou, then California, arriving in Victoria in the 1850s. Lt. Frank Currie, initially an R.A.N. seaman, served as pilot on the western front through 1917 and 1918. After the war, he lived in Melbourne until 1986, aged 92. His brother, Hugh Currie, served from 1916 to 1918 with the 60th Battalion of infantry on the Western Front but was killed in action.

Indigenous Australians in World War One

At the outbreak of war, large numbers of Aboriginal males came forward to enlist in the Australian army, even though, according to the law, because they were not descended from Europeans, they were exempted from military service. It is estimated that over 1,000 indigenous Australians fought in the war. In fact, they were paid the same as non-indigenous Australian soldiers and served under the same conditions. Some vainly hoped that this equality of conditions might prevail in Australia after the war. Sadly, upon returning to Australia, they returned to the same inequality and prejudice.

Noted indigenous Australian soldiers during the war were:

Private Richard Martin, born on Stradbroke Island, Queensland; served in Egypt 1916, and France and Belgium in 1917-18. As Aboriginal Australians were prevented from enlisting, Martin volunteered as a New Zealander with five years-experience in the Light Horse. He was killed while attempting to halt one of the last German offensives of the war at Dernancourt in March 1918.

Corporal Harry Thorpe MM, born near Lakes Entrance, Victoria; served in France and was wounded at Pozieres and Bullecourt. He received the Military Medal and was promoted to corporal but was killed in action in August 1918.

Douglas Grant was born into a traditional community in northern

Queensland, but was adopted by Robert Grant, a Scottish scientist and immigrant. Grant enlisted but was initially barred from leaving Australia by the Aboriginal Protection Board. Enlisting again, he succeeded but was captured at Bullecourt in April 1917. At war's end, Grant was repatriated to Australia, resumed as a draughtsman and factory worker, lobbied for Aboriginal rights, and became active in returned service affairs. He died in 1951, aged 65, and is buried in Botany Cemetery, Sydney.

Australia after the war

The end of the war brought a new era of optimism to Australia. It also brought higher prosperity to many non-indigenous Australians. National and state governments provided medical treatment, financial support, and housing schemes for non-indigenous war veterans.

However, many returned soldiers were haunted by the nightmares of war and suffered mental depression and illness with 'shell shock" and what we know now as post-traumatic stress disorder. Great numbers of returned servicemen and women were unable to cope with life after the war and were taking their own lives. Something had to be done and "into the breach" stepped the RSL.

The formation of the Returned Services League (RSL)

The Returned Services League was formed in 1916 for the care of returned soldiers. It was initially known as the Returned Sailors and Soldiers Imperial League of Australia. Its name was expanded to include Airmen in 1940. However, the name was shortened to Returned Services League of Australia (RSL) in 1983. After the First World War, it grew into creating and administering programs for the caring, wellbeing, commemoration and compensation of returned Australian war veterans and their dependents.

The Returned Services League were responsible for founding the ANZAC Day dawn services and the Remembrance Day commemorations. However, it was also seen as male-centric, conservative, Anglophilic and monarchist. Nevertheless, the RSL has worked actively for the rights and entitlement of ex-soldiers and their dependents and, in the last twenty years, has embraced a more inclusive approach, especially to ex-Vietnam veterans.

Gilbert Dyett and the RSL

Sir Gilbert Dyett (1891-1964) born in Bendigo, was the National President of the Returned Sailors and Soldiers Imperial League of Australia from 1919 to 1946. During the war, Dyett had served as a lieutenant in the Gallipoli campaign and was so badly wounded at Lone Pine that he was left for dead. As he could not walk, he was repatriated back to Bendigo and performed recruiting service with great rigour. It was under Dyett's presidency, the League focused its efforts on supporting returned soldiers. Dyett believed in a policy of 'patience, tact and diplomacy' and consequently gained many concessions on behalf of returned soldiers and their families from the Federal government. Dyett also served as Dominion President of the British Empire Services League from 1921 to 1946, and secretary of the Victorian Trotting and Racing Association from 1919 to 1949. He was awarded Companion of the Order of St Michael and St George in 1927 and Knight Bachelor in 1934.

ANZAC Day

Today, on April 25, ANZAC Day is commemorated by all; however, this was not always the case. In New Zealand, a half-day memorial was gazetted on 30 April 1915, the day that word arrived in New Zealand of the landing. In South Australia, 13 October 1915, Eight Hour Day (Labour Day) was renamed ANZAC Day. In Melbourne, 17 December 1915 was ANZAC Remembrance Day. However, April 25 was agreed by all and it was celebrated on that day from 1916. In London, over

2,000 ANZAC soldiers marched through the streets. In Egypt, General Monash paraded the troops. Marches were held all over Australia, where wounded soldiers were paraded in cars. In New Zealand, 2,000 people attended the service held in Rotorua.

Australians and New Zealanders are not the only ones to commemorate the Gallipoli campaign.

Pictured, left, is a celebratory bottle of 'Suvla', Gallipoli 100th anniversary 1915-2015 white wine. 'Suvla' is a Turkish family-owned winery located at Eceabat on the Gallipoli peninsula.

Picture of the August 1945, 'Victory in the Pacific' service at the Shrine in Melbourne.

After the war, attendance at ANZAC Day parades have had its 'highs and lows'. In 1919, after the soldiers had returned, attendances at each of the memorials in the capital cities numbered in the tens of thousands despite being affected by the 1919 Influenza epidemic, but after a few years these dropped dramatically as soldiers wanted to put the war behind them. In 1926, with the proposal of a new Shrine in Melbourne, attendances there leapt to 12,000, and with the attendance of the Prince Albert, Duke of York, later King George VI, 30,000 ex-soldiers poured into Melbourne. The Shrine in Melbourne was completed in 1934.

Spanish Flu

'Spanish Flu' was an influenza pandemic that passed through the soldiers on the Western Front and killed between 50 to 100 million people across the world and arrived in Australia in 1919, with the return of the soldiers. It was called 'Spanish Flu' not because it began in Spain, but because it was in Spain that it was first widely reported as an epidemic.

Initially, the Australian government acted against the 'flu' was to place incoming ships into quarantine. Of 323 vessels arriving in Australia, 174 carried the infection. Further, the states organised emergency hospitals, vaccination depots, ambulance services, medical staff, and raised public awareness. As medical researchers did not know what caused the infection, vaccines could only treat the secondary infections. Vaccines were initially imported. Later, the Commonwealth Serum Laboratories (CSL) was established to alleviate Australia's dependence on imported vaccines. During a six-month period in 1918/19, Australia produced three million free doses of vaccine.

About 40 percent of all Australians were infected and nearly 15,000 people in Australia died of the disease within a year. Australia's death-rate of 0.27% of population was one of the lowest death rates of any country during the epidemic.

The plight of Aboriginal veterans after the war

Unlike 'white' Australians, Aboriginal veterans returning from the war were ineligible and did not receive any benefits or programs that were available through the national and state governments. They weren't given access to medical treatment nor the soldier settlement program.

After the war, to make way for new housing schemes for 'non-indigenous' veterans, more Aboriginal people were being forcibly removed onto mission reserves and into government-run "assimilation" programs.

Immigration post war

Australia's immigration policies after federation, during the war and after took some interesting turns. The White Australia Policy was still in place, but the government saw a need to encourage immigration from Europe to maintain its connection to the United Kingdom and Europe.

Europe, itself, over the second half of the 19th Century was being torn by revolution and changing empires. As Prussian dominance of German states grew in the 1860s as a counter to its revolutions after 1848, so more German immigrants arrived in Australia, especially in South Australia. As Austria exerted greater control over south eastern Europe, so many displaced people from these regions opted to migrate to Australia. This was especially so with ethnic minorities. As nationalism grew, the identification with one's own nation and support for its interests, especially to the exclusion or detriment of minority interests, in the Eastern Orthodox Russian Empire, so its minority groups, especially Jews from what is now known as the Ukraine and Belarus, sought to avoid the violent pogroms, and were encouraged to migrate. It was during this time, in the early 1900s, my paternal great-grandfather, Chaim Myer Pahoff, a dairy farmer and his family migrated to Australia. Once established in Australia, according to Tess Schwartz, he was to sponsor forty Russian-Jewish families to Australia.

Internment and a wartime change in immigration priorities

During the First World War, Australia's views towards immigration changed dramatically. This war had been largely a European war with European enemies. Migrants from Germany and countries supporting Germany were now looked upon as enemies, even though they had lived in Australia for decades. German and Austrian citizens in Australia were required to report their addresses to the authorities. By February 1915, even those naturalised or born in Australia with German heritage had to report. Internment, imprisonment and confinement, was now used against these people. The Australian authorities chose to hold German and Austrian community leaders and any others deemed suspicious in internment. Camps were erected in state — Rottnest Island (WA), Torrens Island (SA), Enoggera (Qld), Langwarrin (Vic), Bruny Island (Tas), Holsworthy (NSW) and Bourke and Molonglo (Canberra). Over 5,000 German men, women and children were held in the Holsworthy camp alone. Rottnest Island held over 1,000. The men were separated from the women and children, causing great tension. During 1915, the Australian government chose to transfer all interned 'aliens' to the Holsworthy camp in N.S.W., causing further hardship and terror.

The idea for internment or concentration camps had been devised by the British to detain and hold German and Dutch leaders and their families in South Africa during the Boer Wars.

Further, European countries allied to Australia, whose citizens were residing in Australia, were looking to the Australian government to assist the return of these citizens so they could be drafted and serve in the war. When Italy changed it allegiance and joined Britain and France in the war, the Italian government directly approached the Australian government to send back their Italian citizens who had migrated to Australia so they could serve in the Italian army. Many in Australia objected to the government's policies as it discouraged Europeans from migrating to Australia and therefore put a growing "White Australia" at risk.

After the war, as revolutions had swept through Europe, those deemed to be revolutionaries or suspected of revolutionary activity, especially communists, were prohibited from migrating to Australia. However, it did bring some opportunities.

Revolution in Turkey and subsequent Turkish nationalism, led by Kemal Attaturk, the Turkish hero of Gallipoli, meant massacres of Pontic, Ionian and Cappadocian Greeks had occurred. These Greek communities had lived along the Black Sea and Mediterranean coasts of Turkey since ancient times for over two thousand years. Those Greeks surviving the Turkish massacres migrated, and many migrated to Australia. Thea Halo's "Not Even My Name" is an account of that genocide. Australia became a refuge for those displaced by the First World War. Many of these people had lived in the biggest cities in Europe and had expert trades and professions. Australia needed these skills and the country provided opportunity to these new migrants.

Armenian immigration

Although the first Armenians are recorded as arriving in Australia during the 1850s gold rush, there was a large contingent of Christians that arrived after the First World War as a result of the Armenian Genocide that begun in 1915. The Armenians were accompanied by many Pontic Greeks who were also escaping Islamic nationalism.

The Armenian community has grown in Australia now to around 50,000. Mainly based in Sydney, famous Armenians include Gladys Berejiklian (politician), Joe Hockey (politician), George Donikian (newsreader), Brian Goorjian (basketball), among others.

New projects

Science and Medicine

Prior to Federation, Australian science had largely been focused on its fauna, flora, parasitic organisms and the resulting bacteria and diseases. Thomas Jamison was a surgeon that arrived with the first fleet. There are early records of successful smallpox vaccinations being carried out by John Savage, a surgeon posted to Australia in the early 1800s. His success led to a confrontation with his superior, Jamison, and consequently Savage left Australia to serve elsewhere.

In 1862, the University of Melbourne began teaching its first medical students. One of its early graduates was Harry Allen who served as professor in descriptive and surgical anatomy and pathology. The University of Sydney began training medical students in 1883. The other states followed over time.

In 1910, the Australian Institute of Tropical Medicine was opened in Queensland. It was Australia's first formal medical research facility. It was followed in 1915 by the Walter and Eliza Hall Institute in Melbourne. In 1936, the National Health and Medical Research Council (NHMRC) was established to better understand the causes of diseases and the corresponding treatments.

Sir William Henry Bragg & Professor William Lawrence Bragg

In 1915, Sir William Henry Bragg and Sir William Lawrence Bragg were father and son. William Henry Bragg (1862-1842), born in Britain, was a physicist, chemist, and mathematician. William Lawrence Bragg (1890-1971), born in Adelaide, was a physicist. His brother, Robert, was killed at Gallipoli. In 1915, they were the first Australians to be awarded a Nobel Prize. Their award was in physics for their development of the X-ray Spectrometer and X-ray crystallography.

During the First World War, residing in Britain, father and son were called in by the Royal Navy, who were struggling with the sinking of British ships by German U-boats. They immediately recommended the development of sonar devices that could listen out for the undersea movement sounds of the submarines. They also developed the concept of sound ranging to detect minefields. By the war's end, every British naval vessel had sonar equipment manned by train listeners.

Sir William Henry Bragg was elected Fellow of the Royal Society in 1907 and President of the Royal Society from 1935 to 1940. He was knighted (CBE) in 1917 and awarded Knight Commander (KBE) in 1920.

Sir William Lawrence Bragg was elected Fellow of the Royal Society in 1921 and was knighted in 1941.

William Henry Bragg   *William Lawrence Bragg*

*The X-ray Spectrometer
developed by them.*

Dame Jean McNamara

Annie Jean McNamara (1899-1968), born in Beechworth, was an Australian medical doctor and scientist. Her contribution was towards children's health and welfare. She graduated from the University of Melbourne as a doctor and scientist in 1922. Her graduating class also contained Frank McFarlane Burnett, who was to win a Nobel Prize in 1960 for medicine. In 1923, McNamara became a resident doctor at the Royal Children's Hospital at the time of a polio outbreak. Working with Burnett, they discovered multiple strains of the polio virus, which led to the development of the Salk vaccine. McNamara also contributed to the development of Australian orthopaedics and was awarded Dame of the British Empire in 1935.

New projects

Jean McNamara

Australian stamp commemorating the joint work done by Dame Jean MacNamara and Sir Frank MacFarlane Burnet.

A list of Australian Nobel Prize winners, as follows:

Lawrence Bragg and William Bragg (1915) for work in X-ray Crystallography

Howard Florey (1945) in conjunction with Alexander Fleming and Ernest Chain for their work on penicillin

MacFarlane Burnet (1960) — immunology

John Eccles (1963) — nerve cells

Bernard Katz (1970) — physiology and medicine

Patrick White (1973) — literature

John Cornforth (1975) — chemistry

John Harsanyi (1994) — economics

Peter Doherty and Ralph Zinkernagel (1996) — immunology

John Coetzee (2003) — literature

Barry Marshall and Robin Warren (2005) — medicine (causes of stomach ulcers and gastritis)

Elizabeth Blackburn (2009) in conjunction with Carol Greider and Jack Szostak — chemistry and genetics

Brian Schmidt (2011) in conjunction with Adam Riess and Saul Perlmutter — physics and the universe

Also, Australian-born, but not Australian:

Aleksandr Prokhorov (1964) — physics (left Australia at age 7)

Also, two other famous Australian inventions that should be noted:

1. Dr David Warren (1953) — the first black box flight recorder, and
2. Lance Hill (1945) — the Hills Hoist, for hanging wet clothes to dry.

Electricity

The surrender of Germany in 1918 provided opportunity for the Allied countries to gain information about German technology. One area of interest for Australia, specifically Victoria, was how to generate cheap electricity from brown coal. Two key members of the newly formed State Electricity Commission of Victoria (SEC) — geologist Edgeworth Harper and engineer H.R. Harper — sought out General John Monash, while he was still in London. In the true character of his military operations, Monash targeted the city of Cologne and its Fortuna mine. Methodically, with speed and precision, they obtained a working model of a machine that made briquettes, small bricks of compressed coal, and other important information. By November 1919, they had enough information to report to government their recommendation that Victoria should exploit its brown coal deposits around Morwell for the production of cheap electricity. Later, Monash was to accept the position of Chairman of Commissioners for the SEC, which included a loan appropriation of 1.43 million pounds, the construction of a new power-generating city of Yallourn and an eight-storey head office in Williams Street, Melbourne. That project, accepted by the government in 1919, produced cheap electricity for Victorians for almost 100 years.

Oil and Gas

Although much of colonial Australia's power relied on coal and oil shale, crude oil-like deposits were recorded on the third voyage of the HMS Beagle in 1839. (Note: the HMS Beagle's second voyage, 1831-36 was Charles Darwin's famous journey), This discovery was around the area of the Bonaparte Basin, north-western Australia. However, the first drilling for oil occurred in the Coorong area of South Australia in 1892, and the first operating oil well in Australia was sunk in Albany Harbour in 1907. From the 1920s, as automobile and aeroplane use increased, so too did the demand and import of oil.

In 1946, the Australian Motorists Petrol Company (AMPOL) began exploration for crude oil in Western Australia. AMPOL formed a joint venture with the American oil company Standard Oil of California. It was named Western Australian Petroleum (WAPET). In 1953, at Rough Range on the North West Cape, near Exmouth and the Ningaloo Reef, they sunk their first well and were soon extracting 550 barrels per day. Further discoveries of commercially viable oil deposits were also made at Barrow Island off the Pilbara coast. These commercial operations continue today.

In 1966, Western Australian Petroleum discovered commercially viable quantities of natural gas at Dongara, south of Geraldton. In 1971, the first natural gas pipeline transported gas from Dongara to Perth, Kwinana and Pinjarra. It is still in operation and is known as the Parmelia pipeline.

Retail Innovations

The post First World War period also brought innovation to retail with the foundation of a few of the household names today.

G.J. Coles

Coles store, Collingwood, 1914

Sidney Myer

Myers store, Bendigo, circa 1910.

George James Coles (1885-1977), born in Jung Jung, near Horsham, was an Anglican Australian businessman. In 1914, he opened his first shop in Smith Street, Collingwood, with the slogan "nothing over a shilling." In 1924, a new store in Bourke Street, in the centre of Melbourne was opened. By 1927, there were nine stores in Victoria and, by 1938, G.J.Coles & Co. had 86 stores across Australia.

Sidney Myer (born Simcha Myer Baevski, 1878-1934), was a Russian-born Jewish Australian businessman, emigrating to Melbourne in 1899. Sidney Myer began business with a small drapery store in Bendigo. In 1911, Myer bought the property of Wright and Neil Drapers, on Bourke

Street near the General Post Office and opened a new store in 1914. The store expanded to Lonsdale Street in the 1920s. In 1925, shares in Myer Emporium were listed on the stock exchange and a new store was acquired in Adelaide. Myer has 60 stores across Australia.

Westralian Farmers Co-operative Limited was founded in 1914 by the Farmers and Settlers Association of Australia to provide services and merchandise to the Western Australian rural community. In 1924, it established a radio station 6WF to provide news and advice to farmers. In 1984, the company was reorganised as Wesfarmers Limited. It is the owner of Bunnings Warehouse, Officeworks, Kmart, Target and the Coles Group, among others.

Australian Aviation — early beginnings

John Robertson Duigan was the first Australian to design and fly Australia's first aircraft in July 1910. The biplane, with a four-cylinder engine, travelled 7 metres. By 1911, Duigan had made 60 flights, with the longest being 800 metres and an altitude of 20 metres.

Frank McNamara was the first Australian aviator to receive the Victoria Cross during World War One, at Gaza in 1917. McNamara (left) is pictured with his crew.

In 1919, two Australian aviators, brothers **Keith and Ross Smith** were knighted as the first to fly from England to Australia. Their flight began in a Vickers Vimy at Hounslow, in greater London, on 12 November 1919 and eventually landed in Darwin on 10 December, 28 days with an actual flying time of 135 hours.

In 1919, the Australian Aircraft and Engineering Company was established, flying out of Sydney Airport.

In 1921, it began building aircraft, such as this Avro 504K (left) for the Queensland and Northern Territory Aerial Services.

In 1921, the **Queensland And Northern Territory Aerial Services Ltd (QANTAS)** was founded in Winton, Queensland, by Australian WW1 aviators, Hudson Fysh and Paul McGinness, and Australian businessman, Fergus McMaster.

It began by flying between Longreach and Brisbane, in Queensland. In 1934, it began flying between Brisbane and Darwin; and, in 1935, began flights from Darwin to Singapore. In 1943, it began services from Sydney to Karachi, India, via Perth.

QANTAS is the world's third oldest airline.

In 1921, **Norman Brearley** established Western Australia Airways in Geraldton on the west coast of Australia. It was the first airline in Australia to establish a scheduled air service. It was later purchased by Australian National Airways (ANA).

New projects

In 1928, **Bert Hinkler**, also an Australian aviator, was the first to fly solo from England to Australia. He flew in an Avro Avian from Croydon, south London to Darwin in 15 days.

In 1928, **Charles Kingsford Smith**, was the first to lead a flight from North America to Australia. He flew a Fokker F.VII named 'Southern Cross' from Oakland, California to Brisbane, via Hawaii and Fiji. They flew over 11,000 kilometres in 9 days, with a flying time of about 82 hours.

He kept on flying and was the first pilot to eventually circumnavigate the Earth, via Australia, continuing to fly westward, returning to Oakland in 1930. In 1935, "Smithy" disappeared flying over the Bay of Bengal, India.

In 1930, **Amy Johnson**, an English pilot, was the first female to fly solo from England to Australia. She flew in a De Havilland DH.60 Gypsy Moth from Croydon Airport to Darwin, 18,000 kms in 19 days. The aircraft is preserved in the Science Museum in London.

In 1931, Amy co-piloted a flight from London to Moscow in one day (21 hours), and continued across Siberia to Tokyo, Japan to set a new record.

Maude Bonney was a South African-born Australian pilot, immigrating to Australia as a girl. In 1933, she was the first pilot to fly solo from Australia to England. She flew a De Havilland DH.60 Gypsy Moth from Archerfield Airport, Brisbane, to Croydon Airport, London.

In 1937, she was the first pilot to fly solo from

Australia to South Africa. Flying a Klemm KI 32, she departed Archerfield Airport again, flew across southern Asia and down Africa to Cape Town.

Flynn and the Royal Flying Doctor service

Rev. John Flynn (1880-1951), born in Moliagul, Victoria, was a school-teacher, church minister and founder of the Royal Flying Doctor Service. In the 1920s, as a missionary in the outback, Flynn took an interest and became an advocate for providing medical services to remote areas. In 1928, the first medical flight took off from Cloncurry in a single engine biplane leased from QANTAS. In its first year, the Aerial Medical Service flew 50 flights to 26 destinations, treating 225 patients. It was renamed the Royal Flying Doctor Service in 1955.

Early photo of the Aerial Medical Service.

Australian automobiles — early beginnings

The first automobiles began in Australia with a series of independent car builders. One of the first automobiles, the Highland, by Charles Highland in 1894, was a primitive motorised tricycle driven by a Daimler petrol engine. Two years later, Highland built two-seater, four-wheeled models.

In 1896, Herbert Thomson and Edward Holmes built the first steam-driven car in Australia from their workshop in the Melbourne suburban of Armadale. It was a 5 horse-power single cylinder steam carriage named the Phaeton and used the first pneumatic tyres built in Australia by Dunlop.

In 1898, the German-born Johann Zeigler built two cars with a two-cylinder steam engine in Allansford, Victoria, near Warrnambool. Zeigler's car could sit six people, had a maximum speed of 32 km/h, and had solid rubber tyres.

The Phaeton by Herbert Thomson

The JAC Zeigler

The Tarrant automobile 1901

In 1901, Harley Tarrant built the first petrol-driven car in Australia in his workshop in South Melbourne. The car was driven by a rear-mounted 6 horse-power-engine by Benz. The last remaining Tarrant is displayed at the RACV Club, Melbourne.

Other early small-scale Australian automobile manufacturers were Pioneer (1897-1898), Australis (1897-1907), Caldwell Vale (1907-1913),

Australian Six (1909-1930), Chic (circa 1920s), and Southern Cross (1931-1935). These early Australian automobile manufacturers had focused on manufacturing body parts, while importing engines from the established motor engine companies overseas.

However, the new age of Australian-built cars in the early 1900s was short-lived and was soon replaced by cheaper imports of both engines, chassis, and other major parts. In 1926, the Crosby family negotiated an agency with the British Standard Motor Company and imported many Vanguards to Australia.

Ford Australia was founded in 1925 in Geelong, Victoria, as a subsidiary of Ford Canada to assemble Model T kits manufactured and sent from Canada. In 1928, Ford switched to the Model A, followed by the Ford V8 in 1932.

General Motors arrived in Australia the year after Ford and set up its headquarters at Fisherman's Bend, near Port Melbourne. In 1931, General Motors purchased what had been an Australian saddlery business turned to automobiles in 1905, named Holden, and opened a vehicle assembly plant and operations to service its cars. In 1936, General Motors Holden opened an assembly plant at Fisherman's Bend and another in Pagewood, Sydney, three years later.

By the late 1920s, over half a million new cars had been registered out of a national population of 5 million. However, the rise in car traffic also led to a spike in road accidents and fatalities. In 1928, over 1,000 people were killed in road accidents. This sparked a review of road rules and speed limits in every state.

Art and Literature — new technologies and ideas

The film industry began in Paris, France, by the Lumiere brothers in 1895. By the following year, 1896, their films were being played at the Athenaeum Hall in Collins Street, Melbourne.

Melbourne was also the home to Limelight film studios run by the Salvation Army between 1897 and 1910, who made over 300 films. These ranged from films made for the Salvation Army's own purposes to those made for government purposes under contract, including the filming of the Federation of Australia. In 1899, Herbert Booth and Joseph Perry made their first full length feature film of over two hours, combining 13 short stories about early Christianity.

The earliest feature length narrative film made in Australia, and possibly the world, was 'The Story of the Kelly Gang', a silent film made in Melbourne in 1906 by Charles Tait. It ran for over an hour and its reel length was 1,200 metres. According to Tait the film cost 1,000 pounds and took six months to make.

From 1900 to 1910, the numbers of independently made films in Australia grew dramatically until the Australasian Films and Union Theatres, now known as Greater Union, was established. This film distributor found it increasingly more lucrative to import films from the United States of America. Numbers of Australian made films fell from 51 (1911), to 30 (1912), to 17 (1913), to 4 (1914).

The Australian film industry began to recover in 1930, with the help of Francis William Thring. To promote new cinema, Sydney's Capitol Theatre opened in 1928 and Melbourne's state Theatre and Regent Theatre opened in 1929.

Francis Thring — the rebirth of Australian cinema

Francis William Thring (1882-1936), born in Wentworth, New South Wales, was an Australian film director, producer, and exhibitor.

Thring's career with film began in 1911 as a projectionist at Kreitmeyer's Waxworks in Melbourne. He later married Olive Kreitmeyer. In 1915, Thring opened the Paramount Theatre and, in 1918, became managing director of J.C.Williamson Films, merging with Hoyts in

1926. In 1926, Francis and Olive had a son, who was to become famous in his own right as international actor Frank Thring (1926-1994).

In 1930, he sold his interest in J.C.Williamson Films to Hoyts and used the funds to establish Efftee Films, focusing on film production. Over the next five years, Efftee Films produced nine feature films, including A Co-respondent's Course (1931), Diggers (1931), The Haunted Barn (1931), The Sentimental Bloke (1932), His Royal Highness (1932), Harmony Row (1933), A Ticket in Tatts (1934), The Streets of London (1934), and Clara Gibbings (1934). Notable contributors were poet C.J. Dennis, comedian George Wallace, and actor Frank Harvey. Efftee Films also made over 80 short films as well as stage shows and musicals. During this time, Thring worked relentlessly to establish a quota system for the distribution of Australian made films. Furthermore, Australian government policy was to ban any films made about bushrangers.

In 1935, after the New South Wales government passed the Cinematograph Films Act, a quota system, Thring moved to Sydney an established the Mastercraft Film Corporation but died of cancer the following year. He is buried in Burwood Cemetery, in Melbourne's east.

Ken G. Hall and Cinesound Productions

Kenneth George Hall (1901-1904), born in Paddington, NSW, is arguably the most important figure in Australian film history and was the first Australian to win an Academy Award.

Ken Hall began as a cadet journalist at the age of 15, working his way to the position of nation publicity director, the highest post in Australian film publicity, by the age of 20. In 1924, Hall joined First National pictures, an American film distribution company as a publicist and went to Hollywood. There, he learnt the crafts of filming and editing.

By 1931, Hall had returned to Australia and joined a new company, Cinesound Productions, as assistant to its founder Stuart Doyle.

Between 1931 and 1934, Hall made four feature films being: On Our Selection (1932), on Steele Rudd's 'Dad and Dave' stories; The Squatter's Daughter (1933); The Silence of Dean Maitland (1934); and Strike Me Lucky (1934), starring Roy Rene's character Mo McCackie. Hall made another ten feature films, mostly comedies, between 1935 and 1940.

During the Second World War, Hall's reputation gained legendary status with his wartime newsreels, the most notable being his Oscar-winning Kokoda Front Line (1942).

After the war, Hall produced the film Smithy (1946), about Charles Kingsford Smith. He always wanted to make his own version of Thomas Browne's 'Robbery Under Arms' but Australian government policy blocked his efforts. Hall ended his career as an executive at TV's channel 9 in Sydney.

Charles Chauvel

Charles Edward Chauvel (1897-1959), born in Warwick, Queensland, was an Australian filmmaker, producer and screenwriter, and was the nephew of Australian army General Sir Harry Chauvel.

Chauvel showed an early interest in film making and with the help of his friend, Reginald "Snowy" Baker worked on some films before heading to Hollywood to hone his skills.

In 1926, after returning to Australia, Chauvel directed nine major feature length films being: Moth of Moonbi (1926); Greenhide (1926); In The Wake Of The Bounty (1933), starring Errol Flynn; Heritage (1935); Uncivilised (1936), an Aboriginal story; Forty Thousand Horsemen (1940), a film on his uncle's famous cavalry charge at Beersheba in Palestine, starring Chips Rafferty; Rats of Tobruk (1944), starring Peter Finch; Sons of Matthew (1949); and the renowned Jedda (1955), dealing with the plight of Aboriginal people in outback Australia. He also made short documentary films.

After film, Chauvel turned to television and worked on the BBC's Walkabout series on outback Australia until his death in 1959.

F.W.Thring of Efftee Films   Ken G. Hall of Cinesound Productions   Charles Chauvel

  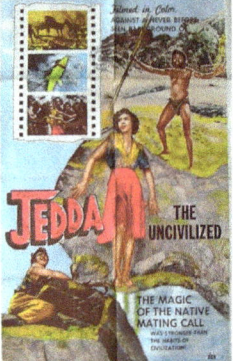

'The Sentimental Bloke' by Efftee Films

'Strike Me Lucky' by Cinesound Productions

'Jedda' by Chauvel

Famous early international Australian actors

May Robson (1858-1942) was born in Moama, New South Wales. Robson was a comedienne and actress on stage and in both silent and sound films. Her career on stage began in New York in 1883, at age 25. In Hollywood, she starred in 13 silent films between 1915-1928, and over 50 sound films between 1931-1942. In 1933, Robson was nominated for a Best Actress Oscar, the first Australian actor to do so, at age 75 in 'Lady for a Day'.

Errol Flynn (1909-1959) was born in Battery Point, Tasmania. He began performing as an actor in 1918, aged nine. Flynn had the charisma to play the leading role in films. In 1933, Flynn played mutineer, Fletcher Christian, in Charles Chauvel's 'In the Wake of the Bounty'. In Hollywood, Flynn starred in 'Captain Blood' (1935), 'The Charge of the Light Brigade' (1936), and "The Adventures of Robin Hood' (1938). Flynn starred in over 50 major Hollywood films until his death, due to ill-health in 1959.

Dame Frances Margaret Anderson (1897-1992), a.k.a. Judith Anderson, was born in Adelaide. Anderson had a successful career on stage, film, and television; won two Emmy awards and a Tony award. In 1915, she began on the stage in Sydney, aged 18, but moved to New York in search of greater success. In 1922, she made her Broadway debut in 'Up the Stairs'. Between 1930-1985, Anderson appeared in over 40 films, including Rebecca (1940), Kings Row (1942), The Ten Commandments (1956), Medea (1983), and Star Trek III: The Search for Spock (1984). In 1960, she was awarded Dame Commander of the Order of the British Empire.

Francis William Thring (1926-1994) was born in Melbourne. After beginning in radio, Thring began acting in 1945, aged 19. He moved to Britain in 1954. He starred in stage, film and television. Thring appeared for the Royal Shakespeare Theatre and in Hollywood films, including 'The Vikings' (1958), 'Ben Hur' (1959), 'King of Kings' (1961), 'El Cid' (1961), and Ned Kelly (1970). Later in life, he returned to the Melbourne Theatre Company.

Peter Finch (1916-1977) was born in London but went to live with his great-uncle in Sydney in 1926. Finch began acting on stage in 1933. His first films were 'The Magic Shoes' (1935), 'Dad and Dave Come to Town (1938), and 'The Power and the Glory' (1941). During the war, Finch served in the army but was given leave to act in films. Between 1935-1976, Finch appeared in over 60 films, including 'The Rats of Tobruk' (1944), 'A Town Like Alice' (1956), "The Nun's Story' (1959), and his Oscar-winning "Network' (1976).

Rod Taylor (1930-2015) was born in Lidcombe. Taylor appeared in more than 50 Hollywood feature films, as well as radio and television productions. He starred in films such as The Time Machine (1960), The Birds (1963), Hotel (1967), Zabriskie Point (1970). On television, Taylor starred in The Bearcats (1973), The Oregon Trail (1976), and Falconcrest (1988-90). In 1960, he was approached to play the role of James Bond in the first film but declined. He was noted to later comment: "Every time a new Bond picture became a smash hit … I tore out my hair."

The Great Depression in Australia

The Great Depression resulted from the Wall Street (New York City, USA) stock share market crash of 1929. As banks and businesses collapsed financially so did people's savings and jobs. As with other parts of the world, Australia too suffered years of high unemployment, low wages for those who had jobs, and high levels of poverty. The Gross Domestic Product (GDP) of Australia fell by 10 percent between 1929 and 1931. Unemployment reached a peak level of 30 percent in 1932. These conditions produced civil unrest and protests, especially in Sydney. Through the Great Depression support grew for both the extreme radical 'left', wanting change, and the extreme reactionary 'right', wanting to suppress change.

Australian Sport before and during 'The Great Depression'.

As the 20th Century unfolded, a wider range of sports became organised with national and international governing bodies. In 1900, the first badminton competition was played in Australia. The first official motorcycle racing event was held at the Sydney Cricket Ground in 1901, followed by the first motorcar race at the Aspendale Racecourse in 1904. The Australian National Rugby Union team won gold at the 1908 London Summer Olympics. Surfing arrived in Australia in 1915, with the first surf lifesaving competition held that same year. Les Darcy began his boxing career in 1915, although controversy occurred when he went to the United States to continue boxing, rather than enlisting into the armed forces during the war. Tragically, he died in the USA and over 100,000 people turned out for the funeral procession when he was returned to Australia. Dick Eve won Australia's first diving gold medal at the 1924 Paris Summer Olympic Games. Also, in 1924, the Australian Rugby Union adopted and wore the team colours of green and gold for the first time by any Australian team.

Women represented Australia for the first time in the Olympics in 1912. In 1922, an Australian sporting committee deemed on what were appropriate sports for women to play as part of physical education. Football was deemed inappropriate. Female participation in tennis, netball, lacrosse, golf, hockey and cricket were discouraged. Swimming, rowing, cycling and horse riding were encouraged, as long as they were not done in a competitive manner. Of course, objections were raised to these limitations and in 1927, netball was first organised into a national female sport under the guise of the All Australia Women's Basketball Association.

Through the glory years of the late 1920s and the hardship of the 1930s, Australians found heroes on the sports fields. To mainstream Australia, there were three great Australian heroes of the 1920s and 1930s — Don Bradman, Phar Lap, and Jock McHale of the Collingwood Football Club.

"Jock" McHale and "Carringbush" glory.
The Collingwood Football Club is often referred to as the "Carringbush". This was because of Frank Hardy's novel "The Power and the Glory". The novel's main character Jack West was a depiction of the infamous John Wren and the tea house, which doubled as West's/Wren's illegal betting venue, and was located in a fictitious suburb named Carringbush, which was Collingwood. The name stuck.

The glory days of the Collingwood Football Club, playing Aussie Rules in Victoria, was led by coach James Francis "Jock" McHale

(1882-1953), born in Botany, NSW, who coached the club from 1912 to 1949, a total of 714 games, a record held until Mick Malthouse exceeded this in 2015. McHale held a 66%-win ratio, 16 grand finals for 8 premierships — 1917 (as playing coach), 1919, 1927, 1928, 1929, 1930, 1935, 1936, plus one (1910) as a player before he coached. The club's four consecutive premierships still stand as a VFL/AFL record. In 1996, McHale was inducted into the AFL Hall of Fame and elevated to Legend status in 2005. Since 2001, the Jock McHale medal has been awarded to the AFL premiership coach.

Phar Lap at full stretch

Phar Lap exhibit at Melbourne Museum

Phar Lap

Phar Lap (1926-1932), born in New Zealand, was a famous Australian racehorse. Phar Lap was a chestnut gelding standing 1.74 metres, owned and trained by Harry Telford. It was also part-owned by American businessman David Davis. Its strapper was a young Tommy Woodcock. Phar Lap won the 1930 Melbourne Cup, two Cox Plates, an AJC Derby, and 19 other weight for age races. At the end of 1931, Phar

Lap went to race in North America. Phar Lap won its first race there, the Agua Caliente Handicap in Mexico, with the largest prize money in North America, in track-record time, carrying 58.5 kgs (129 pounds). In April 1932, while at Atherton, California, Phar Lap fell ill, haemorrhaged, and died. For decades, it was suspected that Phar Lap had been poisoned. In 2008, using modern techniques, equine specialists determined that in the 30 to 40 hours before its death, Phar Lap had ingested massive amounts of arsenic. Phar Lap is exhibited at the Melbourne Museum.

Don Bradman and the Invincibles

Sir Donald George "The Don" Bradman (1908-2001), born in Cootamundra, NSW, is widely acknowledged in cricket as Australia's greatest batsman of all time. Bradman's career Test innings batting average was 99.94 over 52 tests, with a top score of 334. He also represented both New South Wales and South Australia in first class cricket, scoring over 28,000 runs at a 95.14 average, with a top score of 452 not out. Bradman played in the infamous 1932-33 "Bodyline" series, which Australia lost to England, but still scored 396 Test runs at 56.57, an average that any other Test batsman would be proud of as a career Test average.

In 1948, an Australian Test team led by Bradman, nicknamed "The Invincibles", played an English team that had become severely depleted due to the Second World War. "The Invincibles" were famous for being the very first Australian team to go through a full tour without losing a match. Over the entire tour, they played 34 matches, winning 25 and drawing nine. Of the five Test series, Australia won 4-0, with the Third Test drawn. The Invincibles were: Don Bradman (captain), Lindsay Hassett (vice-captain), Ray Lindwall, Keith Miller, Sam Loxton, Neil Harvey, Bill Brown, Arthur Morris, Don Tallon (wicket keeper), Sid Barnes, Ian Johnson, Bill Johnston, Ernie Toshack, Doug Ring, Ron Hammence, Colin McCool and Ron Saggers (wicket keeper). The manager of the team was Australian cricket administrator Keith Johnson.

Eddie Gilbert

Edward Gilbert (1905-1978), born in Woodford, Queensland, was an Aboriginal cricketer. He was taken from his home, as part of government policy, and grew up working on farms around the Barambah Aboriginal Reserve, north of Brisbane. Gilbert played first class cricket as a right arm fast bowler with Queensland. He was the fifth Aboriginal cricketer to play first class cricket after Twopenny (1870), Johnny Mullagh (1879), Jack Marsh (1900), and Albert Henry (1902). Bound by the restrictions of the Aboriginal Protection Act 1897, Gilbert had to receive permission before he could leave the Aboriginal settlement to play his first-class matches. He played 33 first class matches, of which 19 were Sheffield Shield matches taking 73 wickets at 29.75. Against a West Indian team, he took 5/65. Gilbert was only called once for "chucking", a term used for bowling the ball with a bending arm. At the MCG in 1931, Umpire Andrew Barlow called him 13 times for "chucking". He was never called for "chucking" again. Gilbert played two more times against Bradman and also played against Douglas Jardine in the infamous English "Bodyline" tour of Australia in 1932/33. The tour was infamous for the method Jardine connived in having his bowlers deliberately bowl at the bodies of the Australian batsmen. In 2007, a bronze statue of Eddie Gilbert was erected on Greg Chappell Avenue, outside the Alan Border Field at Albion, in Brisbane.

In November 1931, in a match against NSW, Gilbert dismissed the opening batsman with his first ball. To the crease strode the no.3 batsman, Don Bradman. Bradman blocked Gilbert's first ball, the second went down leg. The third ball went straight through Bradman to the wicketkeeper but missed the stumps. The fourth ball hit Bradman directly in his protector and sent him to the ground. The fifth ball was a quick bouncer which Bradman top-edged playing a hook shot and was caught. Gilbert had dismissed Bradman for a duck.

Eddie Gilbert

Photo: Gilbert dismisses Bradman for a duck.

Women's Cricket

The founder of Australian women's cricket was Tasmanian Lily Poulett-Harris, who founded a cricket league in 1894 and captained the Oyster Cove team, deemed to be the first women's league and team in

Australia. This was closely followed by the Rockhampton Ladies Club, who founded a team in Queensland. The Victorian Women's Cricket Association was founded in 1905 and the Australian Women's Cricket Association was founded in 1931. In the summer of 1934/35, an England women's cricket team played Test matches in Australia. Notable Australian players were Nance Clements, I. Cookesley, Peggy Antonio and Anne Palmer. The Australian Women's Cricket Team toured England in 1937. However, the Second World War interrupted cricket and the fortunes of women's cricket did not rise again until the 1970s.

Doug Nicholls and reconciliation's first steps

Sir Douglas Ralph Nicholls (1906-1988) was born in Cummeragunja, on the New South Wales side of the Murray River, north of Echuca. He was an Aboriginal Australian of the Yorta Yorta community. Nicholls was a professional "Aussie-rules" footballer, a church pastor, a ceremonial officer and a pioneering campaigner for reconciliation. He was the first Aboriginal Australian to be knighted and to be appointed to vice-regal office as the 28th Governor of South Australia.

During his teenage years, Nicholls worked as a general hand on sheep stations and played football with Tongala in the Goulburn Valley. In 1927, Nicholls joined the Northcote VFA team in 1927, played on the wing and was a member of their 1929 premiership team. In 1931, he finished third in the competition's best and fairest. In 1932, he joined Fitzroy in the VFL, played 54 senior games, and in 1935 was the first Aboriginal player to be selected in a Victorian representative team. In his early years, Nicholls was often ostracised and sat away from the main group until Haydn Bunton Sr. ensured that he was welcome in the team. Nicholls was also a capable sprinter competing in and winning gift races and a capable boxer. He was also the inaugural chairman of the National Aboriginal Sports Foundation.

After football, Nicholls was a minister and social worker for Aboriginal people. He cared for those affected by alcohol abuse, gambling, and other social problems. He became a pastor of the first Aboriginal Church of Christ in Australia and was fully ordained as a minister. He married his brother's widow, Gladys, in 1942. In 1953, Nicholls was nominated by H.V. Evatt (then opposition leader) to be included in the official Australian contingent to the coronation of Queen Elizabeth II.

In 1957, Nicholls became a field officer for the Aboriginal Advancement League. Both, he and his wife, Gladys, helped set up hostels for Aboriginal children and holiday homes for Aboriginal people at Queenscliff and was a founding member and Victorian Secretary of the Federal Council for the Advancement of Aborigines and Torres Strait Islanders. In 1972, Nicholls was the First Aboriginal Australian to be awarded Knights Bachelor by Queen Elizabeth II. In 1976, he was nominated by Premier Don Dunstan and appointed as South Australia's 28th Governor. He was the first and still only Aboriginal Australian to hold vice-regal office. In January 1977, he suffered a stroke but was able to host the Queen at Government House in March, where he was awarded a second knighthood, Knight Commander of the Royal Victorian Order. Nicholls retired from office the following month, as his ill-health continued, and he died in Mooroopna in 1988. A state funeral was held for him and he was buried at the cemetery at Cummeragunja. His wife Gladys had died in 1981.

The Canberra suburb of Nicholls is named after him, and he has a statue in the Parliament Gardens of Victoria. In 2016, the Indigenous Round of AFL was named after him. He is a great grandfather to Nathan Lovett-Murray, who played 145 senior games with Essendon in the AFL, and great uncle to David Wirrpanda, who played 227 games with Westcoast.

J.F. "Jock" McHale

Sir Donald George "The Don" Bradman

Sir Douglas and Lady Gladys Nicholls

Doug Nicholls, footballer

Nance Clements, circa 1937

Lily Poulett-Harris,
circa 1890s

Clements, Cookesly and Antonio on tour

The Australian Women's Team 1937

Netball in Australia

Netball is the most popular women's sport in Australia. The game was invented in London in 1893 and initially called women's basketball. The rules were modified in 1897 and again in 1899. The first game in Australia was played in early 1897; however, it was not until the 1920s that official competitions were organised. Women were allowed to play without being registered, which allowed the sport to grow quickly.

In 1924, the first interstate competition was founded, still under the name of Women's Basketball. Victoria won the first All-Australia tournament in 1928. The name 'netball' did not become official until 1940. Australia won the first INF World Championship in 1963 and has won 11 times up to 2015. In 1995, it was estimated that there were 360,000 netball participants in Australia. Liz Ellis is Australia's most-capped international representative.

Origins of netball, circa 1890s

Netball in the 1950s

Liz Ellis, circa 2007

Mary Poppins — P.L.Travers & Mary Sheppard

Out of the depression era of the 1930s came arguably Australia's greatest series of children's novels — the Mary Poppins series. The Mary Poppins series were eight novels written by P.L. Travers and illustrated by Mary Shepard, published between 1934 and 1988. The first three books deal with the Banks family's adventures with the magical nanny Mary Poppins in the streets and shops of London, whereas the remainder are more retrospective. In later years, the original versions were revised to exclude any language now deemed inappropriate. The story of Mary Poppins was adapted by Walt Disney into a musical film in 1964, starring Julie Andrews and Dick Van Dyke. The 2018 film, Mary Poppins Returns, is a revision of the original film, rather than an adaption of the second novel, Mary Poppins Comes Back.

P.L.Travers

Pamela Lyndon Travers (1899-1996), was born Helen Lyndon Goff, in Maryborough, Queensland, and wrote novels, short stories and non-fiction. She is best remembered for the Mary Poppins series. Goff began writing poems as a teenager, wrote for The Bulletin, and began performing as an actress in Alan Wilkie's Shakespearean Company, under the name Pamela Lyndon Travers, touring Australia and New Zealand. In 1924, she left Australia for England to act and dance on the stage, which was against her family's wishes. It was in England that she began writing the Mary Poppins series, initially published in 1934, with characters based on her youth. According to a later BBC interview, the phrase 'spit spot' was a favourite saying of her aunt.

During World War Two, Travers moved to the United States, working for the British Ministry of Information. It was then that Walt Disney first approached her regarding gaining the film rights. Disney's daughters loved the books as children, which sparked his interest. Travers declined the rights for many years, until the 1960s. When Travers discovered that Disney had adapted her novel into a musical, she objected, disapproving of his interpretation of the Poppins character. After signing the rights away, she had little influence on the film. It did make her wealthy, as she left an estate of over two million pounds. In 1977, she was appointed Officer of the Order of the British Empire. Travers died in 1996, aged 96, and is buried St Mary the Virgin Church, in Twickenham, England.

As an interesting aside to the Mary Poppins film rights story, Mary Shepard, the English illustrator for the books, was left out of the film rights deal. Shepard had also illustrated A.A. Milne's Winnie the Pooh books, and an edition of Kenneth Grahame's Wind in the Willows. However, in the film, Poppins lands on the ground with feet turned out in ballet's first position. This pose was based on Shepard's illustrations, and is absent in Travers's text, therefore Shepard did eventually receive a one-off payment from Disney of one thousand pounds.

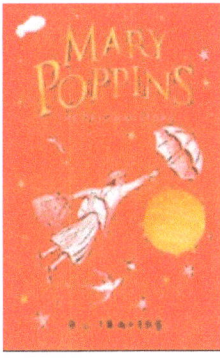

Front cover of Mary Poppins first edition (1934)

Travers in her early acting years, 1924, State Library of New South Wales

Shepard, circa 1924, from E.H. Shepard archive, University of Surrey

The Second World War

After the First World War, often called "the Great War", or "the war to end all wars", no one would have believed that that there would be an even-more devastating war just over twenty years later. However, many believe that the Second World War was a direct consequence of the First World War. The end of the First World War had led to revolutions in Russia, Germany and Austria-Hungary. The Treaty of Versailles 1919 had imposed enormous financial penalties and debt upon Germany. Therefore, not only was there a vacuum of political power in Europe following war but there were also severe financial conditions that led to the Great Depression of the 1930s.

Since 1853, when U.S. Commodore Perry's fleet forced Japan to open its ports, it had felt the full strength of western racism and colonialism. Japan began a process of industrialisation along western lines. In the early 20th Century, it had the opportunity to successfully test its industrialised navy and army against Imperial Russia and Imperial Germany and captured Korea. In the 1930s, many of the world's leading countries attempted to overcome the depression by imposing trade restrictions on other countries. This made matters worse. Japan, now the strongest military nation in Asia and the western Pacific region was restricted in buying iron and other metals on the open market and chose to access these resources by invading neighbouring countries on the Asian mainland. An early success by Japan, in Manchuria in 1931, spurred Japan to continue its war further into China in 1937.

Germany, having suffered over a decade of financial hardship under the democratically elected Weimar government, chose to elect a new

National Socialist (Nazi) government (1933) led by Adolf Hitler. Ordinary Germans connected to Hitler, a populist dictator, who had been a corporal in the German army during the First World War. Many other newly formed nations after the First World War elected populist dictators or had them usurp power. These included Miklos Horthy (1920) in Hungary, Benito Mussolini (1922) in Italy, Miguel de Rivera (1923) and Francisco Franco (1936) in Spain, Josef Stalin (1924) in the Soviet Union, Antonio Salazar (1928) in Portugal, Josef Pilsudski (1926) in Poland, among other European countries. These dictators found minority scapegoats to blame for their each of their country's misfortunes — socialists, communists, Gypsies, and Jews. As each gained early military successes, they were spurred onto further ambition.

In 1933, opposing restrictions to its armed forces, Hitler withdrew Germany from the League of Nations (forerunner to the United Nations) and the World Disarmament Conference. In 1935, the Saarland voted to reunite with Germany. Also, in 1935, Germany increased its army (Wermacht) by six times to 600,000, established an air force (Luftwaffe), and increased its naval forces. Although Britain, France, Italy and other members of the League of Nations condemned this, they did nothing to stop it.

In 1936, Germany occupied the de-militarised zone between itself and France. Germany signed a pact with Italy in 1936 and Japan in 1938. In 1938, German troops marched into Austria then the Sudetenland in western Czechoslovakia. Hitler decided to call off invading the rest of Czechoslovakia due to concerns about his oil supply. The British Prime Minister, Neville Chamberlain, flew to Munich to meet with Hitler and left the meeting declaring "peace in our time". In March 1939, German troops marched into Prague. Still Britain and France did nothing. Hitler's next intention was to invade Poland, but he feared opposition from the giant Soviet Union. In late August 1939, Germany and the Soviet Union signed a non-aggression pact. Their intention was to divide Poland between them. On 1st September 1939, German troops invaded western Poland. Soon after, Soviet troops invaded eastern Poland. On 3rd September 1939, Britain and France declared war on Germany. The Second World War had begun.

For Australia, it joined the rest of the British Empire and declared war on Germany. Australia was even less prepared for the start of the Second World War than it had been for the start of the First World War. The Australian army had 3,000 full time regulars and 80,000 partly trained militia. The navy (RAN) had two heavy cruisers, four light cruisers, and a handful of obsolete destroyers. The air force (RAAF) had just under 250 aircraft but nearly all of these were obsolete. There was one Short Sutherland flying boat patrol bomber from the No.10 Squadron that was deployed in October 1939 over Tunisia, which became the first air force unit to see action.

Australia's immediate threat was not in Europe but closer to home in Asia. Japan had invaded China in 1937 and captured the Chinese capital of Nanjing (Nanking). The Japanese army massacred the population of Nanjing, with some estimates as high as 300,000 dead. The Japanese continued to advance into China, yet the world did nothing. This spurred Japan to plan a Greater East Asia Co-Prosperity Sphere, a giant Asian Empire led by Japan. However, the Japanese were not ready to declare their intentions as yet. That would wait until December 1941. The question of whether to send Australian troops to Europe or whether to retain them for the direct defence of the Australian mainland was to be a dilemma.

Egypt & Libya

The first theatre of action for Australian troops would be in North Africa and the Mediterranean. The HMAS Sydney with five obsolete destroyers accompanied the British Mediterranean fleet. In June 1940, the Sydney sunk an Italian submarine. In July, as part of the British fleet, it engaged Italian light cruisers at the Battle of Cape Spada. The Sydney was relieved from Mediterranean duty by the HMAS Perth in February 1941.

In January 1941, the Australian 6th Division was deployed as part of Operation Compass to attack Italian forces in Libya. Bardia was captured on the 6th of January, Tobruk fell to the Australians on the 22nd, then Benghazi fell to them on February 4th, capturing over 10,000 Italian troops under General Graziani during the campaign. It was then that the 6th Division was relieved by the 9th Division and redeployed to Greece.

In April 1941, the Australian 6th Division was engaged in the unsuccessful defence of Greece and was evacuated to Crete. Subsequently in May, during the battle for Crete, 5,000 Australian soldiers from the division were captured. Also, in April, the German Afrika Korps led by General Rommel reinforced the Italians and they went on the offensive. The 9th Division, led by General Morshead, with a brigade from the 7th Division, were besieged in the town of Tobruk for 241 days until relieved by British units in October.

After the Libyan campaign, Australian army units were brought back to Australia for defence against the invading Japanese army. Australian navy and air force units continued to serve in the Tunisian and Italian campaigns of 1943.

Over 13,000 Australian airmen served in British and Australian squadrons from the Battle of Britain in 1940 through to the end of the war.

Leslie Morshead

Lt General Sir Leslie Morshead (1889-1959), born in Ballarat, was an Australian soldier, teacher, businessman and farmer. Morshead was a schoolteacher until 1914, where he enlisted and was commissioned as a lieutenant in charge of a battalion for the Gallipoli campaign. He later led the 33rd Battalion at various battles during Monash's campaign on the Western Front and was awarded the Distinguished Service Order, the French Legion d'honneur, and knighted a Companion of the Order of St Michael and St George. During the wars, Morshead managed the successful Orient Steam Navigation Company or Orient Line.

With the outbreak of the Second World War, Morshead was given command of the 18th Infantry Brigade as part of the 6th Division. In 1941, he was elevated to command the 9th Division, which he led at the Siege of Tobruk and the First and Second Battles of El Alamein. During the Second Battle of El Alamein, when the British attack began to falter, it was Morshead's 9th Australian Division, suffering very-high casualties, which punched the crucial hole in Rommel's army that won the battle. During the campaign, Morshead was given the nickname "Ming the Merciless", after the Flash Gordon comic strip character. He was awarded the Knight Commander of the Order of the Bath for his efforts.

In 1943, Morshead was redeployed to the Pacific region and commanded the 2nd Australian Corps during the New Guinea campaign. In 1945, he led the 1st Australian Corps during the Borneo campaign. Like General Monash before him, Morshead was to be elevated to higher command for the invasion of the Japanese mainland, but the atomic bomb was dropped, and Japan surrendered before this could occur. After the war, Morshead returned to managing the Orient Steam Navigation Company, and died of cancer in 1959. He is commemorated by Morshead Drive that runs through the Royal Military College at Duntroon; the Morshead War Veterans Home in Lyneham; and the Morshead Fountain, opposite the State Library of New South Wales.

General Sir Leslie Morshead *General Sir John "Shan" Hackett*

John Hackett

General Sir John "Shan" Hackett (1910-1997), born in Perth, was a soldier, painter and university administrator. Hackett's unique notoriety is that he was an Australian-born officer who led British units, rather than Australian units, during World War Two. He was one of the greatest Australian-born generals but in Australia, very few would know it.

Although born in Perth, Hackett received his secondary schooling at Geelong Grammar in Victoria. He then travelled to London and studied at the Central School of Art, then studied history and completed a Master of Arts at New College Oxford, writing a thesis on Saladin's campaign during the Third Crusade.

In 1933, he joined the British Army and was commissioned into the 8th Kings Royal Irish Hussars and served during the Arab Revolt in Palestine (1936-39).

During the Second World War, Hackett fought in the Syria-Lebanon campaign of 1941, where he was wounded and received the Military Cross. Later, during the North African campaign, while leading a tank squadron, he was severely injured when escaping from a burning tank.

In 1944, Hackett raised and commanded the 4th Parachute Brigade that took part in the disastrous parachute assault on the Dutch city of Arnhem, where the Germans were waiting. During the resulting massacre, he was wounded in the stomach and captured. Hackett was hospitalised, operated on, then recovered and escaped with the assistance of the Dutch underground. There he lived, hidden by a Dutch family, until liberated by the Allied army and received the Distinguished Service Order.

After the war, Hackett continued his military career, commanding the Trans-Jordan Frontier Force (1947/48), the 20th Armoured Brigade (1954), the 7th Armoured Division (1956), Commandant Of the Royal Military College of Science (1958), General Officer Commanding in Chief, Northern Ireland Command (1961), Deputy Chief of the General Staff (1963), British Army of the Rhine and NATO's Northern Army Group (1966). In 1968, Hackett wrote an article criticising the British government's support of the army and was subsequently retired. From 1968 to 1975, he served as Principal of Kings College, London. Although he died in Gloucestershire, England in 1997, aged 86, his ashes are interred at Karrakatta Cemetery, in Perth, Western Australia.

Hackett's decorations include the Knight Grand Cross of the Bath, Commander of the Most Excellent Order of the British Empire, Distinguished Service Order and Bar, the Military Cross, among other stars and medals. Although arguably the most decorated Australian-born military officer, as a British officer, he is barely recognised in Australia.

Singapore & Changi — Weary Dunlop

British military strategy in the orient relied in defending its empire and position in south eastern Asia. As British military policy dictated its will to its colonies, so Australian military forces were deployed to Malaysia, rather than being held for the defence of the Australian mainland.

When the Japanese Navy attacked Pearl Harbour by surprise in the early morning of December 7th, 1941, its army immediately deployed to attack British, European and American defensive positions. For the next six months, one by one, they fell to the Japanese — Malaya, Burma, French Indochina, Borneo, Hong Kong, the Dutch East Indies (Indonesia), Rabaul, Singapore, Guam and the Philippines. With the fall of Singapore in February 1942, over 20,000 Australian soldiers had been captured. Many of these were sent to Changi Prison in Singapore and were used to build the Thai-Burma Railway, a 400-kilometre (250 mile) railway, linking and supporting Japanese military supply through Thailand to Burma. It is estimated that 250,000 south-east Asian civilians and 60,000 Allied prisoners of war (POWs) were used to build the railway. Of these 90,000 civilians and more than 12,000 POWs died of starvation and exhaustion.

Changi Prison had in fact been built by the British as a civilian prison in 1936. After the fall of Singapore in February 1942, the Japanese had used it to detain about 3,000 prisoners. The Japanese also used the nearby Selarang Barracks to detain some British & Commonwealth prisoners, including Australians. This also included some women, who were later marched to a new prison camp, some fifteen kilometres away. Many of the prisoners were marched off to labour camps for purposes such as building the Burma railway and to the Sandakan airfield, in what was to be called the Sandakan death marches. The chapel built by prisoners at Changi Prison was later relocated to the Royal Military College, Duntroon, Canberra. There were many notable prisoners of war, including James Clavell, the Australian author, who wrote about his experiences in the novel King Rat, and "Weary" Dunlop, an Australian surgeon.

Weary Dunlop

Lt. Colonel Ernest Edward "Weary" Dunlop (1907-1993), born in Major Plains, near Benalla, Victoria, was an Australian surgeon and was renowned for his leadership as a prisoner of war. From Benalla High School, he progressed through the Victorian College of Pharmacy, then on scholarship to University of Melbourne, graduating with first class honours in pharmacy and medicine in 1934. Also, during his university years, although playing "Aussie Rules", he moved to rugby union, gained state representative honours and was selected and played in the "Wallabies", the national rugby union team. He earned the nickname "Weary" because of the Dunlop tyre, (weary/tired). After university, Dunlop enlisted in the Australian Medical Corps and served as a medical officer in London and was admitted as Fellow to the Royal College of Surgeons.

When World War Two began, Dunlop served in Egypt, Greece, and Libya, at the siege of Tobruk, before being transferred home. On the way, he was transferred to Java, where he was captured. The Japanese noticed his leadership skills and placed him in charge of the Java prisoner of war camps, then transferred him to Changi. Dunlop was placed in charge of the 1st Australian prisoners of war group to work on the Burma-Thai railway. There, he showed much courage and compassion as both a surgeon and leader through the dark years of the war. After the war, "Weary" Dunlop worked for a number of health and care giving organisations, including the Australian Drug Foundation and the Cancer Council of Victoria. He received many honours for his life's work including Officer of the Order of the British Empire (1947), Companion of the Order of St Michael and St George (1965), Knight Bachelor (1969), Companion of the Order of Australia (1987), Knight Commander of the Order of St John of Jerusalem (Knights Hospitaller, 1992), and Knight Grand Cross (1st Class) of the Most Notable Order of the Royal Crown of Thailand (1993). There are statues of "Weary" Dunlop in both the King's Domain, Melbourne, and at the Australian War Memorial, Canberra.

"Weary" Dunlop, Australian War Memorial, Canberra

Statue of Dunlop in the King's Domain, Melbourne

Photo of prisoners inside Changi POW camp, Newcastle Herald

South-West Pacific — Field Marshal Blamey

From December 1941 to March 1942, the Japanese Army had proved invincible in capturing most of south-eastern Asia. In January 1942, it landed in New Guinea with the intent of capturing the island and isolating Australia from the United States of America. Some believe that the Japanese intended invading mainland Australia but there was no Japanese plan discovered to verify this. In May 1942, a series of sea and land battles halted the Japanese advance. In March 1942, in the Coral Sea, the US Navy fleet, led by Admiral Nimitz and two aircraft carriers, fought the Japanese Navy fleet to draw. Each side lost an aircraft carrier sunk. However, the sea battle had stopped the Japanese landing troops directly at Port Moresby. The Japanese army then attempted to march overland across the Owen Stanley Ranges to Milne Bay, in the south-east.

From February 1942 to November 1943, the Japanese conducted air raids on the northern coast of Australia. On the morning of February 19, 1942, 242 Japanese aircraft bombed Darwin, Northern Territory, killing 235 people. Repeated air attacks were made by the Japanese against Darwin, Broome in Western Australia, and as low as Townsville in Queensland. In May and June 1942, Japanese submarines made attacks in Newcastle and in Sydney harbour.

In June 1942, a surprise clash between the Japanese Fleet of 4 aircraft carriers and the US Fleet of 3 aircraft carriers, near Midway Island, saw all 4 Japanese carriers sunk and ended Japanese sea offensive ambitions in the Pacific. Although the result of the battle was an overwhelming and decisive success for the US Navy, the battle was won in a short 10-to-15-minute interval when US torpedo bombers found the Japanese carriers with their planes on deck during a changeover. The US Fleet lost one aircraft carrier, the Yorktown that had previously fought at Coral Sea. The Battle of Midway was the first sea battle in history where neither side's ships came into contact with each other.

In New Guinea, during the Kokoda Trail campaign, July to November 1942, the Australian forces led by General Thomas Blamey fought the Japanese Army to a standstill at Milne Bay, Buna-Gona, and at Wau. The US Army, under General Douglas MacArthur overcame a similar

Japanese attack at Guadalcanal, in the British Solomon Islands, between August 1942 and February 1943. Together, the Allied forces took the Japanese base in Lae and threw the Japanese out of New Guinea.

From 1943, the Allied forces commenced a series of operations called "island hopping", taking key islands one at a time. The sheer number of US troops in the Pacific rendered the Australian troops to secondary operations. In 1944, Australian troops landed at New Britain and Bouganville. In 1945, the Australians were involved in the Borneo campaign until the war ended. In August 1945, following the US atomic bomb blasts on Hiroshima and Nagasaki on the Japanese mainland, the Japanese surrendered.

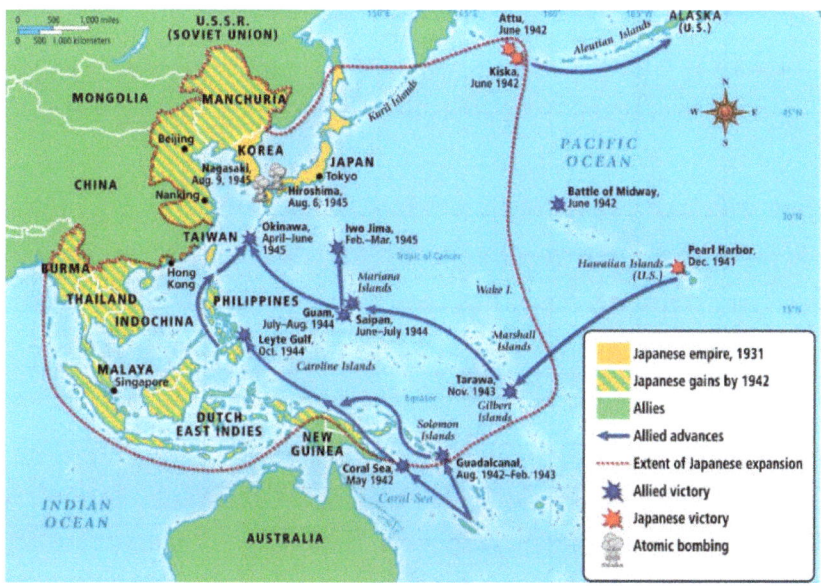

Map of war in the Pacific, Second World War

Field Marshal Thomas Blamey

Thomas Albert Blamey (1884-1951), born Wagga Wagga, New South Wales, was an Australian army officer, serving as a general in both the First and Second World Wars, and the only Australian to achieve the rank of field marshal.

Blamey joined the regular Australian army in 1906 and attended staff college in India. He participated as a staff officer during the Gallipoli campaign of 1915 and was promoted to brigadier general after the Battle of Pozieres (1916) on the Western Front. He led a brigade at both the Battle of Hamel and for the Hindenburg Line 1918.

Between the wars, Blamey served as Deputy Chief of the General Staff and was involved in setting up the Royal Australian Air Force (RAAF). In 1925, following the Victorian Police Strike, he resigned from the regular army to become Chief Commissioner of Police, immediately went to work correcting the grievances that had caused the strike, and held the post until 1936. He did remain in the army militia (army reserve) and was given command of the Australian 3rd Division in 1931 and the 6th Division in 1939.

During the Second World War, Blamey commanded the 2nd Australian Imperial Force 1st Corps in the Middle East. During the Battle for Greece (1941), his main battle was stopping the British generals from dividing and dispersing his brigades into various British divisions. He was given command of all Australian troops in the Middle East in 1941. In 1942, Blamey returned to Australia as military commander of all Australian troops and assumed personal command of the New Guinea force during the Kokoda Trail campaign. He was given command of all Allied land troops in the South Western Pacific Area till the end of the war. He signed the Japanese surrender document aboard the USS Missouri in Tokyo Bay on 2nd September 1945, and accepted another Japanese surrender at Morotai, in Indonesia, a week later. After the war, Blamey retired from active service. He was reinstated to active service briefly to be promoted to the rank of field marshal in 1950. Blamey died in 1951. 300,000 people lined the streets of Melbourne to watch his funeral procession from the Shrine of Remembrance and he was cremated and buried at Fawkner Cemetery, Melbourne.

Blamey's awards were many, extending through both world wars. The list of awards includes Knight Grand Cross of the Order of Orange-Nassau (Netherlands), War Cross (Greece), Distinguished Service Cross (USA), Croix de guerre (France), Commander of the Venerable Order of St John, Distinguished Service Order, Companion of the Order of St Michael and St George, Knight Bachelor, Knight Commander of the Order of the Bath, and Knight Grand Cross of the Order of the British Empire.

Gen Sir Thomas Blamey, circa 1942

Blamey, second from left behind MacArthur, during the Japanese surrender.

Statue of Blamey in King's Domain, Melbourne.

A statue of FM Sir Thomas Blamey stands in the King's Domain, near Government House, Melbourne, opposite the statue of Gen. Sir John Monash. Also, areas of honour are named after him at both the Department of Defence and Australian Defence Force headquarters in Canberra. Blamey Barracks is at Kapooka, NSW, and Blamey Park is in North Ryde, Sydney.

Captain Nancy Wake

Nancy Wake (1912-2011), born in New Zealand, grew up in Sydney. At 16, Nancy left home and worked as a nurse near Mudgee, NSW, later travelling to England to study journalism. In 1935, she visited Berlin, saw the evils of the Nazi regime, then returned to France and married Henry Fiocca, a wealthy French businessman. Fiocca was called up to army service, and Nancy joined the ambulance corps. When France was overrun by the Germans in 1940, Nancy joined the French resistance and the Special Operations Executive as a freelance captain and helped many soldiers and refugees to flee to safety.

After the war, Wake returned briefly to Australia, then returned to England, working as an intelligence officer. In the 1960s, she returned to Australia again and eventually wrote The White Mouse (1980), a recount of her adventures in wartime France. In 2001, she left Australia for the last time to stay in London. She died of a chest infection in 2011. Her ashes were spread in the town of Verneix in France.

Wake received the RSA Badge in Gold (New Zealand), Medal of Freedom (USA), Croix de guerre (France), Officer of the Legion of Honour (France), the George Medal, and the Companion of the Order of Australia.

Nancy Wake, the White Mouse, circa 1945.   Sgt Tom 'Diver' Derrick, circa 1943.   Flt Lt Peter Isaacson, circa 1943.

Sergeant Thomas 'Diver' Derrick

Thomas Currie Derrick (1914-1945) born in Medindie, South Australia, was an Australian soldier who distinguished himself bravely through the war and was awarded the Distinguished Conduct Medal and the Victoria Cross.

Before the war, Derrick had worked odd-jobs, including a fruit-picker, around the Berri and Murray River area. In 1940, he enlisted in the 48th Battalion of the 26th Brigade as a private. His battalion was posted to the Libyan desert and were part of the force that held Tobruk for eight months. After the siege, his battalion was relieved but redeployed within a few days into the First Battle of El Alamein. The German tanks initially broke the Allied line, but individual units attacked the Wermacht infantry marching behind the tanks. Derrick was commended for "outstanding leadership and courage" and received the Distinguished Conduct Medal, as well as being promoted to sergeant. He distinguished himself again in the Second Battle of El Alamein by knocking out three German machine gun posts.

In 1943, the 48th Battalion returned to Australia for jungle training and was deployed in the attack on the Japanese base at Lae, New Guinea. Derrick distinguished himself again by leading the attack, taking out enemy gun posts, at one stage noted as hanging off a cliff with one hand and throwing grenades with the other. His notoriety had grown so much that he had become a legend of the division and was awarded the Victoria Cross and commissioned as a lieutenant. In May 1945, during the attack on Tarakan, Borneo, Derrick was gravely wounded and died a few days later.

In 2004, in a television interview, General Peter Cosgrove was asked his best Australian soldier of all time. He answered, "Diver Derrick". In 2008, the bridge across the Port River in Port Adelaide was named the Tom 'Diver' Derrick Bridge.

Wing Commander Peter Isaacson

Peter Stuart Isaacson (1920-2017) born in London, moving to Melbourne at age 6, was a decorated military pilot and, later, a publisher. In 1940, at 19 years, Isaacson enlisted into the Royal Australian Air Force (RAAF) and trained as a pilot. In 1942, his bomber squadron was deployed for night attacks across Germany. Isaacson was awarded the Distinguished Flying Medal in November 1942.

In a night-raid against the German capital, Berlin, Isaacson's bomber was hit by anti-aircraft fire. Isaacson coolly continued to pilot the damaged bomber despite losing attitude and suffering further damage. He successfully flew the damaged bomber back to base. Over the course of the war, Isaacson was eventually promoted to Wing Commander of the RAF Bomber Command.

After the war, Isaacson became a journalist then a newspaper publisher and established the Melbourne newspapers Southern Cross and The Sunday Observer.

Noted Aboriginal Australians in World War Two

Leonard Waters (1924-1993), born in Boomi, north-western NSW, was the first Aboriginal Australian fighter pilot. He flew almost 100 missions over Japanese-held islands in the Dutch East Indies (Indonesia) and New Guinea. He served in the Royal Australian Air Force from 1942 to 1946 and rose to the rank of Warrant Officer.

After the war, Waters attempted to start a regional air service in south-west Queensland but found that the racism of government officials and financiers stopped every attempt. He felt that as an Aboriginal Australian, his wartime contribution to Australia was not valued.

Reginald Walter "Reg" Saunders (1920-1990), born near Warrnambool, Victoria, was the first Aboriginal commissioned officer in the Australian Army. His father, Chris, fought in the Australian army in World War One.

Reg Saunders served in the Australian army in World War Two, in the North African campaign, Greece, Crete, and in the New Guinea campaign. During the Lae operation, Saunders was recommended as an officer, which was granted in 1944.

Saunders also served in the Korean War (1950-54). In 1953, he was nominated by the RSL to be included in the official Australian contingent for the royal coronation but was rejected by the Federal government.

In 1971, Saunders was awarded a Member of the Order of the British Empire.

Kath Walker

Kathleen Jean Mary Walker (nee Ruska, 1920-1993), born in Minjerribah, Queensland, also known as Oodgeroo Noonuccal, served in the

Australian Women's Army as a signaller during World War Two. It is noted that during her service time, she met many Black American soldiers, who inspired her later advocacy for Aboriginal rights. She joined the Communist Party because it was the only political party of that time opposed to the White Australia policy.

During the 1960s, Kath Walker rose to become a noted political activist and writer, serving as Queensland state secretary of the Federal Council for the Advancement of Aborigines and Torres Strait Islanders and was a key figure in the successful 1967 Aboriginal Citizenship referendum. As a writer, her first book, We Are Going (1964) was the first to be published by an Aboriginal woman.

In 1970, Walker was awarded a Member of the Order of the British Empire (MBE) and later founded the Noonuccal-Nughie Education and Cultural Centre.

In 1974, on her way home from a committee meeting in Nigeria for the World Black and African Festival of Arts and Culture, her plane was hijacked by Palestinian terrorists. During her three days in captivity, she pencilled two poems — "Commonplace" and "Yusuf (Hijacker)".

In 1986, she played the role of Eva in Bruce Beresford's film, The Fringe Dwellers.

In 1987, Walker returned her MBE in protest over the Australian Bicentenary, which she referred to as "200 years of sheer unadulterated humiliation", and permanently changed her name to Oodgeroo Noonuccal.

In 1993, Noonuccal died in 1993 of cancer and she is buried at Moongalba on North Stradbroke Island. Her honours were many — the Mary Gilmore Medal (1970), the Jessie Litchfield Award (1975), Fellowship of Australian Writers' Award, Member of the Order of the British Empire, Honorary Doctorates from the Queensland University of Technology and Macquarie University, and a Doctorate from Griffith University.

In 2017, the Queensland electoral district of Oodgeroo was named after her.

Kath Walker, circa 1944, AWM   Kath Walker, circa 1967   Kath Walker, circa 1986

The End of the Second World War

The war came to an end in Europe in May 1945. As Adolf Hitler had killed himself, rather than surrender, the executive of the German government had passed to Admiral Karl Donitz, head of the German Navy. On May 6th, he advised General Jodl to surrender, which was signed at Reims in France. A more formal surrender document was signed in Berlin on May 8th. Japan surrendered on August 15th, after the devastation of the atomic bomb blasts on Hiroshima and Nagasaki, and documents were formally signed on September 2nd by the Japanese Emperor Hirohito aboard the USS Missouri.

The war saw the devastation of nearly all of Europe and most of Eastern Asia. Casualties of both soldiers and civilians were enormous. It is estimated that between 70 to 85 million people died during the course of the war, 3% of the world's population at the time. 20 to 25 million deaths were soldiers, 50 to 60 million were civilians. A similar number were wounded. The Soviet Union and China suffered the most deaths. Soviet deaths were estimated at over 25 million, Chinese deaths are estimated at 20 million. For Germany and Japan, their total deaths were estimated at 7 million and 3 million, respectively. Poland suffered 6 million deaths, of which 3 million were Jews. The total number of Jews killed during the war was estimated at 6 million. Yugoslavia lost almost 2 million. In Eastern Asia, the Dutch East Indies (Indonesia) lost 4 million dead, and French Indo China (Vietnam and Cambodia) lost 2 million. India lost 4 million. Other countries in Europe and Asia lost tens and hundreds of thousands of people. In Australia, we lost 40,000, nearly all soldiers, and a similar number of wounded.

PART FIVE

MODERN AUSTRALIA TAKES SHAPE

A wave of immigration

The ending of the Second World War had left many countries in Europe and Eastern Asia in ruin. These countries could no longer sustain the remnants of their populations. In Australia, many realised that the population of the country was too low to adequately defend itself from invasion. Ben Chifley, Prime Minister of Australia (1945-49), created a Department of Immigration to manage the process of enticing new immigrants to Australia and made Arthur Caldwell the Minister for Immigration. The popular cry became "Populate or perish", however, Australia still wished to be bound to the White Australia Policy.

Mostly European migrants came to Australia after the war. These migrants were a combination of those who has suffered during the war and those who were seeking refuge from vengeance after perpetrating suffering on others during the war. The "New Australians", the term used by Arthur Caldwell, was coined to replace the bigoted terms of the past decades, such as "Pommy" for a Britainer and "Wog" for any mainland European.

Today, there are members of federal and state parliaments who are the descendants of the oppressed and the oppressors of the war, and there are also ethnic clubs that now celebrate the groups that suffered from and committed atrocities during the war. Others, who could trace European heritage, could arrive from Asia. A small number, who could pass as "white" were allowed to arrive from Asian and African countries. This policy was to hold until 1973, until it was eventually broken by the Whitlam government in 1973.

The Chifley Government

Although, only in government for four years, the Chifley post-war government (1945-49) was one of the great reforming governments in Australian history. In its four years, the Chifley Labour government passed 229 acts of parliament. Ben Chifley (1885-1951), born in Bathurst, was Australia's 16th Prime Minister. His grandparents were Irish immigrants. With limited education, Chifley became a railway worker and engine driver, and worked his way through the trade union movement into a career in politics. He succeeded John Curtin as Prime Minister and leader of the Labor Party. Chifley was the Treasurer of Australia from 1941 to 1949, including being Prime Minister from 1945-49. He led the Labor Party from 1945 until his death in 1951.

The Chifley Government's major innovations were:
- a shift away from British foreign policy towards American foreign policy, due to closer Australian ties to the USA and Britain's declining influence.
- a new, more inclusive immigration policy, the Assisted Migration Program 1945
- the provision of sickness and unemployment benefits, and widows' pensions
- the Commonwealth and State Housing Agreement Act
- the Pharmaceutical Benefits Scheme
- the first massed produced Australian car, Holden
- the formation of the first national airline, Trans Australia Airways (TAA)
- a national university established in Canberra, and
- establishing the Snowy Mountains Scheme (to be dealt with later)

Further, in 1948, Chifley's Minister for External Affairs and

Attorney General, Herbert 'Doc' Evatt served as President of the United Nations General Assembly, the first and only Australian, up to the writing of this book, to do so.

Ben Chifley   *Dr H.V. 'Doc' Evatt*   *Arthur Caldwell*

Caldwell, the Assisted Migration Program 1945 — 10 Pound Poms

In 1945, the Australian government created the Assisted Passage Migration Scheme to encourage migration from Britain. Yet the overtones of racism were clearly stated by Caldwell, "We have 25 years at most to populate this country before the yellow races are down on us." A theme later repeated in 1996 by Pauline Hanson during her inaugural speech in the Parliament of Australia.

The scheme led to the term "Ten Pound Poms" because of the 10-pound adult travel fare by ship, children travelled for free. The derogatory term "Pom" is said to be derived from "pomegranate", Australian rhyming-slang for immigrant. The scheme was also assisted by the Big Brother Movement, a non-profit organisation based in Sydney that sought to bring British youths to Australia to work on rural farms. In 1957, the "Bring out a Briton" campaign. Over one million Brits migrated to Australia between 1945 and 1972. However, even from the onset, the target numbers of an annual 1% increase of population through British immigrants were not being reached. The government had to look further afield and began casting the net for eastern European immigrants.

In 1949, the Menzies government came to office, with Harold Holt as the new immigration minister. The scheme was expanded to include refugees from mainland European countries, with a priority on those who were looking to escape from the growing influence of the Soviet Bloc of communist countries. New immigrants arrived from the Italy, Germany, Netherlands, Greece, Poland, and other European countries. By 1953, non-British European post-war migrants were exceeding those from Britain. Today, Melbourne is the second largest ethnic Greek community beside Athens, including all other Greek cities.

A look at the 1961 Australian census, the year after I was born, indicates the composition of the Australian population, as follows:

Total Persons — 10.5 million, of which 8.8 million were born in Australia. Individual groups born outside of Australia: (Minimum 20,000 to qualify on this list, number rounded to nearest 1,000.)	
England	556, 000
Italy	228,000
Scotland	133,000
Germany	109,000
Netherlands	102,000
Greece	77,000
Poland	60,000
Ireland (Republic, Northern & undefined)	50,000
Yugoslavia	49,000
New Zealand	47,000
Malta	39,000
Hungary	30,000
Austria	24,000

Then compare the above to the list of Asian-born immigrants, as follows:

China	15,000
India	14,000
Cyprus	9,000
Indonesia	6,000

Remembering, Asian-born immigrants complied with the rules of the White Australia Policy.

Also, as no official census records were kept of the Australian Aboriginal population until after 1967, as they were non-citizens, only estimates can be made of the number of Indigenous Australians in 1961. According to the Australian Bureau of Statistics, the estimated number was just below 100,000. However, it spikes heavily after the 1967 referendum, with 150,000 (1976) and 350,000 (1996). The variation in the post referendum figures relate to the terms of a particular census question. From 1967 to 1978, the question was based on "racial origin", and from 1978, the word "racial" was omitted.

American (United States) migration

Although relatively small in number, since 1770 there has always been Americans (United States and territories) coming to Australia. The first was part of Captain Cook's crew, shanghaied from an American schooner, while resting and taking provisions at Funchai in the Madeira Islands. Small numbers of Americans arrived throughout the 1800s, especially during the gold rushes. In 1901, there were 7,448 US-born in Australia.

During the Second World War, there were large numbers of Americans posted on military duty to Australia. At the war's end, 12,000 Australian women migrated to the United States as war brides, and 10,000 United States citizens migrated to Australia. During the 1950s, this continued with ANZUS Treaty obligations. As of 2019, the estimated number of American-born Australians is just over 108,000, and almost the same number claim American heritage.

Famous Australians born in America or with American heritage include Aaron Baddely (golf), Cate Blanchett (actor), Chelsea Brown (comedian), Kate Ceberano (singer), Mel Gibson (actor), Colleen Hewett (singer), Marcia and Deni Hines (singer), Terri Irwin (zoologist), Kristina Keneally (politician), Don Lane (TV presenter), Don Pyke (footballer), Peter Ruehl (journalist), Penny Sackett (astronomer), Brian Schmitt (astrophysicist), Ben Simmons (basketball), among others.

The Foundation of the Liberal Party

The Liberal Party was formed in 1944 by Robert Menzies out of the remains of the previous United Australia Party (UAP). Menzies had previously served as a UAP Prime Minister between 1939-41. The Liberal Party was positioned as a centre-right party alternative to Labor, rather than the more conservative Country (National) Party. However, most of its electoral victories have been in formal or informal alliance with the Country (National) Party. In 1949, Menzies won election as Prime Minister defeating the Chifley government. Menzies was to become Australia's longest serving Prime Minister from 1949 to 1966. This was largely due to the 1955 split in the Labor Party, creating an independent party, the Democratic Labor Party (DLP), a mostly Catholic anti-communist political party, led for the most part by Senators Frank McManus and Vince Gair. The DLP would continually divide the Labor vote and keep the Liberal Party in power until the 1970s.

The 1950s in Australia

The spurt in the Australian population during the 1950s, largely due to immigration saw a sprawling of the major capital cities in Australia. One point was clear. Immigrant groups tended to group and settle together in concentrated areas, usually the capital cities. This was because work, services, opportunity, and mutual support was best found in the capital cities. New suburbs grew and, consequently, many old and new Australians moved from small inner suburban tenements to housing estates on large land blocks. There was a newly found optimism that Australia was the "lucky" country.

In 1950, the Commonwealth Scientific and Industrial Research Organisation (CSIRO) released the myxomatosis virus into the Murray Valley in an effort to eliminate rabbits, which had become a threat to farming and native fauna. In 1955, the Commonwealth Serum Laboratories (CSL) began mass production of a vaccine against poliomyelitis. By the following year, all states and territories had free polio vaccination programs and effectively made Australia polio free.

Australian authors were beginning to look back at Australia's indigenous heritage. In 1950, John Antill wrote the ballet "Corroboree", based on his experiences in Arnhem Land, in northern Australia. Neville Shute wrote the international best-seller "A Town Like Alice". In 1955, Charles Chauvel made the film "Jedda", which highlighted the oppression of Aboriginal people by white Australians and was the first Australian film to star two Aboriginal actors in Robert Tudawali and Ngarla Kunoth.

In 1957, a Danish architect, named Jorn Utzon (1918-2008) won an international competition to design what was to become the Sydney Opera House.

In 1959, an Australian designer, Florence Broadhurst, took the world by storm with her wallpaper designs.

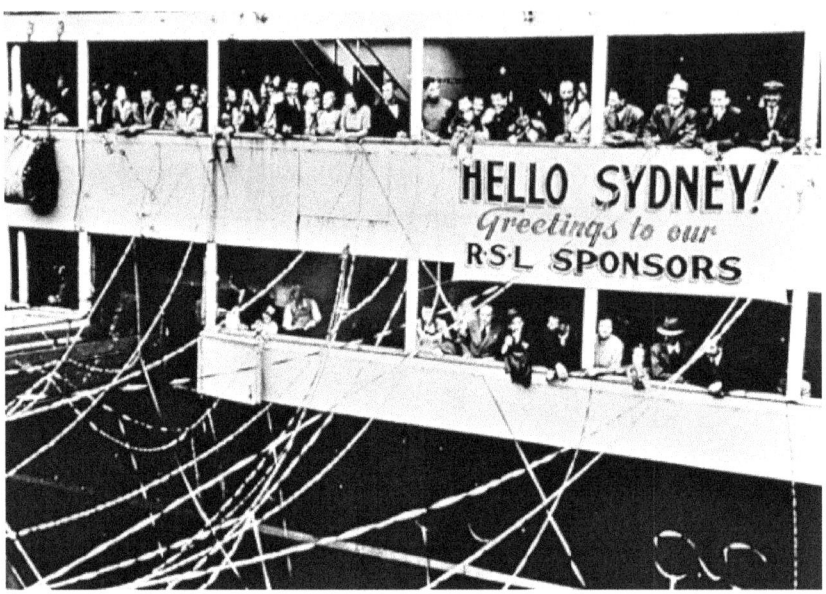

Post-war immigration drive (new arrivals by ship), National Museum of Australia

Jorn Utzon presenting model of Sydney Opera House, circa 1957

Scene from "Corroboree", Empire Theatre, Sydney 1950

The Snowy Mountain Scheme — 1949-1972

One of the major post-war engineering projects was the Snowy Mountain hydroelectricity and irrigation scheme in south-eastern Australia. The scheme was another new policy set down by the Chifley post-war government. The scheme consisted of 16 major dams, 7 power stations, a pumping station, over 200 kilometres of tunnels and pipelines, and 1,600 kilometres of roads and railway tracks. It was located at the Kosciuszko National Park, took 25 years to build, and cost over 800 million dollars (equivalent to between 5 to 10 billion dollars now). The aim of the scheme was to capture water from the Snowy Mountains and Snowy River into dams, use it for hydroelectricity generation, then divert it for irrigation into the Murray and Murrumbidgee rivers.

More than 100,000 people living in 100 camps worked on the Snowy Mountain Scheme over the 25 years. Most of these were immigrants.

The Melbourne Olympics 1956

The highlight for Australia in the 1950s was the Melbourne 1956

Summer Olympic Games. These were the first Olympic Games held in the southern hemisphere and in Oceania. In the final round of voting, Australia won with 21 votes over Buenos Aires, Argentina, with 20 votes — winning by one vote.

Insert from a map of the Snowy Mountains Scheme

Photo of the Snowy Mountains Scheme, ABC

Tunnelling underground

Migrant workers who helped build the scheme.

The Melbourne Olympics ran from November 22nd to December 8th, 1956. 72 nations participated. Over 3,300 athletes competed (about 2,900 men and 300 women). There were over 150 events in 17 different sports. Some countries chose to boycott the Olympics: Egypt, Iraq, Cambodia, and Lebanon, over the Suez crisis; Netherlands, Spain, and Switzerland, over the Hungarian revolution; and mainland China, over Taiwan competing. The Olympic cauldron was lit by the young Australian long-distance runner Ron Clarke, brother of Essendon (AFL) footballing great Jack Clarke.

The main athletics stadium was the Melbourne Cricket Ground (MCG). Swimming, diving, and water polo events were held at the then new Olympic Pool, which has now been converted into the home of the Collingwood (AFL) Football Club. Canoeing and rowing events were held on Lake Wendouree, in Ballarat, Victoria. Other various events were held in venues around metropolitan Melbourne — Broadmeadows (cycling), Laverton and Williamstown (shooting), Port Phillip Bay (sailing), St Kilda (fencing), and Festival Hall, West Melbourne (basketball, boxing, and gymnastics). All equestrian (horse) events for the 1956 Olympics were held in Stockholm, Sweden, as Australian government health regulations at the time forbade the entry of overseas horses into Australia.

Known as the "friendly games", the highlights for Australia were Betty Cuthbert (3 gold medals) and Shirley Strickland (running); and Murray Rose (3 gold medals) and Dawn Fraser (swimming). Other highlights included a much-publicised romance between American hammer-throw champion Hal Connolly and Czech discuss-throwing champion Olga Fikotova. Also, East and West Germany competed together as a unified team.

Ron Clarke lights the cauldron

The Australian team marching

Betty Cuthbert

Shirley Strickland

Murray Rose (middle)

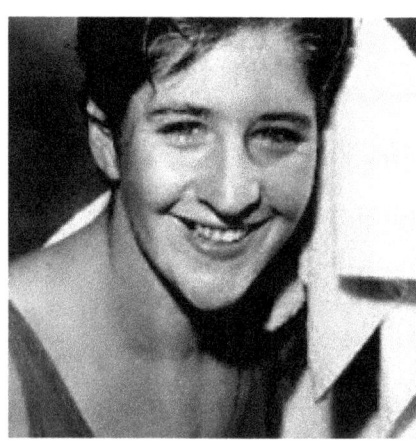

Dawn Fraser

Arguably, the infamous highlight of the Melbourne Olympics was the water polo match between Hungary and the Soviet Union. The Soviet Union was one team composed of a federation of countries including Russia, Ukraine and Belarus. In 1956, Soviet Union tanks and troops crushed a rebellion in Hungary. Hungary, also a communist country, was part of the Soviet bloc. The water polo match between Hungary and the Soviet Union was a bloodbath, a brawl in water turned red.

At the closing ceremony, for the first time, all participants came out together rather than coming out as separate teams, as had occurred previously.

The medal tally indicated the leading countries were:

1st, Soviet Union, 98 medals, 37 gold medals

2nd, United States, 74 medals, 32 gold medals

3rd, Australia, 35 medals, 13 gold medals

The Cold War

The 1950s saw the greater international political pessimism of the Cold War, emanating from the perceived threat of the "Domino Theory" that vulnerable non-communist countries would fall one-by-one to revolution and political domination by communist forces. The Communist forces were made up of those countries led by the Soviet bloc and China. In 1951, the ANZUS Collective Security agreement or military alliance was signed between Australia, New Zealand, and the United States. Australians fought in the Korean War, 1950-53, which saw that country split into the communist North Korea and the capitalist South Korea. That separation still exists today.

Petrov Affair — 1954

Within Australia, authorities and citizens became paranoid over the communist movement and socialist groups. The cry of "Reds under the bed" was used to imply that communists were lurking around corners or in hidden areas, infiltrating society and threatening the homes of ordinary Australians.

The Petrovs in the safety of suburban Melbourne.

The Petrovs in the safety of suburban Melbourne.

For Australia, the Cold War was highlighted by the Petrov Affair, which was a spying incident in 1955, involving the Third Secretary of the Soviet Embassy in Canberra, Vladimir Petrov. Petrov and his wife, Evdokia, were appointed by Josef Stalin. When Stalin died, many of his assistants were executed, including the Soviet Security Chief, Lavrenty Beria. Fearing they would be executed if they were recalled to Moscow, Petrov decided to defect to Australia, although he did not tell his wife. In April 1954, Petrov declared his defection and went into hiding. Two KGB agents (Soviet secret service) immediately escorted Evdokia Petrov to a waiting plane at Sydney Airport. The plane had to refuel at Darwin. The Prime Minister Robert Menzies intervened and ASIO agents (Australian secret service) arrested the KGB agents on suspicion of carrying firearms. They separated Evdokia from the KGB agents, then she chose to defect too. In exchange for security of residence in Australia, the Petrovs promised to provide details of a Soviet spy ring located in Australia. After the affair, the Petrovs lived quietly in suburban Melbourne until their passing.

Indigenous Civil Rights

In post war Australia, white Australians were enjoying the most prosperous time of Australia's history, including full civil rights, full employment, and the "Australian dream" of a family home and car. Conversely, the Australian Indigenous society had no rights, no citizenship, no right to vote, had been stripped of their land and had no right of land ownership, and lived in abject poverty.

The movement for Indigenous civil rights had begun to build momentum with Australia's federation. In 1924, Fred Maynard, born at Hinton in the Hunter Valley, New South Wales, joined with other activists to create the Australian Aboriginal Progressive Association. In 1929, to a Royal Commission on the state of Aborigines, retired Anglican Western Australian Archdeacon Charles Lefroy, representing a London-based Anti-Slavery Society argued for a referendum on the issue of Aboriginal welfare. Edith Jones, President of the Victorian Women's Citizen's Movement presented evidence which contrasted Australia's responsibility for New Guinea, under the rules set down by the League of Nations, and its lack of responsibility towards its own Aboriginal people.

In 1938, on the 150th anniversary of the landing of the First Fleet, William Cooper, a well-respected Aboriginal activist from Cummeragunja, in New South Wales, proposed the first Day of Mourning. In 1944, the first referendum on Aboriginal rights was held but was defeated.

State laws decided where Aboriginal people should live, where they couldn't move, who they should marry, and that their children should be taken away from them to be reared on "white" missions. According to the Aboriginal Preservation and Protection Act 1939, local authorities decided how much of an Aboriginal person's earnings could be given to them and how much was to be retained from them by state trustees. The Queensland Trust Fund was an example of this injustice and was not brought to the public's attention until the campaign of 1969-1972. State laws gave rights to authorities to censor the writings of protest by Aboriginal people. Further, because Aboriginal women had no rights, they were still easy prey to "white" men, who could take full advantage of them, including rape. The campaign to bridge that gap began in the late 1950s and is still being fought today.

The Warburton Ranges Controversy

The first protest began in 1957 after the Australian government began testing nuclear weapons in the Central Desert of Western Australia without care towards the local Indigenous population. Before long, these people fell ill. The Graydon Report of 1956 condemned the conditions under which the Australian government had tested the nuclear weapons and the effect of these on the local Indigenous populations.

Protests were made to the Menzies Federal government of that time, but they deflected responsibility onto the individual state governments. Television became an important tool as the videos of the appalling conditions that Aboriginal people lived in remote conditions was broadcast into the homes of "white" Australians. After the broadcasts, the Menzies government was inundated by letters of protest.

It is interesting to note, Rupert Murdoch, through his papers, chose to publish that people he met in the Central Desert were happy and well fed. The Women's Christian Temperance Union wrote a letter challenging Murdoch's assertions and expressing their disgust and distain. (https://www.nma.gov.au/__data/assets/pdf_file/0007/692368/denying-starvation-in-the-desert.pdf)

In response, Pastor Doug Nicholls joined a Select Group Committee, emanating from the Graydon Report and began filming the plight and impoverishment of Central Desert Aboriginal people. The film, named "Manslaughter", shown on national television, "showed stick-limbed children with the swollen bellies of malnutrition, babies sucking frantically at empty breasts and toddlers too weak or lethargic to brush away the hundreds of flies feeding at their eyes".

Albert Namatjira and excerpts from his paintings

Albert Namatjira and citizenship

Albert Namatjira (1902-1959), an Arrernte Aboriginal person, was born at the Hermannsburg Lutheran Mission, Northern Territory. By the 1950s, Namatjira was Australia's greatest Aboriginal painter and arguably Australia's greatest painter. His paintings were being sold internationally. In 1944, Namatjira was listed in Australia's Who's Who, yet as an Aboriginal person, he was not even an Australian citizen. In 1956, artist William Dargie won the Archibald Prize for his portrait of Albert Namatjira. Yet Namatjira, deemed a notable Australian by the Archibald committee and already a wealthy man, was still not yet an Australian citizen. In 1957, Namatjira was granted restricted Australian citizenship — the right to vote, own land and drink alcohol. However, Arrente law expected him to share everything he owned, which he did. This inevitably brought him into conflict with the Northern Territory law authorities. He was subsequently charged and imprisoned for sharing alcohol to the other Aboriginal people of his community. Paul Hasluck, then Federal Minister for Territories, intervened. Namatjira was released but suffered a heart attack and died soon after. The Australian public was outraged.

In 1957, the Aboriginal-Australian Fellowship launched a petition campaign at the Sydney Town Hall. The petition was the idea of Jessie Street, an Australian suffragette, who had also been Australia's first female delegate to the United Nations. Another petition formed by the Federal Council for Aboriginal Advancement was signed by 25,000 people in 3 months and was presented to Federal Parliament. The aim of the petition was to amend section 51 and section 127 of the Constitution.

Section 51 (xxvi) The Parliament shall, subject to the Constitution, have power to make laws for the peace, order and good government of the Commonwealth with respect to the people of any race other than the Aboriginal race in any State, for whom it is deemed necessary to make special laws.	The aim of the petition was to delete the phrase "other than the Aboriginal race", so that the Federal government could take power away from the individual states and make laws to protect Aboriginal people.
Section 127 In reckoning the numbers of the people of the Commonwealth, or of a State or other part of the Commonwealth, Aboriginal natives shall not be counted.	The aim was to have this section repealed.

The 1960s — Australian Reform, Civil Rights, the Vietnam War and popular music

The 1960s was a decade of change and saw the liberalisation of western thinking, and on Australian society. The areas of liberalised thinking were:

1. Towards civil rights and suffrage for Australian Aboriginal and Torres Strait Islander peoples, culminating in the 1967 referendum that finally recognised the existence of the Indigenous peoples as citizens with the right to vote; 2. Towards the rights and liberation of women in Australian society; 3. Towards questioning the Australian government's blind and unjustified participation in wars, regardless of the harm to our soldiers and to neighbouring men, women and children; 4. Towards the popularisation of that liberalised thinking in popular music and song; and 5. Towards our shopping experiences.

The New Shopping Centres

For many suburban Australians, shopping in the 1960s was to change dramatically. This was also to have an enormous long-term effect on Australian society and economics.

Prior to the 1960s, Australians shopped in independently owned convenience stores. In 1960, Coles opened its first New World supermarket on the corner of Doncaster and Burke Roads, North Balwyn, Victoria. Soon other supermarket brands opened up and independent convenience stores had to revamp their thinking to compete effectively.

Also, in that same year, the Chadstone Shopping Centre was opened on Dandenong Road in Chadstone, Victoria. Today, the 'big chains' — Coles and Woolworths — take up about 70% of the supermarket / grocery business, with only 30% owned by independent traders.

Photo of the first New World (Dickens) Supermarket in North Balwyn.

Photo of Chadstone, circa 1960. Myers store at top, Tim the Toyman at rear, and Pantomime under small white square on upper right of centre.

The effect of the changes in supermarkets and shopping centres have had on Australian society is that retail has been largely taken out of the hands of small business and delivered to large chains, such as Bunnings, Coles, Woolworths, Chemist Warehouse, among others. Further, street shopping has been largely replaced by shopping centres such as Westfield. The structure of Australian society has changed, turning many small business owners into employees of large chains. Inadvertently, in the 1960s, the ethos of the Liberal government, traditionally supporting small business, had moved to supporting big business. Today's growing inequality between the very rich and the rest of society may be traced to this point.

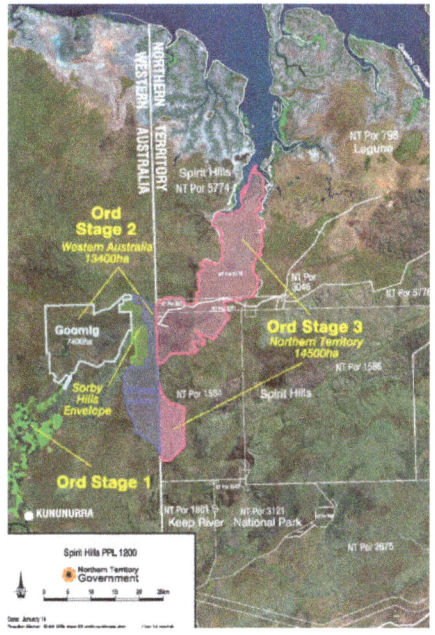

Map of the Ord River Irrigation Scheme

Pictures of the Ord River Scheme (above and below.)

The Ord River Project

The Ord River Irrigation Scheme was originally devised in the 1930s as a series of dams along the Ord River, located on the Kimberley Plateau of northern Western Australia and the Northern Territory border. The idea was conceived during the 1935-1942 drought that affected the greater Kimberley region. In 1939, Australian Michael Durack and the Russian-born Isaac Steinberg were in London and proposed the Kimberley region as an area suitable for the resettlement of Jewish refugees from Europe. After various surveys, the Ord River Irrigation Scheme began in 1960. The first dam, the Ord River Diversion Dam was completed in 1963. The second dam, the Ord River (Main) Dam including Lake Argyle was completed in 1969. A hydro-electric power station was constructed at Lake Argyle in 1996. It is estimated that an average of four billion megalitres of water is discharged into irrigation by the Ord River Irrigation Scheme annually.

Furhter, it has been speculated that many more billions of megalitres are not captured and allowed to run into the Indian Ocean and, if the Australian Government had the will, it could be captured, diverted and used to green the whole of Australia. It is also speculated that this massive project would cost billions of dollars that Australia cannot afford, or does not have the will to perform.

The Decimalisation and Metrication of Australia

Prior to the introduction of the metric counting system, colonial and post-federation Australia used the old Imperial system from Britain. This included measurement of length, area, weight, and currency.

In imperial currency, an Australian pound could be divided into 20 shillings, and each shilling could be divided into 12 pence; therefore, a pound was worth 240 pence. In 1959, the Treasurer, Harold Holt, convened a Decimal Currency Committee to plan for decimalisation. The model for decimalisation was based on the South African rand. One Australian dollar would be divided into 100 cents.

Initially, it was planned for 1963 but was deferred until 14 February (Valentine's Day) 1966. As the Australian dollar was fixed to the UK pound, the exchange rate was set at AU$2 = 1 UK pound. However, in 1967, as the UK pound fell in value, the Australian dollar exchange rate was set against the US dollar instead at a rate of AU$1 = US$1.12.

The first paper Australian banknotes were $1, $2, $10, and $20 notes. The $5 note was added in 1967, the $50 note in 1973, and the $100 note in 1984. The first polymer (plastic) banknotes were issued in 1988. The first coins were the 1c, 2c, 5c, 10c, 20c, and 50c. The $1 coin was introduced in 1984, replacing the banknote, as did the $2 coin in 1988. The 1c and 2c coins were removed from circulation in 1991. Occasionally, there have been commemorative coins circulated to celebrate special events or anniversaries.

An array of advertisements accompanied the introduction of decimal currency in 1966.

The metric system was designed and implemented in France in 1799, during the French Revolution. It was first set up to standardise measurement of length, one metre, and could be multiplied or divided by units of 10. The metric system included units for weight — grams and kilograms — and land area — hectares. All of these could be multiplied or divided by units of 10.

The introduction of metrication into Australia was a slow process, as follows:

- 1966 Introduction of decimal currency.
- 1971 The wool industry converts to metric system.
- 1972 The horseracing industry converts to metric. Air temperatures convert to Celsius.
- 1973 Schools begin teaching in metric system alone.

1974   Packaged products and road signs convert to metric.
1976   The building and construction industries convert to metric.
1987   The real estate industry converts to metric.
1988   Western Australia becomes the last state to fully convert to the metric system.

Aboriginal sports persons in the 1960s

The inclusion and achievements of Aboriginal sports persons in the 1960s was a major factor in the recognition by the wider Australian public of an equal place in Australian society for Aboriginal people.

Polly Farmer

Graham Vivian "Polly" Farmer (1935-1019), born in North Fremantle, Western Australia, was a famous Aussie-Rules footballer and was an advocate for young Aboriginal people.

Farmer played 176 games with East Perth (1952-1961), 101 games for Geelong (1962-1967), and 79 games for West Perth (1968-1971) for a total of 356 games. He also coached West Perth, Geelong, East Perth and Western Australia (1968-1977) in 208 games.

At 191cm (6'3"), Farmer revolutionised ruckwork with agile mobility and handball. His highlights were five WAFL premierships, one VFL premiership, 3 Sandover Medals, and is named in each of the Geelong, East Perth and West Perth Teams of the Century. In 1971, he received a Member of the Order of the British Empire (MBE).

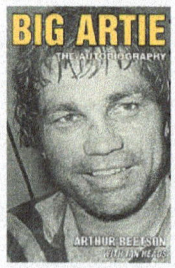
Arthur Beetson

Arthur Henry "Artie" Beetson (1945-2011), born in Roma, Queensland, was a famous Australian Rugby League player.

Beetson was a 188 cm (6'2") prop, second row, and played 233 club games in Australia and England, and played 50 representative games for Australia, Queensland and New South Wales. Also, he coached in 192 club games and 17 representative games — Queensland and Australia.

Beetson was the first Indigenous player to captain Australia in Rugby League. He is named in the Australian, Queensland and Indigenous Teams of the Century and received the Medal of the Order of Australia (OAM).

Lionel Rose

Lionel Edmond Rose (1948-2011), born in Drouin, Victoria, was an Australian Bantamweight boxer and was the first Indigenous Australian to win a world boxing title.

At 166 cm (5'6"), Rose fought in 53 bouts for 42 wins, of which 12 were knock outs. In 1968, Rose won the World Bantamweight title in Tokyo after winning against Masahiko "Fighting" Harada in a points decision. After retiring from boxing, Rose had a hit song with the single, "I Thank You", which was a national "top 5" hit. Rose was awarded Australian of the Year in 1968, the first Indigenous Australian to do so.

Evonne Fay Goolagong Cawley (1951-), born in Griffith, New South Wales, was a famous Australian tennis player and the world's no.1 female player.

Evonne Goolagong

Evonne Goolagong, as she was known in her early career, was a 168cm (5'7") right-hander.

Goolagong won over 80% of her 869 games and won 86 singles titles, including four Australian Opens, one French open, one Wimbledon, and was a finalist in four US Opens. She also won 46 doubles titles, including five Australian Opens, one Wimbledon, and one French Open. She was also a member of three winning Australian Federation Cup teams.

Goolagong was Australian of the Year in 1971, appointed an MBE in 1972 and made an Officer of the Order of Australia in 1982.

Equal wages

The issue of equal wages rose in 1963 because of the inequality of wages in rural communities between "white" stockmen and Aboriginal stockmen. Not only were wage outcomes different, but the meals provided by the station owners were different, with the Aboriginal workers receiving only basic food that did not meet nutritional needs, often merely salt beef, damper, sugar and tea. The issue also remained that while the Aboriginal stockmen were still out looking after the cattle, "white" stockmen were returning to camp and taking advantage of the Aboriginal women. In a 1966 submission, the pastoralists stated that if an equal wages outcome occurred, they would stop employing Aboriginal stockmen. In 1968, after Aboriginal people were granted citizenship, the Conciliation and Arbitration Commission ruled that equal wages should apply. Immediately, pastoralists reacted by "sacking" their Aboriginal stockmen and forcing Aboriginal communities off the stations that they had worked for generations. Subsequently, Aboriginal people began drifting into the towns, unemployed and idle, receiving unemployment benefits, and often spending the money on alcohol.

The Freedom Ride 1965

Inspired by a similar Freedom Ride in the United States in 1964, Australian students were inspired to look at the plight of impoverished Aboriginal communities. In February 1965, a group of University of Sydney students went on a bus tour of New South Wales coastal towns. It was led by third-year student and Arrente man, Charles Perkins. The purpose was to draw the public's attention to the impoverished state of Aboriginal health, housing and education, the discrimination Aboriginal communities faced by "white" residents, and to encourage the Aboriginal people to resist that discrimination. The Freedom Ride visited towns including Walgett, Gulargambone, Kempsey, Bowraville and Moree. The group were refused service in shops and hotels. At one point outside Walgett, one of the group Jim Spigelman, captured on camera a convoy of cars of local residents who intentionally ran the bus off the road. In each town, the group was met with hostility. In Moree, a violent scuffle broke out. The videos of each incident were sent to and reported by the Australian Broadcasting Commission (ABC) on television, highlighting the discrimination and revealing to the general public something it had not seen. It made most of the Australian general public realise the injustice done to Aboriginal peoples and the discrimination that they were still facing. It also showed that strong activism could create change in the public's mind.

Student Action for Aborigines

The 1967 Referendum

In 1965, the Legislative Reform Committee of the Federal Council for the Advancement of Aborigines and Torres Strait Islanders (FCAATSI) took responsibility for constitutional reform. FCAATSI included Doug Nicholls, Charles Perkins, Kath Walker (Oodgeroo Noonuccal), Harry Penrith (Burnum Burnum), Joe McGinness, Faith Bandler, Stan Davey, Bert Groves, Bill Onus and Chicka Dixon. In 1967, Federal Attorney General, Nigel Bowen, recommended to cabinet the amendment of section 57 and the repeal of section 127. The churches across Australia came out in favour of the referendum.

The bus in Bogabilla

Charles Perkins speaks to Moree Aboriginal residents.

The crowd confronting the students at Moree

On May 27th, 1967, over 90% of the Australian electorate voted 'YES'. The sheer number of 90% was important in seeing the legislation changed through parliament. In June 1967, Charles Perkins wrote an important letter to then Prime Minister Harold Holt and they met in London. Kath Walker also wrote an important letter of recommendation, and Holt responded with a short letter of affirmation.

It was to be more than a decade before Australia had its first Aboriginal Member of Parliament.

In December of 1967, Prime Minister Harold Holt was to disappear at Cheviot Beach near Point Nepean on the Victorian coast. He was never seen again, and no one really can be certain what happened to him, although he was deemed to have drowned while swimming. Rather ironically, in what can be considered a humorous twist, Harold Holt is memorialised by having a swimming pool named after him.

Victory celebration, Tranby College, Sydney, June 1967

Victory celebration, Tranby College, Sydney, June 1967

Neville Bonner

Neville Bonner (1922-1999) was the first Aboriginal Australian to be a member of the Parliament of Australia. Bonner was born on Ukerebagh Island, located at the mouth of the Tweed River, in New South Wales. Without any formal education, he worked on cane fields and as a stockman, settling in Palm Island in 1946 as assistant to the settlement overseer.

Neville Bonner as acting President of the Senate (Museum of Australian Democracy, Old Parliament House).

In 1960, Bonner moved to Ipswich, joining the board of directors of an indigenous rights organisation, the One People of Australia League (OPAL). He became its Queensland President in 1970. In 1967, Bonner had joined the Liberal Party and in 1971 was asked to fill a casual vacancy in the Senate. Bonner had become the first indigenous Australian to sit in the Australian Parliament, re-elected four times until 1983, where he left the Liberal Party to run as an independent. Bonner was well known for crossing the floor on particular issues, including opposing drilling on the Great Barrier Reef. The Hawke Government then appointed him to the board of directors for the Australian Broadcasting Corporation (ABC).

In 1979, Neville Bonner was named Australian of the Year, was awarded an Officer of the Order of Australia in 1984 and sat on the Griffith University Council from 1992 to 1996, being awarded an honorary doctorate in 1993. He sat in the 1998 Constitutional Convention, supporting the constitutional monarchy. Bonner died in Ipswich in 1999.

From a different perspective, this is one of Australia's great moments of hope and shame. Australian athlete Peter Norman finished in second place in the men's 200 metre sprint in the 1968 Mexico Summer Olympics. On the podium, he supported the 'human rights' salutes of the two U.S. athletes. Consequently, Norman was alienated by Australian athletics and was ignored for the 1972 Munich games, though qualifying over a dozen times.

The Vietnam War (1962-1975)

The Vietnam War ran from 1955 until 1975, however Australia's involvement in it began in 1962. The war began in 1945, when the Vietnamese people sought independence from the old colonial French Indochina.

The Vietnamese leader, Ho Chi Minh, rejected a French proposal for limited self-government and the Viet Minh began a war of rebellion. In 1950, both China and the Soviet Union recognised the communist Democratic Republic of Vietnam (North Vietnam). The United States offered help to the French-led government (South Vietnam). In 1954, French troops were decisively defeated by the Viet Minh at Dien Bien Phu. In retaliation the United States entered the war against the Viet Minh. In 1962, as part of ANZUS treaty obligations, Australia sent troops to assist the Americans in Vietnam.

From 1962 to 1973, almost 60,000 Australian troops were sent to Vietnam; over 500 died and over 3,000 were wounded. The war was the first to be broadcast live on national television with pictures in newspapers and magazines.

Scenes from the Vietnam War

It was the first time that war was portrayed in its full horror while occurring. It was the first war where Australians were drafted, rather than volunteered, which resulted in conscientious objection, 'draft dodgers', and public protests against the war. The war saw the United

States (US) Airforce indiscriminately bomb, massacre, and burn Vietnamese cities, towns and villages. It escalated in 1970, when the US Airforce began bombing into the neighbouring country of Cambodia. The Viet Minh never fought in open battle as they were technologically inferior to the United States. Instead, they chose to resist using guerrilla warfare. By 1973, the Viet Minh had taken Saigon, the South Vietnamese capital and the last of the Australian troops were withdrawn. The Vietnam War was the first war in Australian history when the return of Australian soldiers was not celebrated. The Vietnam War officially ended in 1975, with Ho Chi Minh as leader of a united Vietnam.

The Arts in '60s Australia

As Australia's post-war economy grew, so did its arts. A number of Australians became internationally famous through the various arts — music, painting, and acting.

Joan Sutherland (1926-2010), born in Sydney and nicknamed 'La Stupenda', was Australia's most successful opera star, performing from the late 1940s through to the 1980s. An international star, Sutherland was the first Australian to win a Grammy Award, Best Classical Performance — Vocal Soloist, in 1962. Sutherland studied at St Catherine's School in Waverley, NSW, then at the Royal College of music in London. She had a tremendous upper range in her repertoire, although critics often complained of the Australian 'twang' in her diction.

Sutherland was awarded Commander of the Order of the British Empire (CBE) and Australian of the Year in 1961. She was elevated to Dame Commander (DBE) in 1979. Sutherland received many other awards.

Robert Helpmann (1909-1986), born in Mount Gambier, South Australia, was an Australian ballet dancer, actor, director, and choreographer in a career that spanned from the 1930s to the 1980s.

In 1926, Helpmann was a student ballet apprentice to Anna Pavlova, who was touring Australia. Helpmann left for London in 1932. He danced with Margo Fonteyn and Alicia Markova, acted with Ralph Richardson and Vivian Leigh on stage, directed opera at Covent Garden, choreographed 12 ballets, acted in 16 films as diverse as 'Henry V' (1944), '55 Days in Peking' (1963), and 'Chitty Chitty Bang Bang' (1968).

Helpmann was awarded the Royal Order of the Polar Star (Sweden, 1954), Knight of the Cedar (Lebanon, 1957), Commander of the Order of the British Empire (CBE, 1964), Australian of the Year (1965), and Knight Bachelor (1968). The Helpmann Academy in South Australia is named in his honour and the Helpmann Awards for performing arts have been presented annually since 2001.

Richard Bonygne (1930-), born in Epping, Sydney, is an Australian conductor and pianist, and conducted all of Sutherland's performances from 1962. Bonygne studied piano at the Sydney Conservatorium of Music then the Royal College of Music. He became a coach for singers, including a young Joan Sutherland, whom he had previously accompanied in Australia. They married in 1954 and performed as a duo. In 1962, Bonygne took over as conductor for Sutherland.

Bonygne was awarded Commander of the Order of the British Empire (CBE) in 1977, among other awards.

Kevin Charles 'Pro' Hart (1929-2006), born in Broken Hill, NSW, was a famous Australian artist and is considered the father of Australian 'Outback' painting. He painted in various styles over his career and established his own unique style using 'cannon painting' and 'balloon painting'. Unfortunately, Hart was regularly criticised by the art 'establishment' yet earned popularity and acclaim despite it. His painting often explored political themes. He is well known for his series of 'Ned Kelly' paintings. He was warded a Member of the Order of the British Empire (MBE) in 1976.

Florence Broadhurst

Florence Broadhurst (1899-1977), born in Mount Perry, Queensland, was an Australian painter, fabric and wallpaper designer. She also went by the names Bobby Broadhurst and Madame Pellier. In her early years, Broadhurst established herself as a touring singer and ran a music school. After a car accident, she left for England and married a British businessman. There she called herself Madame Pellier. After World War Two, she returned to Australia and began painting the Australian landscape. She produced 144 paintings that were displayed in 1954 at the David Jones Art Gallery.

Florence Broadhurst

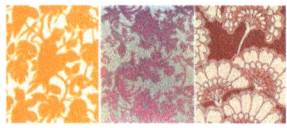
An array of her floral wallpaper designs

In 1959, Broadhurst established Australian (Hand Printed) Wallpapers. Her wallpapers were a hit worldwide. By the 1970s, she had 800 different designs in 80 colours, exporting worldwide. In 1977, she was mysteriously killed at her home in Paddington and the perpetrator was never apprehended.

Popular Music in the '60s

Prior to the 1960s, Australian popular music had been based on ballads, folk and country music. Famous country musicians included Smokey Dawson (1913-2008), Buddy Williams (1918-1986), Shirley Thoms (1925-1999), Gordon Parsons (1926-1990) Slim Dusty (1927-2003), Reg Lindsay (1929-2008), Stan Coster (1930-1997) and Jimmy Little (1937-2012).

From 1962 to 1963, an English-born Australian singer, Frank Ifield, had four no.1 singles on the U.K. charts, being: I Remember You, Lovesick Blues, The Wayward Wind, and Confessin' (That I Love You), as well as his U.K. no.4 hit Nobody's Darlin' But Mine. His songs did better in the U.K. than in Australia.

In 1962, three boys from Melbourne High School — Athol Guy, Keith Potger and Bruce Woodley — formed a band called The Seekers and recruited a young female, Judith Durham, as lead singer. The band was heavily influence by the rising popularity of folk music in the early 60s. The Seekers found opportunity as the resident band on a Sitmar Lines cruise to London. Upon arriving there, they found regular work and became connected to Dusty Springfield's brother, Tom Springfield, who was to have a profound effect on the band. He penned, I'll Find Another You, which was recorded by The Seekers and went to no.1 in both the UK and Australia and no.4 in the USA, becoming the seventh largest single in 1965. In 1966, their next hit, The Carnival Is Over, their own, did even better. The Seekers continued with hit singles such as A World of Our Own, Morningtown Ride, and the famed Georgy Girl, eventually adapted to film, starring Vanessa Redgrave and James Mason. In 1967, they returned to Australia for a homecoming tour. The highlight was the sold-out concert at the Myer Music Bowl, Melbourne.

After the tour, the band broke up. The band has reunited a number of times over following decades.

The greatest contribution of The Seekers was in 2015, when on a reunion, the band introduced a new song penned by Bruce Woodley and Dobe Newton (of Bushwackers fame). The song was called I Am (you are, we are) Australian, which expressed all the views that unite a multicultural Australia and, arguably, should be the national anthem of a future generation.

Frank Ifield *The Seekers* *The Easybeats*

In late 1964, an Australian rock band, The Easybeats was formed in Sydney. The Easybeats were to become one of the most important bands in Australian rock music history. Interestingly, none of the band was born in Australia. All were members of migrant families that come to Australia during the "wave of immigration" and the band was formed in the Villawood Migrant Hostel. Members Stevie Wright and Gordon "Snowy" Fleet were from England; George Young was from Scotland; Harry Vanda and Dick Diamonde were from the Netherlands (Holland). The Easybeats had their first hit in 1965 with She's So Fine, followed by further hits, Wedding Ring, Women (Make You Feel Alright), and Come and See Her. After moving to England, The Easybeats had an Australian no.1 hit and a U.K. no.6 hit with Friday on My Mind at a time when The Beatles and The Kinks were dominating the U.K. charts. Soon after, the band fell into decline and returned to Australia. Guitarist George Young learnt from his experience with The

Easybeats and almost a decade later went onto manage his younger brothers' band, AC/DC, arguably Australia's greatest ever rock band.

Brian Cadd was a Perth-born, Australian Singer-songwriter. His music career spanned Australia, Europe and America. He wrote and played keyboards for a number of bands — The Groop (1966-69), Axiom (1969-71), The Bootleg Family Band (1972-75), The Flying Burrito Brothers (1991-93) — as well as having a successful solo career. Cadd also produced other acts and his own record label — Bootleg Records. His song-writing hits include Woman You're Breaking Me, When I Was Six Years Old (later recorded by Manfred Mann), Arkansas Grass, A Little Ray of Sunshine, Ginger Man, Don't You Know It's Magic, and the theme to the film 'Alvin Purple'.

Brian Cadd

Two Great Australian Sportswomen

No history of Australia would be complete without noting the tennis achievements of Margaret Court and the achievements in squash of Heather McKay.

Margaret Court

Margaret Court (nee Smith, b.1942-), born in Albury, New South wales, is Australia's greatest tennis player and the greatest tennis player of all time. She won 24 Grand Slam singles titles, more than any other tennis player in history. At the time of this book's writing, Serena Williams had won 23 Grand Slam titles and Roger Federer had won 20 Grand Slam titles.

Court, a 175 cm (5'9") right-hander began playing professional tennis in 1960. She was world no.1 ranked female tennis player by 1962. Over her career, Court won 192 singles titles, including eleven Australian

Opens, five French Opens, three Wimbledons, and five US Opens. She also won 40 Grand Slam Doubles and Mixed Doubles titles. Court was also a member of four winning Federation Cup teams. She retired in 1977 and was elected to the International Tennis Hall of Fame in 1979.

Having grown up as a Roman Catholic in her youth, after her retirement, Court entered the Pentecostal Church and was ordained a minister in 1991. She has come under recent criticism and censure for her views on LGBT rights and same-sex marriage.

Margaret Court's honours include receiving a Member of the Order of the British Empire (MBE) in 1967, aged 25 years. She was made an Officer of the Order of Australia (AO) in 2007 for services to tennis and the community, among other achievements. The main tennis court at Melbourne Park, the home of the Australian Open, is named after her. Margaret Court is to tennis, as Don Bradman was to cricket.

Court with Evonne Goolagong, Wimbledon Doubles, 1971

Court with Evonne Goolagong, Wimbledon Doubles, 1971

Heather McKay

Heather McKay (nee Blundell, b.1941-), born in Queanbeyan, New South Wales, is considered to be greatest female squash player of all time, and also arguably Australia's greatest sportswoman. McKay dominated female squash tournaments through the 1960s and 70s, winning 16 consecutive British Open squash titles from 1962 to 1977. She won the inaugural women's squash World Open in 1976 and, again,

Heather McKay, circa 1970

in 1979, before retiring. In 1980, McKay turned her attention to the game of racquetball and was soon the world champion, after winning the pro-nationals in 1980, 1981 and 1984. In 1997, she was inducted into the US Racquetball Hall of Fame.

For her achievements, McKay was awarded ABC Sportsman of the Year (1967), Order of the British Empire (1969), Order of Australia (1979), Officer of the Order of Australia (2018), among others.

Australia and Women's Lib — Greer, Reddy & Roxon

There were many contributions to the Women's Liberation movement in the 1960s and 1970s. Australia had been one of the first countries to give women the vote in 1902.

In the 1960s and 1970s there were three notable women who made an international contribution to women's rights — Germaine Greer, Helen Reddy and Lillian Roxon.

Germaine Greer

Germaine Greer (1939-), born in Melbourne, is a noted author of feminism. From a Catholic family, Greer won a scholarship to Star of Sea College in Gardenvale. She studied at the University of Melbourne, the University of Sydney, and attained her Ph.D at Newnhan College, Cambridge. Greer's most famous and internationally acclaimed and bestselling book, 'The Female Eunuch', a critique on the plight of women, womanhood, and femininity. Greer dedicated 'The Female Eunuch' to Lillian Roxon, facing page.

Helen Reddy (1941-2020), born in Melbourne, is a noted international singing star. Reddy was born into an acting and performing family. At 17, she won a contest on Bandstand, with the prize, a free trip to New York. Singing in clubs, Reddy had an early Australian hit with 'One Way Ticket'. In 1972, she co-wrote 'I Am Woman', with Ray Burton of Delltones fame. The song became an anthem for women around the world. From 1972-76, Reddy had nine U.S. #1 hit singles, including 'Delta Dawn', 'Angie Baby', among many others.

Helen Reddy

Lillian Roxon (1932-73), born in Italy, was a noted journalist and author. Her Jewish family, originally Ropschitz, migrated to Brisbane in 1937. Lillian anglicised the family name to Roxon. She moved to Sydney and became the New York correspondent for the Sydney Morning Herald. She is best known for her interest and articles on women's

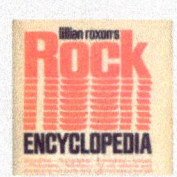

Lillian Roxon

affairs and feminism, and new wave pop music in the '60s. In 1968-69 was commissioned to write the first 'Rock Encyclopaedia'. She is often referred to as 'the mother of rock and roll journalism'. Her niece is Australian politician Nicola Roxon.

In 1972, **Shane Gould** (b. 1956, Sydney), at age 16, became Australia's most renowned freestyle swimmer. At the 1972 Munich Olympics, she won 3 gold, 1 silver, and 1 bronze. Between December 1971 and September 1972, Gould simultaneously held the world record times for all freestyle events and the 200m individual medley. After the Munich  Olympics, she retired from competitive swimming. In the early 2000s, Gould returned to swimming, competing and setting records in the Australian Masters series, as well as a world record in 2003, in the 45-49 year 200m individual medley. In 2018, at age 62, she appeared and won the reality TV series, Australian Survivor.

Gould was awarded Best Sportswoman in the World (1971), ABC Sportswoman of the Year (1971 & 1972), Australian of the Year (1972), International Swimming Hall of Fame (1977), Member of the Order of the British Empire (1981), Sport Australia Hall of Fame (1985), among many other awards.

Free Trade and Anti-Censorship — 1970s

In the 1970s, world economists, largely from America, began spouting the benefits of free trade. At that time, the manufacturing sector was about 42% of the Australian economy, with textile manufacturing being 40% of that. In 1973, the Whitlam government introduced a 25% reduction in tariffs across the board. The immediate effect of the tariff cuts was that the Australian textile manufacturing industry was by 1980 wiped out, with many textile distributers choosing to import from south eastern Asia instead. This was followed by further quota removals and tariff reductions in 1987, 1988, 1991, 1993, 2010 and 2015. The final 2015 cut saw the last of the Australian car manufacturers — Holden, Ford, and Toyota — close Australian manufacturing. Today, the manufacturing sector is around 5% of the Australian economy — an enormous reduction from the 40% of the 1970 Australian economy — with only a few boutique manufacturers remaining.

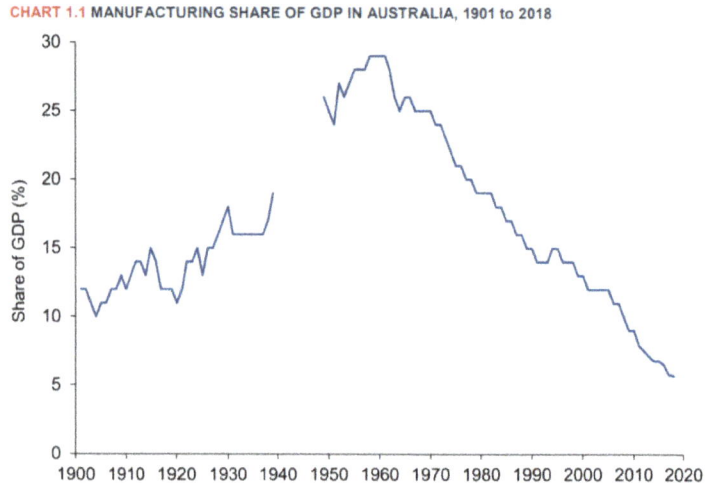

Trend of Australian manufacturing as a % of GDP from 1901, peaking in the 1960s, declining through to now. (Source: AI Goup)
https://cdn.aigroup.com.au/Economic_Indicators/Economic_Outlook/Australian_Manufacturing_in_2019.pdf

Censorship has been an issue in Australia since federation. In 1929, the D.H. Lawrence novel, 'Lady Chatterley's Lover', was banned, using importation laws. In 1969, Philip Roth's novel, 'Portnoy's Complaint', was also banned but public opinion had changed. In 1970, the newly formed Australian Classification Board created a Restricted (R) rating, for adults only.

Alvin Purple (1973)

The first and most notable 'R' rated films to be produced in Australia were 'Stork' (1971) starring Bruce Spence; 'The Adventures of Barry McKenzie' (1972), starring Barry Crocker and Barry Humphries; and 'Alvin Purple' (1973), starring Graeme Blundell. In 1993, the classifications were watered down to allow the MA15+ rating, allowing films with some sex and violence, e.g., 'Silence of The Lambs' (1991) to be shown to the adolescent public.

The Adventures of Barry McKenzie (1972)   The Adventures of Barry McKenzie (1972)

Trans-Tasman Agreement — New Zealand and Pacific Island migration

New Zealand became a separate colony in 1840. Since then, there has been a steady exchange of people between the two countries. However, this was almost entirely for 'white' persons. For those that were not 'white', it was a very different story. The first group of 67 southern Pacific islanders arrived in 1863. From then, until federation, over 60,000 Pacific Islanders were kidnapped or coerced into working on the sugar plantations and the farms of northern Queensland. In 1901, influenced by a growing 'White Australia Policy', the federal government passed the Pacific Island Labourers Act, which saw the deportation of most Pacific Islanders from Australia.

In 1973, following the ending of White Australia Policy, the Whitlam government entered into the Trans-Tasman Travel Agreement, which allowed for the free movement of citizens between Australia and New Zealand, including employment. Many of the provisions of free movement have been eroded by subsequent Australian governments on the basis that many Pacific Islanders had come to Australia via New Zealand. In 1982, passports were required. In 1994, the Keating government introduced special visa arrangements. In 1998, the Howard government reduced welfare arrangements to two years. In 2001, new arrangements removed all welfare and civic rights.

In 2014, the Abbott government introduced character tests for New Zealanders arriving in Australia, and the deportation of those that had broken the law. By July 2018, over 1,000 New Zealanders had been deported from Australia on the basis of the character test, with the majority of these being from either Maori or Pacific Islander descent. In 2018, the ABC aired a documentary that exposed the discriminatory nature of the character test. Subsequently, the Australian government was heavily criticised.

Following the Covid-19 pandemic, negotiations between Australian and New Zealand Prime Ministers, Morrison and Ahern respectively, saw the extension of 'Job-Keeper' payments to New Zealanders. There are about 650,000 New Zealanders living in Australia, mainly living in Queensland and New South Wales.

1975 — Constitutional Crisis

The dismissal of the Whitlam government by the Governor-General, Sir John Kerr, on 11 November 1975 set off a constitutional crisis in Australia. The Whitlam government had been elected in 1972, with the slogan "It's time", and had implemented a series of reforms to Australian society. The key reforms were: 1. the introduction of a national health scheme, Medicare; 2. the abolition of capital punishment (death) for national crimes; 3. a national sewerage program;

4. the introduction of legal aid; 5. reforms to family law; 6. abolition of university fees; and 7. the replacement of the national anthem to 'Advance Australia Fair' — all within only 3 years in office. The Whitlam government also ended Australia's involvement in the Vietnam War and abolished military conscription.

1972 election poster of Gough Whitlam and his wife, Margaret

Governor-General, Sir John Kerr

Opposition leader, Malcolm Fraser

Whitlam speaking on the steps of Parliament House.

However, as the Whitlam government rushed through its reform agenda while still maintaining control of both parliamentary houses, it began losing financial control of the budget supporting its agenda and was 'rocked' by a growing number of scandals. During 1975, due to the need to replace a Queensland senator, the Whitlam government lost control of the Senate. Upon this, the Opposition, led by Malcolm Fraser, blocked all fiscal supply and budget bills by the government. A crisis was growing, and Whitlam refused any compromise offered by Kerr at a 1pm meeting in the Governor-General's office. Whitlam did not know that Fraser was sitting in the office's ante room. Refusing the compromise, Kerr terminated Whitlam as Prime Minister. Whitlam left the office and Fraser entered immediately to be installed as caretaker Prime Minister. When Whitlam was sacked, he delayed informing his government colleagues. In that short time, at 2pm the budget bill was introduced to Senate and passed by a knowing opposition, giving Fraser the funds that he needed as caretaker. Later that day, a large and noisy crowd assembled on the steps of Parliament House, where Whitlam uttered the famous words, "Well may we say, "God save the Queen", because nothing will save the Governor-General!" A general election was called for December. Labor focused on the dismissal, with the slogan "Shame Fraser Shame". The Opposition focused on the declining economy. A letter bomb sent to the Governor-General's office was discovered and defused. Fraser won the election in a landslide.

In 2020, the release of the Buckingham Palace correspondence between the Governor General, John Kerr and Her Majesty's Secretary indicated that Kerr had communicated with the Queen's office regarding the circumstances and options leading up to the dismissal, although he did not notify the Queen of his decision until after the dismissal. Further, Kerr had not communicated any of his intensions prior to dismissing Prime Minister Gough Whitlam.

Photo of the Chamberlain family after the incident, 1980.

"A dingo's got my baby" — The Lindy Chamberlain Case

In August 1980, the Australian public woke to the news of a two-month baby girl who had been killed by a dingo on a family camping trip to Uluru (Ayers Rock) in the Northern Territory. However, the mother, Lindy Chamberlain was charged with murder and spent the next three years in prison. The police investigation and subsequent trial became the widespread focus of the Australian public. The police claimed crucial evidence of blood found in the family's car. In 1986, a piece of Azaria Chamberlain's clothing was found at a dingo's lair near the place of the incident. Later investigation found that the Northern Territory coroner had mistaken the blood residue of the car when it was in fact clay. Although released in 1986, Lindy Chamberlain had to wait 32 years, 2012, before her version of events was supported by the coroner. She received over $1 million in compensation for false imprisonment. The case serves as an example of how media bias can affect the result of a trial. In 1985, John Bryson wrote an account called Evil Angels, which was turned into film by Fred Schepisi in 1988, starring Meryl Streep. The story has also been produced into an opera, 'Lindy' (2002), and a TV mini-series, 'Through My Eyes' (2004), starring Miranda Otto and Craig McLachlan.

The HIV/AIDS Epidemic

Human Immunodeficiency Virus (HIV) and Acquired Immune Deficiency Syndrome (AIDS) refers to a virus that notably spread across the world during the 1980s. The virus led to rare types of fatal pneumonia and lung cancer. It is believed to have originated from chimpanzees in Central Africa and transferred to humans in the 1920s. By the 1970s, there were already over 100,000 people infected over five continents. Originally, it was thought only to be transferred between gay men and people injecting themselves with drugs. However, there were also reports of HIV and AIDS being acquired by haemophiliacs and heterosexual women. In 1985, the Hollywood actor Rock Hudson died of AIDS. By the end of the 1980s, it was estimated by the World Health Organisation (WHO) that about 500,000 people had AIDS.

The Grim Reaper bowls over unsuspecting Australians during the HIV/AIDS adverts of the 1980s.

In Australia, the first recorded case of AIDS was detected in Sydney in 1982, and the first death from AIDS was in Melbourne in 1983. Community and television advertising about AIDS featured a "grim reaper' bowling over people like ninepins with bowling balls, causing fear and paranoia across the country. In 1985, a three-year-old, Eve van Grafhorst contracted AIDS after blood transfusions, due to complications after premature birth. She was ostracized from her pre-school, and after the news hit network television, from Australia too. Her family moved to New Zealand, where she died at eleven.

Eventually, the world found methods to treat HIV/AIDS through anti-retroviral drugs, although it still remains, and in 2017 it is estimated that over 20,000 people live with some sort of HIV in Australia.

In 2003, it was reported that a division of the international medical supply company Bayer had been sourcing blood supplies in the 1980s from HIV/AIDS-infected prison populations in the United States and supplying infected blood, thereby spreading the virus to the rest of the world. By 2003, Bayer had secretly paid out over US$600 million (AU$1 billion) to settle cases. However, the report was effectively covered up and Bayer has not been prosecuted.

New Waves of Immigration

In 1966, the Holt Liberal government reviewed and enacted changes in the Migration Act, effectively dismantling the White Australia Policy. The number of non-European migrants grew from 746 in 1966 to 2,696 in 1971. However, the old Labor opposition, under Caldwell, was still clinging to the White Australia Policy. This was to change. In 1973, the newly elected Whitlam Labor government amended legislation, preventing any racial aspects to immigration law. This was followed by the Racial Discrimination Act 1975, which made racial criteria for any official purpose illegal. Between 1978 and 1981, the Fraser Liberal government removed the last traces of any racial elements or country of origin from Australian law. This allowed non-European immigrants to come to Australia from Asia, Africa, and the Americas.

Ceylon / Sri Lanka — 1970s
The first Ceylonese persons to come to Australia were Drum Major William O'Dean (a Sri Lankan Malay) and his wife Eve (Sinhalese) in 1816. The recorded first group of Sinhalese arrived in Australia in 1870 as sugar cane plantation workers in Queensland. From 1948, after the Second World War and Sri Lankan independence, Burghers (of Euro-Asian ethnicity) began arriving in Australia as they qualified as European under the terms of the White Australia Policy. In the 1950s and 1960s, Sinhalese, the main ethnic group of Sri Lanka, began arriving with the introduction of the Colombo Plan. This was a cross-cultural economic and educational development plan set up between Asia-Pacific nations. In the early 1970s, I met the Sinclair family from

Sri Lanka, through our local cricket club. They lived in Mount Waverley, in Melbourne.

After the dismantling of the White Australia Policy and the Sri Lankan Civil War, more Sinhalese, Tamils and Moors (Muslim Tamils) have migrated to Australia. Half of the Sri Lankan communities in Australia live in the Melbourne greater suburbs of Dandenong, Glen Waverley, Clayton, Hallam, and Keysborough. Another quarter live in Sydney's suburbs of Pendle Hill, and Homebush. Current Australian cricketer Ashton Agar is of Sri Lankan ancestry.

Latin American migration – 1970s on

Due to the economic and political unrest of South and Central American countries during the 1970s, Australia experienced a surge in immigration from that region. According to the 2006 Census, the largest groups were from Chile (23,305), El Salvador (18,000), Argentina (11,369), Uruguay (9,376), Brazil (6,647), Peru (6,322) and Columbia (5,706). Since 2011, Brazil which has overtaken Chile. As of 2014, there were 4,960 Mexican-born living in Australia. The estimated number of Latin American-born in Australian is about 200,000 people.

Vietnam – 1975

Prior to 1971, less than 700 persons in Australia stated that Vietnam was their country of birth. After the fall of Saigon to the North Vietnamese, ending the Vietnam war, many who were part of or collaborated with the South Vietnamese government feared persecution. When Australia relaxed its immigration laws, a wave of 'boat people' from South Vietnam arrived. By 1985, over 80,000 persons of Vietnamese origin resided in Australia. By 2011, this number had increased to over 180,000.

Many of the 'boat people' endured great hardship getting to

Australia. One 1982 newspaper report from Thailand detailed the plight of Mrs Dang Thai Dung. She travelled on a boat with her husband and baby boy. On the way, the boat was intercepted by Thai pirates. Her husband, with 23 other men, were thrown into the ocean to drown. She was raped repeatedly by the pirates. Another, Vo Thi Thua, saw her three children drowned in the ocean and she was repeatedly raped over a period of eleven days, before being rescued by a friendly ship. Yet when they arrived in Australia, the Vietnamese refugees were labelled as 'queue-jumpers' and received negative public sentiment from the Australian public.

Tuong Quang Luu was a senior diplomat for the South Vietnamese government. He disguised himself in ordinary clothing and made his way to the Vietnamese coast to catch a boat to Australia. Mr Luu reflected that 'the White Australia Policy had been abolished. The public opinion had not turned around" and "... the policy of the Fraser government was a courageous one and very visionary".

Today, the Vietnamese communities are an important part of the greater Australian community, with representatives in public service and government. Hieu Van Le is the current Governor of South Australia.

Cambodia (Khmer Rouge, 1975-1986)

The first Cambodians to arrive in Australia were a family of nine, arriving in the late 1940s. After Cambodian independence from French rule, Cambodian students began to study in Australia under the Colombo plan. However, the decision by the United States military to involve Cambodia in the Vietnam War was to have a devastating effect on the country. During the early 1970s, the indiscriminate bombing, killing, and starvation saw the Khmer Rouge regime replace the political vacuum that had been created. It is estimated that over one million Cambodians died of starvation or execution during the tenure of the regime between 1975 and 1978.

Prior to 1975, there were about 1,000 Cambodian-born Australians; however, many Cambodians fled their homes into the refugee camps of other south-eastern Asian countries. Australia increased its intake and by the mid-1980s, about 10,000 Cambodians had arrived and most eventually settled in Melbourne's south-eastern suburbs (Clayton/Springvale). Today, the Cambodian community are also an important part of the Australian community. Hong Lim was the Labor Member of the Legislative Assembly of Victoria from 1996 to 2018 for Clayton, then Clarinda. Meng Heang Tak replaced him in 2018, also from the Labor Party.

Lebanese Civil War – 1975-1990

The first Lebanese people arrived in Australia during the late 1800s. They were a combination of Maronite Catholics, Greek Orthodox, and Muslim migrants, primarily because they were seeking a better life.

The earliest recorded Lebanese, Massoud El-Nashbi, arrived in Australia in 1880 from Kfasghabi in northern Lebanon. He sold souvenirs of the Holy Land for large sums of money to Australians then returned home. Upon hearing good words about Australia, some families from northern Lebanon migrated to Australia and worked in the Broken Hill mines. This is how the Joseph, Kardachi and Abdullah families established the beginnings of the Lebanese communities initially in Adelaide, Broken Hill, then Sydney.

The Joseph family, also from Kfasghabi, began arriving in Adelaide in the 1880s. An early member of the Joseph family, Mary Joseph, also known as Shalbeh Isaac, arrived with her husband Antoni Abdullah Simon around 1900. George Joseph, son of Khalil Youssef Kanaan, was Mayor of Adelaide from 1977 to 1979.

The Abdullah family were from Referset, in the northern mountains of Lebanon. Antoni Abdullah Simon and Mary Joseph were married in 1895, in Referset, before migrating to Australia. They arrived in Gordonvale, in the Atherton tablelands, inland of Cairns, around 1902. Antoni and Mary settled and ran a drapery in Gordonvale. They owned the grounds, lived, and eventually donated the land where St Mary's Catholic Church now stands. In 1923, the Abdullah family moved to Sydney and their descendants reside there today.

In late 1975, during the first Lebanese Civil War, prominent members of the Lebanese-Australian community sought permission from the Immigration Minister, Michael Mackellar, for Lebanese Christians from Beirut to join their relatives already in Australia. Under prevailing rules, they were only allowed if they stated that they were fleeing the civil war and had Australian relatives. As it was, many Christian Lebanese opted to stay in Lebanon, but many Sunni and Druze Lebanese from rural areas took the opportunity. Between 1975 and 1990, more than 30,000 Lebanese people came to Australia.

Many members of the Lebanese communities throughout Australia have become leaders. Some of these are: Steve Bracks, Victorian Premier (1999-2007); Marie Bashir, Governor of NSW (2001-2014); Bob Katter, Australian MP since 1993; David Malouf, writer and poet; Joe Saba, fashion designer; Joe Hasham, actor; Bachar Houli, AFL footballer; Benny Elias, NRL player; John Symond, Aussie Home Loans; Jacques Nasser, Ford Company; Ahmed Fahour, Australia Post; among others.

Sir Nicholas Shehadie

Nicholas Michael Shehadie (1926-2018) born in Coogie, New South Wales, is a noted Australian of Lebanese descent. In his sporting career, Shehadie was front row/second row for Randwick DRUFC, New South Wales and Australia in Rugby Union from 1942 to 1958. In politics, he was an Alderman of the City of Sydney (1962-67, 1969-77) and Mayor of Sydney (1973-75). Furthermore, Shehadie was the 2nd Chairman of the Special Broadcasting Service (SBS) from 1981 to 1999. His awards include Officer of the Order of the British Empire (1971), Knight Bachelor (1976), Companion of the Order of Australia (1990), Knight of the Order of St John (2001). He was inducted into the Sport Australia Hall of Fame in 1985. His wife was Dame Marie Bashir (see above). Shehadie is buried in Waverley Cemetery.

Khalil Youssef Kanaan, From Dr Leo Joseph, his grandson.

Nicholas Shehadie, Rugby union player.

Sir Nicholas Shehadie, Lord Mayor of Sydney.

Baha'i refugees

In 1981, the Fraser government released the Special Humanitarian Assistance Scheme (SHP) seeking preference for refugee immigrants. This policy was focused on the Baha'i community of Iran (Persia). The first members of this community had arrived in Sydney in 1920 from the United Sates. The Baha'i faith is a unique faith, quite separate from Islam. This community was facing extinction at the hands of the fundamentalist Muslim government in Iran under Ayatollah Khomeini. By 1988, 2,500 members of the Baha'i community had arrived in Australia through refugee programs.

Multiculturalism, the ABC Charter, and SBS

Multiculturalism is a term that recognises and celebrates the public acceptance of cultural diversity — identity, language, and religion — of the Australian population. Multiculturism as a set of policies and acts of parliament began with the dismantling by the Whitlam Labor Government of the White Australia Policy (1973) but gained its first ground with the establishment by the Fraser Liberal Government of the Australian Institute of Multicultural Affairs (AIMA) in 1979. Its aims were to promote cultural diversity, social cohesion, understanding and tolerance.

In the 1980s and 90s, the Australian Governments enacted two reforms that were to fundamentally change the way that Australians understood multiculturalism.

The Australian Broadcasting Corporation Act (1983), the ABC Act. Section 6 is the ABC Charter, which includes:

(1) The functions of the Corporation are:
(a) to provide within Australia innovative and comprehensive broadcasting services of a high standard as part of the Australian broadcasting system consisting of national, commercial and community sectors and, without limiting the generality of the foregoing, to provide:
  (i) broadcasting programs that contribute to a sense of national identity and inform and entertain, and reflect the cultural diversity of, the Australian community; and
  (ii) broadcasting programs of an educational nature;
(b) to transmit to countries outside Australia broadcasting programs of news, current affairs, entertainment and cultural enrichment that will:
  (i) encourage awareness of Australia and an international understanding of Australian attitudes on world affairs; and
  (ii) enable Australian citizens living or travelling outside Australia

to obtain information about Australian affairs and Australian attitudes on world affairs; and

(ba) to provide digital media services; and

(c) to encourage and promote the musical, dramatic and other performing arts in Australia.

Note: See also section 31AA (Corporation or prescribed companies to be the only providers of Commonwealth-funded international broadcasting services).

(2) In the provision by the Corporation of its broadcasting services within Australia:

(a) the Corporation shall take account of:
  (i) the broadcasting services provided by the commercial and community sectors of the Australian broadcasting system;
  (ii) the standards from time to time determined by the ACMA in respect of broadcasting services;
  (iii) the responsibility of the Corporation as the provider of an independent national broadcasting service to provide a balance between broadcasting programs of wide appeal and specialized broadcasting programs;
  (iv) the multicultural character of the Australian community; and
  (v) in connection with the provision of broadcasting programs of an educational nature—the responsibilities of the States in relation to education; and

(b) the Corporation shall take all such measures, being measures consistent with the obligations of the Corporation under paragraph (a), as, in the opinion of the Board, will be conducive to the full development by the Corporation of suitable broadcasting programs.

(3) The functions of the Corporation under subsection (1) and the duties imposed on the Corporation under subsection (2) constitute the Charter of the Corporation.

(4) Nothing in this section shall be taken to impose on the Corporation a duty that is enforceable by proceedings in a court.

(https://about.abc.net.au/how-the-abc-is-run/what-guides-us/legislative-framework/)

The independence of the ABC is still being argued today, with the conservative press led by Murdoch's Newscorp seeking to have it broken up, privatised, and made ineffective.

The Special Broadcasting Service Act of 1991, included the SBS Charter, as follows:

(1) The principal function of the SBS is to provide multilingual and multicultural radio, television and digital media services that inform, educate and entertain all Australians, and, in doing so, reflect Australia's multicultural society.
(2) The SBS, in performing its principal function, must:
 (a) contribute to meeting the communications needs of Australia's multicultural society, including ethnic, Aboriginal and Torres Strait Islander communities; and
 (b) increase awareness of the contribution of a diversity of cultures to the continuing development of Australian society; and
 (c) promote understanding and acceptance of the cultural, linguistic and ethnic diversity of the Australian people; and
 (d) contribute to the retention and continuing development of language and other cultural skills; and
 (e) as far as practicable, inform, educate and entertain Australians in their preferred languages; and
 (f) make use of Australia's diverse creative resources; and
 (g) to the extent to which the function relates to radio and television services—contribute to the overall diversity of Australian television and radio services, particularly taking into account the contribution of the Australian Broadcasting Corporation and the community broadcasting sector; and
 (h) to the extent to which the function relates to radio and television services—contribute to extending the range of Australian television and radio services, and reflect the changing nature of Australian society, by presenting many points of view and using innovative forms of expression. (https://saveoursbs.org/sbscharter)

In 1987, The Hawke Labor Government replaced the AIMA Act with the Office of Multicultural Affairs (OMA) and followed this up with the National Agenda for a Multicultural Australia (1989), which had bipartisan (Labor and Liberal) support. Despite the Howard Liberal Government absorbing the OMA into the Department of Immigration and Multicultural Affairs, multiculturalism has continued to gain ground, with major works being: the Parliamentary Statement on Racial Tolerance (1996), a new National Multicultural Advisory Committee (1997), Australian Multiculturalism for a New Century: Towards Inclusiveness (1999), Multicultural Australia: United in Diversity (2003), the Australian Multicultural Advisory Committee (2008), The People of Australia — Australia's Multicultural Policy (2011), and Multicultural Australia — united, strong, successful (2017).

Blainey's All for Australia 1984

In 1984, Geoffrey Blainey published the book "All for Australia", which criticised the Australian government's immigration policies. Blainey's main criticisms were: 1. Some Asian immigrant groups had not assimilated into Australian society; 2. Australian immigration had become over-balanced in favour of Asian refugees; 3. Immigration policy was 'top-down' and not democratic; 4. Multi-culturalism was emphasising ethnic identity, alienating many Australians; and 5. Immigration policy had moved from one extreme to another.

Howard's One Australia policy 1988

In response, the Howard opposition released a reactionary approach to immigration, attempting to 'turn the clock back' on multiculturalism and replacing it with a "One Australia Policy" of assimilation into the stereo-typed 'Anglo-Australian' identity. The Hawke government responded that Howard's policies were more about dividing

Australians rather than uniting them. A decade later, the Howard government attempted to implement a One Australia Policy but, by then, the children of Asian immigrant families were already assimilating into Australian society without losing their cultural identities.

Pauline Hanson — 1996

In opposition to Australia's migration policies, Pauline Hanson in her 1996 maiden-parliamentary speech expressed that Australia "was in danger of being swamped by Asians". In 1996, journalist Tracey Curro interviewed Hanson on 60 Minutes and asked whether she was xenophobic. Hanson replied with "Please explain?" This became a much-parodied catchphrase. Hanson went onto form the One Nation Party in Queensland and won nearly a quarter of the vote in the 1998 Queensland state election. One Nation members were manual workers and trade union members, who had traditionally aligned themselves to the Labor Party. The One Nation vote was a key factor in maintaining the Howard (Liberal/National) government in office. However, the One Nation Party declined after that. It has had a resurgence since 2016. In a reformed One Nation Party, Pauline Hanson claimed that Halal certification (on Muslim permissible food) was funding terrorism. After the Orlando nightclub shooting of 2016, she again called for cuts to Australian migration.

South Africa 1980s

In South Africa, a system of segregation called 'Apartheid' had been applied by the 'white' Anglo-Dutch peoples and government over the indigenous African population from the early 1900s. In 1980, Rhodesia became Zimbabwe, and the minority 'white' government was replaced by a majority indigenous government. 'White' Rhodesians began arriving in Australia. In South Africa, the threat of civil war and growing violence, especially in cities such as Johannesburg, saw many 'white' South Africans immigrate to Australia. The early South African immigrants were restricted from taking much of their wealth with them. After the overthrow of Apartheid in the early 1990s, the restrictions were relaxed, and 'white' South Africans were allowed to take their wealth.

Tiananmen Square 1989

In June 1989, the Australian newsreaders were woken to stories that Chinese students were protesting against their government in Tiananmen Square. The students wanted a change in the political policies of the Chinese government, allowing private enterprise and individual land ownership. Many Chinese students on student visas, studying in Australia, took the opportunity to criticise the Chinese government. The Hawke government in Australia allowed Chinese students in Australia to convert their student visas into residential visas. Between 2000 and 2005, the number of skilled Chinese immigrants tripled from 4,000 to over 12,000 people.

Balkan wars 1991-2001

With the fall of the Soviet Bloc in 1990 and its economic collapse, many eastern Europeans migrated to Australia. As the old Yugoslavia broke up into smaller ethnic-based counties — Serbia, Croatia, Bosnia — so hostilities grew, especially between the Christian and Muslim communities. The Muslims had migrated to the Balkans during and after the Ottoman invasions of Europe in the 15th century, and the region had regularly been in conflict — Bosnian Crisis (1908-09) and the Balkan War (1912-13). After the creation of a united Yugoslavia, the region began to settle down. Although, immediately after the Second World War, many Yugoslavs migrated to Australia, seeking to escape retribution, or fleeing communism. In 1954, Yugoslav migrants to Victoria numbered 6,000. However, with the break-up of Yugoslavia, the ethnic communities set upon each other in violent conflicts, including the Bosnian genocide (1992-95), in and around Srebrenica. As a consequence of the wars, many Albanians, Bosnians, Croats, and Serbs migrated to Australia. Many of these were Muslims who settled in western Sydney (Fairfield/Liverpool) and south-eastern Melbourne (Dandenong/Keysborough).

1983 — Australia and its droughts

Since the 1860s, when official recordings began, there have been nine major droughts in Australia. Of these, the four major droughts have been 1895-1903, 1937-1947, 1964-1968, 1981-86, and 2003-2010. Droughts usually last around seven years. There is a relationship between droughts and the temperature of warm water currents in the Indian, Pacific, and Southern oceans.

An excellent study was published by the Government of Western Australia, Department of Primary Industries and Regional Development.

All weather on Earth begins with the Sun. There is a theory that our Sun undergoes a cycle of solar storms on its surface. This cycle runs from 7 to 11 years. When the Sun's storms rage frequently, these storms affect the electro-magnetic surface of the Earth's atmosphere and cause floods. When the Sun's storms quieten and the Sun "goes to sleep" the lack of storms negatively affect the electro-magnetic surface of the Earth's atmosphere and result in droughts. There is uncertainty as to how much the sun causes variability in the Earth's climate.

Drought is a matter that Australia is still finding a solution to. In 2006, the Perth Seawater Desalination Plant was built. It produces 140 megalitres of water per day and supplies 17% of Perth's water supply.

In 2012, the Victorian Desalination Plant was completed at Dalyston on the Bass Coast. Although largely ridiculed at the time for its cost, $5.7 billion, and being completed after the August 2010 drought break, it has recently played a critical role in supplying Melbourne with water. The Victorian Desalination Plant can produce 440 megalitres per day, with an

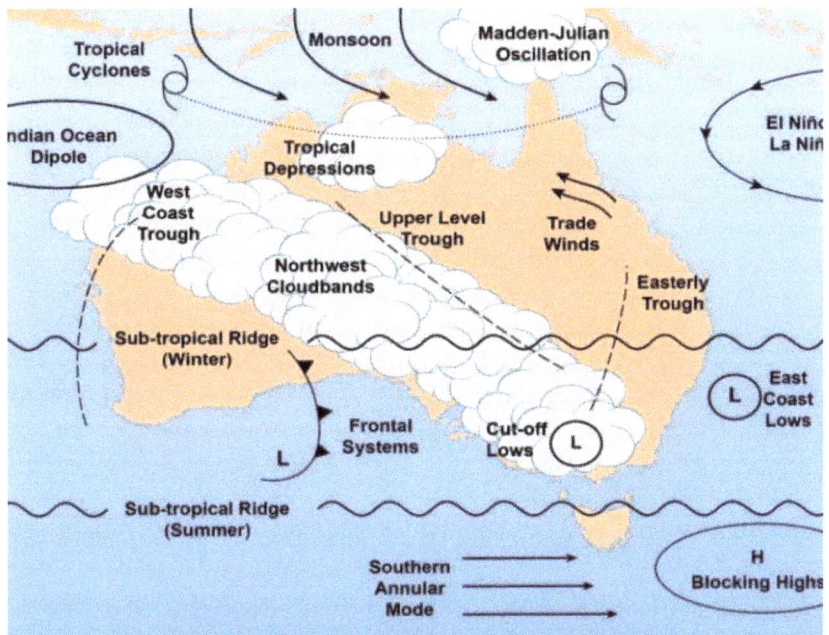

A map of Australia showing the main climate drivers.
https://www.agric.wa.gov.au/climate-weather/
climate-drivers-south-west-land-division

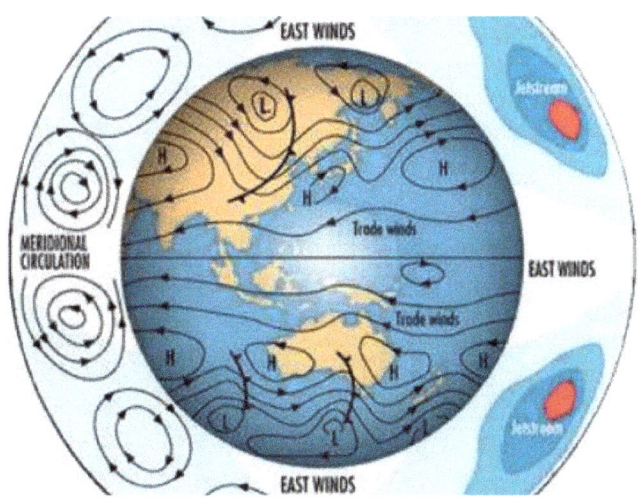

The sub-tropical ridge is a belt of high pressure that runs along the globe's middle latitudes. It moves south during drier, warmer months and north during wetter, cooler months.

extended output of 550 megalitres per day. In 2019, the Victorian Desalination Plant supplied 150 billion litres of drinking water to Melbourne, its maximum capacity. The same order was placed again in 2020. Without this desalination plant, Melbourne water storages would be more than 10% lower than its current level of around 60% of full capacity.

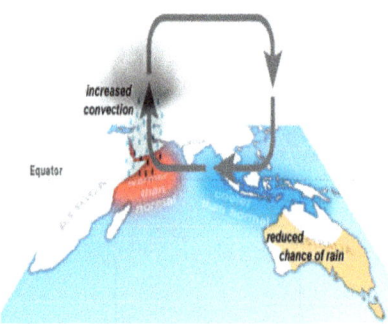

The positive phase of the Indian Ocean Dipole (IOD) of warmer ocean currents near Africa mean cooler currents near Australia, reducing rain.

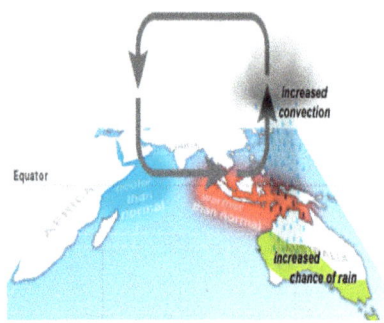

The negative phase of the Indian Ocean Dipole (IOD) of cooler ocean currents near Africa mean warmer currents near Australia, increasing rain.

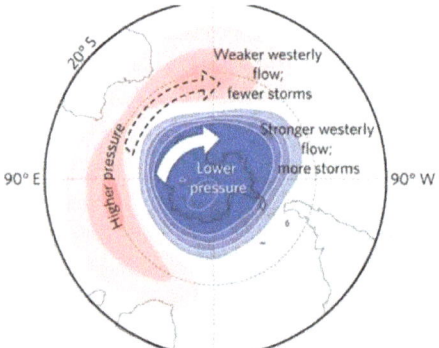

The Southern Annular Mode (SAM) affects Australia's southern climate.

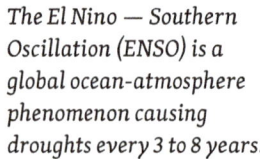

The El Nino — Southern Oscillation (ENSO) is a global ocean-atmosphere phenomenon causing droughts every 3 to 8 years.

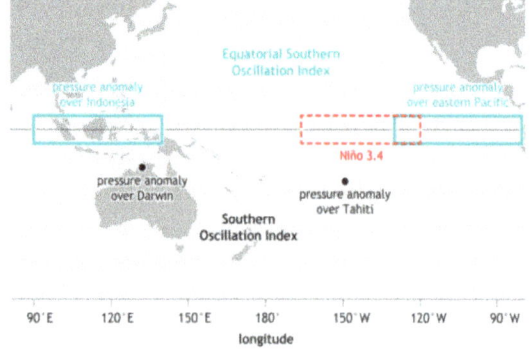

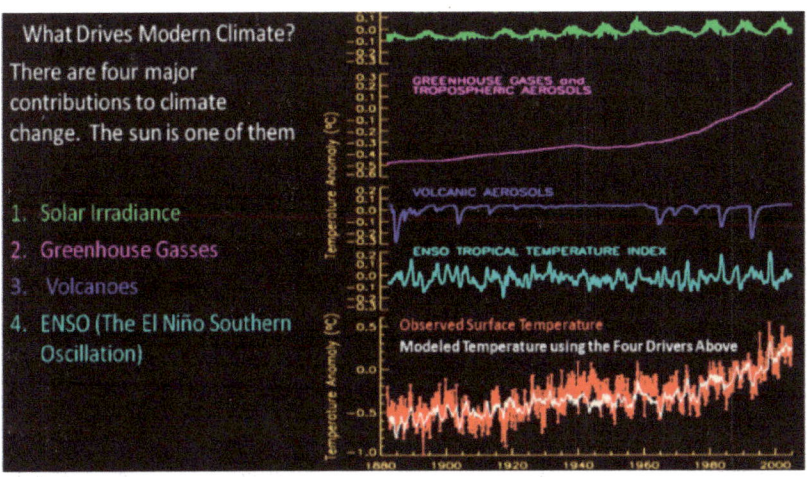

A study published by the National Oceanic and Atmospheric Administration (NOAA) indicate four main factors influencing the modern climate. According to the study, greenhouse gases is the key driver in global temperatures. However, there appears to be a direct relationship between solar irradiance (solar storms) and The El Nino — Southern Oscillation (ENSO).

https://www.swpc.noaa.gov/impacts/space-weather-impacts-climate

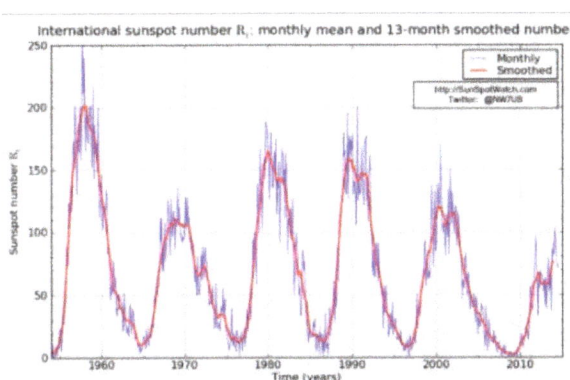

A graph of solar irradiance (solar storm activity) taken over a 60-year period (1955 to 2015) appears to show a positive relationship between the variation of solar storms and the variations in climate. Years of declining levels of solar storms correspond to years of drought in Australia.

In 1983, the drought was so severe that a giant windstorm lifted red dust from the deserts and sent it over Melbourne.

1986 — Australia becomes truly independent

When the constitution of Australia was enacted in late 1900, it not only had to passed by the parliament of Australia but, also, by the parliament of the United Kingdom in London. The constitution provided that although Australia was to be self-governing, all amendments and major pieces of legislation, especially those involving other countries, needed to be passed by the UK Parliament too, to ratify the decisions of the Australian parliament, like a parent or guardian. Furthermore, through the judiciary, there was also a right of appeal where decisions in Australia's highest court, the High Court of Australia, could be appealed against and taken to the Privy Court in London for review. That changed in 1986.

The Australia Act 1986 is the short name for a set of two pieces of legislation; one an Act of the Parliament of Australia; the other an Act of the Parliament of the United Kingdom. The Acts, almost the same in words, effectively freed Australia technically and legally from its United Kingdom overlordship. From then on, Australia was free to make its own constitutional amendments and legislation, without approval from the British parliament, and its High Court could deliver final decisions, without the right of appeal to the Privy Council in London. It was passed on March 3rd, 1986. It is the date when Australia technically became an independent country. The 3rd of March 1986 is Australia's Independence Day. (It is my hope that in future generations, it will be gazetted as the date that all Australians will be able to celebrate as 'our day'.)

Uluru returned (1985)

Uluru is a large sandstone rock formation in central Australia that lies 335 kilometres (just over 200 miles) south west of Alice Springs. It is located on the lands of the Anangu people. Anthropological findings estimate that the region was first inhabited 10,000 years ago. In 1873, the first European to gazette it was surveyor William Gosse, who named it after the Chief Secretary of South Australia, Sir Henry Ayers (Ayer's Rock). Uluru is home to numerous waterholes, rock caves, ancient paintings, fauna, and flora. The Uluru-Kata Tjuta National Park also includes Kings Canyon and Mt Olga.

In the 1950s, Uluru began to be popularised as a tourist attraction. In 1964, a chain handrail was embedded into the rock, and extended in 1976, to assist tourist climbers. (Regretfully now, I climbed Uluru as a 13-year-old boy in the spring of 1973.)

Uluru at sunset

In December 1983, the Labor Prime Minister, Bob Hawke, promised to hand back the title of Uluru to its traditional owners, the Anangu people. The government agreed upon a 10-point plan for the return, which included the stopping of climbing on the rock. However, in its lease back agreement, the government pushed through a 99-year lease, instead of the proposed 50-year lease and allowed climbing.

The official return of the title to the Pitjantjatjara and

Yankunytjatjara communities of the Anangu people occurred in October 1985. After several incidents, the Uluru-Kata Tjuta National Park Board voted unanimously to prohibit climbing of Uluru. In October 2019, the chain assisting climbers was removed.

Mabo v Queensland (1986 & 1992)

In June 1992, the High Court of Australia held that residents, led by Eddie Mabo, held ownership of Mer (Murray Island). In its decision, the High Court recognised that native title existed for all indigenous people and acknowledged that terra nullius was a legal fiction.

In May 1982, a group of residents of Murray Island (Meriam) lodged a case with the High Court of Australia. The group included: Eddie Koiki Mabo, David Passi, Sam Passi, Celuia Mapo Salee and James Rice. Over a 10-year period, 33 Meriam people, including the plaintiffs, generated 4,000 pages of evidence. The evidence proved that eight clans of the Mer had shown clear and continuous occupation of the island from before European settlement.

Eddie Mabo

Mabo with his legal team.

While the High Court case progressed, the Queensland government through the Torres Strait Islands Coastal Islands Act 1985 attempted to "extinguish without compensation" any indigenous land claims. In February 1986, the High Court, in its first decision, held that the Queensland governments legislation contravened the Racial Discrimination Act 1975. This allowed the High Court to rule on the Meriam's land rights case.

In June 1992, in its second decision, six of the seven High Court judges held that the Meriam held traditional land rights over Mer territory. The decision led to the Native Title Act 1993, allowing a framework for future land rights cases. Unfortunately, by the time the High Court decision was handed down, Eddie Mabo, Sam Passi and Celuia Mapo Salee had died.

1990s — Was it "the Recession we had to have"?

Following a short-term economic boom in the mid-1980s, largely set off by the deregulation of global banking controls, a stock market correction occurred in October 1987. The stock market crash began in New York on October 19. The Australian Treasurer, Paul Keating, later Prime Minister, had deregulated Australian banking controls too, allowing a lending boom. The Australian stock market followed the New York crash. In response to the stock market crash, Keating intervened by implementing a budget surplus policy and implementing severe interest rates. The result was in Paul Keating's infamous words, "The recession we had to have."

By 1991, Australia's Gross Domestic Product (GDP) had fallen significantly, unemployment had risen to over 10%, and homeowners were paying interest rates of 17% or more. Bankruptcies spiralled, including the collapse of the Victorian Pyramid Building Society, the State Bank of Victoria, and the State Bank of South Australia. The recession lasted until 1994, when Australia began working its way again into economic growth.

Nicky Winmar — 1993

In 1993, photographer Wayne Ludbey snapped one of the most important pictures in Australian history. In an AFL match against Collingwood, St Kilda players Nicky Winmar and Gilbert McAdam were continually taunted by racial abuse from Collingwood supporters. In response, Winmar, a Noongar man, lifted his jumper and pointed to his skin. It became an iconic image.

In 2020, Winmar received a $100,000 settlement from three AFL commentators, which he donated to the Michael Long Foundation to fund educational programs for indigenous children.

The Internet and Online development

By the mid-1990s, Australian families were connecting to the internet. The internet first became available to Australian universities in 1989. The first permanent link was between the Australian Academic Research Network (AARNet) and the Advanced Research Projects Agency Network (ARPANet). It linked the University of Melbourne to the University of Hawaii via a 2,400 bits per second satellite connection.

By 1992, Pegasus Networks, located in Byron Bay, was supplying public internet services along Australia's east coast, while DIALix provided services in Perth. In 1994, Telstra acquired all the assets of the AARNet and set up a commercial dial-up operation running out of Canberra. By 1995, a node linked to Los Angeles in the USA ran at 1.5 megabits per second (Mbps). Rather than charging for time spent on the internet, as had been the previous standard, Telstra was the first internet provider in the world to charge based on megabits downloaded. It became the new world standard. Soon after, Telstra opened a new link to the USA allowing for an additional 45Mbps. This continued to increase as public and commercial use of the internet grew in

Australia through 1995 and 1996. In the late 1990s, Telstra and Optus began rolling out cable internet services, using Hybrid Fibre Coaxial (HFC), along Australia's eastern coast. In 2000, the first consumer Asymmetric Digital Subscriber Line (ADSL) was established, allowing faster data transmission over copper telephone lines.

In 2006, Telstra set up ADSL2+ to cope with faster data transmission speeds and announced their intention to establish a Fibre To The Node (FTTN) network, where fibre would be run to mini-exchanges near premises, however this was scrapped. There had been growing concern that rural areas were being left out of the internet. Under instructions from the Howard Government, the Department of Communications, Information Technology, and the Arts (DCITA) began tenders for a broadband network that would reach rural areas. The tender was awarded to OPEL Networks who intended to provide ADSL2+ internet to rural areas through the existing telephone exchanges.

In 2008, with a change of government, the new Communications Minister, Stephen Conroy, cancelled the agreement with OPEL networks and awarded a new agreement to the National Broadband Network (NBN), which would provide Fibre To The Premises (FTTP), with "guaranteed uniform wholesale pricing". As the roll-out of NBN began, criticism grew as costs blew out as increasing difficulties occurred in laying down the fibre through the old 'asbestos-ridden' telephone pits. In 2013, with another change in government, FTTP was altered to Fibre To The Curb (FTTC), with copper wiring to complete the connection from the curb to premises, allowing a significant saving in costs. By 2015, the NBN had set up a network running at 25Mbps and that capacity would increase as demand increased. As of 2020, there are packages with download speeds of up to 100Mbps available. In 2019, the NBN Co.'s CEO, Stephen Rue announced that the project would be completed in June 2020 at a cost of $51 billion.

PART SIX

THE NEW MILLENNIUM

The Y2K Bug

Through the late 1990s, the new millennium approached with fear as well as celebration. As the world — government, institutions and business — had become reliant on computer systems that controlled all their key operations, it became known that the software these computers ran on had only been configured showing years as the last two digits only and had not been configured for the new millennium. It was named the "Y2K Bug" or "Millennium Bug". The fear was that all the computer systems in the world would stop running and chaos would occur. Fortunately, a software upgrade was devised and distributed to allow computer clocks to turnover into the year 2000. The fear was overcome. At any rate, the computer systems that did not have the upgrade installed merely clicked back to the year 1900 and continued running, later to be upgraded.

Sydney 2000 Summer Olympics

Joy was brought to Australians as Sydney hosted the first Summer Olympics of the new millennium. The games hosted over 10,000 athletes from 199 nations. There were 300 events in 28 sports. It ran from September 15 to October 1, chiefly at the Homebush stadium, now called Stadium Australia. During the opening ceremony, the cauldron was lit by Cathy Freeman, who would eventually win gold in the women's 400 metres.

The medal tally was led by the United States with 37 gold medals and 93 medals in total, followed by Russia 32 gold, 89 in total then China 28 gold, 59 in total. Australia was fourth with 16 gold and 58 in total medals.

For Australia, the highlights were a 17-year-old Ian Thorpe winning the men's 400-metre freestyle swimming, winning the 4 x 100-metre freestyle, and the 4 x 200-metre freestyle, and Cathy Freeman winning the 400 metre athletics. However, controversy occurred when Freeman carried both the Aboriginal and Australian flags in her victory lap, despite unofficial flags being banned at the Olympics. Controversy had also preceded the event, when Freeman's main competitor, France's Marie-Jose Perec withdrew from the Olympics and flew home before the event for what she described as "harassment from strangers". There was enormous pressure on Cathy Freeman to win gold at the Olympic Games, and Perec was singled out by the Australian media as a threat to that outcome.

Nova Peris (1971-), born in Darwin in the Northern Territory is a famous indigenous sportswoman and politician and was the first indigenous Australian to win a gold medal at the Olympic Games. At 170cm (5'7"), Peris won gold for field hockey in the 1996 (Atlanta) Summer Olympics; at the 1994 (Dublin) World Cup; and the 1993 and 1995 Champions Trophies. Peris also won gold at the 1998 (Kuala Lumpur) Commonwealth Games for athletics in the 400m and 4 x 100m relay. She competed in the 2000 Sydney summer Olympics in athletics.

In 1997, Nova Peris was Young Australian of the Year. While an athlete, Peris showed an interest in politics, participating in the Constitutional Convention 1998 on an Australian republic. In 2013, upon initially being invited to join the Australian Labor Party (ALP) by Julia Gillard, Peris was elected the first female indigenous parliamentarian in the national Senate.

Catherine Freeman (1973-), born in Mackay in Queensland is a famous indigenous Australian sprinter/runner. At 164cm (5'5"), Freeman won gold at the 2000 Summer Olympics (400m sprint); in the 1997  (Athens) and 1999 (Seville) World Championships; and 1990 (Auckland), 1994 (Victoria, Canada) and 2002 (Manchester) Commonwealth Games. Since her retirement, Freeman has acted as an ambassador for various foundations. Cathy Freeman was Australian of the year in 1998 and was awarded the Medal of the Order of Australia in 2001, among other awards.

The Oarsome Foursome of Nick Green, Mike McKay, Samuel Patten, and James Tomkins, won gold in the coxless four rowing at the 1992 (Barcelona) Olympics, and in the 1996 (Atlanta) Olympics, although Andrew Cooper had replaced Patten.

Kieren Perkins won gold in the 1992 and 1996 Summer Olympics and silver in the 2000 Summer Olympics for 1500-metre freestyle swimming. Overall, Perkins won 15 gold medals in international competition.

Ian Thorpe won three gold in the 2000 (Sydney) Olympics and two gold in the 2004 (Athens) Olympics, nine Olympic medals overall. Thorpe won 13 gold in the World Chamiopnships (1998-2003), nine gold in Pan-Pacific Games (1999-2002), and ten gold in Commonwealth Games (1998 to 2002)

Grant Hackett won gold in the 2000 and 2004 Summer Olympics for the 1500-metre freestyle swimming, and gold in the 4 x 200m freestyle relay in Sydney. Overall, Hackett won 36 gold medals in international competition.

Further waves of immigration

Since the arrival of European settlers, the Australian population has seen waves of new immigrants looking for better opportunities. These waves have come from different parts of the world have been devastated by hardship, devastation, and war. It began with Anglo-Celtic immigrants, through to other European, Asian, and American immigrants. Initially, each wave finds hardship then prosperity and inclusion in following generations. The new millennium has brought new waves of immigration presenting new challenges for the inclusiveness of Australian society.

The Sudanese Wars, 1997 and after

Since Sudan gained self-government and independence, from 1953 to 1956, it has been racked by drought, famine, and war. The main conflict has been between Black African Christian Sudanese and Arab Muslim Sudanese. Between 1997 and 2007, over 20,000 refugees from Sudan have arrived in Australia through the Refugee and Special Humanitarian Program (SHP). According to figures supplied by the Department of Immigration and Citizenship (2007), 74% of Sudanese migrants have come though SHP provisions, settling in Victoria (34%), New South Wales (24%), Queensland (14%) and other states and territories (28%).

In 2017, **Deng Adut** won the New South Wales Australian of the Year. Deng arrived in Australia as a refugee after being kidnapped and forced to serve as child soldier in South Sudan, where he was shot and almost bled to death. In Australia, Deng graduated in law from Western Sydney University and is now a criminal defence lawyer and refugee advocate.

Afghan War, 2001 on

The earliest Afghan migrants to Australia were the Afghan cameleers in the 1880s, settling in South Australia. Prior to the 1996 invasion of Afghanistan, there were just over 6,000 Afghan-born Australians. Since the invasion, according to the 2016 census, this community has increased to over 45,000, with almost 30,000 arriving between 2006 and 2015. Those that arrived were: 1. part of the persecuted Hazara group from the mountains of central Afghanistan; 2. intellectuals and activists; 3. those who assisted the Australian military presence in Afghanistan, e.g., interpreters; and 4. women and children at risk, under the Special Humanitarian Program (SHP).

The Arab Spring (Nightmare) 2010

In 2010, the Arab countries of the Middle East and northern Africa erupted in a series of protests, uprisings, rebellions, and civil wars. These occurred in repressive regimes where there were low standards of living, human rights violations, unemployment, and Muslim sectarianism. They were also very heavily influenced by social media emanating from the First World (NATO) countries, espousing democracy, and a better way of life. Tunisia (2010) erupted first, spreading the following year to Algeria, Libya, Egypt, Yemen, Syria and Bahrain. In the cases of Libya, Syria and Yemen, rebels were armed by NATO countries. In Libya, Syria and Yemen, civil wars continue. Since the Arab Spring, there has been an estimate of up to 140,000 deaths from recorded data. It is estimated that the Arab Spring has displaced almost 25 million people. Since 2010, over 200,000 migrants have settled in Australia, many of which continue to arrive under refugee and humanitarian status.

Indian migration — 2016 on

As described earlier in this book, there is evidence of Indians having settled in Australia from about 4,000 years ago. Also, Indians also arrived as part of the companies of household servants brought by British officers to Australia from the early times of British settlement. At Federation, it is recorded that about 5,000 people born in India lived in Australia. From 1951 to 2000, the number of Indian Australians steadily grew from under 2,000 to over 35,000. However, in 2006, with a change in Immigration Department priorities, the number of Indian Australians jumped to over 150,000 by 2011, and over 600,000 by 2016. The significant factor in Indian migration to Australia was economic migration. Indians arriving in Australia since 2000 are skilled professionals working as doctors, nurses, commercial managers, IT specialists and engineers.

2K Australian music rules the world

In the millennium, the Australian popular music industry has gone from strength to strength. In the last few years, Australia is even represented in the annual Eurovision song competition. There have been three major internationally-renowned Australian music acts worth noting here — AC/DC, INXS, and Nick Cave.

AC/DC is an Australian rock band formed in Sydney in 1973 by Angus and Malcolm Young, both born in Glasgow, Scotland. Although changing members over time, AC/DC's heavy metal / hard rock style  has remained consistent, selling over 200 million records worldwide. Their hits include Back in Black, Highway to Hell, Thunderstruck, You Shook Me All Night Long and T.N.T..

AC/DC have recorded 18 studio albums and performed on over 20 tours. They have won five Grammy awards and 3 ARIA awards, among many others. AC/DC is arguably Australia's greatest rock band ever, and still performing.

INXS (in excess) was also an Australian rock band formed in Sydney. INXSs 'new wave' became popular in the 1980s, with their first hit Original Sin (1983). The band's popularity stemmed largely from their lead-singer Michael Hutch-  ence, who died in 1997. Their most popular hits were Need You Tonight, Never Tear Us Apart, New Sensation and Don't Change.

INXS recorded 12 studio albums, selling 60 million records worldwide, and won seven ARIA awards. In 2019, the film Mystify documented Hutchence's life.

Nick Cave (1957-), born in Warracknabeal, Victoria, is a singer, songwriter, and author. Cave fronted 'The Boys Next Door' a.k.a. 'The Birthday Party' (1973-83), a punk band, then 'Nick Cave and the Bad Seeds'(1984-  present), also in a 'gothic' style. Cave also fronted 'The Grinderman' (2007-10), as an alternative project, as well as writing film scores, essays, novels, and screenplays. Cave has recorded 24 studio albums, five live albums, numerous soundtracks, contributions, collaborations, and awards. He is Australia's greatest songwriter.

A great array of players

In the last half-century, no other area of endeavour reflects the multicultural change in Australia than Australian Rules football. From 1970, there has grown a proliferation of players with international backgrounds. Some of the listed players have links to more than one group; however, I have only listed each player once.

Albania	Adam Yze
Austria	Alex Jesaulenko, Justin Leppitsch
Barbados	Josh Gibson
Chile	Jose Romero
China	Danny Deow, Lin Jong
Cook Islands	Karmichael Hunt
Croatia	Alan Didak, Ray Gabelich, Darren Gaspar, Ilija Grgic, Alan Jakovich, Glenn Jakovich, Addam Maric, Ivan Maric, Val Perovic, Steve Salopek, Peter Sumich, Jacob Surjan, Jon Dorotich
Cyprus	Andrew Demetriou
Czech Republic	Paul Vinar
Denmark	Tom Boyd, Jim Marchbank
Egypt	Ahmed Saad
England	Chris Burton, Brandon Jack, Brad Moran, Clive Waterhouse, Garrick Ibbotson, Chris Mayne, Paul Medhurst, Matthew Scarlett, Andrew Swallow, David Swallow, Jack watts, John Worsfold
Estonia	Dane Rampe

Fiji	Alipate Carlile, Nick Natanui, David Rodan, Esava Ratugolea
Germany	Jordan Doering, Jack Riewoldt, Nick Riewoldt, Alex Ruscuklic, David Schwarz , Dean Terlich
Ghana	Joel Amartey
Greece	Ang Christou, Josh Francou, Gary Frangalas, John Georgiadis, John Georgiou, Con Gorozidis, Athas Hrysoulakis, Patrick Karnezis, Paul Koulouriotis, Spiro Kourkoumelis, Anthony Koutoufides, Angelo Lekkas, Stephen Malaxos, Spiro Malakellis, Tony Malakellis, Alex Marcou, Daniel Metropolis, John Rombotis, Jim Toumpas, Jason Triainides, Zeno Tzatzaris, David Zaharakis
Hungary	Jack Veszpremi
India	Daniel Kerr, Jordan McMahon, Clancee Pearce, Alex Rance
Ireland	Colm Begley, Dermott Brereton, Conor McKenna, Pearce Hanley, Tadgh Kennelly, James Magner, Conor Nash, Mark O'Connor, Brett O'Hanlon, Jamie O'Reilly, Setanta O'Hailpin, Michael Quinn, Jim Stynes, Brian Stynes, Zac Tuohy, Tom Walsh, Sean Wight, Aidan Corr
Israel	Mordechai Bromberg
Italy	Steven Alessio, Mario Bortolotto, Vin Catoggio, Reece Conca, Stephen Coniglio, Adam Contessa, Steven Da Rui, Ron De Iulio, Danny Delre, Brett Deledio, Andrew Dimattina, Frank Dimattina, Paul Dimattina, Robert Dipierdomenico, Alec Epis, Alex Fasolo, Brendan Fevola, Michael Firrito, Silvio Foschini, Anthony Franchina, Tony Liberatore, Paul Licuria, Frank Marchesani, Alan Martello, Peter Matera, Phil Matera, Wally Matera, Mark Mercuri, Joe Misiti, Anthony Morabito, Romano Negri, Christian Petracca, Paul Puopolo, Simon Prestigiacomo, Peter Riccardi, Mark Ricciuto, Guy Rigoni, Anthony Rocca, Saverio Rocca, Renato Serafini, Alex Silvagni, Sergio Silvagni, Steven Silvagni, Shane Valenti, Bill Valli
Kenya	Aliir Aliir

Latvia	Mark Blicavs, Arnold Briedis, Andrejs Everitt, Peter Everitt
Lebanon	Bachar Houli, Mil Hanna, Robin Nahas, Adam Saad, Christian Salem
Lithuania	Adam Ramanauskas
Macedonia	Josh Daicos, Peter Daicos, John Gastev, Mark Nicoski, Nick Malceski
Malaysia	Robert Ahmat, Paul Medhurst
Malta	Jason Attard, Tony Buhagiar, Jaryd Cachia, David Calthorpe, John Formosa, Blake Grima, Nathan Grima, Adam Saliba,
Myanmar	Andrew Embley, Trent Dennis-Lane
Netherlands	Robert Klomp, Paul van der Haar, David Hale, Matthew Kreuzer, Ben Rutten, Billie Smedts, Richard Vandenburg, Jay van Berlo, Nathan van Berlo, Nick Vlastuin
New Zealand	Simon Black, Paul Bower, Greg Broughton, Adam Campbell, Trent Croad, Danny Dickfos, Donald Dickie, Aaron Edwards, Max Gawn, Heath Grundy, Kurt Heatherley, Jarrad Jansen, Dustin Martin, Beau Maister, Rowan Marshall, Daniel McAllister, Sam Mitchell, Brent Peake, Brian Peake, Daniel Pearce, Jasper Pittard, Jordan Russell, Shane Savage, Wayne Schwass, Brent Renouf, Marley Williams
Nigeria	Joel Wilkinson
Northern Ireland	Conor Glass
Papua New Guinea	Mal Michael
Philipinnes	Mathew Stokes, Alex Woodward
Poland	John Pitura, James Podsiadly, Jared Polec
Russia	Bodhan Jaworskyj, Oleg Markov
Samoa	Aaron Edwards

Scotland	Matthew Dick, Sam Docherty, Jim Edmond, Grant Lawrie, Luke McGuane, Rhys Palmer, Paul Stewart, Ewan Thompson
Seychelles	Matt Thomas
Serbia	Ray Boyanich, Brian Kekovich, Sam Kekovich, Lazar Vidovic, Lukas Markovic
Slovenia	Nick Suban, Rene Kink, Dayne Zorko
South Africa	Damian Cupido, Jack Darling, Eugene Kruger, Stephen Lawrence, Ian Muller, Jason Johannisen,
South Sudan	Reuben William
Spain	Paul Licuria
Sri Lanka	Hayden Crozier, Paul Jacotine, David Gallagher, Enrico Misso,
Sudan	Aliir Aliir, Majak Daw, Mabior Chol
Sweden	Kris Massie
Switzerland	Matthew Leuenberger
Thailand	Sudjai Cook
Tonga	Israel Folau, David Rodan
Turkey	Taylin Duman, Sedat Sir
Tuvalu	Scott Harding
Uganda	Emmanuel Irra
Ukraine	Jason Daniltchenko, Alex Ishchenko, Alex Jesaulenko, Jake Kolodjashnij, Kade Kolojashnij, Steven Kolyniuk, Jared Petrenko, Jason Porplyzia, Justin Staritski, Shane Woewodin
Wales	James Gwilt, John McCarthy
Zimbabwe	Tendai Mzungu, Ian Perrie

Australian Rules football also has a great array of indigenous players. Indigenous participation began from Sir Doug Nicholls in the 1930s, and Eddie Jackson in Melbourne's glorious 1948 premiership win. In the 1960s, indigenous players such as Graham "Polly" Farmer,

Barry Cable, Stephen Michael, Jim and Phil Krakouer, Wally, Peter and Phil Matera, Nicky Winmar and Byron Pickett were champion players with Noongar (WA) heritage. Carlton champion Sydney Jackson's indigenous heritage, as part of the stolen generation, is still unknown. Maurice Rioli was the first noted Tiwi Island player in the VFL/AFL. There have been many other champion indigenous players.

In 2019, the AFL Players Association updated their survey of current female and male players and produced an indigenous player map, shown below. Some of the listed players have links to more than one group; however, I have only listed each player once. Please note that the list does not include indigenous players who completed their AFL or AFLW careers prior to the 2019 season.

Anmatjerre (NT)	Ben Long, Jake Long
Arabana (SA)	Luke Lavender
Arrente (NT)	Shane Edwards
Barkindji (NSW)	Derek Eggmolesse-Smith, Jarmaine Jones
Balardong (WA)	Kirby Bentley, Cassie Davidson, Jeffrey Garlett, Ian Hill, Kyron Hayden, Lewis Jetta, Neville Jetta, Sydney Stack, Quinton Narkle, Jared Pickett, Sam Powell-Pepper
Bunuba (WA)	Toby Bedford
Dja Dja Wurrung (Vic)	Madison Prepakis
Gangulu (Qld)	Ally Anderson
Gunai Kurnai (Vic)	Paul Ahern
Gunnandji (Qld)	Jay Kennedy-Harris
Iwaidja (NT)	Nakia Cockatoo
Jaru (WA)	Cedric Cox, Jasmin Stewart
Kamilaroi (NSW)	Natalie Plane, Taryn Thomas
Kaurna (SA)	Chad Wingard

Kija (WA)	Jason Carter, Liam Jones, Shane McAdam, Irving Mosquito, Sam Petrevski-Seton
Kokatha (SA)	Eddie Betts, Cameron Ellis-Yomen
Kukatja (WA)	Francis Watson
Lardil (Qld)	Charlie Cameron, Jarrod Cameron
Larrakia (NT)	Steven May, Steven Motlop, Danielle Ponter
Malak Malak (NT)	Ben Long
Mara (NT)	Joel Garner
Meriam Mir (Qld)	Delma Gisu, Alicia Janz
Minang (WA)	Durak Tucker
Miyartuwi (NT)	Sean Lemmens
Narangga (SA)	Wayne Milera, Travis Varcoe, Robert Young
Ngarrindjerri (SA)	Tobin Cox, Jarrod Lienert, Izak Rankine
Ningy Ningy (Qld)	Aliesha Newman
Noongar (WA)	Harley Bennell, Ebony Dawson, Bradley Hill, Stephen Hill, Tim Kelly, Nathan Kreuger, Brandon Matera, Michael Walters, Nathan Wilson
Noonocal (Qld)	Karl Amon
Nyikina (WA)	Brendon Ah Chee, Callum Ah Chee,
Quandamooka (Qld)	Paige Parker
Thursday Island (Qld)	Ben Davis
Tiwi (NT)	Allen Christensen, Jake Long, Anthony McDonald-Tipungwuti, Daniel Rioli, Willie Rioli,
Wajarri (WA)	Liam Ryan
Wajuk (WA)	Shai Bolton, Lance Franklin, Jarrod Garlett, Matthew Parker,
Wangkatha (WA)	Daniel Wells
Warramungu (NT)	Jed Anderson, Brandan Parfitt
Warray (NT)	Shaun Burgoyne
Wirangu (SA)	Kim Lebois, Tyson Stengle

Wirradjuri (NSW)	Aidyn Johnson, Zac Williams
Yamatji (WA)	Patrick Ryder,
Yidinjdi (Qld)	Blake Schlensog
Yindjibarndi (WA)	Gemma Houghton,
Yirrganydji (Qld)	Jarrod Harbrow
Yorta Yorta (Vic)	Jeremy Finlayson, Jade Gresham, Joel Hamling, Jarman Impey, Jy Simpkin, Mathew Walker
Yuin (NSW)	James Bell

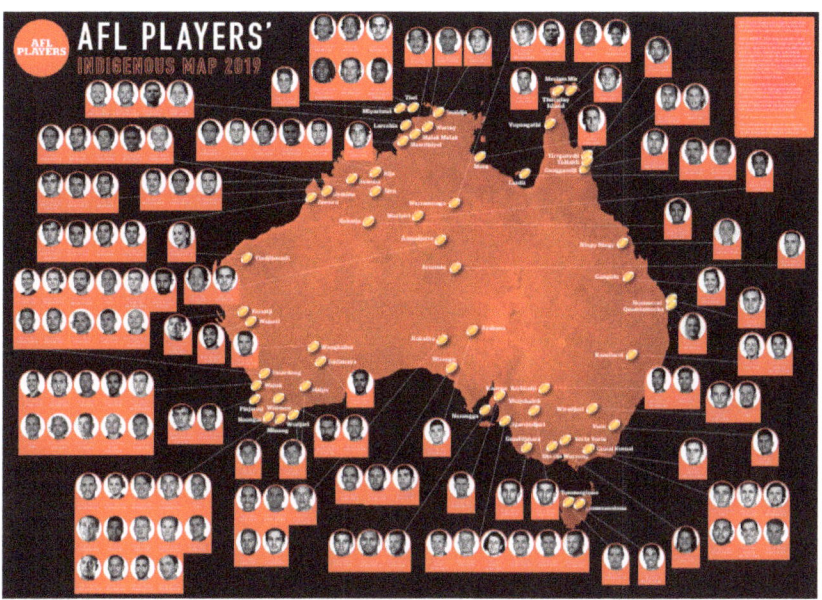

Stolen Generations, Deaths in custody, and Sorry

As described previously, the 'Stolen Generations" were children of Australian Aboriginal people and Torres Strait Islanders who were taken away from their parents by the police and other government authorities to be adopted or fostered out to non-Aboriginal parents, or to church missions and orphanages. The apparent logic of the authorities was the long term assimilation of the Aboriginal people into 'white' Australia.

Many of these children received abuse and were often held as servants within their adopted families. Many, as they grew into adulthood, were alienated from their adopted families and communities.

In 1989, a study published in Bereson's 'Decades of Change: Australia in the Twentieth Century' noted that "removed Aboriginal people were less likely to have completed a secondary education, three times as likely to have acquired a police record, and were twice as likely to use illicit drugs than as were Aboriginal people who grew up in their ethnic community.

In 1995, the 'Bring Them Home' report, as part of the Australian Report of the National Inquiry into the Separation of Aboriginal and Torres Strait Islander Children from Their Families, estimated that at least over 100,000 children were taken from their parents.

Furthermore, a disproportionate number of indigenous Australians have died in prison while in prisons or under police custody. The Royal Commission into Aboriginal Deaths in Custody (RCIADIC), between

1987 and 1991, highlighted deficiencies in the standards of care given to indigenous Australians in custody.

Palm Island Death in Custody 2004

In 2004, the Palm Island death in custody of resident Cameron Doomadgee (Mulrunji) allegedly at the hands of Queensland police officer, Sergeant Christopher Hurley. It was alleged that Hurley, 201 cm and 115 kg, fell on Doomadgee, 181 cm and 74 kg, resulting in fatal injury. The death in custody led to civil rioting on the island, where the police barracks and Hurley's house were burnt down. Police retreated and barricaded themselves in the hospital until reinforcing police in full riot gear, wearing balaclavas and heavily armed carried out a punitive action on the island's residence.

In 2007, noted lawyer and civil rights activist Noel Pearson openly criticised the Queensland Director of Prosecutions, Leanne Clare, for her failure to press charges against the police. In response, the police officer was indicted by Queensland Attorney-General, Kerry Shine. Although acquitted, Hurley was later medically retired from the police force after a range of other charges. Police were found to have breached the Racial Discrimination Act 1975 with their actions deemed "unnecessary" and "disproportionate" and that police "acted in this way because they were dealing with an Aboriginal community". The raids resulted in a class action that saw a settlement of AU$30 million and an apology by the Queensland government.

Sorry — 2008

On 13 February 2008, the Australian Prime minister Kevin Rudd presented an apology to Indigenous Australians for the Stolen Generations, as part of a motion in Parliament. The apology is as follows:

(Kevin Rudd) I move:

That today we honour the Indigenous peoples of this land, the oldest continuing cultures in human history.

We reflect on their past mistreatment.

We reflect in particular on the mistreatment of those who were Stolen Generations—this blemished chapter in our nation's history.

The time has now come for the nation to turn a new page in Australia's history by righting the wrongs of the past and so moving forward with confidence to the future.

We apologise for the laws and policies of successive Parliaments and governments that have inflicted profound grief, suffering and loss on these our fellow Australians.

We apologise especially for the removal of Aboriginal and Torres Strait Islander children from their families, their communities and their country.

For the pain, suffering, and hurt of these Stolen Generations, their descendants and for their families left behind, we say sorry.

To the mothers and the fathers, the brothers and the sisters, for the breaking up of families and communities, we say sorry.

And for the indignity and degradation thus inflicted on a proud people and a proud culture, we say sorry.

We the Parliament of Australia respectfully request that this apology be received in the spirit in which it is offered as part of the healing of the nation.

For the future we take heart; resolving that this new page in the history of our great continent can now be written.

We today take this first step by acknowledging the past and laying claim to a future that embraces all Australians.

A future where this Parliament resolves that the injustices of the past must never, never happen again.

A future where we harness the determination of all Australians, Indigenous and non-Indigenous, to close the gap that lies between us in life expectancy, educational achievement, and economic opportunity.

A future where we embrace the possibility of new solutions to enduring problems where old approaches have failed.

A future based on mutual respect, mutual resolve and mutual responsibility.

A future where all Australians, whatever their origins, are truly equal partners, with equal opportunities and with an equal stake in shaping the next chapter in the history of this great country, Australia.

A Champion Indigenous Footballer

Adam Roy Goodes (1980-), born in Wallaroo, South Australia, was a champion AFL footballer with the Sydney Swans. Through his mother, he is linked to the Adnyamathanha (Flinders Ranges) and Narungga (Spencer Gulf) peoples. At 191 cm and 100 kg, Goodes played the key role of Centre Half Forward in

Adam Goodes

many of his 372 games and 464 goals for the Sydney Swans. Goodes represented Victoria once and Australia three times. His list of achievements is extraordinary, winning two Brownlow Medals (2003,

2006); two AFL Premierships (2005, 2012); three club best and fairests (2003, 2006, 2011); three club leading-goalkicker (2009, 2010, 2011); four All-Australian Team selections (2003, 2006, 2009, 2011); Indigenous Team of the Century selection; and Australian of the Year (2014).

In 2019, two documentaries were made about the controversial end to Adam Goodes' career and racism in Australia, being: 'The Final Quarter' by Ian Darling, and 'The Australian Dream' by Stan Grant.

In May 2013, during a Sydney and Collingwood football AFL match played during Reconciliation Week, Sydney star Adam Goodes was confronted by a 13-year-old female Collingwood supporter calling him an 'ape', after he had kicked a breath-taking goal. He was interviewed after the match.

(Adam Goodes) "Yeah look, I'm pretty gutted to be honest. The win was the first of its kind in 40 years. To win by 47 points against Collingwood, to play such a pivotal role just sort of means nothing, you know, to come to the boundary line and hear a 13-year-old girl call me an ape. And it's not the first time on the footy field I've been referred to as a monkey or an ape. It was shattering.

I turned around and when I saw it was a young girl and I thought she was 14, that was my initial thought, I was just like 'really?'. I just thought how could that happen? And all this week, you know, this week is a celebration of our people and our culture and the absolute privilege of meeting the great man Nicky Winmar two days ago now and what he's been able to do for us 20 years ago and to be able to make a stand myself and say racism has a face last night and, you know, it was a 13-year-old girl but it's not her fault.

She's 13, she's still so innocent, I don't put any blame on her. Unfortunately, it's what she hears, the environment she's grown up in that has made her think it's ok to call people names. I can guarantee you right now she would have no idea, you know, how it makes anyone feel by calling them an ape. Um, I think, you know, it was just the name calling that she was doing and unfortunately it cut me deep and it affected me so much that I couldn't even be on the ground last night to celebrate a victory to indigenous round and I'm still shattered personally, yeah it's tough. Loving the support of my friends and family and people in the social media, it's fantastic.

But I think the person that needs the most support is the little girl, you know. People need to get around her, she's 13, she's uneducated. You know if she wants to pick up the phone and call me and apologise, I'll take that phone call and I'll have a conversation with that girl about 'You know what, you called me a name, this is how it made me feel', and it's school stuff, it is school stuff."

From then on, in every game he played, Goodes was constantly "boo-ed" by opposition fans. In 2015, upon his retirement, he was invited to participate in a commemorative lap but declined in fear of being "boo-ed" again. In 2017, Goodes was awarded an honorary doctorate by the University of Sydney for his contribution to Australian society.

In 2021, Adam Goodes declined his nomination to the AFL Hall of Fame citing alienation from the game.

Australia's first female Prime Minister

Julia Gillard (1961-), born in Wales, UK, was Australia's 27th Prime Minister and first and only female Australian Prime Minister at the time this book was written. Her family migrated to Adelaide in 1966, where she later attended the University of Adelaide, where she served as president of the university's student union. Transferring to the University of Melbourne, Gillard became the second female to lead the Australian Union of Students. After graduating in law and arts in 1989, she joined Slater and Gordon, working in industrial law.

Julia Gillard

In 1996, Gillard became Chief of Staff to Victorian Labor Party leader, John Brumby, and in 1998, won the House of Representatives seat of Lalor in the Federal election. Between 2001 and 2007, Gillard served in the Shadow Ministries of Immigration then Indigenous Affairs. In 2007, Gillard became the Deputy Opposition Leader to Kevin Rudd. From 2007 to 2010, she served as Deputy Prime Minister implementing the controversial NAPLAN educational assessment program.

In 2010, Gillard led a successful coup against Rudd and was installed as Australia's first female Prime Minister. In 2012, Gillard made a speech on the misogyny of politics, directed at the Leader of the Opposition. In 2013, Gillard became the victim of a coup by a returning Kevin Rudd as Prime Minister, where she promptly resigned and retired from politics. In 2017, she was appointed Companion of the Order of Australia.

Other current well-known Australians

Rupert Murdoch (b.1931, Melbourne, Vic), is a media publisher and was the Chief Executive Officer for Newscorp and Fox. Rupert's father was Keith Murdoch, a journalist, who covered Australian operations during World War One and created a newspaper empire upon his return.

Upon Keith's death, Rupert was left with the Adelaide Herald only, which he subsequently turned into another news empire, expanding into both the UK and the USA. Rupert's great accomplishment was foreseeing electronic news and building Sky News then BSkyB, the Fox Corporation, then with the decline of print media, Murdoch has moved into online media. In 1984, Rupert Murdoch received a Companion of the Order of Australia.

Anthony Pratt (b.1960, Melbourne, Vic), is the Global Executive Chairman of Visy Industries, the largest privately owned paper packaging and recycling company. Visy Board was founded in 1948 by Anthony's grandfather, Leon Pratt, a Polish-Jewish immigrant. In 1969, upon Leon's death, Richard Pratt took over

and expanded the Australian operations. In 1988, Anthony became Deputy Chairman and expanded the operations into the United States, then Asia. Since that time, Visy Industries has increased its turnover many-times over. Visy has won numerous awards internationally for its environmentally sustainable manufacturing.

Catherine 'Cate' Blanchett (b.1969, Ivanhoe, Vic), is a globally acclaimed actress, producer, and theatre director. Blanchett graduated from the National Institute of Dramatic Art (NIDA) in 1992 and worked with the Sydney Theatre Company and made her film debut in Paradise Road (1997). Since, she has starred in many blockbuster films, including the 'Lord of the Rings' trilogy.

Blanchett has won 2 Academy Awards (Oscars), 3 British Film Awards, 7 Australian Film Academy Awards, 3 Golden Globes, and 4 Helpmann Awards, among many other stage and film awards. She was awarded an Order of Australia (2017).

Lauren Jackson (b.1981, Albury, NSW), 196cm, 85kg, was a former basketball player, with a playing career from 1996 to 2016, as a power forward / centre. Jackson has represented the Australian Institute of Sport (1997-99), Canberra Capitals (1999-2006, 2009-13, 2014-16), Seattle Storm (2001-12), Spartak Moscow (2007-10), among other teams.

Lauren Jackson, Basketball Australia

Amongst her many awards include 7 times WNBA All-Star (2001-03, 2005-07, 2009); 3 times WNBA MVP (2003, 2007, 2010); 2 times NBA champion (2004, 2010); WNBA All-Decade Team (2006), among many, many other awards.

In 2019, Jackson was inducted into Australia's Basketball Hall of Fame and, in 2020, she was inducted into the Women's Basketball Hall of Fame and, in 2021, she was inducted into the overall Basketball Hall of Fame, the first and only Australian player to do so.

Ashleigh 'Ash' Barty (b.1996, Ipswich, Qld.), 166 cm, is an indigenous Australian, right-handed, professional tennis player and in June 2019 was ranked no.1 in the world by the Women's Tennis Association (WTO).

Between 2014 and 2016, Barty rested from tennis and played cricket for the Brisbane Heat in the inaugural Women's Big Bash League.

To mid-2021, she has won 11 titles, including the French Open Singles (2019), the US Open Doubles (2018), and Wimbledon (2021). Barty becomes the first Australian to win the Women's Singles since Evonne Goollagong Cawley in 1980.

Emma McKeon (b.1994, Wollongong, NSW) is Australia's latest Olympic swimming star. Already having won a gold, two silver, and a bronze at the 2016 Rio Olympics, McKeon made Australian Olympic history by winning  four gold and three bronze medals in the recent 2021 Tokyo Olympics.

There were and are many more great and well-known Australians that I might have included in this book, who have contributed within the realms of science, humanities, the arts, entertainment, and other fields of endeavour. However, this was always intended to be a concise history. Although a more inclusive history of Australia, it was not meant to be a 'Who's Who'. The most difficult part was creating an end as time continued to move on and new history was created. It was especially hard to cover areas such as pandemics and Covid-19, as situations were changing daily. To this, I have addressed some of Australia's current and future challenges.

My other reflection is that it is extremely hard to end an Australian history as the finish line is constantly moving. An unknown future quickly becomes our present. The latest news in Covid-19, the Tokyo Olympics, or a new political corruption become possible new additions to the book. So, here I finish with a changing present.

Same-sex Marriage

Same-sex marriage became legal in Australia in December 2017, with the passing of the Marriage Amendment Act 2017 through Federal parliament. The legal implications of relationships have slowly developed with the liberalism of the 1970s.

The first Marriage Act was passed in 1961 to standardise the laws of marriage across Australia, although they have been amended since. The Family Law Act 1975, allowed for 'De facto' relationships, those that exist in reality, although not officially recognised by law. This allowed couples living together to receive most of the same legal rights and responsibilities as married couples. However, in 2004, the Howard government amended the law to exclude same-sex couples from these rights.

Between 2004 and 2017, there were 22 unsuccessful attempts in the Federal Parliament to pass amendments allowing for same-sex marriage. In 2013, the Australian Capital Territory (ACT) passed its own legislation recognising same-sex marriage; however, it was overturned by the Courts on the basis that only the Federal Parliament had the right to amend the laws of marriage.

In 2017, the Turnbull Coalition government took the brave but controversial step of implementing a voluntary postal survey across Australia as a plebiscite on same-sex marriage, to gain public support and place pressure on parliament. The survey returned a 61.6% vote in favour of same-sex marriage. The Marriage Amendment Act 2017 was passed in December 2017, which recognised the rights and responsibilities of same-sex marriage couples and provided protections for celebrants and ministers performing same-sex marriages.

Euthanasia

Throughout Australia, a patient can choose not to receive medical treatment for a terminal illness and can have life support turned off. However, until 1996, euthanasia or assisted suicide was illegal in all states and territories. The laws regarding euthanasia have always been a matter for each of the state governments and the federal government for the territories. For a short time between 1996 and 1997, euthanasia was legal in the Northern Territory before this decision was overturned by the federal government. In June 2019, an assisted suicide scheme was passed by the Victorian government. In 2021, a similar scheme should be implemented in Western Australia. However, in all other states and territories euthanasia and assisted suicide is illegal.

Covid-19

Coronavirus Disease 2019 (Covid-19) is a pandemic affecting Australia and the whole world now, as this book is being written. It is caused by Severe Acute Respiratory Syndrome Coronavirus 2 (SARS-CoV-2). The first SARS virus appeared in China in 2002 (SARS-02) and spread through eastern Asia within a few months. Those countries learnt then how to react to a SARS virus, which should have provided a lesson for the world. Unfortunately, it did not.

Further, in 2012, Middle East Respiratory Syndrome (MERS), otherwise known as 'camel flu' was identified in Saudi Arabia. The symptoms were similar to SARS including fever, cough, diarrhea and shortness of breath. Of those diagnosed with MERS, 35% died from it. Other outbreaks of MERS occurred in South Korea 2015 and again in Saudi Arabia in 2018. About 2,500 cases of MERS were diagnosed as of January 2020.

Covid-19 was first identified in the city of Wuhan, China in December 2019, and was reported to the World Health Organisation (WHO) that same month. However, the WHO did not issue a worldwide warning until mid-January. The first case of Covid-19 was identified in Australia in late-January, a returning visitor to Victoria from Wuhan. However, it was not until late-March that the federal and state governments took actions such as closing borders, closing non-essential services, lockdowns, and social-distancing.

As of mid-February 2021, in Australia, there have been over 28,000 Covid-19 cases reported, with over 25,000 recoveries, but with over 900 deaths. The state of Victoria, so far, has had significantly more cases and deaths than any other state or territory, with over 20,000 cases, and over 800 deaths.

World-wide, Covid-19 has recorded almost 110 million cases, and almost 2.5 million deaths. As of mid-February 2021, the most affected country is the United States of America (USA) with over 27 million cases and half a million deaths. The other most highly affected countries are India, Brazil, United Kingdom, and Russia. Other eastern Asian countries, having learnt the lesson of SARS-02, have had relatively fewer cases of Covid-19. New Zealand, with 2,340 cases and 26 deaths so far, provides an example of good Covid-19 minimization and treatment.

Further complications have occurred with the original corona virus mutating into different streams, causing severe complications in the northern hemisphere during its last 2020/21 winter, particularly the United Kingdom.

As of February 2021, there have been four different types of Covid-19 vaccines, as follows:

1. RNA, a synthetic version of the Covid genetic code, triggering a protein resistance spike. The Pfizer-BioNTech and Moderna vaccines are based on this version. The RNA versions rely on maintaining the vaccines in freezing temperatures.
2. Viral Vector, using a harmless virus that duplicates the Covid genetic code, also triggering a protein resistance spike. The Oxford-AstraZeneca, the CanSino Biologics, Gamaleya Research Institute, and the Johnson & Johnson vaccines are based on this version.
3. Whole virus, using weakened versions of Covid-19, directly triggers an immune response. Sinovac, Bharat Biotech, Sinopharm and Medicago Inc. supply these versions.
4. Protein Sub-unit, using fragments of the spike protein to trigger

an immune response. Novavax and the Chinese Academy of Sciences supply these versions.

All the vaccines seem to require or have recommended two doses. The Pfizer-BioNTech vaccine must be kept below -70°Celsius (C) in storage and can remain up to 5 days between 2-8°C. The Moderna vaccine must be kept below 20°C in storage and can remain up to 30 days between 2-8°C. All the other vaccines can be maintained in storage at between 2-8°C.

The Australian government has chosen to distribute the Pfizer-BioNTech and the Oxford-AstraZeneca vaccines. It has already imported over 50 million doses of the Pfizer-BioNTech vaccine from overseas and intends producing the Oxford-AstraZeneca vaccine in Australia through CSL as soon as it is approved by the appropriate medical authorities.

The WHO has reported a decline in the reported new cases of Covid-19, although it is uncertain whether this is a long-term trend. Also, the WHO has already expressed its concern that vaccines appear to have been distributed on the basis of political influence and alliances. The U.S./German Pfizer-BioNTech has distributed its vaccine on a commercial basis with wealthier countries, like Australia, receiving preference. While the Russian Gamaleya Research Institute 'Sputnik V' vaccine and the Chinese Sinopharm vaccines appear to be distributed on a more social basis to poorer countries, although the Sinopharm vaccines have been distributed in the wealthier U.A.E. and Bahrain too. India is producing the Oxford-AstraZeneca and Bharat Biotech vaccines. Further, new strains of Covid-19 have emerged in South Africa, the United Kingdom and India. The full extent of the subsequent waves of the Covid-19 viruses and the effect of these vaccines are yet to be reckoned and concluded.

PART SEVEN

FUTURE CHALLENGES

As Australia moves further into the new millennium it contends with numerous challenges. These challenges appear not to be new challenges but repetitions of past issues or a continuation of themes. In some ways, as our population and policies evolve and grow, so our solutions to these challenges have developed and improved. However, on each of these major challenges, there is still much more progress to be made.

Immigration

All Australians have an ancestry of immigration, from the Aboriginal peoples migrating over 60,000 years ago till now, and beyond. As each new wave of immigrants arrive in Australia there appears to be fear and resentment by many already living here. Some of the fears relate to competition for jobs, living space, wealth distribution, and other resources. Some of the resentment relates to legal versus illegal immigration, and racial, religious, and cultural differences, and the cost of migrant integration. Again, these are not new but are a continuing theme apparent from first European settlement, soldiers and settlers versus indigenous Australians, soldiers versus convicts, European settlers versus Chinese settlers, and so on.

The benefits of migration are that it produces a much more diverse culture, it helps reduce labour shortages, migrants are more prepared to take on jobs where there is an insufficient supply of labour. Some of these may be skilled professionals, e.g., doctors and I.T. technicians, or unskilled labourers, e.g., labourers and agricultural workers. Many have come to Australia on temporary visas as seasonal workers in agriculture and tourism, before migrating permanently. Yet, as we look around our communities, many migrants and their descendants have grown to be our leading professionals, entrepreneurs, and politicians. According to Henry Sherrell, a political analyst for the Immigration Council of Australia, there will be significant benefits to Australia from migration. In 2050, Australia's population is projected to be 38 million, with migration contributing $1,625 billion to the Australian Gross Domestic Product (GDP).

Indigenous Rights

There still remain many challenges regarding achieving indigenous rights and full equality with the rest of the Australian population. The issues are also a continuation of a theme: land rights, lack of services, especially to remote areas; lack of medical care and the age-mortality differential between indigenous versus other Australians; lack of education; high unemployment; decaying infrastructure; broken families; high crime rates, high rates of Aboriginal incarceration, and Aboriginal deaths in custody.

Currently, security of land control and heritage is a major issue, emphasised by the recent destruction of 46,000-year-old Aboriginal sacred heritage caves by the Rio Tinto mining company at the Juukan Gorge in the Pilbara region of Western Australia, devastating the Puutu Kunti Kurrama and Pinikura people living in the area. Initially, the Rio Tinto CEO apologises for what he explained as a 'miscommunication'. However, further investigation alleged that the destruction had been planned as far back as 2012 and had been prioritised for May 2020 before Western Australian legislation permanently banned mining in the area. An inquiry is currently in process with a result yet to be determined. However, there are many other sites of similar heritage that stand in the way of various mining companies operating in Australia.

In hand with land rights is the issue of consent for land use. It is not enough to award land ownership to Aboriginal peoples, if mining companies are making land use agreements with non-representative, minority Aboriginal groups, which often leads to bribery, corruption, and subsequent misuse. Therefore, it is the obligation of federal and state authorities to ensure land rights are protected. This can be achieved by raising public awareness, including more indigenous representatives into the conversation, building a bridge between policy and practice, and holding states more accountable for the mistreatment or discrimination against indigenous Australians.

Australia is still the only commonwealth country not to have a treaty with its indigenous peoples. New Zealand had the Treaty of Waitangi signed in 1840. However, in North America, hundreds of treaties have been signed by Canada and the United States with their indigenous peoples with most being broken. Even recently, the United States government broke a long-standing treaty with the indigenous tribes of South Dakota, building an oil-pipeline across its sacred sites. Predictably, a major oil spill from the pipeline has devastated and ruined much of this sacred land.

An indigenous treaty may provide solutions to important issues, such as symbolic recognition of prior occupation to European settlement; redefining the relationships and rights between indigenous and other Australians; better protection of indigenous rights; improving regional self-government; providing guidelines for state, regional and local treaties; and improving structures, systems and processes for regional decision-making. In 2017, the 'Uluru Statement from the Heart' was passed by a constitutional convention made up of over 250 Aboriginal and Torres Strait Islander leaders. However, debate will continue as to what the precise form of the treaty will take and whether a treaty will take a minimalist or more comprehensive solution to these issues.

Uluru Statement from the Heart

We, gathered at the 2017 National Constitutional Convention, coming from all points of the southern sky, make this statement from the heart:

Our Aboriginal and Torres Strait Islander tribes were the first sovereign Nations of the Australian continent and its adjacent islands and possessed it under our own laws and customs. This our ancestors did, according to the reckoning of our culture, from the Creation, according to the common law from 'time immemorial', and according to science more than 60,000 years ago.

This sovereignty is a spiritual notion: the ancestral tie between the land, or 'mother nature', and the Aboriginal and Torres Strait Islander peoples who were born therefrom, remain attached thereto, and must one day return thither to be united with our ancestors. This link is the basis of the ownership of the soil, or better, of sovereignty. It has never been ceded or extinguished and co-exists with the sovereignty of the Crown.

How could it be otherwise? That peoples possessed a land for sixty millennia and this sacred link disappears from world history in merely the last two hundred years?

With substantive constitutional change and structural reform, we believe this ancient sovereignty can shine through as a fuller expression of Australia's nationhood.

Proportionally, we are the most incarcerated people on the planet. We are not an innately criminal people. Our children are aliened from their families at unprecedented rates. This cannot be because we have no love for them. And our youth languish in detention in obscene numbers. They should be our hope for the future.

These dimensions of our crisis tell plainly the structural nature of our problem. This is the torment of our powerlessness.

We seek constitutional reforms to empower our people and take a rightful place in our own country. When we have power over our destiny our children will flourish. They will walk in two worlds and their culture will be a gift to their country.

We call for the establishment of a First Nations Voice enshrined in the Constitution.

Makarrata is the culmination of our agenda: the coming together after a struggle. It captures our aspirations for a fair and truthful relationship with the people of Australia and a better future for our children based on justice and self-determination.

We seek a Makarrata Commission to supervise a process of agreement-making between governments and First Nations and truth-telling about our history.

In 1967 we were counted, in 2017 we seek to be heard. We leave base camp and start our trek across this vast country. We invite you to walk with us in a movement of the Australian people for a better future.

Lowitja O'Donohue   *Mick Dodson*   *Noel Pearson*

Galarrwuy Yunupingu   *Michael Long*

Fortunately, although through many challenges, the indigenous population of Australia has continued to grow since federation. In the last half century, since the 1967 referendum and subsequent reforms, Indigenous Australians are receiving more opportunities in education, politics, sport, and professional careers. We can only hope for this to continue. Through the new millennium, the cause for indigenous rights has continued, led by people such as Lowitja O'Donoghue (ATSIC Chair); Mick Dodson and Noel Pearson (law); Galarrwuy and Mandawuy Yunupingu (Yothu Yindi), and Archie Roach (music); Michael Long and Adam Goodes (sport), and the number of leaders continues to grow.

Even today, in Western Australia, mandatory sentencing laws send people to jail for minor crimes, such as women for unpaid parking tickets. In the Northern Territory, almost all, if not 100% of juveniles in detention are indigenous Australians. Incarceration and deaths in custody remain major problems.

David Gulpilil

David Gulpilil Ridjimiraril Dalaithngu (born in the Arnhem Land, 1953) is one of Australia's great actors. From the Mandipingu tribe of the Yolngu people, Gulpilil was already an accomplished hunter, tracker, and ceremonial dancer when British filmmaker, Nicholas Roeg, cast the 16-year-old boy in a lead role for his film Walkabout (1971). Since, Gulpilil has starred in Storm Boy (1976), The Last Wave (1977), The Right Stuff (1983), Crocodile Dundee (1986), Rabbit Proof Fence (2002), Ten Canoes (2006), Australia (2008), among many other film and television productions. He was awarded the Member of the Order of Australia (1987), the Centenary Medal (2001), Best Actor at the Cannes Film Festival (2014), NAIDOC lifetime achievement award (2019), among others.

Pandemics

Viruses, infections, and diseases have always affected humanity. The first recorded influenza epidemic, according to Sanskrit records, occurred in Mesopotamia and western Asia in 1200BC. Within a year of European settlement of Sydney (1789-90), there was a major smallpox epidemic that estimated deaths among the Aboriginal population as high as 50 to 75%. In 1828, another year-long major smallpox epidemic in New South Wales is estimated to have killed almost 20,000 people. In 1857, another smallpox epidemic killed an unknown number.

In 1867, a measles epidemic in Sydney killed over 500 people. In 1875, a year-long Scarlett Fever epidemic killed over 8,000 people. In 1900, bubonic plague broke out in Sydney killing over 100 people, reoccurring in Fremantle three years later (1903).

From 1915 to 1926, Australia was affected by a worldwide encephalitis epidemic killing 1.5 million people. This was coupled with the worldwide 'Spanish Flu' epidemic (1918-1920) killing well over 20 million people. In 1937, a major polio epidemic broke out in Australia, followed by 'Asian Flu' (1957-1958), Hong Kong Flu (1968-1970), HIV/Aids (1981 on), SARS (2002-2004), Mumps (2009), Swine Flu (2009), Dengue Fever (2019-20), and Covid-19 (2020 on).

New diseases, epidemics, and pandemics, as well as recurring ones, will always be a challenge to Australia's health. Infectious disease hospitals need to be set up to isolate and treat the ill. As each state controls its own health policies, there should be at least one infectious disease hospital in each state. In Victoria, Fairfield Infectious Diseases Hospital was founded in 1904 but closed in 1996, due to the infamous Kennett government assets sell-off. During our current Covid-19 epidemic crisis, Victorians might wish that the Fairfield Hospital still existed in an updated mode. Disease, virus research and vaccination remain a priority.

Infrastructure, Land Use, and Climate Change

As an inhabited continent, Australia is more than 60,000 years old. As a westernised settlement, it is almost score off being 250 years old. As a sovereign nation, Australia is about 120 years old. Yet, in many ways, Australia's infrastructure and land use reflect its colonial past. This is reflected in its population density of each state that still centres around its six capitals. Sydney, Melbourne, Brisbane, Perth, Adelaide, and Hobart are still the largest cities in each of their states. However, the sprawl of these capitals has seen the growth of satellite centres such as the Gold Coast/Tweed Heads (Qld/NSW), Newcastle/Maitland (NSW), Sunshine Coast (Qld), Wollongong (NSW), and Geelong (Vic). Geelong has grown by over 50% in the last decade. Also, Canberra, our national capital city, with Queanbeyan (NSW) is now Australia's 8th largest city by population. Yet Darwin, the northern-most capital city, still remains in a mediocre 15th place, between Cairns and Toowoomba. Although the north of Australia is rich in climate, vegetation, and minerals, and is closest to our trading neighbours, it remains relatively poorly developed.

Further, Australian land use has remained largely the same since colonial days. A 2018 study, edited by Richard Thackway, titled 'Land Use in Australia: Past, Present and Future' shows the proportions of land use in Australia, as follows:

Land Use	Percentage
Grazing — native vegetation	46.3%
Minimal use (desert)	16.2%
Protected areas	13.2%
Grazing — modified pastures	9.4%
Nature conservation	7.4%
Cropping — dry land	3.3%
Water (rivers & lakes)	1.63%
Forestry — non-plantation	1.5%

Forestry — plantation	0.3%
Residential — urban	0.22%
Cropping — irrigated	0.17%
Grazing — irrigated pastures	0.13%
Residential — rural	0.12%
Mining & waste	0.02%
Other various	0.11%

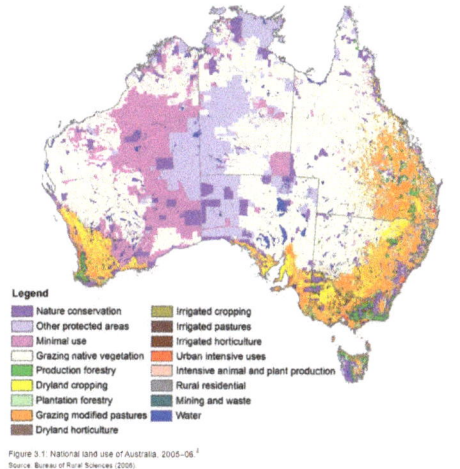

Figure 3.1: National land use of Australia, 2005–06.[4]
Source: Bureau of Rural Sciences (2006).

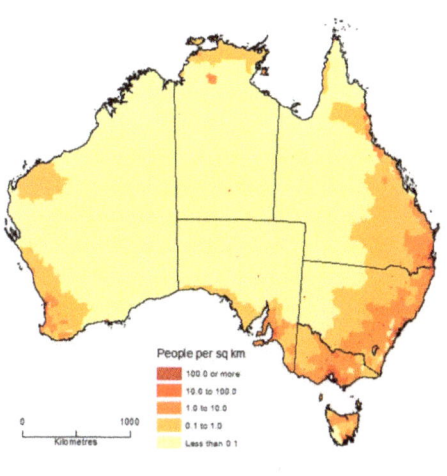

POPULATION DENSITY BY SA2, Australia - June 2016

Source: ABS

From another perspective, Australia is a continent of over 7.5 million square kilometres with a population of 25 million people.

Compare this to one of our neighbours Indonesia, which has islands totalling 1.9 million square kilometres but has a population of 275 million people. Yet 85% of Australia's population lives within 50 kilometres of the coast. There is a lot of empty room for land development, increased infrastructure, and anti-desertification measures, e.g., greening the land.

For decades, our government has been obsessed with balancing the annual budget. Yet, relative to many other countries, Australia has a low Public Debt to Gross Domestic Product (GDP) of 45% (increased by 5% from 40% to 45%, due to Covid-19 pandemic spending).

Public Debt to Gross Domestic Product (GDP), sample of countries by region					
Europe / Asia / Oceania		North & South America		Africa	
Greece	177%	United States	107%	Cape Verde	124%
Italy	135%	Canada	90%	Angola	111%
United Kingdom	80%	Argentina	89%	Djibouti	104%
India	70%	Brazil	76%	Egypt	90%
Germany	60%	Mexico	46%	South Africa	62%
China	51%	Haiti	33%	Sudan	62%
Australia	45%	Chile	28%	Zimbabwe	53%
New Zealand	19%	Peru	28%	Nigeria	18%
Russia	12%	Cuba	18%	Libya	17%

It has been argued that if all the water that ran from the top end of Australia into the ocean was captured and diverted south, there would be enough water to green the whole of Australia. Already, two metres of water falls on Darwin each year, running out to the ocean. Building a dam would cost billions of dollars. Building several dams and running pipelines may cost 'tens' of billions of dollars. As of March 2020, our current public debt is $573 billion, having increased by $20 billion since 2017, and a further $60 billion since Covid-19, yet still only remains 45% of our national GDP. Our country has the resources to build the necessary infrastructure for better land use, but do we have the will?

Climate change and global warming is an area of concern that has become popular in the new millennium, although these subjects are much older and need to be looked at over the Earth's long history. According to the USA's National Aeronautics and Space Administration (NASA), the two have distinct definitions. "Climate change is a long-term change in the average weather patterns that have come to define the Earth's local, regional, and global climates." However, "Global warming is the long-term heating of the Earth's climate system observed since the pre-industrial period due to human activities, primary fossil burning, which increases heat-trapping greenhouse gas levels in the Earth's atmosphere." Therefore, when we focus on climate change, we look at those changes since the Earth began, or as far as we can go, millions of years; whereas, global warming only looks at the human influence on Earth over less than two hundred years.

In the early to mid-1970s, as high school students, the science teachers presented to my cohort, as it probably did to other cohorts, a film on climate change and rising global temperatures that would result in a new ice age. According to scientists, the cycle for recurring major ice ages occurs every 250,000 years, and we are now due for another one.

Currently, there is a heated debate (excuse the pun) between climate change or global warming activists and deniers. The subject of human expansion and resource devastation actually goes back to the writings of British natural philosopher Thomas Malthus before the industrial revolution. In 'An Essay on the Principle of Population (1798), he writes:

"Population, when unchecked, increases in a geometric ratio. Subsistence increases only in an arithmetic ratio. A slight acquaintance with numbers will show the immensity of the first power in comparison of the second."

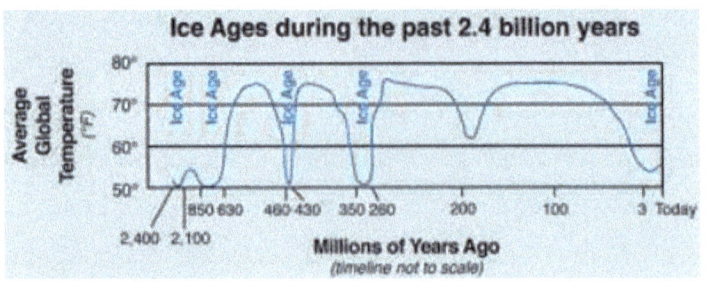

The chart by the University of Utah Geology shows the variations in average global temperatures over 2.4 billion years, indicating that intense global warming precedes every ice age, and that our current global temperature is below the peaks. This infers that the peaks go beyond that of global human endurance.

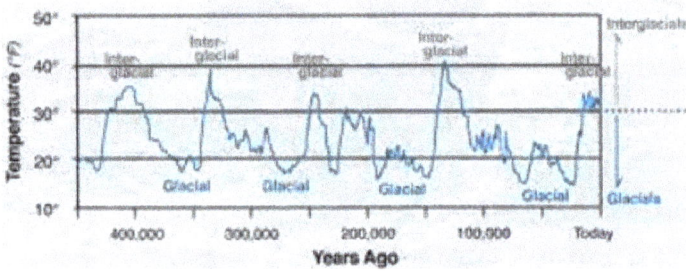

Another chart by the Utah Geology looks at the variations in temperature and the cycle of ice ages over the last 450,000 years. The window of human existence over the last 100,000 years. The indication is that there has been continual global warming over the last 20,000, and we may be heading into another ice age.

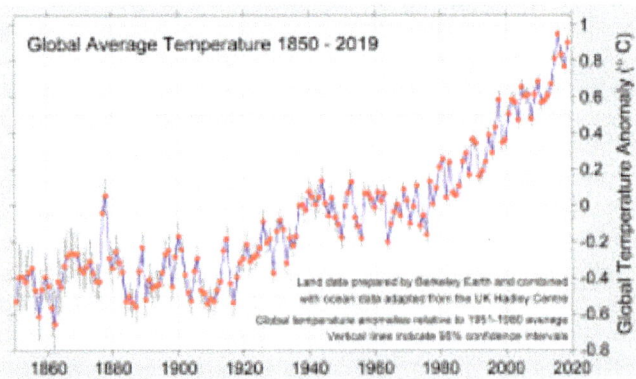

Berkley Earth looks at the variation of temperatures over the last 170 years and clearly indicates global warming from 1850.

Research indicates that both climate change and global warming is occurring, one cannot argue against it. However, we need to look at global warming, the human effect of global temperature changes over the last 200 years, within the context of the Earth's long history and cycle of climate change cycles.

Recently, in a Maths tutorial with a Year 5 student, I was trying to convey an understanding of large numbers with the following details. According to science:

1. The Universe is...   13,770,000,000 years old,
2. Earth is...   4,543,000,000 years old,
3. Human existence is...   100,000 years old, and
4. European settlement in Australia is... 233 years old.

As humans, we link our existence to that of the Earth, rather than looking at our existence upon the Earth. Human existence on Earth began about 100,000 years ago. The Earth will continue to exist through further ice ages and volcanic peaks long after human existence has ended. We can prolong human existence on Earth by making technology and resource changes, but we are battling against much larger natural elements. Further, although the people of the world may wish to take action on global warming, concern must be raised over the power of corporations to circumvent these intentions.

Corporate Governance

Recently, Australia had the Banking Royal Commission (2017-19) into the banking sector. The result of which was a scathing judgement of how banks were run, the greedy policies they administered, and the damage they caused to the community. The Royal Commission held that Australia's leading banks, superannuation and other financial services had acted illegally by facilitating money-laundering for drug-syndicates, terrorist organisations, as well as overcharging ordinary customers on a range of transactions. The banks were fined millions of dollars and some banking chief officers, among other officers, were forced to resign.

The Federal and State governments of Australia have problems in legislating and governing for corporations. In essence, corporations supersede national boundaries. Laws differ from country to country, and corporations are structured to advantage the laws that best suit them.

The founder of modern economics, Adam Smith, in his second volume of his illustrious work, An Inquiry into the Nature and Causes of the Wealth of Nations (1776), expressed his opposition to what were then called joint-stock companies, now called corporations. Of shareholders, he said:

"... (They) seldom pretend to understand anything of the business of the company; ...but receive contentedly such half-yearly or yearly dividend, as the directors think proper to make to them."

Of directors, Smith stated:

"... being the managers rather of other people's money than of their own, it cannot well be expected that they should watch over it with the same anxious vigilance with which the partners in a private copartnery (partnership) frequently watch over their own. ...and very easily give themselves a dispensation from having it. Negligence and profusion, therefore, must prevail, ..."

Almost prophetically, Adam Smith had described the problems that corporations beset over society from the corruption of the Dutch and British East India companies of the 18th Century through to the global financial, commodity, manufacturing, and service corporations of today.

In Australia, 40% of taxation income comes from workers income, 18% from corporate income, 12% from goods and services tax (GST), 14% from non-GST goods and service taxes, and 5% from payroll tax.

Many international corporations use transfer payments to minimise their tax obligations and pay little if any tax at all.

Australia's annual GDP is $1.89 trillion. Its public spending is $0.09 trillion, about 4.7% of GDP. Australia might consider a more equitable taxation system where each individual, organisation and corporation pays 5% of its gross income in Australia, without deduction. Pricing would factor in this 5%. The introduction of the GST in July 2000 had a short-term 1% effect on that year's GDP, much less than the long-term effect of the Covid-19 virus of over 5%. Such reform would bring a fairer tax system.

Outside of taxation, corporations pay little heed to national laws, the property rights of individuals and groups, and the environment and heritage of our great country, none more so than the recent destruction by Rio Tinto of the 46,000-year-old indigenous heritage site within the Juukan Gorge. Further concern is raised by the practice of 'fracking', otherwise known as hydraulic fracturing, which is injecting a mix of water, sand, and chemicals into underground rock to fracture it and force gas and oil to the surface. The concern over fracking relates to polluting the underground water supplies in and around the respective areas, consequently affecting vegetation, fauna and communities relying on the water.

Further issues of corporate governance have been raised recently between international and global corporate giants, such as Facebook and Google, and the Australian government. The Australian government has legislated to determine the ownership rights of news and its commercial distribution. The corporate giants have threatened to overpower this legislation. Google has threatened to cut supply of its Google online services to Australia, although it has recently negotiated positive outcomes to suppliers and users of its services. However,

Facebook has threatened to cut part of its services to Australia and appears not to be moving towards a resolution.

Australian independence — constitutional monarchy v republic

Since federation, debate has continued about the level of Australian independence and self-government, including continuing a constitutional monarchy or moving to a republic.

True legal and constitutional independence for Australia occurred on March 3, 1986, with the Australia Act. Personally, this is our true Independence Day. We celebrate 35 years of independence this year, 2021, and is a day we can celebrate together.

Further, since the English Civil War of the 1640s, parliament has sat at a higher level with more power than the monarch. King Charles was beheaded for treason against parliament. We inherited this through their system, although the monarch and its representative, the governor-general, are given the ceremonial title, head of state. Recently, the United States of America has shown us that we may be better off with a seemingly powerless constitutional monarchy than under the apparent power of a megalomaniac president.

Appendices

Appendix 1 — Australian Governor Generals and Prime Ministers

Decade	Governor-General	Prime Minister and Party
1900	John Hope (1901-02), Hallam Tennyson (1903-04), Henry Northcote (1904-08), William Ward (1908-11)	Edmund Barton (1901-03), Protectionist Alfred Deakin (1903-04), Protectionist Chris Watson (1904), Labor George Reid (1904-05), Free Trade Alfred Deakin (1905-08), Protectionist Andrew Fisher (1908-09), Labor Alfred Deakin (1909-10), Commonwealth Liberal
1910	Thomas Denman (1911-14), Ronald Ferguson (1914-20)	Andrew Fisher (1910-13), Labor Joseph Cook (1913-14), Commonwealth Liberal Andrew Fisher (1914-15), Labor Billy Hughes (1915-23), Labor, National Labor, Nationalist
1920	Henry Forster (1920-25), John Baird (1925-30)	Stanley Bruce (1923-28), Nationalist James Scullin (1928-32), Labor
1930	Isaac Isaacs (1931-36), Alexander Hore-Ruthven (1936-45)	Joseph Lyons (1932-39), United Australia Earl Page (1939), Country Robert Menzies (1939-41), United Australia

Decade	Governor-General	Prime Minister and Party
1940	Prince Henry (1946-47), William McKell (1947-53)	Arthur Fadden (1941), Country John Curtin (1941-45), Labor Frank Forde (1945), Labor Ben Chifley (1945-49), Labor
1950	William Slim (1953-60)	Robert Menzies (1949-66), Liberal
1960	William Morrison (1960-61), William Sidney (1961-65), Richard Casey (1965-69)	Harold Holt (1966-67), Liberal John McEwen (1967-68), Country John Gorton (1968-71), Liberal
1970	Paul Hasluck (1969-74), John Kerr (1974-77), Zelman Cowen (1977-82)	William McMahon (1971-72), Liberal Gough Whitlam (1972-75), Labor Malcolm Fraser (1975-83), Liberal
1980	Ninian Stephen (1982-89)	Robert Hawke (1983-91), Labor
1990	Bill Hayden (1989-96), William Deane (1996-2001)	Paul Keating (1991-96), Labor John Howard (1996-2007), Liberal
2000	Peter Hollingworth (2001-03), Michael Jeffery (2003-08)	Kevin Rudd (2007-10), Labor
2010	Quentin Bryce (2008-14), Peter Cosgrove (2014-19), David Hurley (2019-)	Julia Gillard (2010-13), Labor Kevin Rudd (2013), Labor Anthony Abbott (2013-15), Liberal Malcolm Turnbull (2015-18), Liberal Scott Morrison (2018-), Liberal
2020		

Appendix 2A — List of New South Wales Governors and Premiers

Decade	Governors	Premiers and Party
1780	Arthur Phillip (1788-92)	
1790	John Hunter (1795-1800)	
1800	Philip King (1800-06), William Bligh (1806-08)	
1810	Lachlan Macquarie (1810-21)	
1820	Thomas Brisbane (1821-25), Ralph Darling (1825-31)	
1830	Richard Bourke (1831-37), George Gipps (1838-46)	
1840	Charles Fitzroy (1846-55)	
1850	William Denison (1855-61)	Stuart Donalson (1856), No Party Charles Cowper (1856), No Party Henry Parker (1856-57), No Party Charles Cowper (1857-59), No Party William Forster (1859-60) No Party
1860	John Young (1861-67), Earl Belmore (1868-72)	John Robertson (1860-61), No Party Charles Cowper (1861-63), No Party James Martin (1863-65), No Party Charles Cowper (1865-66), No Party James Martin (18666-68), No Party John Robertson (1868-70) No Party
1870	Hercules Robinson (1872-79)	Charles Cowper (1870), No Party James Martin (1870-72), No Party Henry Parkes (1872-75), No Party John Robertson (1875-77), No Party Henry Parkes (1877), No Party John Robertson (1877), No Party James Farnell (1877-78), No Party Henry Parkes (1878-83), No Party

Decade	Governors	Premiers and Party
1880	Augustus Loftus (1879-85), Lord Carrington (1885-1890)	Alexander Stuart (1883-85), No Party George Dibbs (1885), No Party John Robertson (1885-86), No Party Patrick Jennings (1886-87), No Party Henry Parkes (1887-89), Free Trade George Dibbs (1889), Protectionist
1890	Earl of Jersey (1891-93), Robert Duff (1893-95), Viscount Hampden (1895-99), Earl Beauchamp (1899-1901)	Henry Parkes (1889-91), Free Trade George Dibbs (1891-94), Protectionist George Reid (1894-99), Free Trade William Lyne (1899-1901), Protectionist
1900	Harry Rawson (1902-09)	John See (1901-04), Progressive Thomas Waddell (1904), Progressive Joseph Carruthers (1904-07), Liberal Reform Charles Wade (1907-10), Liberal Reform
1910	Lord Chelmsford (1909-13), Gerald Strickland (1913-17), Walter Davidson (1918-23)	James McGowen (1910-13), Labor William Holman (1913-20), Labor, Nationalist
1920	Dudley de Chair (1924-30)	John Storey (1920-21), Labor James Dooley (1921), Labor George Fuller (1921), Nationalist James Dooley (1921-22), Labor George Fuller (1922-25), Nationalist Jack Lang (1925-27), Labor Thomas Bavin (1927-30), Nationalist
1930	Philip Game (1930-35), Lord Gowrie (1935-36), David Anderson (Aug-Oct 1936), Lord Wakehurst (1937-46)	Jack Lang (1930-32), Labor Bertram Stevens (1932-39), United Australia Alexander Mair (1939-41), United Australia
1940	John Northcott (1946-57)	William McKell (1941-47), Labor James McGirr (1947-52), Labor

Appendices

Decade	Governors	Premiers and Party
1950	Eric Woodward (1957-65)	Joseph Cahill (1952-59), Labor
1960	Roden Cutler (1966-81)	Robert Heffron (1959-64), Labor James Renshaw (1964-65), Labor Robert Askin (1965-75), Liberal
1970		Tom Lewis (1975-76), Liberal Eric Willis (1976), Liberal
1980	James Rowland (1981-89), David Martin (1989-90)	Neville Wran (1976-86), Labor Barry Unsworth (1986-88), Labor
1990	Peter Sinclair (1990-96), Gordon Samuels (1996-2001)	Nick Greiner (1988-92), Liberal John Fahey 1992-95), Liberal Bob Carr (1995-2005), Labor
2000	Marie Bashir (2001-14)	Morris Iemma (2005-08), Labor Nathan Rees (2008-09), Labor Kristina Keneally (2009-11), Labor
2010	David Hurley (2014-19), Margaret Beazley (2019-)	Barry O'Farrell (2011-14), Liberal Mike Baird (2014-17), Liberal Gladys Berejiklian (2017-), Liberal
2020		

Note: William Denison served as Tasmanian Governor (1847-55) then serving as New South Wales Governor (1855-61).

Appendix 2B — List of Tasmanian Governors and Premiers

Decade	Governors	Premiers and Party
1780		
1790		
1800		
1810	Thomas Davey (1813-17), William Sorrell (1817-24)	
1820	George Arthur (1824-36)	
1830	John Franklin (1837-43)	
1840	John Eardley-Wilmot (1843-46), William Denison (1847-55)	
1850	Henry Young (1855-61)	William Champ (1856-57), No Party Thomas Gregson (1857), No Party William Weston (1857), No Party Francis Smith (1857-60), No Party
1860	Thomas Browne (1862-68)	William Weston (1860-61), No Party Thomas Chapman (1861-63), No Party James Whyte (1863-66), No Party Richard Dry (1866-69), No Party
1870	Charles Du Cane (1869-74), Frederick Weld (1875-80)	James Wilson (1869-72), No Party Frederick Innes (1872-73), No Party Alfred Kennerley (1873-76), No Party Thomas Reiby (1876-77), No Party Philip Fysh (1877-78), No Party Willian Giblin (1878), No Party William Crowther (1878-79) No Party

Appendices

Decade	Governors	Premiers and Party
1880	John Lefroy (1880-81), George Strahan (1881-86), Robert Hamilton (1887-92)	William Giblin (1879-84), No Party Adye Douglas (1884-86), No Party James Agnew (1886-87), No Party Philip Fysh (1887-92), Liberal
1890	Viscount Gormanston (1893-1900)	Henry Dobson (1892-94), No Party Edward Braddon (1894-99), Free Trade
1900	Arthur Havelock (1901-04), Lord Strickland (1904-09)	Neil Lewis (1899-1903), No Party William Propsting (1903-04), Liberal-Democrat John Evans (1904-09), No Party Neil Lewis (1909), Liberal John Earle (1909), Labor
1910	Harry Barron (1909-13), William Ellison-Macartney (1913-17), Francis Newdegate (1917-20)	Neil Lewis (1909-12), Liberal Albert Solomon (1912-14), Liberal John Earle (1914-16), Labor Walter Lee (1916-22), Liberal-Nationalist
1920	William Allardyce (1920-22), James O'Grady (1924-30)	John Hayes (1922-23), Liberal Walter Lee (1923), Liberal Joseph Lyons (1923-28), Labor
1930	Ernest Clark (1933-45)	John McPhee (1928-34), Liberal Walter Lee (1934), Liberal Albert Ogilvie (1934-39), Labor Edmund Dwyer-Gray (1939), Labor
1940	Hugh Binney (1945-51)	Robert Cosgrove (1939-47), Labor William Brooker (1947-48), Labor
1950	Ronald Cross (1951-58)	Robert Cosgrove (1948-58), Labor

Decade	Governors	Premiers and Party
1960	Lord Rowallan (1959-63), Charles Gairdner (1963-68)	Eric Reece (1958-69), Labor
1970	Eric Bastyan (1968-73), Stanley Burbury (1973-82)	Walter Bethune (1969-72), Liberal Eric Reece (1972-75), Labor William Neilson (1975-77), Labor Douglas Lowe (1977-81), Labor
1980	James Plimsoll (1982-87), Phillip Bennett (1987-95)	Harold Holgate (1981-82), Labor Robin Gray (1982-89), Liberal
1990	Guy Green (1995-2003)	Michael Field (1989-92), Labor Raymond Groom (1992-96), Liberal Anthony Rundle (1996-98), Liberal
2000	Richard Butler (2003-04), Willian Cox (2004-08)	James Bacon (1998-2004), Labor Paul Lennon (2004-08), Labor David Bartlett (2008-11), Labor
2010	Peter Underwood (2008-14), Kate Warner (2014-)	Lara Giddings (2011-14), Labor William Hodgman (2014-20), Liberal
2020		Peter Gutwein (2020-), Liberal

Note: Tasmanian Governors Harry Barron (1909-13), William Ellison-Macartney (1913-17) and Francis Newdegate (1917-20), all immediately went onto serve as Western Australian Governors — Barron (1913-17), Ellison-Macartney (1917-20) and Newdegate (1920-23).

Later, Charles Gairdner served as Western Australian Governor (1951-63) then as Tasmanian Governor (1963-68).

Appendix 2C — List of Western Australian Governors and Premiers

Decade	Governors	Premiers and Party
1780		
1790		
1800		
1810		
1820		
1830	James Stirling (1832-39)	
1840	John Hutt (1839-46), Andrew Clarke (1846-47), Frederick Irwin (1847-48)	
1850	Charles Fitzgerald (1848-55), Arthur Kennedy (1855-62)	
1860	John Hampton (1862-68), Benjamin Pine (1868-69)	
1870	Frederick Weld (1869-75), William Robinson (1875-77), Harry Ord (1877-80)	
1880	William Robinson (1880-83), Frederick Broome (1883-90)	
1890	William Robinson (1890-95), Gerard Smith (1895-1901)	John Forrest (1890-1901), No Party
1900	Arthur Lawley (1901-03), Frederick Bedford (1903-09)	George Throssell (1901), No Party George Leake (1901), No Party Alf Morgans, (1901), No Party George Leake (1901-02), No Party Walter James (1902-04), No Party Henry Daglish (1904-05), Labor Hector Rason (1905-06), Ministerialist Newton Moore (1906-10), Ministerialist
1910	Gerard Strickland (1909-13), Harry Barron (1913-17), William Ellison-Macartney (1917-20)	Frank Wilson (1910-11), Ministerialist John Scaddon (1911-16), Labor Frank Wilson (1916-17), Liberal Henry Lefroy (1917-19), Nationalist Hal Colebatch (1919), Nationalist

Decade	Governors	Premiers and Party
1920	Francis Newdegate (1920-23), Willian Campion (1924-31)	James Mitchell (1919-24), Nationalist Philip Collier (1924-30), Labor
1930	vacant (1931-48)	James Mitchell (1930-33), Nationalist Philip Collier (1933-36), Labor John Wilcock (1936-45), Labor
1940	James Mitchell (1948-51)	Frank Wise (1945-47), Labor Ross McLarty (1947-53), Liberal
1950	Charles Gairdner (1951-63)	Albert Hawke (1953-59), Labor
1960	Douglas Kendrew (1963-74)	David Brand (1959-71), Liberal
1970	Hughie Edwards (1974-75), Wallace Kyle (1975-80)	John Tonkin (1971-74), Labor Charles Court (1974-82), Liberal
1980	Richard Trowbridge (1980-83), Gordon Reid (1984-89)	Ray O'Connor (1982-83), Liberal Brian Burke (1983-88), Labor Peter Dowding (1988-90), Labor
1990	Francis Burt (1990-93), Michael Jeffery (1993-2000)	Carmen Lawrence (1990-93), Labor Richard Court (1993-2001), Liberal
2000	John Sanderson (2000-2005), Ken Michael (2006-11)	Geoff Gallop (2001-06), Labor Alan Carpenter (2006-08), Labor
2010	Malcolm McCusker (2011-14), Kerry Sanderson (2014-18), Kim Beazley (2018-)	Colin Barnett (2008-17), Liberal Mark McGowan (2017-), Labor
2020		

Note: William Robinson (1834-97) served as Governor of Western Australia (1875-77) and (1880-83), Governor of South Australia (1883-90), then returned as Governor of Western Australia (1890-95). He also served as Falkland Islands (1866-1870), Prince Edward Island (1870-73), Leeward Islands (West Indies) (1874), and The Straits Settlements (Singapore) (1877-79).

Appendix 2D — List of South Australian Governors and Premiers

Decade	Governors	Premiers and Party
1780		
1790		
1800		
1810		
1820		
1830	John Hindmarsh (1836-38), George Gawler (1838-41)	
1840	George Grey (1841-45), Frederick Robe (1845-48)	
1850	Henry Young (1848-54), Richard MacDonnell (1855-1862)	Boyle Finniss (1856-57), No Party John Baker (1857), No Party Robert Torrens (1857), No Party Richard Hansen (1857-60), No Party
1860	Dominic Daly (1862-68)	Thomas Reynolds (1860-61), No Party George Waterhouse (1861-63), No Party Francis Dutton (1863), No Party Henry Ayers (1863-64), No Party Arthur Blyth (1864-65), No Party Francis Dutton (1865), No Party Henry Ayers (1865), No Party John Hart (1865-66), No Party James Boucaut (1866-67), No Party Henry Ayers (1867-68), No Party John Hart (1868), No Party Henry Ayers (1868), No Party Henry Strangeways (1868-70), No Party

Decade	Governors	Premiers and Party
1870	James Fergusson (1869-73), Anthony Musgrave (1873-77), William Jervois (1877-83)	John Hart (1870-71), No Party Arthur Blyth (1871-72), No Party Henry Ayers (1872-73), No Party Arthur Blyth (1873-75), No Party James Boucaut (1875-76), No Party John Colton (1876-77), No Party James Boucaut (1877-78), No Party William Morgan (1878-81), No Party
1880	William Robinson (1883-1889)	John Bray (1881-84), No Party John Colton (1884-85), No Party John Downer (1885-87), No Party Thomas Playford II (1887-89), No Party John Cockburn (1889-90), Liberal
1890	Earl of Kintore (1889-95) Thomas Buxton (1895-99)	Thomas Playford II (1890-92), Conservative Frederick Holder (1892), Liberal John Downer (1892-93), Conservative Charles Kingston (1893-99), Liberal Vaiben Solomon (1899), Conservative Frederick Holder (1899-1901), Liberal
1900	Lord Tennyson (1899-1902), George Le Hunte (1903-09)	John Jenkins (1901-05), Liberal Richard Butler (1905), Conservative Thomas Price (1905-09), Labor Archibald Peake (1909-10), Liberal
1910	Day Bosanquet (1909-14), Henry Galway (1914-20)	John Verran (1910-12), Labor Archibald Peake (1912-15), Liberal Crawford Vaughn (1915-17), Labor Archibald Peake (1917-20), Liberal
1920	William Weigall (1920-22), Tom Bridges (1922-27)	Henry Barwell (1920-24), Liberal John Gunn (1924-26), Labor Lionel Hill (1926-27), Labor Richard Butler (1927-30), Liberal
1930	Alexander Hoare-Ruthven (1928-34), Winston Dugan (1934-39)	Lionel Hill (1930-33) Labor Robert Richards (1933), Labor Richard Butler (1933-38), Liberal Thomas Playford IV (1938-65), Liberal

Appendices

Decade	Governors	Premiers and Party
1940	Malcolm Barclay-Harvey (1939-44), Willoughby Norrie (1944-52)	
1950	Robert George (1953-60)	
1960	Edric Bastyan (1961-68), James Harrison (1968-71)	Frank Walsh (1965-67), Labor Don Dunstan (1967-68), Labor Steele Hall (1968-70), Liberal
1970	Mark Oliphant (1971-76), Douglas Nicholls (1976-77), Keith Seaman (1977-82)	Don Dunstan (1970-79), Labor Des Corcoran (1979), Labor
1980	Donald Dunstan (1982-91)	David Tonkin (1979-82), Liberal John Bannon (1982-92), Labor
1990	Roma Mitchell (1991-96), Eric Neal (1996-2001)	Lynn Arnold (1992-93), Labor Dean Brown (1993-96), Liberal John Olsen (1996-2001), Liberal
2000	Marjorie Jackson-Nelson (2001-07), Kevin Scarce (2007-14)	Rob Kerin (2001-02), Liberal Mike Rann (2002-11), Labor
2010	Hieu Van Le (2014-)	Jay Weatherill (2011-18), Labor Steven Marshall (2018-), Liberal
2020		

Appendix 2E — List of Victorian Governors and Premiers

Decade	Governors	Premiers and Party
1780		
1790		
1800		
1810		
1820		
1830		
1840		
1850	Charles Latrobe (1851-54), Charles Hotham (1854-55), Henry Barkly (1855-63)	William Haines (1855-57), No Party John O'Shanassy (1857), No Party William Haines (1857-1858), No Party John O'Shanassy (1858-59), No Party William Nicholson (1859-60), No Party
1860	Charles Darling (1863-66), Viscount Canterbury (1866-73)	Richard Heales (1860-61), No Party John O'Shanassy (1861-63), No Party James McCulloch (1863-68), No Party Charles Sladen (1868), No Party James McCulloch (1868-69), No Party John McPherson (1869-70), No Party
1870	George Bowen (1873-79)	James McCulloch (1870-71), No Party Charles Duffy (1871-72), No Party James Francis (1872-74), No Party George Kerferd (1874-75), No Party Graham Berry (1875), No Party James McCulloch (1875-77), No Party Graham Berry (1877-80), No Party

Decade	Governors	Premiers and Party
1880	Marquess of Normanby (1879-84), Henry Loch (1884-89)	James Service (1880), No Party Graham Berry (1880-81), No Party Bryan O'Loghlen (1881-83), No Party James Service (1883-86), No Party Duncan Gillies (1886-90), No Party
1890	Earl of Hopetoun (1889-1895), Lord Brassey (1895-1900)	James Munro (1890-92), No Party William Shiels (1892-93), No Party James Patterson (1893-94), No Party George Turner (1894-99), No Party Alan McLean (1899-1900), No Party
1900	George Clarke (1901-03), Reginald Talbot (1904-08), Lord Carmichael (1908-11)	George Turner (100-1901), No Party Alexander Peacock (1901-02), No Party William Irvine (1902-04), Reform Thomas Bent (1904-09), Reform
1910	John Fuller (1911-13), Arthur Stanley (1914-20)	John Murray (1909-12), Liberal William Watt (1912-13), Liberal George Elmslie (1913), Labor William Watt (1913-14), Liberal Alexander Peacock (1914-17), Liberal John Bowser (1917-18), Nationalist Harry Lawson (1918-24), Nationalist
1920	Earl of Stradbroke (1921-26), Lord Somers (1926-31)	Alexander Peacock (1924), Nationalist George Prendergast (1924), Labor John Allan (1924-27), Country Edmund Hogan (1927-28), Labor William McPherson (1928-29), Nationalist Edmund Hogan (1929-32), Labor
1930	Lord Huntingfield (1931-39)	Stanley Argyle (1932-35), United Australia Albert Dunstan (1935-43), Country

Decade	Governors	Premiers and Party
1940	Lord Dugan (1939-49)	John Cain Sr (1943), Labor Albert Dunstan (1943-45), Country John Cain Sr (1945-47), Labor Thomas Hollway (1947-50), Liberal
1950	Dallas Brooks (1949-63)	John McDonald (1950-52), Country Thomas Hollway (1952), Independent John McDonald (1952), Country John Cain Sr (1952-55), Labor Henry Bolte (1955-72), Liberal
1960	Rohan Delacombe (1963-74)	
1970	Henry Winneke (1974-82)	Rupert Hamer (1972-81), Liberal
1980	Brian Murray (1982-85), Davis McCaughey (1986-92)	Lindsay Thompson (1981-82), Liberal John Cain Jr (1982-90), Labor
1990	Richard McGarvie (1992-97), James Gobbo (1997-2000)	Joan Kirner (1990-92), Labor Jeff Kennett (1992-99), Liberal
2000	John Landy (2001-06), David de Kretser (2006-11)	Steve Bracks (1999-2007), Labor John Brumby (2007-10), Labor
2010	Alex Chernov (2011-15), Linda Dessau (2015-)	Edward Ballieu (2010-13), Liberal Denis Napthine (2013-14), Liberal Daniel Andrews (2014-), Labor
2020		

Appendix 2F — List of Queensland Governors and Premiers

Decade	Governors	Premiers and Party
1780		
1790		
1800		
1810		
1820		
1830		
1840		
1850		
1860	George Bowen (1859-68)	Robert Herbert (1859-66), Conservative Arthur McAllister (1866), No Party Robert Herbert (1866), Conservative Arthur McAllister (1866-67), No Party Robert McKenzie (1867-68), Conservative Charles Lilley (1868-70), No Party
1870	Samuel Blackall (1868-71), George Phipps (1871-74), William Cairns (1874-77), Arthur Kennedy (1877-83)	Arthur Palmer (1870-74), Conservative Arthur McAllister (1874-76), No Party George Thorn (1876-77), No Party John Douglas (1877-79), No Party
1880	Anthony Musgrave (1883-88)	Thomas McIlwraith (1879-83), Conservative Samuel Griffith (1883-88), No Party Thomas McIlwraith (1888), Conservative Boyd Morehead (1888-90), Conservative

Decade	Governors	Premiers and Party
1890	Henry Norman (1889-1895), Charles Cochrane-Baillie (1896-1901)	Samuel Griffith (1890-93), No Party Thomas McIlwraith (1893), Conservative Hugh Nelson (1893-98), Ministerial Conservative Thomas Byrnes (1898), Ministerial Conservative James Dickson (1898-99), Ministerial Conservative Anderson Dawson (1899), Labor
1900	Herbert Chermside (1902-04), Frederic Thesiger (1905-09)	Robert Philp (1899-1903), Ministerial Conservative Arthur Morgan (1903-06), Liberal William Kidston (1906-07), Labor Robert Philp (1907-08), Conservative William Kidston (1908-11), Liberal
1910	William McGregor (1909-14), Hamilton Goold-Adams (1915-20)	Digby Denham (1911-15), Liberal Thomas Ryan (1915-19), Labor
1920	Matthew Nathan (1920-25), John Goodwin (1927-32)	Edward Theodore (1919-25), Labor William Gillies (1925), Labor William McCormack (1925-29), Labor
1930	Leslie Wilson (1932-46)	Arthur Moore (1929-32), Country William Smith I(1932-42), Labor
1940	John Lavarack (1946-57)	Frank Cooper (1942-46), Labor Edward Hanlon (1946-52), Labor
1950	Henry Abel Smith (1958-66)	Vince Gair (1952-57), Labor Frank Nicklin (1957-68), Country
1960	Alan Mansfield (1966-72)	Jack Pizzey (1968), Country Gordon Chalk (1968), Liberal Johannes Bjelke-Peterson (1968-87), Country/National
1970	Colin Hannah (1972-77)	

Decade	Governors	Premiers and Party
1980	James Ramsey (1977-85), Walter Campbell (1985-92)	Mike Ahern (1987-89), National Russell Cooper (1989), National Wayne Goss (1989-96), Labor
1990	Leneen Forde (1992-97), Peter Arnison (1997-2003)	Rob Borbidge (1996-98), National Peter Beattie (1998-2007), Labor
2000	Quentin Bryce (2003-08)	Anna Bligh (2007-2012), Labor Campbell Newman (2012-2015), Liberal National
2010	Penelope Wensley (2008-14), Paul De Jersey (2014-)	Annastacia Palaszczuk (2015-), Labor
2020		

Appendix 3 — Events in Australia and the rest of the world

	Australia	Rest of the world
200 million years ago	One super-continent on Earth — Pangea.	
100 million years ago	Australia breaks apart from southern continents.	All continents begin moving to their current positions.
40 million years ago	Australia has moved to about its current position.	Most continents have moved to about current positions. Africa and India still have to connect to Asia. Last major global Ice Age (1.5 MYA)
100,000 years ago	Last major ice age occurs. Australia is connected by land-bridge to New Guinea.	Land bridges connect all continents. Human journey begins out of Africa.
60,000 years ago	First Aboriginal people (Pama-Nyangan) arrive in Australia	Humans meet and assimilate with Neanderthals in Europe and Asia.
15,000 years ago	Last ice age is past its peak. Aboriginal people have settled throughout Australia.	North-eastern Asians cross land-bridge across Bering Sea into North America then South America. End of last minor Ice Age (11K YA). Global water levels rise, and most continental land-bridges are sub-merged. Britain and Ireland separate from European mainland.
4,000 years ago	Macro-Gunwinyguan people arrive in northern Australia.	Maori people have arrived and settled in New Zealand.

Appendices

	Australia	Rest of the world
1400	Chinese explorer Zheng He's treasure fleet travels around Australia (1420s) and may have landed.	Ming Empire rules over China. Ottoman Empire takes Constantinople (1453) and shuts Europe off from overland trading routes with Asia (Silk Road). Aztec and Inca dominate American continents. Slave trade as a European business begins (1452). Leonardo Da Vinci lives (1452-1519).
1520	Portuguese explorer, Mendonca, visited Australia.	European colonisation of Africa, Asia and Americas begin. Copernicus publishes first book on modern solar system (1543).
1600	Janszoon visited Cape York Peninsula (1606), near Weipa.	Russian Empire has expanded into Siberia. Shakespeare lives (1533-1603). Kepler publishes on elliptical orbit of planets (1609).
1610	Dirk Hartog (1616), Janszoon (1618), and Houtman (1629) landed on west coast	Thirty Years War begins in Europe (1618-48).
1640	Abel Tasman sails to Tasmania and names it, Van Dieman's Land (1642).	Moliere lives (1622-73). English Civil War (1642-51). Newton publishes Theory of Gravity (1686).
1700		Great Britain established (1701). War of Spanish Succession (1701-13).
1710		First Freemason Grand Lodge (1716).
1720		Halley becomes Astronomer-General (1720). Peter the Great made Emperor of Russia (1721).
1730		First Great Awakening (Evangelical Revival) begins (1730-60).
1740		Frederick the Great takes Prussian throne (1740).

	Australia	Rest of the world
1750		Peak of Little Ice Age (1750) spawns age of invention. Diderot begins compiling "Encyclopedie" (1751). Samuel Johnson publishes Dictionary (1755). Voltaire publishes Candide (1759).
1760		Catherine the Great takes Russian throne (1762).
1770	Cook expedition arrives (1770)	Diderot publishes "Encyclopedie" (1772). Goethe writes Faust and Sorrows of Young Werther (1770s). Adam Smith publishes '... Wealth of Nations' (1776). American Declaration of Independence signed (1776).
1780	First Fleet settle at Sydney Cove, home of Eora people, and at Norfolk Island (1788).	Treaty of Paris signed ending American Revolutionary War (1783). Schiller writes poem 'Ode to Joy' (1785). French revolution begins (1789). Mutiny on the Bounty (1789).
1790	Second Fleet (1790) & Third Fleet (1791). First Aboriginal massacre in NSW at Prospect Hill (1791). Bennelong sails to England (1792). Bass and Flinders circumnavigate Tasmania (1798).	Malthus writes Principle of Population (1798). Napoleonic Wars begin (1799-1815).
1800	Massacres of Aboriginal people continue in NSW. Flinders completes circumnavigation of continent (1803). Settlement founded at Risdon (1803). Massacres of Tasmanian Aboriginal people begins at Risdon Cove (1804). Castle Hill convict rebellion (1804). Rum Rebellion (1808)	United Kingdom established (1801). Civil Code of Napoleon compiled (1800-04), upholding civil rights in France. Napoleon crowned Emperor of France (1805). Napoleon invades Spain (1808). Beethoven completes Fifth Symphony (1808).

	Australia	Rest of the world
1810	Massacres of Aboriginal people continue in NSW and Tasmania. Blaxland, Wentworth and Lawson cross Blue Mountains (1813). Name "Australia" first used in dispatches by Flinders (1813). Bank of New South Wales established (1817).	Mexico declares independence (1810). Venezuela and Paraguay declare independence (1811). Battle of Waterloo, Napoleon's last battle (1815). Argentina declares independence (1816). Chile declares independence (1818).
1820	Massacres of Aboriginal people continue in NSW and Tasmania. Penal colony founded at Moreton Bay (1824). First recorded massacre of Aboriginal people in Northern Territory region at Raffles Bay (1827). Perth founded (1829).	Beethoven completes Ninth Symphony (1824). Bolivia declares independence (1825). Greece gains independence (1829).
1830	Massacres of Aboriginal people continue in NSW. "Black Line" six-week genocide of Tasmanian Aborigines by English soldiers and settlers ends autonomous Aboriginal existence in Tasmania (1830). First massacre of Aboriginal people in Western Australia at Fremantle (1830). Port Arthur penal colony established (1833). First massacre of Aboriginal people in Victoria begins at Portland (1833-34). Batman and Fawkner establish village at Port Phillip (1835), now Melbourne. First Germans arrive in South Australia (1838). Strzelecki climbs peak of Mt Kosciuszko (1839). HMS Beagle sailed into Darwin Harbour (1839).	Darwin sails around South America aboard HMS Beagle (1831-36). British trafficking of opium into China spirals in Opium War (1838).

	Australia	Rest of the world
1840	Massacres of Aboriginal people continue in NSW, Victoria, and Western Australia. First massacre of Aboriginal people in Queensland at Kilcoy (1842). Last massacre of Aboriginal people in Victoria at Cape Otway (1846). First recorded massacre of Aboriginal people in South Australia near Guichen Bay (1848). Last recorded massacre of Aboriginal people in SA at Waterloo Bay, Eyre Peninsula (1849).	New Zealand separates from New South Wales (1841). Babbage creates first mathematical calculator engine (1840s). The Communist Manifesto published by Marx and Engels (1848). European 'Year of Revolutions' (1848).
1850	Massacres of Aboriginal people continue in NSW, Qld and WA. University of Sydney founded (1850). Victoria separates from New South Wales (1851). Gold discovered in New South Wales and Victoria (1851). Last recorded massacre in NSW of about 50 Bundjalung people at East Ballina (1854). Eureka Stockade (1854). Van Dieman's Land changes to Tasmania (1856). Australian Rules codified (1859). Queensland separates from New South Wales (1859).	Perry lands in Japan (1853). Crimean War (1853-56). Darwin publishes Origin of the Species (1859). Franco-Austrian War (1859) leads to founding of Red Cross (1863).
1860	Massacres of Aboriginal people continue in Qld and WA. Stuart reaches central Australia (1860). Burke & Wills expedition (1861). Removal of Aboriginal children from families begins (1869).	Abraham Lincoln elected US President (1860). US Civil War (1861-65). 'Das Kapital' published (1867). Meiji Restoration (modernisation) commences in Japan (1868).

Appendices

	Australia	Rest of the world
1870	Massacres of Aboriginal people continue in Qld and WA. Uluru first sighted by Europeans (1873). Massacres of Aboriginal people resume in Northern Territory at Barrow Creek (1874). First cricket Test in Australia at MCG (1877).	Unification of Italy completed (1871). Unified German Empire completed, dominated by Prussia (1871). Bell transmits first telephone call (1876).
1880	Massacres of Aboriginal people continue in Qld, WA & NT. Ned Kelly hanged (1880). Last recorded massacre of Aboriginal people on Queensland mainland at Diamantina River (1888).	Pasteur develops vaccine for rabies (1880s).
1890	Massacres of Aboriginal people continue in WA & NT. Employees of Eastern and African Cold Storage Company perform indiscriminate massacres of Yolngu people in Arnhem Land, while NT Police maintain "conspiracy of silence". (1890s). "Man from Snowy River", by Banjo Paterson published (1890). National Australian Convention meets (1891). "Waltzing Matilda" written by Banjo Paterson (1895).	Japanese annihilate Chinese army in Sino-Japanese War (1894). Vaccinations for tetanus and diphtheria are developed (1890s). Benz creates first standardised motor car (1895).

	Australia	Rest of the world
1900	Massacres of Aboriginal people continue in WA. Australia becomes a federation, first parliament in Melbourne (1901). Immigration Restriction Act begins White Australia Policy (1901). Franchise Act, 'white' women given right to vote (1902). The Defence Act, Australian government takes full control of Australian army (1903). First powered aeroplane flies in Australia (1909).	Boxer Rebellion in China (1900). Wright Brothers fly first powered airplane (1903). Russo-Japanese War (1904-05), Japanese annihilate Russian army and navy. Einstein publishes Theory of Relativity (1905). New Zealand gains self-government (1907).
1910	Massacres of Aboriginal people continue in WA. Canberra is named Australia's capital (1913). Australia enters World War One (1914). Bentinck Island Massacre off Queensland coast of Kaiadilt people (1918). World War One ends — 60,000 Australians dead (1918).	Mexican civil wars (1910-20). Chinese revolution ends China's last imperial dynasty (1911). World War One begins (1914). Gallipoli campaign begins (1915). Battle of Beersheba (1917). Battle of Amiens (1918). Russian Revolutions (March and November 1917). World War One ends, German, Austrian and Turkish empires end with revolutions (1918). Treaty of Versailles (1919). League of Nations formed (1919).

Appendices

	Australia	Rest of the world
1920	Massacres of Aboriginal people continue in WA and NT. QANTAS is founded (1920). Edith Cowan was first female elected to Australian parliament (1921). Vegemite first produced (1923). Last recorded massacre of Aboriginal people in WA in Kimberley Region (1926). Canberra opens its first parliament (1927). Hinkler flies from UK to Australia (1928). Coniston Massacre in Northern Territory is last recorded massacre of Aboriginal people in Australia (1928). Kingsford Smith flies from USA to Australia (1928). Great Depression hits Australia (1929).	Irish Free State created (1921). Turkish republic begins (1923). Civil war in China, nationalists come to power (1925). Hubble discovers other galaxies (1925). Mussolini begins fascist regime in Italy (1926). Oil discovered in Iraq (1927). Lindbergh's trans-Atlantic crossing by airplane (1927). World's stock markets crash, Great Depression begins (1929).
1930	Phar Lap wins Melbourne Cup (1930). Don Bradman scores highest Sheffield Shield score (452n.o.) and highest Test score (334), (1930). Mawson charts Antarctica (1931). Sydney Harbour Bridge opened (1932). Tasmanian Tiger becomes extinct (1936). Australia Day declared 'day of mourning' by Aboriginal population (1938). Australia enters World War Two (1939).	Post-depression unemployment begins to decline (1932). Iraq gains independence (1932). Hitler appointed chancellor of Germany (1933). Spanish Civil War (1936-39). Japan invades China, sacks Nanking (1937). League of Nations collapses (1937). Franco begins dictatorship in Spain (1939). Germany invades Poland, World War Two begins (1939).

	Australia	Rest of the world
1940	Howard Florey helps invent penicillin (1940). Pharmaceutical Benefits Scheme introduced (1944). Australia becomes founding member of United Nations (1945). First Sydney to Hobart Yacht Race begins (1945). Holden begins building cars (1948). Snowy Mountain Scheme begins (1949).	Siege of Tobruk (1941). Battles of Coral Sea, Midway and Kokoda Trail, and Second battle of El Alamein (1942). Exterminations begin at Auschwitz (1942). Atomic bombs dropped on Japan, World War Two ends (1945). United Nations begins (1945). India and Pakistan gain independence (1947). Berlin blockaded: Cold War begins (1948). Gandhi assassinated (1948). Israel proclaimed (1948). Maoist regime begins in China (1949). Indonesia gains independence (1949).
1950	ANZUS begins (1951). Television launched in Australia (1956). Melbourne Olympics (1956). Edna Everage first appears on Australian stage (1956).	Queen Elizabeth II crowned (1953). Vietnam gains independence (1954). Rosa Parks arrested (1955). USSR supresses Hungary (1956). European Economic Community (EEC) formed (1957). Castro regime in Cuba begins (1959).
1960	The Beatles tour Australia (1964). Australian decimal currency begins (1966). Aboriginal Australians given right to vote (1967).	Wave of African states gaining independence (1960-62). USSR crushes Czech uprising (1968). Martin Luther King assassinated (1968). Apollo 11: first Moon landing (1969).

	Australia	Rest of the world
1970	Neville Bonner becomes first Aboriginal Australian Member of Parliament (1971). Daylight saving first introduced (1971). Sydney Opera House opened (1973). Governor-General Kerr dismisses Prime Minister Whitlam (1975).	Britain, Ireland, and Denmark join EEC (1973). Death of Franco (1975). Death of Mao (1976). USSR invades Afghanistan (1979). Iranian revolution: Khomeini regime begins (1979).
1980	"Advance Australia Fair" proclaimed as national anthem (1984). Uluru given back to Mutitjulu people (1985). Australia Act passed, making Australia legally independent (1986). Brisbane hosts World Expo (1988).	Gorbachev introduces Glasnost and Perestroika to USSR (1985). Nuclear reactor explodes in Chernobyl (1986). Collapse of Marcos regime in Philippines (1986). USSR and USA agree to disarm (1986). Collapse of Soviet Bloc (1989). Russians pull-out from Afghanistan (1989).
1990	Carmen Lawrence becomes first female Premier of an Australian state (1990). Mabo decision delivered (1992). Wik decision (1996). Port Arthur Massacre, gun laws introduced (1996).	First Iraq War (1990). USSR dissolved (1991). Civil war in Rwanda (1993). Multi-racial elections in South Africa (1994).
2000	Sydney Olympics (2000). Bali Bombings (2002). Cronulla racial riot (2005). Prime Minister Rudd delivers 'Sorry' speech (2008).	Al-Queda attacks USA (2001). USA begins war in Afghanistan (2001). Second Iraq War begins (2003). Indian Ocean tsunami (2004). Global financial crisis (2007-08).
2010	Julia Gillard becomes first female Prime Minister of Australia (2010). Same-sex marriage is legalised in Australia (2017).	Covid-19 Virus break-out (2019). Aung San Suu Kyi released from house arrest (2010).
2020		Covid-19 declared pandemic (2020). Aung San Suu Kyi re-placed into house arrest (2021).

References:

Some online content was viewed on multiple occasions and could not be given a precise retrieval date.

Allam, Lorena and Evershed, Nick; The Killing Times Project, A massacre map of Australian frontier wars; The Guardian Australia; as retrieved on 6 June 2019 at https://www.theguardian.com/australia-news/ng-interactive/2019/mar/04/massacre-map-australia-the-killing-times-frontier-wars

Australian Broadcasting Corporation (ABC); Jandamarra's War; 2011; as retrieved on 27 December 2018 — http://www.abc.net.au/tv/programs/jandamarras-war.htm

Australian Institute of Aboriginal and Torres Strait Islander Studies; https://aiatsis.gov.au/

Australian National University; (1966), Australian Dictionary of Biography, Melbourne University Publishing.

Australian Petroleum Production and Exploration Association (APPEA): The voice of Australia's oil and gas industry; as retrieved on 17 December 2019 at https://www.appea.com.au/

Australian Science and Technology Heritage Centre 1996-2006; Technology in Australia 1788-1988; http://www.austehc.unimelb.edu.au/tia/

Barker, W.R., Greensdale P. J. M.; Evolution of the Flora and Fauna of Australia; Australian Systematic

Berkeley Earth (2021); http://berkeleyearth.org/

Botany Society, Peacock Publications/Australian Systemic Botany Society, 1982

BBC History; Captain Cook and the scourge of scurvy; http://www.bbc.co.uk/history/british/empire_seapower/captaincook_scurvy_01.shtml

Bladen, F. M., ed. (1978). Historical records of New South Wales. Vol. 2. Grose and Paterson, 1793–1795. Lansdown Slattery & Co.

Blainey, Geoffrey; A Very Short History of the World; Penguin Books; 2004

Blainey, Geoffrey; The Tyranny of Distance; Pan MacMillan Australia; 2001

References:

Chalk, Frank and Jonassohn, Kurt; The History and Sociology of Genocide: Analyses and Case Studies. Yale University Press, 1990.

Clark, Ian D.; Aboriginal Language Areas in Victoria, A Report to the Victorian Aboriginal Corporation For Languages; 1996 — https://vacl.org.au/home

Clark, Mavis T; Pastor Doug: the story of Sir Douglas Nicholls, Aboriginal leader; 1972

Colwell, Max; (1970), The Voyages of Matthew Flinders; Paul Hamlyn, Sydney.

Dreamtime: Welcome to the Dreamtime; http://dreamtime.net.au/

Fang, Jason (2018); 200 Years of Chinese Australians: First settler's descendants reconnect with their roots; ABC News, as retrieved on 19 September 2018 — http://www.abc.net.au/news/2018-06-10/first-chinese-settlers-descendants-reconnect-with-their-roots/9845804

Farooqui, Amar; Smuggling as Subversion: Colonialism, Indian Merchants, and the Politics of Opium, 1790-1843; Lanham, Md.: Lexington Books.; 2005.

First Fleet Fellowship Victoria; They came from many lands; https://firstfleetfellowship.org.au/convicts/they-came-from-many-lands/

First Hellenes in Australia; The Athenian Association of Sydney and NSW; 2013

Frindall, Bill; The Wisden Book of Test Cricket, 1876-77 to 1977-78; Macdonald and Jane's, London, 1979

Frost, Alan (2012). The First Fleet: the real story. Collingwood: Black Inc.

German Australia; German Speakers in Australia from 1788 to the Present; Dave Nutting; 2001-19; as retrieved on 7/1/2019 from http://www.germanaustralia.com/

Gillen, Mollie (1989). The Founders of Australia: A Biographical Dictionary of the First Fleet. Library of Australian History

Halo, Thea; Not Even My Name; Angel Hat, New York, USA, 2000

Hocking, Jenny, and Reidy, Nell, 'Marngrook, Tom Wills and the continuing denial of Indigenous History', Meanjin, Winter 2016: 83-93, as retrieved on 13 February 2019 at https://meanjin.com.au/essays/marngrook-tom-wills-and-the-continuing-denial-of-indigenous-history/

Hogan, Paul; The Tigers of Old; Richmond Football Club, Australia, 1996

Howard, Bruce; A Nostalgic look at Australian Sport; Rigby Ltd, Australia; 1978

Johns Hopkins University, Coronavirus Resource Center; https://coronavirus.jhu.edu/map.html

Kaartdijin Noongar — Noongar Knowledge; Sharing Noongar Culture; South West Aboriginal Land & Sea Council — https://www.noongarculture.org.au/

Keneally, Thomas; (2006), A Commonwealth of Thieves, Random House, Sydney.

Kimberly. W.B.; History of West Australia : A Narrative Of Her Past Together With Biographies Of Her Leading Men; F.W. Niven & Co; Australia, 1897, as retrieved on 3 March 2019 at https://trove.nla.gov.au/work/19050170?q&versionId=22370156

Malaspinas, Anna-Sapfo, et al; A Genomic History of Aboriginal Australia; McMillan Publishers; 2016; https://www.nature.com/articles/nature18299.epdf

Manning Clark; A History of Australia, Vol.1, Melbourne University Publishing, 1999

Manning Clark; A Short History of Australia, Sydney, Tudor Distributors, 1969

Manning Clark; Sources of Australian History, Melbourne, Oxford University Press, 1977, first published 1957.

McIntyre, K.G. (1977) *The Secret Discovery of Australia, Portuguese ventures 200 years before Cook*, Souvenir Press, Menindie

Megalogenis, George; The Football Solution; Penguin Random House; Australia, 2018

Migration Heritage Centre, New South Wales; The Enemy at Home: German Internees in World War One Australia; retrieved on 12 March 2020 at http://www.migrationheritage.nsw.gov.au/exhibition/enemyathome/the-camps-and-the-system-of-internment/

Museums Victoria, Collections, Sudanese migration in Australia; retrieved On 5 May 2020 at https://collections.museumvictoria.com.au/articles/2997

My Place for Teachers: Australia in the 1800s; http://myplace.edu.au/

National Archives of Australia; Documenting a Democracy: Secret Instructions to Lieutenant Cook 30 July 1768 (UK); https://web.archive.org/web/20080721065703/http://foundingdocs.gov.au/item.asp?dID=34

National Chinese Museum of Australia; Golden Dragon Museum, Yi Yuan Gardens & Guan Yin Temple, Origins brochure; Bendigo, Australia, 2018

National Museum of Australia; The White Australia Policy; as retrieved on 2 July 2019 at https://www.nma.gov.au/defining-moments/resources/white-australia-policy

National Museum of Australia; Fights for Civil Rights; as retrieved on 25 April 2020 at https://www.nma.gov.au/explore/features/indigenous-rights/civil-rights

Percival Searle (1949); Dictionary of Australian Biography, Volumes 1 & 2; Angus and Robertson Ltd, Sydney.

Pollard, Elizabeth; Worlds Together Worlds Apart; W. W. Norton & Co., New York; 2015.

References:

Presland, Gary (1994); The Land of the Kulin: Discovering the lost landscape and the first people of Port Phillip; McPhee Gribble, Penguin Books, Australia.

Prior, Tom; A Pictorial History of Bushrangers; Paul Hamlyn, Sydney; 1970

Project Gutenberg Australia: a treasure trove of literature; http://gutenberg.net.au/

Roberts, Andrew; The Art of War: Great Commanders of the Modern World; Quercus Books, UK, 2008

Robinson, Tony; History of Australia from New Holland to Neighbours; Viking, Penguin Group; 2011

Schaffer, Kay; Manne's Generation: White Nation Responses to the Stolen Generation Report; Australian Humanities Review, June 2001; as retrieved on 8 July 2019 at http://australianhumanitiesreview.org/2001/06/01/mannes-generation-white-nation-responses-to-the-stolen-generation-report/

Shermer, David; World War I; Octopus Books Limited, London, UK, 1973

Sherrell, Henry; Economic Impact of Migration (2015); Migration Institute of Australia, retrieved on 13 August 2020 at https://www.mia.org.au/documents/item/752

Schwartz, Tess; The First of Forty Families: Bringing My Family Tree and Forest to Life; Makor Jewish Community Library, Australia, 2001

Sovereign Union — First Nations Asserting Authority; Prisoners of Frontier Wars — Backbirding and Chain Gangs; as retrieved on 22 July 2019 at http://nationalunitygovernment.org/content/prisoners-frontier-wars-blackbirding-chain-gangs

Stunden, L.O. (Lina); Lord Kitchener's One Hundred, World War 1 Surgeons, Biographies and Diaries; Symphony of Peace Pty Ltd, Australia, 2015

Thackway, Richard; Land Use in Australia: Past, Present and Future; Australian National University, 2018

The Economist; An Antipodean Raj; January 19th 2013 Edition, retrieved on 25 May 2020 at https://www.economist.com/science-and-technology/2013/01/19/an-antipodean-raj

The Sydney Gazette and New South Wales Advertiser; New South Wales; National Library of Australia

Trove, The National Library of Australia; The Founders of Brisbane: Captain Henry Miller — retrieved 12 September 2018 from https://trove.nla.gov.au/newspaper/article/20617350

University of Newcastle; Colonial Frontier Massacres in Central and Eastern Australia 1788-1930; as retieved on 6 June 2019 at https://c21ch.newcastle.edu.au/colonialmassacres/

University of Utah, Geology; https://geology,utah.gov

Vincent Smith, Keith (2009); Bennelong Among his People; http://press-files.anu.edu.au/downloads/press/p74631/pdf/ch0156.pdf

Wellcome; News; What different types of Covid-19 vaccine are there; https://wellcome.org/news/what-different-types-covid-19-vaccine-are-there

Wharton, WJL; Captain Cook's Journal During the First Voyage Round the World, London, 1893 — http://www.gutenberg.org/files/8106/8106-h/8106-h.htm#ch6

Wikipedia; https://en.wikipedia.org/

Acknowledgements:

I would like to thank family and friends who have supported me through the writing of this book, especially to Natasha who worked while I wrote, and Delysia and Reuben for repeatedly asking if I'd completed it yet.

Thanks to Lucy, Chris, Natalie, and Maddy, who approved of the book's structure in the early stages. Special thanks to Chris and Tim, who reviewed this book in great detail and offered many constructive options.

Thanks to Anton, who kept me supplied with new references.

Thanks to Luke and his network for advice during the publication process.

Thanks to Sasha, who provided two special inspirations for this book.

The crediting task has not been an easy one. I have attempted to seek approval and give credit where references and images have been used. Some were personal photographs, while others were sourced through the internet.

Some online content was viewed on multiple occasions and could not be given a precise retrieval date.

www.ingramcontent.com/pod-product-compliance
Lightning Source LLC
Chambersburg PA
CBHW062030290426
44109CB00026B/2580